Mughal India

Mughal India
Studies in Polity, Ideas, Society, and Culture

M. Athar Ali

OXFORD
UNIVERSITY PRESS

OXFORD

UNIVERSITY PRESS

Oxford University Press is a department of the University of Oxford.
It furthers the University's objective of excellence in research, scholarship, and
education by publishing worldwide. Oxford is a registered trademark of Oxford
University Press in the UK and in certain other countries

Published in India by
Oxford University Press
22 Workspace, 2nd Floor, 1/22 Asaf Ali Road, New Delhi 110002

First Edition published in 2006
Oxford India Paperbacks 2008
29th impression 2025

ISBN-13: 978-0-19-569661-5
ISBN-10: 0-19-569661-1

Typeset in 10.5/12, Times New Roman
by All India Press, Pondicherry 605 001
Printed in India by Manipal Technologies Limited, Manipal

The publishers regret that Professor M. Athar Ali could not live to see this book in print. We are deeply grateful to Professor Irfan Habib for his help in facilitating its publication.

Contents

MAPS
between pages 148–9
Akbar's Progress from Ajmer to the Salt Range 1577–8

between pages 328–9
India's North-West Frontiers from the 13th to the 19th Century

Preface

When the author of this collection of papers, M. Athar Ali, died of cancer in a Delhi hospital on 7 July 1998, an association between us of some fifty years was brought to a close. From the Intermediate to MA in history we had studied together at the Aligarh Muslim University (1947–53). We were both fortunate that, as we passed our MA examination, there came to be openings for us in the same university, because of an ambitious programme of research and publications in medieval Indian history instituted by the Government of India. The fields in medieval history that we took up were different and reflected the different approaches we had. Athar Ali felt strongly that the Mughal empire had not had a good press because the primary Persian material had not been studied extensively enough. My own concerns, rooted in a commitment to Marxism, were with the study of economy, social structure, and class exploitation. Athar Ali, in line with his own interests, took the Mughal nobility for the subject of his PhD thesis, while I attempted a study of the agrarian system of Mughal India. It is not surprising that the conclusions we arrived at on the performance of the Mughal empire, were also different. In his thesis which in its published form (*Mughal Nobility under Aurangzeb,* Delhi, 1966) came after mine, Athar Ali duly took me to task for my adverse judgement on the Mughal agrarian administration. From those early days, while debating with each other, we constantly exchanged both information and ideas, as we sat for long hours on adjacent desks. (The third desk was that of Professor Iqtidar Alam Khan, who, I am glad to say, generally took my side.)

Those early days were to be followed by years in which Athar Ali, by his two major published works and numerous papers won considerable acclaim in the academic world both in India and abroad. He was appointed Professor at Aligarh in 1977 and was subsequently the UGC National Professor in 1980–1. After his retirement from Aligarh in 1990, he was elected a National Fellow of the Indian Council of Historical Research, 1990–3. He served as Secretary of the Indian History Congress, 1977–80, and was elected its General President in 1989–90. He was elected Smutts Fellow at the University of Cambridge, 1974–5, and Wilson Fellow at the Woodrow Wilson

International Centre for Scholars, Washington, DC, 1986. He worked
as a Visiting Fellow at the School of Oriental and African Studies,
London, twice, in 1970 and 1973–4. He was appointed Visiting
Professor at the Centre for South Asian Studies, University of Virginia,
Charlottesville, 1978–9, and at Centre d'etudes del'Inde et de l'Asie
du Sud, Paris, 1980.

That these honours were well deserved cannot admit of doubt. It
would be difficult for anyone to match the industry that Athar Ali put
in for his thesis and for compiling his second major work, *The
Apparatus of Empire: Awards of Ranks, Offices and Titles to the Mughal
Nobility (1574-1658)*, New Delhi, 1985. He collected his data not only
from numerous official and private histories, published and manuscript,
and a mass of documentary material, especially at the Andhra Pradesh
State Archives, Hyderabad, but also from a number of out-of-the-way
texts which he read through just in case they contained chance
information on any official's antecedents or appointment to rank or
office. In a sense *The Apparatus* completed his study of the Mughal
nobility, for he had now covered in this and his earlier book the entire
period from the middle of Akbar's reign (1574) to the death of
Aurangzeb (1707). But he still wished to extend his comprehensive
biographical record of the Mughal nobility to the whole of Aurangzeb's
reign as well, so as to produce a companion volume to his *Apparatus*.
Many years of intense work (involving repeated trips to Hyderabad)
followed; and the data from 1659 to 1685 was ready partly in processed
and partly in handwritten form, when he was suddenly forced by illness
to abandon the work altogether early in 1998. Sad though it is, it is
difficult to see how this product of many years' labour can now be
retrieved, and put into a form that the author would have approved of.

Athar Ali's work on the Mughal nobility, with the massive
information that he was able to deploy, has naturally greatly
influenced much of the subsequent work on the Mughal empire, its
structure and functioning. His *Mughal Nobility under Aurangzeb*,
therefore, acquired the status of a landmark in Mughal historiography.
In the last two decades or so, Athar Ali's perceptions of the Mughal
political and administrative structure have attracted criticism from
some who have in effect questioned the validity of the Persian
evidence itself. Athar Ali's own detailed response to such objections
came in what is now Chapter 8 in the present volume and then in his
introduction to the second edition of *Mughal Nobility under
Aurangzeb*, published by the Oxford University Press, New Delhi,

1997.

In later years Athar Ali tended to take an exceptional degree of interest in cultural history, to which earlier he had paid little attention. It is, perhaps, possible to trace this broadening of the scope of his work by reference to two of his earlier essays. In one (Chapter 6), written in 1973, he gave his general perception of the Mughal empire, arguing that it had very strong conventions which limited the personal powers of the emperor, and that in some respects it was a 'quasi-modern' state. Such a perception of Mughal polity led him to look anew for the factors behind its decline. This came in Chapter 27, in which, while not overlooking factors internal to that empire, he attributed the decline of all major Asian states at that time to what he called a 'cultural failure' in their confrontation with the West. The implication was that there was an ideology, a cultural ethos, which had sustained the Mughal empire, but which was now getting obsolete in the world-context.

It is this, I think, which made him take special interest in the history of religion and ideas in his later studies. It will be seen that no less than eleven essays in this collection (Chapters 2, 11–20) belong to this field. He said much that was original in regard to Akbar's ideas, and it seems that his admiration for this extraordinary man grew much with time: it is most notably to be seen in Chapter 10, where he assesses Akbar as a proponent of the idea of India as well as a protagonist of the cause of reason. It is no accident surely that what is perhaps his last essay (Chapter 19) is devoted to the author of the *Dabistan-i Mazahib* (*c.*1652) who proceeded with the avowed purpose of giving an unbiased account of all religions. Such a work, Athar Ali argued, could only have been written (and become popular) in the Mughal empire.

Since his student days Athar Ali remained a steadfast friend of the Communist movement. But while he recognized Marxism as an important trend within modern historiography, he himself did not accept many of its premises. At the same time he was irritated at any tendency towards introducing religious or sectarian sentiments into history: Chapter 1 is a product of his anxiety to show that Islamic history too must be held to be susceptible to a rational interpretation. He usually avoided polemics; but in Chapters 8 and 28, he took issue with approaches which he thought were becoming fashionable, without having much basis in real fact. Chapter 28 was, perhaps, the first major critique anywhere of the conceptions of the eighteenth century that C.A. Bayly and some others have put forward.

Any collection of papers of a historian who often wrote, like many of us, for conferences and seminars, without a thought of these going into a book, runs the risk of appearing miscellaneous, its quality uneven, its contents overlapping or repetitious. It is a tribute to Athar Ali's choice of themes, clarity of thought and fluent prose that the reader gets here a large amount of information on medieval India in such lucidly analysed form, where one can recognize a consistency of approach, without any sense of hearing the same thing over and over again. We can see him going out to explore with an open mind, as ready to criticize as to admire what he finds. Athar Ali was no apologist of any cause (even of the Mughal Empire!). He always felt the excitement of pursuing enquiry for the joy of it. And the reader too may well sense this as he goes through his written word.

It will be manifest to the reader that though Athar Ali was never afraid of investigating minor matters, there is hardly an occasion where his extensive researches do not produce important facts not considered before or do not suggest new ways of looking at historical problems. The present volume may for this reason supply a far better comprehension of Mughal India than any conventional history of it. Irrespective of whether one is not here or there fully in agreement with him, one can still admire the rigorous rationality and critical spirit with which Athar Ali goes to his materials and the straightforwardness with which he takes his position.

The papers in the present collection were assembled by the author himself. He also made a rough thematic arrangement, which has largely been followed here. Unfortunately, Athar Ali decided to have the papers retyped (not word-processed), and he fell ill before he could check the typescript. When the material was seen by me after his death, it became clear that the entire text needed to be checked, and compared with the original. I have corrected typing errors, made some spellings uniform and slightly amended the text where I felt that there could otherwise be some confusion. Athar Ali did not sometimes give the full publication details of the texts he used; these, as far as possible, have been supplied. Needless to say in all this I have been greatly helped by the excellent copy editor from the Oxford University Press. The reader is assured, however, that there is no deviation of substance, even on any minor point, from the text as the author had put it in a revised form.

There is one matter in which the reader's indulgence is sought. Athar Ali's papers appeared in diverse publications, some of which may have had no provision for diacritical marks, while others followed their own special systems of transliteration. Different papers in this volume therefore spell some of the Persian terms and names differently; moreover, such diacritical marks as there were in the printed articles were dropped when these were typed. To spell all the names and terms according to a uniform transliteration system and to apply the appropriate diacritical marks to all of them would now be too onerous a task. The non-English words and terms therefore largely appear as they appeared in the original publications, but without any diacritical marks.

Before closing, I should like to add a few words on matters outside of Athar Ali's academic work. He possessed a wonderful fund of commonsense and a surprisingly acute legal acumen. These capacities were always put at his friends' service, and of others too who called upon him for assistance. In however critical a situation he never lost his wits or nerve, and when he knew death was not far away he faced it with the same calmness that one had come to expect from him in all circumstances.

During the last ten years of his life he did not hide his growing concern at the rapid advance of communalism in the country. The secular India, with a strong commitment to the scientific spirit, which we had all so long taken for granted, was now in danger. Athar Ali joined three other distinguished historians, Professors R.S. Sharma, Suraj Bhan, and D.N. Jha in penning a Historians' Report to the Nation on Ayodhya (1991). It was translated and printed in almost every important language of India. His assistance was made available to every organization that joined the fight for secularism, whether it was the Indian History Congress, or SAHMAT, or the Association for the Study of History and Archaeology (ASHA), or the Aligarh Historians Society. His anxieties on this score are reflected in some of his later papers in this volume (see the conclusion of Chapter 2 and Chapter 10).

Athar Ali was always given steadfast support by his wife, Feroza Khatoon, and his family. An apology is due to them, and to the Oxford University Press, as well as to readers, for the time I have taken in preparing the press copy.

IRFAN HABIB

Acknowledgements

'The Islamic Background to Indian History: An Interpretation of the Islamic Past', *Journal of the Economic and Social History of the Orient*, Vol. XXXII, October 1989, Leiden.

'Encounter and Efflorescence: The Genesis of the Medieval Civilization', Presidential Address, *Proceedings of Indian History Congress*, 1989, Gorakhpur session.

'Nobility under Muhammad Tughluq', *Proceedings of Indian History Congress*, 1981, Bodh Gaya session.

'Capital of the Sultans: Delhi during the Thirteenth and Fourteenth Centuries', in R.E. Frykenberg ed., *Delhi Through the Ages*, 1986, Oxford University Press, New Delhi.

'The Punjab between the Thirteenth and Fifteenth Centuries', Presidential Address, Medieval Section, *Proceedings of Punjab History Conference*, 1981, Patiala session.

'Towards an Interpretation of the Mughal Empire', *Journal of the Royal Asiatic Society*, Vol. 1, 1978, London.

'The Pre-Colonial Social Structure and the Polity of the Mughal Empire', *Proceedings of Indian History Congress*, 1984, Annamalai session.

'The Mughal Polity: A Critique of Revisionist Approaches', *Modern Asian Studies*, Vol. 27, 1993, Cambridge.

'Political Structures of the Islamic Orient in the Sixteenth and Seventeenth Centuries', in Irfan Habib ed., *Medieval India 1*, 1992, Oxford University Press, New Delhi.

'The Evolution of the Perception of India: Akbar and Abu'l Fazl', in Irfan Habib ed., *Akbar and his India*, 1996, Oxford University Press, New Delhi.

'The State in Islamic Thought in India', Symposium Lecture, *Proceedings of Indian History Congress*, 1982, Kurukshetra session.

'Evolution of Social Justice in Medieval Islamic Thought', *Proceedings of Indian History Congress*, 1996, Madras session.

'The Vision in the Salt Range, 1578: An Interpretation', *Proceedings of Indian History Congress*, 1993, Mysore session.

'Sulh-i Kul and the Religious Ideas of Akbar', *Studies in History*, Vol. IV, No. 1, 1982, New Delhi.

'Translations of Sanskrit Works at Akbar's Court', in Iqtidar Alam Khan ed., *Akbar and his Age*, 1999, Northern Book Centre, New Delhi.

'The Religious World of Jahangir', *Proceedings of Indian History Congress*, 1990, Calcutta session.

'The Religious Environment under Shah Jahan and Aurangzeb', original place of publication not traceable.

'Sidelights into Ideological and Religious Attitudes in the Punjab During the Seventeenth Century', in S. Nurul Hasan ed., *Medieval India: A Miscellany*, Vol. III, 1972, Asia Publishing House, Bombay.

'Pursuing an Elusive Seeker of Universal Truth: The Identity and Environment of the Author of the Dabistan-i Mazahib', *Journal of Royal Asiatic Society*, Vol. 9, No. 3, 1999, London.

'Muslims' Perceptions of Judaism and Christianity in Medieval India', place of original publication not traceable.

'The Religious Issue in the War of Succession, 1658-59', *Medieval India Quarterly*, Vol.V, 1963, London.

'Causes of the Rathor Rebellion of 1679', *Proceedings of Indian History Congress*, 1961, Delhi session.

'Provincial Governors under Aurangzeb: An Analysis', in S. Nurul Hasan ed., *Medieval India: A Miscellany*, Vol. I, 1969, Asia Publishing House, Bombay.

'International Law or Conventions Governing Conduct of Relations between Asian States, Sixteenth and Seventeenth Centuries', paper presented at 34th International Congress of Asian and North African Studies, 1993, Hong Kong.

'Jahangir and the Uzbeks', *Proceedings of Indian History Congress*, 1964, Ranchi session.

'The Objectives behind Mughal Expedition into Balkh and Badakhshan, 1646–47', *Proceedings of Indian History Congress*, 1967, Patiala session.

'The Passing of the Empire: The Mughal Case', *Modern Asian Studies*, Vol. 9, No. 3, 1975, Cambridge.

'Recent Theories of Eighteenth-Century India', *Indian Historical Review*, Vol. XIII, Nos 1–2, 1986, New Delhi

'History in Indo-Muslim Tradition', original place of publication not traceable.

'The Use of Sources in Mughal Historiography', *Journal of Royal Asiatic Society*, NS, Vol. 5, No. 3, 1995, London.

'The Correspondence of Aurangzeb and its Historical Significance', original place of publication not traceable.

ANTECEDENTS

1

The Islamic Background to Indian History

An Interpretation of the Islamic Past

The medieval period of Indian history, as conventionally fixed by historians, c. 1000 to c. 1750, had so deep an imprint of Islam, that during much of the period India could be held to have belonged culturally to the Islamic world, not on its periphery, but close to its core. It is, of course, the uniqueness of India's situation that at the same time, strictly in terms of its Hindu component, it could be said to have been a world in its own right, with Islam only as a peripheral phenomenon. Yet, since the Islamic connection greatly influenced the political structure, the fiscal system and even much of the network of internal commerce and external trade, it is crucial to understand the background that Islam provided to Indian history, or in other words, to understand Islamic history till the arrival of Islam in northern India, c. 1200.[1] A splendid effort to do so was provided by Professor Mohammad Habib in his introduction to a reprint of Volume II of Elliot and Dowson's *History of India as Told by its Own Historians* (1952). A year later Hamilton Gibb came out with his well-known essay, 'An Interpretation of Islamic History', published in the *Journal of World History* (1953).[2] Nearly thirty-five years have passed since then, years during which much has been written, and many new insights obtained. The present essay proposes to offer a rather personal reappraisal of the first six hundred years of Islamic history based, admittedly, on only a partial reading of the vast literature on the subject and with a confessed bias towards what seems more relevant from an Indian point of view, though not deliberately neglecting other possible angles of vision.

I

In any narration of the events of the past, the emergence of Islam within a neglected, seemingly 'wild' desert, and its rapid transformation into one of the great historical cultures of the world, presents a subject of great drama and wonder. There have been greater and more rapid conquests. The Mongols in the thirteenth century too arose out of the steppes to create the one sole world empire in pre-modern history, twice or thrice the size of the Islamic caliphate at its greatest extent; and they achieved it in far less time. But the Mongols created no international culture; their own language was overwhelmed by the babel of tongues of their subjects; instead of assimilating, like the Arabs, they were themselves assimilated by others. Clearly then, without denigrating the claims of *Pax Mongolica* for historical analysis, one may still assert that an analysis of Islam is likely to tell us much more about what has happened in a large part of Asia and Africa during the last fifteen hundred years.

How does one set about the task? There has recently been a spate of criticism of the 'Orientalists'. Amidst this protest, Edward W. Said's critique is perhaps the most comprehensive as well as reasonable.[3] In so far as 'Orientalism' is conceived as an attempt to study eastern cultures, especially Islam, in the way one studies Zoology, or animals of lower orders, many of the criticisms are, perhaps, quite valid. From this valid objection, however, there has been a tendency to go on to assert that Islamic history can be understood only by those who believe in Islam, who can study it on its own terms, and still better, interpret it *in its terms*. This is a very attractive notion, and by ruling out all comparisons with other cultures or systems (for each of them must then be studied on its own terms), it sweeps away the possibility of any arrogantly Eurocentric interpretation of Islamic history. One may, perhaps, see the most learned practitioner of this kind of exposition in Hamidullah, with his well-known biography of the Prophet in two volumes.

Without totally denying the claims of this school to legitimacy, I would still argue that the basic premises here are not acceptable. A believer has a perfect right to expound the tenets of Islam 'on its own terms', in its own terminology; but this would be theology, without any indignity necessarily attaching to that term. Can it be history? Islam as a historical phenomenon has always interacted with other elements that have indisputably originated and existed outside its fold. Will it be valid to see them on terms supposedly proper only to Islam? If not, how is the interaction to be interpreted? For if one is to understand the Islamic phenomenon in a historical perspective, the interaction is not peripheral but central to any analysis. The conclusion is inescapable that whether it is the history of feudal Christendom or of Lama-Buddhism or of Islam, one would need the same critical apparatus, the same freedom from assumptions or given premises, and the same sharp critical faculty.

This can be illustrated with the very first problem one faces: the emergence of Islam within the womb of what Muslims call the *Jahilliya*, the society and culture in which the Prophet was born. Is Jahilliya to be understood 'on its own terms' (hardly known to us now, at first hand) or on those of Islam, whose followers understandably exaggerated the allegedly evil customs of the Jahilliya? One must now rather examine the degree of exaggeration in the Islamic traditions about that period and reconstruct, by additional use of other sources, what was really happening in the Arabian peninsula before the rise of Islam. There is no proof that the pre-Islamic Arabian society was in a primitive communal stage, as E.A. Belyaev has argued; nor, as he further asserts, that it was being converted into a slave-owning one.[4] One would rather say that the bedouin society, based on tribe, was indeed pastoral; but it had long developed individual property, even if this was counted in terms of camels and date palms rather than money. Slavery was a convenient, but not an essential, prop of this property system. Outside Yemen agriculture was only of secondary importance; but this, along with date palm cultivation, would again emphasize individual right and economic and social differentiation. Thus, clearly, private property, which is the basis of Islamic civil law, already existed in Arabia. Islam helped at best to standardize and systematize its norms. As far as slavery is concerned, it is possible that slavery became more important after Islamic conquests (with the train of captive slaves they generated); but it is unlikely that here too Islam either greatly modified or intensified slavery. It recognized slavery virtually just as it had found it.

Where then was there, in a sphere other than ideological, a true break with Jahilliya? Montgomery Watt's thesis of town–nomad conflict may be taken to develop a proposition of the triumph of urbanism over pastoral rusticism.[5] The essential difference between the town-dweller and the bedouin is recognized in the Quran, where the nomad is spurned.[6] There is no doubt that the initial success of Islam is related to the existence of commercial oases, notably Mecca, within the desert wastes of the peninsula. One can trace this situation, perhaps, to the discovery of the monsoons that occurred around the time of Christ. This discovery suddenly shifted the main ports to the mouth of the Red Sea. The Red Sea itself is unaffected by the monsoon winds, and so posed a tedious barrier to sailing ships within its waters. The trade between the Mediterranean and India must needs, therefore, pass overland through Hijaz, connecting the Levant and Egyptian ports with those of Yemen. Of this overland caravan trade, Mecca became the undeclared capital. It also became, apparently, the entrepôt from where some of the luxuries of civilization were distributed among the nomadic tribes (or rather among their chiefs and 'wealthy' families). Mecca sealed its position by installing, in the Ka'bah, the images of gods (including the one called Allah) and goddesses to establish for itself a position of a pilgrimage centre for the tribes of the peninsula. The response of Mecca to Islam was governed, among other factors, by this alliance of commerce with religion. Could Islam offer a more attractive alternative in terms of persuading the tribes to respect the security of the Quraysh in the name of religious sanctity? As Shaban and Rodinson argue, the moment Islam would be shown to offer a far more effective claim on the nomad than Lat and Manat,[7] the Ka'bah would assume an even greater sanctity under its banner. The Meccan reaction to Islam passed quickly from surrender to reconciliation, and ultimately, to dominance.[8]

If these are reasonable notions, do we assume that Islam was simply a development of institutions already present in Arab society and economy? This indeed is precisely Shaban's conclusion. Islam 'was definitely Arab, based on Arab traditions, and shaped in Arab forms'.[9] It seems to me that this represents an exaggeration that may dangerously mar our understanding of early Islamic history.

What is missing in Shaban's thesis is any recognition that the essential elements of the Islamic faith cannot be shown to have grown historically out of Arabian soil. If one does not care to contest the believer's faith in the message of Abraham, that message had admittedly long been forgotten in Mecca and it had left no living tradition. What was intruding into Arabia were the ideas of Judaism and Christianity radiating from the Roman Empire, and later Byzantium. The notorious missionary gibe that Islam is a rehash of Judaism and Christianity has undoubtedly inhibited free discussion of the matter. But the link with both religions is explicitly recognized in the Quran, where God's message to Prophet Muhammad clearly reinforces, succeeds or supersedes that sent through Moses and Christ; the tradition of the Old Testament is appealed to in considerable detail. Its hearers did not deem these to be strange and incomprehensible narrations, for already all over Hijaz and Yemen there were Jewish and Christian communities of tradesmen, peasants and even pastoralists, who often lived as at Madina, among pagan populations. The basis, introduced from outside, for challenging pagan beliefs already existed; without it the reception given to Islam in pagan Arabia, after an initial hesitation, would have been inconceivable. The ideology of Islam was, then, by no means 'Arab', if it is intended to mean that its acceptance was the product of internal questionings spontaneously sprouting in nomad Arabia.

The core of what was new to pagan Arabia was umma, a concept which rapidly evolved from the sense of a federation of tribes or communities, pagan, Jewish and Muslim, with the Prophet as the arbitrator, into a community of Believers. There was no precedent of this in Arabia. The only precedents were external to the Arabs, in the Jewish community, for instance, but still more, the Christian realm, embracing all, irrespective of race and tribe, who believed in God, His Son and the Holy Ghost. If Allah was central to the faith of Islam, the umma was central to its organization; and the latter at any rate, was in its evolved form a purely external phenomenon.

Here one might also note that 'Arabism' in the age of the Prophet would have been a total anachronism. The Arabs were conscious of no sense of superiority; there were grounds for lack of such consciousness. They envied the wealth and prosperity of their neighbours; they were themselves visibly primitive and backward. That Allah in His mercy had sent them the last of the Prophets was a matter of Divine Grace, not a thing expected or natural. Believers could be proud if those other than Arabs became Muslims; Islam was thus, quite self-consciously, not an Arab but a universal faith. Things were to change only later, when the Arabs subjugated other people in the name of Islam. Then alone could Islam become, in the eyes of its neo-aristocratic believers, the peculiar privilege of the conquering race.

Yet, it was the externally introduced concept of umma that made the conquests possible; a unity to which tribal diversity became subordinate, and a unity that could, therefore, give cohesion and direction, if its leadership came into such able hands as those of Abu Bakr and Umar, the first two caliphs. The unity did not, however, imply equality or democracy. For one thing, the Quraysh, as the sacred tribe of the past and now the tribe of the Prophet, enjoyed a rising prominence. Within the tribes the chiefs (saiyyids, shaykhs) had from the beginning retained their places upon joining the Islamic banner. There were thus all the elements present for a

rapid evolution of an aristocracy within the umma, though such
evolution could not but bring in the infusion of family and tribal
feuds—the real 'Arab' heritage.

II

On the actual process of conquests little need be said, since much
has been written. It is difficult to know what the initial reactions of
the conquered people were. The Byzantine Empire was undoubtedly
ridden by sectarian quarrels, and the Sassanid Empire had been
shaken by a revolt of the poor, led by Mazdak in the preceding
century. But the factors behind the first successes of the Arabs lay
probably more within their own new-found unity of purpose than in
any support they would arouse among the ranks of their opponents.
Yet once the initial military advantage had been attained, the Arab
conquests were relatively swift, and the vast structures of the two
empires, with their taxes and rents, lay in the hands of the conquerors,
even before the Pious Caliphate came to an end (AD 661).

What took place may now be studied from two angles: what
happened to the conquerors, and what happened to the conquered.
First, I venture to think that Wellhausen's analysis, though
demanding modifications in detail, still stands in its essentials.[10] On
a close scrutiny of the traditions incorporated in Tabari, Wellhausen
argued that with the ultimate rise to dominance of the aristocratic
Qurayshite house of the Ummayyads, there developed three basic
contradictions among the ruling classes of Islam: (a) between the
tribal leaders of two great tribal federations, which evolved within
the aristocracy of tribal leaders, namely the Muzarites and the
Yemenites; (b) between the Arab tribal leaders settled in Iraq (the
conquerors of Persia) and the Syrians (who hosted, so to speak, the
Ummayyad Caliphate); and (c) between the Arabs, in general, and
the non-Arab Muslims who tended to increase with 'unauthorized'
conversions, that is with people becoming Muslims without actual
acceptance as clients (mawwali) by any Arab tribe. I do not think
that Shaban in his *The Abbasid Revolution* has really brought down
Wellhausen's major thesis, though one would readily agree that
Wellhausen's implied supposition of the continuation of pagan—
Arab rivalries in an Islamic form, probably goes too far.[11] The Abbasid
Revolution was seen by Wellhausen as an alliance of the Iraqites
with the mawwali, with loyalty to the House of the Prophet (the
Alids) as an ideological cloak for their ambitions. One could, of

course, agree that the natural result of such an alliance, when successful, was bound to be 'the assimilation of all Muslims', but whether this was a conscious immediate 'objective' of the Abbasid Revolution, as Shaban supposes may perhaps be doubted.

This brings us to the question: who were the mawwali? We must now ask the second question, what was happening to the conquered? It may be seen from the actual records of the Arab conquests, for example of Sind, given in splendidly detailed narration in the *Chachnama,* that the first converts to Islam, the 'clients' accepted by Arabs, belonged to the high and middle nobility rather than the masses who remained unconverted for a much longer time. Muhammad ibn Qasim, the conqueror of Sind and his successors, even continued the Brahmanical restrictions on the pastoral 'unclean' community of the Jatts.[12] The conquerors also continued the earlier taxation, so that a very heavy tax (*kharaj*) assimilated and incorporated the earlier burdens. It is doubtful if Arab conquests meant any kind of liberation or even relief to the poor of the conquered lands.

The converted aristocracy, such as the *marzban*s and *dihqan*s of the Sassanid regime, became inevitable adjuncts and middlemen to the Arab rulers. In course of time they would be Arabicized in culture, and, perhaps, speech; they would never be tribalized. In essence, therefore, they came to represent a more coherent and homogeneous class than the tribally divided Arab rulers. As conversions percolated downwards, Hajjaj ibn Yusuf could inveigh against the rising mawwali, but in vain. The future belonged to them.

III

We may yet, with Wellhausen, suppose the Abbasid Revolution to have been the work of a coalition between the Iraqite Arabs and the mawwali, the latter still probably a minority among the subject population, but indispensable to Iraqite rule.

The Abbasid caliphate was the period when the classical world of Islam really took shape: A subterranean Persian basis, influx of Hellenic and Hellenistic thought and sciences, Arabic as the vehicle of expression—such was the trinity of Abbasid high culture. It was the emergence of the great juridical schools, the formulation of the orthodox (Ash'arite) theology, the beginnings of Sufism. This high culture, with Arabic as its main vehicle, was the obvious result of a tremendous cross-cultural fertilization.

Alongside the development of this culture whose last great representatives in the eastern lands were Avicenna and Alberuni (early eleventh century), there seems to have occurred a process whereby Islam, from being the religion of an elite minority, became the faith of the masses. By the time of the Mongol conquests, the Muslims obviously formed the vast bulk of the population of western and central Asia. The Christians, Parsis and Buddhists had been reduced to small minorities. It was probably this basic fact that saved Islam when its splintered political fabric was all but destroyed by the Mongols in the thirteenth century.

The process of conversion, as it neared completion, created new problems for Islamic polity: a state where the rulers and subjects were both Muslims, and where, therefore, the Muslims must bear the brunt of the taxation. For such a state neither the practices of the Prophet, more suitable for a semi-pastoral economy, nor the policies of Umar I, when the Muslims were the conquerors and all other people their subjects, could form a precedent. If Muslims were to pay *ushr* or one-tenth of the produce, no state could subsist financially. Inevitably, law adjusted to circumstance. The notion of kharaj as a tax on all peasants, comprising the surplus, irrespective of the faith of the taxpayer, came to be conceded by the jurists of the Hanafite School.[13] In practice this prevailed from the Atlantic to the Altai mountains. Conversely, the ruling class could no longer claim legitimacy on the basis of its Arab or Islamic origins. The Arab tribal claims on conquered lands in the form of *ziya'*, which the early caliphs had had to admit, similarly disappeared as the *iqta* or transferable revenue charge became universal. The ruling classes came to be detached from earlier roots, and, but for exceptional cases like the Siljuq tribe under the Siljuqids, the nobility became a class totally dependent not on hereditary claims, but on the pleasure of the ruler. The classic new state was that of Ghaznin, whose ruler Mahmud (999–1030), the great conqueror, was supposed to be the first Sultan of Islam. Thus arose the characteristic state of Medieval Islam, which seems to have formed the model of Marx's 'Asiatic Despotism'.[14]

In spite of these rather ominous features, the medieval states of the Islamic world (from the thirteenth century) had many positive contributions which may be readily admitted: patronage of commerce, a high level of urbanization, a minimum degree of security. There were other features, which no longer appeal to the modern mind: oppression of the peasantry, growing orthodoxy and stagnation in science and learning. But these questions, though important, are outside the area of our present concern, which has only been to raise issues about the stages of evolution of the Islamic polities and societies of the early period, before their arrival in India with the Ghorian conquests of *c.*1200.

NOTES

1. Here I am ignoring the Arab conquest of Sind, in the early eighth century, the Muslim communities in various parts of India in the subsequent period, and the Ghaznavide conquests of the eleventh century. Islam, as an important social and cultural factor in Indian history, begins its history only with the Ghorian conquests and the establishment of the Sultanate around the beginning of the thirteenth century.

2. Reprinted in H.A.R. Gibb, *Studies on the Civilization of Islam*, ed. Stanford J. Shaw and William R. Polk, London, 1912, pp. 3–33.

3. Edward W. Said, *Orientalism*, New York, 1979.

4. E.A. Belyaev *Arabs, Islam and the Arab Caliphate*, London, 1969, p.115.

5. Watt's major works are *Muhammad at Mecca*, Oxford, 1953; and *Muhammad at Madina*, Oxford, 1956.

6. Sura IX, 98.

7. Maxime Rodinson, *Mohammed*, Penguin edn, 1973, esp. pp. 264–5. M.A. Shaban, *Islamic History, A.D. 600–750: A New Interpretation*, Cambridge, 1971, pp. 13–14.

8. Ibid., p. 15.

9. Ibid.

10. J. Wellhausen, *The Arab Kingdom and its Fall*, tr. Margaret Graham Weir, Calcutta, 1927. One of the important modifications was introduced by D.C. Dennet in respect of Wellhausen's theory of the history of *kharaj* and *jizya* (Dennet, *Conversion and the Poll Tax in Early Islam*, Cambridge, Mass, 1950).

11. M.A. Shaban, *The Abbasid Revolution*, Cambridge, 1970, esp. p. XIV. Clearly Shaban is much harsher on Wellhausen than the evidence warrants.

12. *Chachnama*, ed. N.A. Baloch, Islamabad, 1983, pp. 163–4.

13. The most useful compilation for the jurists' opinions on the taxation is Aghnides, *Theories of Mohammadan Finance*, Lahore, 1961.

14. For the characteristics of the state now formed in the Islamic world, see the chapter 'Political Structures of the Islamic Orient in the Sixteenth and Seventeenth Centuries', in this volume.

2
Encounter and Efflorescence
The Genesis of the Medieval Civilization

There is much introspection, in these times, and gropings towards conflicting 'identities'. History (often, unhappily, appearing only in a garb of part-mythology and part-fiction) has become a court of appeal for all rival interests. It is time, therefore, that we interpret, as objectively and critically as possible, our heritage. This address offers my own understanding of that long and fateful encounter between two civilizations which took place in the medieval times, and which I believe to have not only been fateful but also immensely creative.

At first sight it may look odd why anyone should elaborate namely on a theme which would now seem to be well-worn, 'the intrusion of Islam' in Indian history. My own excuse for doing so is a twofold one. First, the debate on the question, far from being closed, has intensified, and it is not likely to go away, even if the present phase of its violent expression would hopefully pass, being perhaps only one of those periodical bouts in which we have learnt, by our action, to belittle the greatness of our own civilization. Secondly, it has seemed to me that much of previous writings, despite the extensive research and scientific outlook on which so much of it was based, did not fully take into account the perceptions of Islamic history, generated by modern research, but rather took either the old-fashioned missionary's or the apologist's view of Islam for its basis.

This is unfortunate. Wellhausen in his *Arab Kingdom and its Fall* had, for example, long ago shattered the stereotype picture of Arabs appearing with a sword in one hand and the Quran in the other, and asking every one to stand up and be converted. For Indian scholars there was little excuse to have waited. We had in the *Chachnama*, the thirteenth-century Persian translation of a virtually contemporary set of narratives of the Arab conquest of Sind, an authentic, detailed account of the process of the Arab conquest (710–14) and its aftermath. Here we see the Arab conquerors easily slipping into the shoes of the Indian rulers. The *Chachnama* tells us how the Brahmans were continued as revenue collectors, how their mode of worship and sanctity of images was guaranteed, including the right of the priests to a share in tax collection, and how the lowly Jatts continued to be subjected to the same humiliating restrictions that remind us of the *Manusmriti*'s injunctions against the *Chandalas*.[1] On the last point, we have an independent confirmation from Balazuri.[2] The same tolerance of the established religion extended to the Buddhists: they continued to make votive offerings of Arab coins at the great Stupa of Mirpur Khas.[3] Epigraphy attests to a similar attitude of the Arab rulers in an area further northward. In 857–8 in the Tochi Valley, North–West Frontier Province (Pakistan), an Arab Governor Fayy ibn 'Ammar constructed a pond, and then had a bilingual inscription set up, in Arabic (Kufic) and Sanskrit (Sharda), the latter duly beginning with '*Om*'.[4]

These actions belie the picture of the Arab conquerors as uncouth, avaricious, barbarian nomads coming out of the desert, fired with a fanatical belief that God was on their side. The picture is by no means a modern one. In the eleventh century Firdausi put the following words of indignant portrayal of the Arab victor in the mouth of the vanquished Persian aristocrat:

> From living on camel's milk and lizard's flesh
> The Arabs have suddenly reached a state
> That they have set their sights on the throne of the Emperors,
> Fie upon thee, ever altering Fortune.[5]

But the picture, though early, is overdrawn, even for the Arabs who overthrew the Persians in the 630s. The overdrawing was aided by the Muslims' own tendency to stress the pagan Arabs' barbarous ways in order to highlight the change wrought by Islam. Recent research has tended to discount much of this, and to suggest, by an interpretation of the word *ummi*, that the Prophet himself was not unlettered but only a 'gentile', in the Jewish and Christian meaning of the term, and that, even the early Arabs obtained leadership and organization from the mercantile and sophisticated Quraysh.[6] By the end of the seventh century, the situation was different. The bedouin element in the conquering Arabs had been suppressed, through a series of bloody civil wars by the Umayyads—the cream of the Quraysh — relying upon the Syrians, the most Hellenized of the Arabs. (We must remember that it was through Syriac that Arabic was to receive the wealth of Greek science and learning under the Abbasids.)

By the time the Arabs invaded Sind, other civilized elements had entered the scene: the non-Arab Muslims, largely from Iran, called the mawwali. Their existence was essential to the Arab regime, yet their pretensions had to be severely suppressed in the interest of the Arab ruling class.[7] The elite position of the Syrians and the contempt for mawwali, are duly attested by the *Chachnama*.[8] It is this hierarchical structure pre-existing among the Arab conquerors which explains their readiness immediately to accommodate the existing hierarchy in Sind. They had already achieved an accommodation with the dihqans, or the rural aristocracy of the Sassanid regime in Iran, and the move to accept Brahmans and possibly *Thakkuras* (*Takurs*),[9] as subordinate ruling class was thus in conformity with their tradition. Their scorn for the mawwali moderated their zeal to create a large population of converts in Sind: the *Chachnama* thus records not a single forcible conversion to Islam.

If this was the attitude of the conquerors, how were they looked at by the vanquished? The only source for this is the *Chachnama*. It is by no means an unreliable source. The presence of an entire local chronicle for the history of the pre-Arab dynasty—reminding us of the later, celebrated *Rajatarangini* of Kalhana—and of constant reports from the Indian side on the war, including much hero-worship of Dahar's son, Jaisiya, shows that it can claim some authenticity as conveyer of the Indian sentiments. It represents Dahar's sister preparing for self-immolation to escape from captivity under those 'cow-eating *Chandalas*'.[10] But, after the settlement at Brahmanabad, the Brahman officials are said to have dispersed over the country and to have thus addressed the 'notables' everywhere:

Dahar is dead; the power of the 'infidels' has come to an end. In the whole of Sind and Hind, the writ of the Arabs has been established. The big and small of this territory, from town and village, have become one (under subjection), and our affairs are to be held to be managed under a great Empire. We have been sent by them to give you good assurances.[11]

Thus the response was of a dual kind. In the first instance, a bitter rejection of an alien invader: in the second, a realistic acceptance of conditions in which the invader became familiar, and life with honour, though with reduced authority, undoubtedly, was possible. The question one tends to ask is whether the response could have been very greatly different if the invaders had not been the Arabs, but, say, another north Indian power. Certainly, when King Harsha of Kashmir was overthrown by an internal revolt (AD 1101), the scene of fiery immolation of the queens and women of the royal family[12] was no different from that described by the *Chachnama* in respect of Dahar's family faced with seizure by the Arabs.[13]

Undoubtedly, the Arabs were foreigners in that they represented a visibly different cultural tradition. But our present understanding that 'foreign' invasions have been detrimental to a country derives from a natural but illogical confusion between pre-modern 'foreign' (a concept again based on modern national boundaries) and modern colonial acquisitions. There is in all advanced historiographies a much more critical attitude towards the role played by conquerors from different cultural areas. V. Barthold, the Soviet historian, had strongly opposed the negative assessment of the Mongol conquests pronounced by his Russian colleagues. It is thus equally important that we should not try to read back our present national sentiments into those of the people a millennium earlier, and feel awkward if these do not appear to have been shared by them.

Conformable to this view, one tends to forget that during the subsequent centuries too Sind remains part of Indian history. This ought not to be forgotten if for the single reason that during this period it represented a strong contrast to the conditions of 'Indian feudalism'. The ruins of the large city of Mansura (encompassing Brahmanabad and Mahfuza) that the Arabs built, extended in a band about two and a half miles long and a half to three-fourths of a mile wide, exhibiting dense occupation with 'thousands' of wells.[14] Nor is the coinage issued by the Arab rulers of Sind to be despised for its size: the copper coins recovered are numerous, and the silver, though small and relatively 'rare',[15] suggest commerce on a considerable scale. One would respectfully take issue with Professor R.S. Sharma, who holds that the Arab conquests adversely affected India's external commerce during the first two or three centuries of Islam.[16] The statement is perhaps based on Henry Pirenne's famous hypothesis of the genesis of feudalism out of the blocking of Mediterranean commerce through the Islamic presence.[17] This argument, however, was contested long ago by W.C. Dennett and others, and has now been virtually abandoned.[18] Conditions were, on the other hand, quite the opposite. Spain in Arab hands was a thriving region of commerce with the western empire, as Marc Bloch notes.[19] Arab-held Sind might well have played a similar role in 'feudal' India.

II

Textbook writers often tend to view the 'coming' of Islam into India as the work of three principal figures, Mohammad ibn Qasim (d. 714), Mahmud of Ghaznin (d. 1030) and Shihabuddin of Ghor (d. 1206). This leaves out of account the fact that there had occurred considerable changes in the Islamic world in the three centuries that separated the Arab conqueror of Sind from the Ghaznavid empire-builder, and that the nature of interests and ambitions of the two were widely different.

What happened during the three intervening centuries was the flowering in the Asian and African worlds of a single great civilization, and the construction, side by side, of the brutal institutions of despotic polities. Under the great Abbasids (eighth and ninth centuries), Greek philosophy and science found a home in Arabic, through one of the greatest processes of translations made in pre-modern history; and it became the starting point of an intellectual renaissance. Islam was given its classic shape, with Asharite theology and the great schools of jurisprudence. There came a deep new probing into the motives of conformist ethics, and this was to lead to Islamic mysticism or *tasawwuf*, the refuge of souls unimpressed by orthodoxy. By the eleventh century the Iranian revival had begun in the eastern portion of this world, making its own contribution to the growth of a sceptical spirit.

Along with these developments in higher culture, new political institutions evolved, as the caliphate waxed and waned. The claim to the entire agrarian surplus as royal tax (kharaj), the transferable tax assignment (iqta), the slave-soldiers and officers (largely Turkish) gave enormous strength to the centralized regional states, which now arose, their rulers ultimately claiming the old Arabic title of Sultan. The power of the new states lay not only in these fiscal and administrative instruments: the new techniques of war made the Arab infantryman and camel-rider obsolete and brought in the mounted archer, his horse provided, besides the saddle, with the stirrup and iron-shoe.[20]

The successes of Mahmud of Ghaznin were undoubtedly due not only to his military genius, but also to the institutions of centralized despotism and the military system that had been steadily built up. He only put them skilfully to use for his self-aggrandizement.

From minds truly nurtured in the civilization that had been created in the world of Islam, Mahmud could call for little sympathy. Sa'di (thirteenth century) saw him as an avaricious man, jealous that his empire should pass after his death to another, and contrasted him with

Naushervan, whose name would be gratefully remembered for ever because of his pursuit of justice.[21] Al-Beruni, the great scientist and contemporary of Mahmud, did not conceal his true sympathies when he wrote:

Mahmud utterly ruined the prosperity of the country (India), and performed there wonderful exploits, by which the Hindus became like atoms of dust scattered in all directions, and like a tale of old in the mouth of the people. Their scattered remains cherish, of course, the most inveterate aversion towards all Muslims.[22]

It was only the fanatically inclined who would interpret Mahmud's exploits as contributing to the glory of Islam, and for reasons which would be hardly edifying for any religion. Isami (writing in 1350) was to say in verse:

If I and you, O wise one, find a place in this realm,
Sometime to convert a temple into mosque, or break sacred threads,
Or make the women and children of Hindus into concubines and slaves —
All of this is due to the legacy of his (Mahmud's) work. This is the truth, all else is mere talk.[23]

Glorification in vulgar terms like this has given Mahmud the image of an 'arch-fanatic he never was'. Professor Mohammad Habib was right to argue that Islam won infamy in India, not only from the original depredations of Mahmud, but also from admiration 'by such Mussalmans as have cast off the teachings of Lord Krishna in their devotion to minor gods'.[24]

But it is equally right to look at some other evidence as well: Was Mahmud so vastly different from other conquerors and marauders as to leave in India an everlasting bitter memory? It does appear strange as we seek such evidence that he should not be mentioned in any Sanskrit source, except for one, Kalhana's *Rajatarangini*. In that single Sanskrit account of one of Mahmud's invasions, a campaign against Trilochanpala, we are told of the defeat of the combined armies of the Shahi and Kashmir rulers, attributed by Kalhana to the Kashmir general Tunga's lack of acquaintance with 'Turushka warfare'. Kalhana sincerely mourns the fall of the Kashmir general brought about by Hammira (Amir Mahmud), 'skilled in stratagem'. But there is no particular denunciation of the 'fierce Chandalas', the Turushkas, who descended 'on the whole surface of the earth'.[25] There is no reference to any plunder, enslavement, desecration of temples, flight of Brahmans to Kashmir, which one might naturally have expected

Kalhana to dilate upon if only to stress the baneful consequence of Tunga's ineptitude. It is, seemingly, just one of the episodes in political history, a conquest like any other. One begins to wonder whether the sensitive Alberuni and the vainglorious chroniclers have not presented a picture of Mahmud's depredations that is heavily overdrawn. Nor should Mahmud be allowed to overshadow Alberuni. The compilation of Alberuni's *Kitabul-l Hind*[26] was a unique event in the history of mankind, unique because there has been no other instance in pre-modern times, of one of the greatest intellectuals of one civilization studying and analysing, with such range and depth, the major aspects of another civilization. To borrow words from reviews of Needham's great work on China, it was at once an 'act of recognition' and a great act of 'intercultural communication'. We are here introduced to a rigorously scientific spirit, a detailed, balanced, scrutiny of Sanskrit materials, a close knowledge of Greek philosophy and science, which the author calls upon to assess the level of Indian cultural and intellectual development, and a truly critical approach as well to the ideas and institutions of his own Islamic milieu. Sachau wonders how Alberuni, under the shadow of Mahmud, could speak of Hindu scholars 'who enjoy the help of God'.[27] He was ready to seek reason behind many of the myths in his texts and rituals that he examined with such care, just as he could condemn in his texts with straightforward frankness the inanities or concealments that he found. It was surely a seminal moment when Alberuni conveyed to his readers the view, tentatively nurtured in India, that 'the earth moves while the sun is resting'.[28]

Surely, Alberuni's immense achievement is not only a tribute to his own genius; it is equally a tribute to the civilization which produced him and which provided readers for his great work. There was a duality in Islamic civilization—as in any other—greatness rubbing shoulders with pettiness, an Alberuni by the side of Mahmud; but it would be unhistorical, when assessing the consequences of that civilization's arrival in India, to absolutely forget one side of it and remember only the other.

III

The bilingual coinage of Muizzuddin bin Sam of Ghor (the Shihabuddin Ghori of our textbooks) proclaimed the establishment of what was to become essentially an Indian Sultanate. The coinage is not only bilingual: In two gold coins, it carried the figure of a seated Lakshmi—

a concession to Hindu sentiments so unique that Brown pronounces it 'without a parallel in Muhammadan history'.[29] In other gold and silver coins the figure of a horseman is provided, as also of Shiva's bull, without any thought of Islamic reserve about representation of living beings.[30] When Iltutmish created the silver *tanka* of 168 grains or so, he did not import 'Islamic' metrology, but clearly tried to base his coin on the *tola*-weight. The billon coins of Iltutmish and his successors continued to be bilingual and carry the horseman and the bull, down to Muizzuddin Kaiqubad (d. 1290).

The coinage suggests a polity which was not alien. Originally planted by invasions, it was seeking to spread roots into the soil. How far and fast they had spread is divulged by a chance exclamation of that scrupulous chronicler, Minhaj Siraj. When in 1255 Uzbak Tughril Khan declared himself King and marched from Bengal to Awadh, in rebellion against Sultan Nasiruddin Mahmud, 'this act of defiance of his was disapproved by all the people of Hindustan, the divines and the nobles, Muslims and Hindus.'[31] By 1260, then, when Minhaj Siraj was writing, it was already politically important what Hindus, and not just a section of Muslims (the 'divines and the nobles'), thought of the claims of a pretender.

In the next century, the Sultanate was to embark on an experiment that could have very few parallels in the pre-modern world, though it was to be repeated in the Mughal empire on a still bolder scale: the creation of a ruling class not confined to followers of a single religion. Thakkura Pheru, who has left valuable information on coinage and other economic and cultural matters in Sanskrit tracts, was an officer of Alauddin Khalji's mint.[32] Another important Hindu officer of the treasury under the same Sultan (1296–1316), Sadharana by name, makes his appearance in the Ladnun Sanskrit inscription.[33] Their number and influence increased under Muhammad Tughluq: We hear of Ratan, the governor of Siwistan (Sind);[34] Bharan or Sharan, the governor of Gulbarga;[35] Kishan, 'the market-man of Indri', the governor of Awadh;[36] and Dhara, the *naib wazir* of Deogir.[37] The general statement that Hindus were given high offices by that Sultan occurs in Isami.[38]

Other sections of Hindus not in official employment also obtained a position of protection and prosperity, such as the merchants, especially the Multanis. Already in the thirteenth century, they were large-scale creditors to the Sultanate nobility and greatly benefited from this relationship.[39] Jalaluddin Khalji (1290–6) is said to have commented on their prosperity and pretensions.[40] And, apart from the nobility, they were said to have been the people who retained their wealth under Alauddin Khalji.[41] They were wealthy enough to have left step-wells, with classical Sanskrit inscriptions praising the Sultans in the same way as a Kshatriya ruler would be praised in any *prasasti*.[42] They would go accompanied by Brahmans to welcome Sultan Firuz upon his successful bid for the throne,[43] and acquire 'lakhs and crores' under that sovereign.[44] Moreland long ago clarified that there is no basis for identifying Hindus wholesale with the village aristocracy (*muqaddams, khuts*, etc.), whom Alauddin Khalji tried to contain and impoverish.[45] In any case, not only does Barani say that when Firuz Tughluq ascended the throne in 1351, 'the Muslims and Hindus had their hearts comforted',[46] but notes that by 1357 the khuts and muqaddams had become prosperous, with numberless horses and cattle.[47]

This evidence of accommodation of Hindus in the political and economic framework of the Sultanate had its counterpart in the official recognition (however limited in terms of the secularism of today) of the coexistence of the two religions. One may begin by recalling that the extensive reconstruction of the Mahabodhi temple of Bodh Gaya, under Arakanese auspices, took place in 1305–6, during the regime of the Sultans.[48] A spirit of accommodation and even identification is apparent in the famous poet Khusrau's *Nuh Sipihr* (1318), a long panegyric on Qutbuddin Mubarak Khalji (1316–20): Not only is India superior to other countries, the Hindus are superior to many others in their religious beliefs, language, learning and science.[49] This spirit was obviously shared by Muhammad Tughluq when during a famine he shifted his capital from Delhi to a new settlement on the Ganga, and gave his new seat the Sanskrit name *Swarga-duari* or 'Gate of Heaven'.[50] He would play Holi, and converse with yogis.[51] There is documentary proof too of his solicitude for the Jains: Two religious leaders of the community were to be allowed to go wherever they wished, and be rewarded and honoured.[52] Under Muhammad Tughluq's successor Firuz, well known for his espousal of orthodox views, a sun temple was built at Gaya in 1352, its Sanskrit inscription containing the Sultan's name twice.[53]

A similar attitude was adopted by Hindu rulers. A Sanskrit inscription of 1246 at Verawal, Gujarat, tells us of the erection of a mosque there by Nuruddin Firuz of Hormuz, under the partronage of the Chaulukya king Arjunadeva, said to be powerful through the grace of 'Siva'.[54] Some two hundred years later, when Rana Kumbha built his famous victory tower, he had the word 'Allah' in Arabic recorded nine times on the third storey and eight times on the eighth storey, on pillarettes in excellent workmanship. This led an English observer (1883–84) to say:

This discovery opens up a problem, of which the only solution which presents itself to me is that the barrier dividing the Hindus and Musalmans three (*rect.* four) centuries ago, was far less impassable than it is at the present day.[55]

IV

The rulers' indulgence towards the 'other' religion could not, indeed, have existed had the barrier between Hindus and Muslims been as impassable as Garrick thought it was in his own time. The evidence on what relations between Hindus and Muslims in everyday life were like is not large, but it is fairly clear.

I shall first offer what the dated conversations of the mystic Shaikh Nizamuddin of Delhi, recorded by Amir Hasan Sijzi, in the first two decades of the fourteenth century, provide us. In assessing the evidence, it should be noted that the view that the Sufis or dervishes were liberal men, with little care for orthodoxy, is simplistic. They accepted the shariat, or Muslim law, in its entirety; theirs, as Professor Mohammad Habib once remarked, was a 'post-graduate creed'. Shaikh Nizamuddin himself was sufficiently orthodox to find fault with Abu Hanifa, the founder of the juridical school of Muslim Law prevalent in the larger part of the eastern world of Islam, for saying that on the Last Day, the unbelievers too would see the Light and be pardoned. This could never be, said Nizamuddin, with an assured knowledge of Divine intentions, of which only the most religious and the most orthodox are capable.[56] Yet, he tells us of his own friendly conversations with yogis (*jogis*), and treats their beliefs and principles with much respect. At one meeting at his preceptor's seat at Ajodhan, a yogi told him that in man's body the navel marks the division of two spheres, the higher concerned with spiritual matters and truth, the other, the lower, concerned with good morals. The Shaikh commended this.[57] Or, again, he tells of obtaining from a yogi what qualities the offspring conceived on different days would have.[58]

Even more telling is Nizamuddin's assertion that the actual ethics of Muslims being what they were, a Hindu could not be asked to convert to Islam. He said this when a Muslim disciple brought his Hindu brother to Nizamuddin in the hope of attaining his conversion.[59] Elsewhere, Nizamuddin contrasts the upright business ethics of the

Hindus of Gujarat with the improbity of the Muslim merchants of Lahore.[60] He commended the compiler Amir Hasan's action in restoring a slave girl to her Hindu parents, although this meant that she would apostatize.[61] 'The theologians concerned with matters of appearance would condemn such action, but one must understand what he did', said Nizamuddin of a similar freeing of a slave maidservant by a mystic to enable her to return to her Hindu sons in Katehr.[62]

If these were ethical values being established, in spite of the narrow letter of the law, this was surely on account of an increasing appreciation of the vast learning and wisdom of Hinduism (even if seen only by encounters with yogis) and a recognition of the ethical stature of the Hindus—early products of living side by side with them in towns and villages.

I am not aware of any text in which appraisals from a Hindu divine of this period can be obtained. The late Dev Raj Chanana wrote an interesting essay on the Sanskritist and Indian society. In this he argued that the Sanskritists were prone to sing loyally of whomever had power, and that the prasasti-like compositions in which the Muslim rulers appear in the same guise as the Kshatriya rulers were not an expression of a 'communal fraternity of an intellectual kind', as J.B. Chaudhuri had thought, but a pure practising of an old tradition of opportunism.[63] I believe Chanana went a little too far in arguing a partly legitimate case. A poet or writer, whether Amir Khusrau, the court poet, or Pandita Yogiswara, the composer of the Palam Baoli inscription, would equally be ready to serve their patrons and write what they wished them to, whether the patron was the Sultan in one case, or a merchant in another. The question really is why the patron should have wished the Sanskritists to write as they did. It is difficult to believe that the Hindu merchants who got the laudatory verses for Muslim rulers inscribed on their step-wells at Palam or Sarban were under any pressure to do so; it is unlikely that officials would have read the Sanskrit inscriptions to find out whether the Sultan had been sufficiently praised. What is more likely is that the Sultans fitted into an existing tradition of lauding contemporary rulers; and Muslims had become so familiar a participant in everyday life that they and their faith no longer seemed alien. Thus Balban could be praised for doing all of Vishnu's work for the god, and Muhammad Tughluq could be described as the 'crest-jewel of all rulers of the earth' under whom at Delhi 'sin is expelled through the chanting of the Vedas'.[64] No contradiction was discerned in Vishnu leaving his work to a Muslim ruler, or the Vedic hymns purging a Muslim capital.

How was a Muslim loyal to his faith looked at? An unclean *mlechha*, exciting bitter hatred, as Professor R.C. Majumdar would like us to believe?[65] Majumdar cites no authority for his assumption of the Hindu urge to exterminate 'the *mlechhas* (Muslims)' altogether in India. But one can cite a contrary view. Nanak (*fl.* 1500) was a Khatri, born a Hindu. His concept of an ideal Muslim, in an oft-quoted verse, is as follows:

> Let him heartily obey the will of God,
> Worship the Creator, and efface himself—
> When he is kind to all men, then, Nanak,
> Shall he be indeed a Musalman.[66]

This was not the image of a fierce, fanatical religion, but of one held to preach ethics and benevolence. How far the image was accurate is not relevant; its existence in the mind of men like Nanak is the essential fact.

V

The 'intrusion of Islam' in Indian history, in its first three centuries (thirteenth to fifteenth) helped to create a political structure, based on the iqta (transferable territorial assignment). This allowed the creation, even for half a century, of the first all-India empire after nearly fifteen hundred years, the only preceding one being that of the Mauryas. It clearly reinforced the concept of India as a country, if not a nation. The Palam Baoli inscription of 1281 already gives a geographical description of India, the whole of which it inaccurately claims for Balban.[67] When less than forty years later the claim became a fact, Amir Khusrau proudly claims for India a primary position in all aspects of nature and culture. He gives us a description of the languages of the different regions of the country but reminds us that the Hindawi is the country's lingua franca, and Sanskrit its classical language.[68] Khusrau knows India as 'Hind'. In 1350, Isami could write a glowing ode to Hindustan, the name that was to become so common:

> Great is the prosperity of the country of Hindustan.
> Heaven itself is jealous of this garden.
> Its territories are an ornament to the face of the Earth
> As a beauty spot on the face of a lovely maiden.

And so he goes on.[69]

This lends support to Tara Chand's conclusion that the all-India empire under the Sultans created 'a political uniformity and a larger allegiance'.[70] The larger allegiance coalesced with a love for the larger land, seen and loved with a new vividness and pride as a single country.

This country now began to develop a composite culture in which the language, literature, ideas and arts, brought from outside merged with those existing earlier. Tara Chand gave an account of this in a book justly regarded as a classic and just quoted. It is pointless to repeat in summary what he has spelt out so well. I would only remind readers that Tara Chand's survey was not intended to be exhaustive; and that the influence of the earlier culture on Muslims in India was excluded from the scope of his work, though this factor too was crucial in the creation of a composite culture. The exchange took place at high intellectual levels besides the level of ordinary social intercourse. Much knowledge of Indian arts, for example, was transferred to Persian.

In 1374–5, under the patronage of Firuz Tughluq's governor of Gujarat, came the first-known Persian work on Indian music, with the most competent knowledge of Sanskrit terms imaginable.[71] Nearly a hundred and forty years later (1512–13), Bhuwa, son of Khawas Khan, prepared a wonderfully comprehensive compendium of Indian medicine (Ayurveda), *Ma'dan-i Shifa-i Sikandar Shahi,* with extensive use of Sanskrit texts.[72] Alberuni's cause was by no means dead, however pale in terms of brilliance his successors might have been.

The cultural efflorescence was accompanied by economic changes of some significance. There was an influx of technology, to which Kosambi had briefly referred and which Irfan Habib has studied in so much detail.[73] It was in these three centuries (thirteenth to fifteenth) that India received the spinning-wheel, the pedals of the loom, cloth-printing, paper, magnetic compass, techniques of large-scale arcuate construction, lime mortar, pindrum gearing (to complete the apparatus of the Persian wheel), more effective devices for distillation and sericulture. These undoubtedly led to an expansion of craft production, possibly even to greater cloth production per captia, and certainly to more extensive use of masonry. There is evidence, literary as well as numismatic, that commerce expanded; and archaeology attests to the fact that the urban decline postulated for the previous period[74] was over, and an urban economy of impressive size rapidly developed. The economy had its own unhappy features, such as heavy agrarian taxation and, at least in the initial phase, an extensive urban slavery;

but these features (by no means necessarily new) were linked to what, in comparison to its immediate predecessor, was a distinctly expanding economy.[75]

The cultural and economic changes generated consciousness of unities and inequities that had not existed before. It expressed itself in a religious upsurge of a kind never witnessed since the emergence of Buddhism. A new comprehension of the unity of man, beyond castes, classes and other frontiers, reflected itself in an uncompromising assertion of the Unity of God. Never in India before, neither from the pen of a Hindu nor a Muslim, had there been such an outpouring of the rejection of the concepts of purity and pollution — the basis of the Indian *homo hierarchicus*[76] and the theoretical justification of the oppression of the untouchables. Learned scholars have argued whether the religious upsurge had been fertilized by Islamic, especially Sufic, ideas, or whether it was a logical development from premises inherent in early Indian philosophy. One can deduce from the first, as does R.C. Majumdar, that the movement was outside the pale of Hinduism;[77] from the second, as does Ishtiaq Hussain Qureshi, that it was a conspiracy by Hinduism to thwart the spread of Islam by borrowing its very colours.[78] These are matters which may concern only those who identify themselves with one particular religious denomination, as delimited by themselves. To me, the signal feature of the popular monotheistic movements of the fifteenth and sixteenth centuries was that it was a movement of the Small Man; its leaders came from his ranks and addressed him in his language; and they had an ethical message of substance to deliver to him.

The social character of the movements is best expressed in verses that Guru Arjan (d. 1606) composed in the name of Dhanna Jat:[79]

> In Gobind, Gobind, Gobind was Namdev's heart absorbed;
> A calio-printer worth half a *dam*, he became worth a lakh.
> Abandoning weaving and stretching thread, Kabir devoted his love to God's feet;
> Though a weaver of low family he obtained untold virtues.
> Ram Das who used to remove dead cattle, abandoned the world;
> Became distinguished, and in the company of the saints obtained a sight of God.
> Sain, barber and village drudge, (but now) well known in every house;
> In whose heart the supreme God dwelt is numbered among the saints.
> Having heard all this I, a Jat, applied myself to God's service;
> I have met God in person; and great is the good fortune of Dhanna.

Or the proud declaration on behalf of the lowly composed by Guru Amar Das:

Nanak, the gate of salvation is very narrow; only the lowly can pass through.[80]

To Kabir and Nanak and other teachers, denominations were meaningless. They denied they were Hindus or 'Turks' (Muslims); it is useless putting such tags on them. With almost a seeming foreknowledge of the current controversy, Kabir had sung:

> Hindus call Him Ram, Muslims Khuda.
> Says Kabir, Whoever lives,
> never bothers with this duality—
> Ka'bah then becomes Kashi, Ram becomes Rahim.[81]

When Kabir died, so the tradition runs, Hindus and Muslims came to claim him for their own.[82] He thus conformed to the aspirations of Urfi, the great Persian poet at Akbar's court in a verse which the author of the *Dabistan-i Mazahib* (*c.* 1655) uses for Kabir's epitaph:

> Urfi, live so well with people, good and bad,
> that when you die
> The Muslims should wash your body in *zamzam* water,
> and the Hindus should cremate it.

In 1590–91, the famous theologian Abdul Haqq, closing his biographical dictionary of Muslim saints, writes that his father when a child asked the author's grandfather whether Kabir, whose verses were current among the people, was a Muslim or a Hindu. The answer was: he was a monotheist (*muwahhid*). To the question further whether a monotheist, then, is neither a Hindu nor a Muslim, the old man replied: 'To understand this is difficult: you will understand when you grow up.'[83]

It seems from some recent events and disputes that many of us have still to grow up to understand. But so long as the Indian people cherish a love for their heritage, in ideas and values, the message of medieval cultural efforescence should surely live with us.

NOTES

1. *Chachnama*, ed. Umar bin Muhammad Daudpota, Hyderabad, 1939, pp. 208–16.

2. *Futuh at Baldan*, portion tr. Elliot and Dowson, *History of India as Told by its Own Historians*, I, London, 1867, p. 129.

3. Henry Cousens, *Antiquities of Sind*, Calcutta, 1929, p. 93.

4. *Epigraphia Indo-Moslemica*, 1925–6, pp. 27–8; B.N. Mukherjee, *Central and South Asian Documents on the Old Saka Era*, Varanasi, 1973, pp. 56–8.

5. *Zi-shir-i shutar khurdan*, etc. (*Shahnama*).

6. Modern research on the earliest phase of Islam, seen through a biography of the Prophet, is best presented in Maxime Rodinson, *Mohammed*, Eng. tr. Penguin Books, 1973. The term *ummi* is referred to on p. 240.

7. Wellhausen's interpretation of the main structure of the Umayyad rule in *Arab Kingdom and its Fall*, essentially based on a detailed analysis of the materials in Tabari, still stands, despite criticism by Shaban in the *Abbasid Revolution*, Cambridge, 1970.

8. *Chachnama*, pp. 95–6; pp. 181 and 182 for the exalted position of the Syrians; p. 192 for the low position of the mawwali.

9. *Chachnama* has many references to thakkuras, for example pp. 169, 177, 191, 232, but more explicitly to their adjustment with the Arab regime.

10. *Chachnama*, p. 195.

11. Ibid., p. 211.

12. *Rajatarangini*, tr. M.A. Stein London, 1990, I, pp. 388–9.

13. *Chachnama*, pp. 186, 194–5.

14. Cousens, *Antiquities of Sind*, pp. 48ff and plate IV (plan of the city).

15. Ibid., pp. 178–83.

16. R.S. Sharma, *Indian Feudalism*, Calcutta, 1965, p. 61. The statement is retained in the second edn, New Delhi, 1980, pp. 54–5.

17. See Pirenne's *Mohammad and Charlemagne*, Eng. tr., 1939, esp. part 2, ch.I, sect. 2.

18. Cf. R. Hilton, in *Transition from Feudalism to Capitalism*, London, 1953, pp. 65–6; B. Lewis, *Arabs in History*, London, 1958, pp. 87–92.

19. *Feudal Society*, Eng. tr., London, 1965, p. 65.

20. For the introduction of stirrup among the Arabs, see Lynn White Jr. *Medieval Technology and Social Change*, New York, 1966, pp. 18–19. The nailed horseshoe had reached Byzantium early in the tenth century (ibid., p. 58). For the Arabic and Persian evidence, see Irfan Habib, *Proceedings of the Indian History Congress (PIHC)*, Varanasi (1969), p. 159.

21. *Hikayat* in *Gulistan*, beginning *Yake az muluk-i Khurasan*, etc.

22. Edward C. Sachau (tr.), *Alberuni's India*, London, 1910, I, p. 22.

23. Isami, *Futuh-us Salatin*, ed. A.S. Usha, Madras, 1948, p. 29.

24. Mohammad Habib, *Sultan Mahmud of Ghaznin*, Aligarh, 1951, p. 87.

25. *Rajatarangini*, I, pp. 272–3. Kalhana does not give the date of the encounter, but puts it in the reign of Samgaramaraja (1003–28).

26. Edward C. Sachau has rendered all of us in debt by his excellently annotated translation of *Kitabul-i-Hind (Alberuni's India)* in two volumes (London, 1910). Professor Qeyamuddin Ahmad has edited an abridged version of this translation, published by the National Book Trust, New Delhi, 2nd edn (revised), 1983.

27. Tr. Sachau, II, p. 108. Alberuni is actually quoting Varahamihira here. Cf. Sachau, I , p. xviii. Perhaps, in real life, Mahmud could not care less!

28. Tr. Sachau, I, p. 276–7.

29. C.J. Brown, *The Coins of India*, Calcutta, 1922, p. 70.

30. H. Nelson Wright, *The Coinage and Metrology of the Sultans of Delhi*, Delhi, 1936, pp. 6–12 (catalogue), 67 (commentary). It is only fair to say that Muizzuddin was continuing a tradition of bilingual coinage established by the Ghaznavids.

31. *Tabaqat-i Nasiri*, ed. Abdul Hayy Habibi, Kabul, 1343 H. II, pp. 31–2. Raverty, the erudite translator of the work into English, notices the implications of this statement (*Tabaqat-i Nasiri*, tr. Raverty, p. 764). For the date of Tughril's rebellion, see A.B.M. Habibullah, *The Foundation of Muslim Rule in India*, 2nd (revised) ed, Allahabad, 1961, p. 130.

32. Cf. S.R. Sarma in *Aligarh Journal of Oriental Studies* I (1), 1984, pp. 3–4.

33. *Journal of Indian History (JIH)*, xv (2), 1936, pp. 182–3.

34. Ibn Battuta, *Rihla*, tr. Mehdi Husain, p. 8.

35. Isami, *Futuh-us Salatin*, pp. 484–8; Barani, *Tarikh-i Firuz Shahi*, ed. Saiyid Ahmad Khan, Bib. Ind., Calcutta, 1862, p. 488.

36. Barani, p. 505.

37. Ibid., p. 501.

38. *Futuh-us Salatin*, pp. 464–5.

39. Barani, p. 120.

40. Ibid., pp. 216–17.

41. Ibid., p. 113.

42. See the Palam Boali Inscription of AD 1281 (*Journal of Asiatic Society of Bengal*, henceforth *JASB* xxxxIII (1), 1874, pp. 104ff); and the Sarban Inscription of 1328 (Mehdi Husain, *Rise and Fall of Mohammad Tughluq*, London, 1938, pp. 246–7).

43. Barani, p. 546.

44. Ibid., p. 554 (read *Sahan* for *Sipahan*).

45. W.H. Moreland, *Agrarian System of Moslem India*, Cambridge, 1929, pp. 32, 225, 230.

46. Barani, p. 547.

47. Ibid., p. 554.

48. Cunningham, *Archaeological Survey Reports*, III, pp. 103–5.

49. *Nuh Sipihr*, ed. Mohammad Wahid Mirza, London, 1950, pp. 151–95.

50. Barani, p. 485; Isami, p. 472 (where for material reasons, perhaps, the name is given as *Sargadari*, but a reference to heaven in the couplet shows *sarg* represents *swarga*).

51. Isami, p. 515. For Muhammad Tughluq's interest in yogic practices, see Ibn Battuta, p. 266.

52. Order issued to officials in 1329. Simon Digby of Channel Islands, UK, possesses a clear photograph of the document.

53. Cunningham, *Archaeological Survey Reports*, III, pp. 103–5.

54. *JIH*, xv (2), p. 181.

55. H.B.W. Garrick, in Cunningham, *Archaeological Survey Reports*, XXIII, pp. 116–17.

56. *Fawaid-ul Fowwad*, ed. Mohammad Latif Malik, Lahore, 1996. pp. 118–19.

57. Ibid., p. 118.

58. Ibid., pp. 417–18; Nizamuddin's preceptor, Farid, told him not to bother with this, not because what the yogi was furnishing him with was wrong, but because he would not have any use for it, since he was not to marry himself. See also ibid., pp. 404–5.

59. Ibid., pp. 305–6, 308.

60. Ibid., pp. 201–2.

61. Ibid., pp. 339–40.

62. Ibid., pp. 278–9.

63. *Enquiry*, Delhi, New Series II (2) (Old series, no. 11), 1965, pp. 49–67. He contests J.B. Chaudhuri's view on p. 56.

64. In respectively the Palam and Sarban inscriptions: see references given above.

65. R.C. Majumdar, Preface to *History and Culture of Indian People*, vol. v, p. xiv.

66. Majh ki War, *Guru Granth Sahib*. The translation is that of Macauliffe.

67. See references to this inscription above.

68. *Nuh Sipihr*, pp. 179–81.

69. Isami, pp. 604–5.

70. Tara Chand, *Influence of Islam on Indian Culture*, 2nd edn, Allahabad, 1963, p. 141.

71. The work, *Ghunyat-ul Munya*, which is unfortunately anonymous, has been edited by Shahab Sarmadee, Bombay, 1978.

72. Nawal Kishore editions, Lucknow, 1877, 1889 (page-to-page correspondence with the earlier edn).

73. D.D. Kosambi, *Introduction to the Study of Indian History*, Bombay, 1956, p. 370. Irfan Habib, 'Technology and Society in the 13th and 14th Centuries', *PIHC*, Varanasi, 1969, pp. 139–61, and 'Medieval Technology: Exchange between India and the Islamic World', *Aligarh Journal of Oriental Studies*, II (1–2), 1985, pp. 196–222.

74. R.S. Sharma, *Urban Decay in India*, c. 300–1000, New Delhi, 1987.

75. Cf. Irfan Habib, 'Economic History of the Delhi Sutanate', *Indian Historical Review (IHR)* IV (2), 1978, pp. 287–303.

76. Cf. Louis Dumont, *Homo Hierarchicus*, English, edn, London, 1972.

77. This follows from Majumdar's identification of Hinduism with 'temples and monasteries and Brahmans' (*History and Culture of Indian People*, I, pp. xxxi, xxxiii).

78. I.H. Querishi, *History of Freedom Movement*, Karachi, 1957, I, pp. 17,20.

79. Asa, *Guru Granth Sahib*, Macauliffe's translation modified.

80. Gurjari Kiwar, *Guru Granth Sahib*, Macauliffe's translation.

81. *Kabir Granthavali*, ed. Shyam Sundar Das, Kashi, p. 54.

82. Abul Fazl, *Ain-i Akbari*, ed. Blochmann, I, p. 393. Elsewhere Abul Fazl says of Kabir: 'Some of the truth was revealed to him, and he rejected the obsolete customs of society'.

83. The passage is in *Akhbar-ul Akhyar*, Deoband, AH 1332, p. 306. The word used for Hindu is *kafir*. Abdul Haqq's grandfather Sa'dullah died in 1523, when his father was eight years of age.

3

Nobility under Muhammad Tughluq

The reign of Muhammad Tughluq (1325–51) spans a critical period in the history of the Delhi Sultanate. Under him it reached its largest extent as well as greatest power; it also underwent an acute crisis which led to its veritable collapse, masked and only partly delayed by the stability and 'prosperity' of the reign of Firuz Tughluq.

Muhammad Tughluq is doubtless a controversial figure, full of 'contradictory qualities', as Barani and Ibn Battuta tell us, or of devilish hypocrisy as Isami assures us. Was he an ingenious author of failed projects (Barani) or a genius seeking pleasure in human distress (Isami)? The argument can go on and on, but the tendency initiated by Moreland,[1] and continued by Ishwari Prasad and Mehdi Husain,[2] is to see his various measures in the light of the requirements of the actual situation rather than in primitive psycho analysis.

One major aspect of the crisis that developed in Muhammad Tughluq's reign was the internal conflicts in the Sultanate nobility, which led to the spate of rebellions in the various provinces which not only resulted in the final secession of large parts of the empire, but gravely weakened its power even in areas that nominally remained under its control.

Barani suggests as if the Sultan's 'punishments' were the major reason for these outbreaks. But it is clear that the roots of the crisis lay at least partly in the composition of the nobility. Ibn Battuta refers to the jealously between the indigenous and foreign nobility;[3] Isami to the provocation given to Muslims by the appointment of Hindu officers;[4] and Barani himself, a personal aide (muqarrab) of the Sultan, inveighs against the appointment and promotion of men of low birth.[5] In addition, he speaks of the intransigence of officers known as amiran-i sada who suddenly appear very prominently during the closing years of the Sultan's reign. What their grievances were does not immediately become clear but needs investigation.

It seems that even under Ghiyasuddin Tughluq, whose reign

(1320–5) Barani describes in almost idyllic terms, there were certain suspicions in the hearts of the previous 'Alai' nobility (i.e. those who had served under Alauddin Khalji) as to the intentions of the new regime towards them. Certainly, most of them had been either passive or lukewarm in supporting Ghiyasuddin Tughluq against the 'usurper' Khusrau Khan. When Muhammad Tughluq (then Ulugh Khan) had gone on an expedition against Warangal, these suspicions ignited a conspiracy of Alai nobles.[6] Bahram Aiba Kishlu Khan, who governed Multan and had supported Ghiyasuddin Tughluq against Khusrau Khan, rebelled against Muhammad Tughluq.[7] Subsequently, Ali Shah, a Khalji kinsman of the famous commander of Alauddin, Zafar Khan, revolted in the Deccan.[8]

It is, therefore, probable that a part of the nobility inherited from the Khaljis was not loyal to Muhammad Tughluq, and this in part necessitated the recruitment of new elements.

In the first phase, this probably represented nothing more than the promotion of those already in service. The outstanding case was that of Ahmad, (son of) Ayaz, who from his name appears originally to have been a slave, and who was kotwal of Delhi in 1320.[9] Ahmad Ayaz became the principal minister of Muhammad Tughluq.[10] He was a foreigner (Turk) and his daughters were married to Iranian immigrants.[11] Ahmad Ayaz was a pure bureaucrat and financier,[12] and this was apparently reflected in his title of Khwaja Jahan (Khwaja meant a financial official, a moneyed man).

Another officer who probably came from the older service was Ainul Mulk 'Mahru', the last being his father's name (presumably title). He is to be distinguished from Ainul Mulk Multani, a commander under Alauddin Khalji, whose last assignment was as Governor of Malwa at the time of Ghiyasuddin Tughluq's victory against Khusrau Khan.[13] This distinction has unfortunately not been made.[14] Unlike Ainul Mulk Multani, Ainul Mulk Mahru was a bureaucrat who had no experience of military matters. He had his own apprehensions on being transferred to the Deccan, but his revolt in 1340–1 was supported by Indian *amir*s, for they were jealous of the Khurasani and other foreigners, who were being invited and given posts in large numbers by Sultan Muhammad Tughluq.[15]

Others were favourites of the reigning Sultan appointed directly to office. Qutlugh Khan, the viceroy of the Deccan, had been a tutor of Sultan Muhammad, and this was responsible for his high appointment as well as the promotion of his brother Nizamuddin.[16]

A somewhat different example was that of Kannu, an officer under the Rai of Warangal. Captured, he became formally a slave of Muhammad Tughluq and was given the Muslim name Maqbul.[17] He became deputy prime minister (naib wazir) under Sultan Muhammad,[18] and prime minister in the next reign.[19]

It was obviously a part of the attempt to create his own nobility which made Muhammad Tughluq open the doors so wide to foreign immigrants. Ibn Battuta has left a detailed account of how rich and well-born persons from central Asia and Iran were rewarded. He gives particulars of how Khudawandzada and his brothers were received at Sultan Muhammad's court, and in this connection he names a number of other foreign-born nobles of high station.[20]

Barani not only corroborates Ibn Battuta, even mentioning the case of Khudawandzada,[21] but also tells us that Muhammad Tughluq paid special attention to immigrant Mongol nobles, 'Commanders of 10,000, (*amiran-i tuman*), of 1000 (*amiran-i hazara*), ladies of high status (*Khatun*) and children (*ughli*s).[22] Among those welcomed were a son-in-law of the Khan Tarmashirin,[23] and two others who remained very high officers under Firuz Tughluq.[24]

It is likely that Muhammad Tughluq wanted to attract officers to his service who would not have any local base of their own and would be dependent on him. Ibn Battuta tells us that only those foreigners received rewards who agreed to enter the Sultan's service, as Ibn Battuta did himself. His entertainment of Mongol commanders probably indicated his desire to reinforce the Delhi Army with Mongol methods of organization and tactics. We shall revert to this point when we discuss the question of amiran-i sada.

A similar anxiety drove Muhammad Tughluq to take into service people from communities which had so far not been the source or recruitment for the nobility. The increase in the number of Afghans was probably owing to this cause. The rebellions of the Afghan Qazi Jalal in Gujarat and Nasiruddin in the Deccan as well as another Afghan revolt described by Ibn Battuta,[25] bring to light the fact that the Afghans now held a considerable position in the nobility as against the period before Qutbuddin Mubarak Shah (acc. 1316), during which not a single Afghan officer is heard of.

Barani tells us that Muhammad Tughluq denounced men of low birth in words but appointed a large number of such officers. Two of those whom he mentions are well known. Aziz Khummar (*khummar* means wine distiller) was the revenue official (*wal'ul-kharaj*) of Amroha,[26] then in charge of a *shiq* (province) in the Deccan[27] and finally governor of Dhar (Malwa).[28] He killed a number of amiran-i sada and then went into Gujarat where he was captured and killed by the rebels. Aziz Khummar is repeatedly designated *bad-asl* (base-born) by Barani. A person still more bitterly denounced, Muqbil had been a slave of Ahmad Ayaz, and served in Gujarat, where he ultimately became governor (*naib-i wazir*).[29] He too was defeated and driven out by the rebels.[30] Among other officers he recalls Najaba, a dancer's son who was given charge of territories like Gujarat, Multan and Badaun. Pira Mali, 'the lowest of the meanest castes of India', was appointed to head the finance ministry (*diwan-i-wizarat*); Kishan Bazaran Indri, similarly low in status, was given Awadh.[31]

Kishan was probably a Hindu (who did not, like Maqbul above, change his faith), but all Hindus were not of low caste. There was a Hindu astronomer, Ratan, who was appointed governor of Siwistan (Sehwan, Sind).[32] Bharan, governor of Gulbarga, was a Hindu who was treacherously killed by rebels.[33] It was probably this policy of appointing Hindus to administrative posts that led to the criticism that Muhammad Tughluq sat with jogis and played Holi, or that he stopped congregation prayers.[34] Muhammad Tughluq probably had a genuine interest in Hinduism, but his policy of appointing Hindus had political objectives to serve irrespective of his own ideological liberalism.

Barani speaks as if in the last days of Muhammad Tughluq the basic danger to him came from the amiran-i sada (commanders of 100) whom he set out to destroy. Now it is clear that this term was a new one; it first occurs for an office in a system of a chain of decimal commands, in words put by Barani into Bughra Khan's mouth. We also hear of *amiran-i panjah bandgan* (captains of 50).[35] These are almost certainly officers over hundred and fifty cavalry respectively. The names also suggest Mongol associations since captains of Mongol army are described by Barani himself as amiran-i hazara and amiran-i sada.[36]

It is possible that the grievance of the military officers arose because of the prominence Muhammad Tughluq gave to the bureaucracy. This appears from Ibn Battuta's account of the fracas at Amroha, where Aziz Khummar as the chief tax collector (wal'ul-kharaj) was besieged by the army commander.[37] The cases of Nusrat Khan and Nizam Main show that Muhammad Tughluq was also farming out revenues to speculators in order to get fixed amounts.[38]

It is probable that Muhammad Tughluq was trying to divide the army command from revenue collection and so reduce the extra revenues which went to commanders as *muqtis*. This could have provided enough provocation to rise against the Sultan; but the material is perhaps not sufficient to warrant a very definite conclusion.

Muhammad Tughluq's policy of creating a heterogeneous nobility might have been influenced partly by eccentricity, but it was also partly the response to a certain alienation already existing between the Sultan and the established nobility. Unfortunately for him, the heterogeneous elements could not be combined together into a composite nobility. This was achieved by Firuz Tughluq by virtually freezing its composition. This might have helped to overcome the pressing difficulties of the moment, but it cost the Sultan the lever (new recruitments) by which the nobles could be controlled. A decline in the Sultan's power was thus inevitable.

NOTES

1. W.H. Moreland, *Agrarian System of Moslem India*, Cambridge, 1929, pp. 45–52.

2. Ishwari Prasad, *History of Qaraunah Turks in India*, Allahabad, 1936; Mehdi Husain, *Rise and Fall of Muhammad bin Tughluq*, London, 1938.

3. Ibn Battuta, *Rehla*, tr. Mehdi Husain, Oriental Institute, Baroda, 1953, pp. 105–6.

4. Isami, *Futuh-us Salatin*, ed. A.S. Usha, Madras, 1948, p. 515.

5. Barani, *Tarikh-i Firuz Shahi*, ed. Saiyid Ahmad Khan, Calcutta, 1862, p. 504.

6. Ibid., p. 448.

7. On Bahram Aiba, son of Malik Ghazi, see Barani, pp. 379–8, 479.

8. Isami, pp. 483–7; Ibn Battuta, p. 111.

9. Isami, p. 425.

10. Ibn Battuta, p. 54.

11. Ibid., p. 24.

12. Barani, p. 540.

13. Ibid., p. 419.

14. As in Professor S.A. Rashid's introduction to *Insha-i Mahru*, ed. S.A. Rashid and Bashir Husain, Lahore, 1965, pp. 1ff.

15. Ibn Battuta, pp. 105–6.

16. Barani, pp. 479–81.

17. Afif, *Tarikh-i Firuz Shahi*, Bibliothica Indica (Bib. Ind.) edn, Calcutta, 1890, pp. 394–405.

18. Barani, pp. 544–5.

19. Afif, pp. 394–405.
20. Ibn Battuta, pp. 12, 81, 118.
21. Barani, pp. 461–2.
22. Ibid., p. 499.
23. Ibid., p. 584.
24. Ibid., p. 585
25. Ibid., pp. 482, 514–16; Isami, pp. 503, 531–2; Ibn Battuta, pp. 113–16.
26. Ibn Battuta, p. 144.
27. Barani, pp. 501–2.
28. Ibid., p. 502; Isami, p. 507.
29. Isami, p. 505; Ibn Battuta, pp. 113, 116.
30. Isami, p. 505.
31. Barani, p. 505.
32. Ibn Battuta, p. 8.
33. Isami, pp. 522–3.
34. Ibid., p. 515.
35. Barani, pp. 373–6.
36. Ibid., pp. 461–2.
37. Ibn Battuta, pp. 144–6.
38. Barani, pp. 481, 487–8.

4

Capital of the Sultans
Delhi during the Thirteenth and Fourteenth Centuries

The Sultanate monuments of Delhi have received much attention. Saiyid Ahmad's *Asarus Sanadid*[1] and Carr Stephen's *Archaeology and Monumental Remains of Delhi* (1876), are old but competent descriptions. But everything else is overshadowed by the great survey, *Delhi: Architectural Remains of the Delhi Sultanate Period* by Tatsuro Yamamoto, Matsuo Ara, and Tokifusa Tsukinowa, published in Tokyo in 1970, with its detailed descriptions (all in Japanese), scientific diagrams and magnificent photographs. Handling it, one feels in the presence of a definitive work.

The purpose of this essay is, however, not to offer a short view of the monuments, but to focus on the settlements; for this purpose the existing archaeological evidence is undoubtedly very important, but our attention here is basically directed towards literary evidence, and on what it tells us about the settlement history of Delhi during the thirteenth and fourteenth centuries. Such a correlation has been surprisingly lacking until now, and the intention here is to fill the gap.

When one looks at Delhi on the map, one feels a little surprised that its importance in the historical period should date only from the twelfth century. The spurs of the Aravalli range reaching deep into the great alluvial plains of north India have their terminal point in the Delhi Ridge. The Yamuna river is thereby diverted from its seemingly natural south-westerly course (parallel to the Indus tributaries) to an easterly one (parallel to the Ganga) by the interposition of the Ridge under which it flows. Thus heights for commanding positions, rocks for stone quarries, and the river for water supply, navigation and defence from the east, all should have combined to attract to Delhi the attention of rulers and merchants alike.

Yet, so far as we know, when Prithvi Raja was defeated at Tarain in 1192, there was only a small fort amidst the present ruins on the rocky ground now called Qila Rai Pithora. It was this fort which

Qutbuddin Aibak occupied on behalf of Shahabuddin of Ghor in 1192,[2] and which became the nucleus of the Delhi of his successor Iltutmish— the Delhi known as Dihli-i Kuhna or 'Old Delhi' in the fourteenth century.[3]

It was natural that the Ghorian–Turkish conquerors should, upon choosing Delhi for their headquarters, start building their city around the fortress they had captured. So was built the Jama Majid, with the Qutb Minar, and a new fort (Hisar-i Nau) close to the north of the mosque.[4] This latter was probably the walled enclosure now known as Lal Kot. Probably adjacent to the mosque was a religious school founded as early as the reign of Muizzuddin of Ghor, since it was know as Madrasa-i Muizzi. Outside its gate was a market for cloth-merchants (Bazar-i bazzazan) through which a party of Carpmthian heretics had tried to break into the mosque, in AH 724/AD 1324, having mistaken the madrasa for the mosque.[5]

An obvious deterrent to the growth of the city, which during the first half of the thirteenth century could not have been very large, was the problem of water supply. The Yamuna was far away from the site of the town; the nearest point on the Yamuna is 18 Km from the Qutb Minar as the crow flies. The rocky ground on the Aravalli spurs precluded the digging of wells at most places. It proved, therefore, incumbent upon Iltutmish, (1210–36) to lay out a large tank, Hauz-i Sultani or Hauz-i Shamsi from which citizens of Delhi could fetch water.[6] When during the 1260s, the Meos became turbulent and began to come up to the walls of Delhi, they prevented the citizens from enjoying a walk up to the tank and harassed the water-carriers and the slave girls who came to fetch water.[7] It subsequently dried up because the channels feeding it were dammed up by 'dishonest men'. Firuz Shah (1351–88), however, claims to have broken down these dams and so opened the supply of water to the tank again.[8] The Hauz-i Shamsi was situated to the south of the then city, about three kilometres from the Qutb complex. It received rain-water[9] drained off from the large, higher, fairly level catchment area to its west. The present mapped dimensions of the 'Shamsi Talab' as it is now called suggest that it was rectangular, about 200 metres long and 125 metres broad.[10] (Ibn Battuta's statement that it was two 'miles' (*mil*) long and one mile broad [11] indicated its roughly rectangular shape; it also suggests that his mil is a unit of length far short of the English mile.) A tank of this size, large as it was, could not have met the needs of a large population; and the difficulty in carrying water from it to the populated parts of the city must have been considerable.

It was, therefore, natural that a tendency should emerge to shift towards the Yamuna river. A suburb first developed at Ghayaspur, whose name suggests its settlement during the reign of Sultan Ghyasuddin Balban. Since Shaikh Nizamuddin established his Jammat Khana in this suburb,[12] the present Dargah Nizamuddin fixes its site pretty will. Quite obviously, it owed its settlement to its being near the bank of the river[13] which just below here takes a turn towards the east; the point was thus nearest the then city of Delhi, while being close to the river. Still the distance between the Qutb Minar and Dargah Nizamuddin is about seven miles in a straight line.

Between this settlement and the Yamuna, Balban's grandson and successor, Muizzuddin Kaiqubad (d. 1289) began building a walled palace (*qasr*), which was either named Kilokhari or was on the site of a village of that name.[14] It was about half a *kuroh* (less than a mile) from Ghayaspur;[15] this broadly suits too the position of the 'Kilokhari' palace which fronted the river, although there is said to have been space enough in between for Jalaluddin Khalji (1290–6) to lay out a garden.[16] Under this Sultan, who harboured suspicions about the loyalty of the leading citizens of the old city, a 'New City', the Shahr-i Nau, developed around the palace.

Sultan Jalaluddin ordered his own nobles and commanders as well as the great men of the city to build houses in Kilokhari and erect high edifices, and bring certain merchants from the (Old) city. Large markets came to be established, and Kilokhari was named Shahr-i Nau, Moreover, a stone-fort was built, of very great eminence.[17]

The population seems to have extended up to the present Purana Qila, if the latter represents correctly the position of the then village of Indpat or Indarpat (Indraprastha). During Jalaluddin Khalji's reign, a number of Mongols (Mughals) are said to have settled in Kilokhari and Ghayaspur as well as Indarpat and Bakula (?), their settlements being known as Mughalpur.[18]

It is almost certain that the shift of the town from the dry rocky zone to the riverside would have continued, had not certain circumstances occurred during the reign of Jalaluddin Khalji's nephew and successor, Alauddin Khalji, to force the Sultan to adopt a new policy.

The circumstances were, perhaps, dual in nature. On the one hand, the combination of the Ogetai and Chaghatai hordes in Central Asia under the leadership of Qaidu, gave a new intensity and ferocity to the Mongol raids into India. Delhi itself became the target of Mongol

attack and was subject to siege twice.[19] It therefore became necessary
for the population of the capital to be kept within fortified walls. This
meant that the vicinity of the rocky zone where the supply of stone
was easier must continue to contain the capital. Barani clearly says as
much:

The terror of the Mongols became all pervasive. Mughal horsemen began
to come up to the platform of Subhani (*Chabutara-i Subhani*), and the
villages of Mori and Hadhi, and the banks of the Hauz-i Sultani (Hauz-i
Shamsi)—after the disaster of Targhi's invasion—which was a great
disaster, Sultan Alauddin woke up from his sleep of negligence and gave
up the projects of taking away the army on campaigns and reducing forts
(in India). He now built his palace (*kaushak*) in Siri and began to reside at
Siri; he designated Siri his capital (*Darul Khilafa*) and made it well
populated. He also built up the fort of Old Delhi.[20]

Siri was in fact a plain waste ground (*sahra*) almost adjoining the
old city of Delhi to its north-east;[21] Alauddin had camped his army
here before entering the walled capital in 1296.[22] He had also come
out of the walled capital (Old Delhi), and pitched his tent on this plain
when the Mughal commander Qutlugh Khwaja came to make an
attempt on the capital.[23]

In the beginning the settlement at Siri seems to have been called
Lashkar or Lashkargah (army encampment) in contrast to the Qutb
Delhi knows as Shahr (City). Nizamuddin commented upon the
distance between Shahr and Lashkar.[24] His disciple and recorder of
his conversations, Amir Hasan Sijzi, himself an army officer, had built
a house in Lashkar, and this enabled him to offer his Friday prayers at
the Friday mosque in Kilokhari.[25] Subsequently, Lashkargah, situated
in Siri, was named Darul Khilafa,[26] a statement corroborated by Ibn
Battuta[27] and Barani.[28]

Apparently, local memory of where Siri was situated was lost; it
was Cunningham who identified it with a vast area enclosed by raised
mounds of earth and containing the village of Shahpur Jat. The
identification is now held to be definitive and the name Siri appears
on the survey sheets. It indeed meets all the indications of the position
of Siri in our sources; an expanse of level ground between Qutb Delhi
and Kilokhari. The enclosed area amounts to some 1.7 square
kilometres.[29] The Statement in Yazdi's *Zafarnama*, that the walled
enclosure (*sura*) of Siri was roughly 'circular' is broadly correct in
that it is not rectangular.[30]

Alauddin Khalji's attention seems, however, mainly to have centred on Qutb Delhi. The vast extensions he made to the Friday Mosque[31] suggest not only his interest in that city, but also the fact that an enormous increase in the population of the city had occurred since Iltutmish's time so that the old space no longer sufficed. Indeed, this was the Shahr par excellence in contrast to the Darul-Khilafa that was Siri and Sahr-i Nau (new city) that was Kilokhari.[32] It was the major commercial centre, as Barani's description of Alauddin Khalji's price regulation so definitely tells us.

Alauddin decreed that the cloth markets should be established on an open ground (sahra) within (i.e. inside the city wall at) Badaun Gate in the direction of Kaushak-i Sabz, that had for years remained unoccupied.[33] The market came to be known as Sara-i 'Al. The Badaun Gate is mentioned as the 'greatest gate' of (Qutb) Delhi by Ibn Battuta,[34] and is often mentioned in our authorities.[35] Outside the gate were excavated dry wells which served as dungeons for the imbibers and purveyors of wine.[36] The grain market (*manda* or *mandi*), so often referred to by Barani,[37] was situated at yet another gate of the city, the Mandavi Darwaza.[38]

The dry wells outside Badaun Gate should remind us of the problem of water supply in the enlarged city, a problem more acute for the settlement around the Qutb than for Siri, where underground water could be reached more easily by digging wells through alluvial soil.

Alauddin Khalji tried to alleviate this problem by re-excavating Iltutmish's Hauz-i Sultani or Hauz-i Shamsi. That tank is said to have run dry and to have only contained some pools. Large amounts of mud and silt were therefore removed from inside the tank and a platform (*chabutra*) and domed pavilion (*gumbad*) built in the middle.[39]

However, as Amir Khusrau remarks with engaging exaggeration, the waters of the Nile and Euphrates would have been insufficient to meet the needs of the increased population of Qutb Delhi.[40] In any case, the Hauz-i Shamsi would have been too far south for the quarters and suburbs situated to the north of the Qutb Minar.

Alauddin Khalji, therefore, excavated another tank about two miles north of the Qutb, the Hauz-i Alai or Hauz-i Khas (now the name of a well-known part of upper-class New Delhi); the banks of the tank are still traceable; it is a square, each side some 600 m in length, the total space enclosed by the banks amounting to over 70 acres.[41] Ibn Battuta describes it as larger than the Hauz-i Shamsi.[42] Yazdi calls it a 'small sea' (*daryacha*), and says it was filled during the rainy season and served to supply the needs of the inhabitants of Delhi for the whole year[43]. The catchment area of the tank lay to the south behind the present-day Indian Institute of Technology and Jawaharlal Nehru University, and some channels which probably took water to the tank can still be traced. Like Hauz-i Shamsi, this too was at some distance from the more closely inhabited parts of the city. Plain vacant ground (sahra) adjoined it, interposing itself between the tank, on the one hand, and Siri on the other, and stretching to the fortified wall of Qutb Delhi. In this ground Khusrau Khan had planted orchards.[44] Women singers and dancing women lived on one side of the tank.[45] Fetching water from the tank must have been strenuous business and must have involved the labour of many maidservants or slaves and professional water-carriers.

The major part of Delhi under Alauddin Khalji (1296–1316) was thus the Qutb Delhi with Siri as an isolated extension. When Barani later on recollected how large numbers of people came to visit Shaikh Nizamuddin, the Chishti mystic settled at Ghayaspur (near Kilokhari in Shahr-i Nau), he thought of the crowds coming from the Shahr, the city, or Qutb Delhi. The road by which they came probably passed through much uninhabited waste or unpopulated terrain:

The freemen (*hurrs*) and philanthropists laid out platforms at many places from the Shahr to Ghayaspur; there they set up thatched huts, dug wells, and kept ready water-filled basins with clay vessels, and with matting spread out. Every platform and thatched hut had a watchman and servants so that the disciples, followers and pious men should not have anything to worry about in regard to ablutions and performing of prayers during their visit to and return from the Shaikh's house.[46]

It seems that the increase in the population of Delhi and Siri led Ghiyasuddin Tughluq (1320–5) to lay out yet another settlement, namely Tughluqabad.[47] The site is at a considerable distance (about eight kilometres) due east of the Qutb Minar (and so of 'Old Delhi'); it sits upon a southern terminal of the Ridge towards the Yamuna, from which it is almost as much distant as from the Qutb Minar. The advantage of the site lay in its stone quarries which provided building material, and the scraps that could be used to reinforce the elevation of fortifications. There was the possibility too of setting a dam against the natural eastward drainage line, which narrowed here; and so of creating a tank and source of water supply. Isami writes: 'The sagacious sovereign ordered the digging of a tank under the elevated fort. Every moment the tank was beset by waves like the seven oceans beneath the Caucasus Mountains'.[48]

The great survey of Sultanate Delhi by Yamamoto and others, contains excellent photographs of the tank, the surrounding walls and the main dam with its three arches containing the sluices.[49]

Unfortunately, besides the outstanding monuments, namely the tomb of Ghayasuddin Tughluq and the fortress walls, it is difficult to reconstruct the plan of Tughluqabad. Across the tank Muhammad Tughluq constructed the fort of Adilabad, with which Tughluqabad is corrected by a cause way. It would seen that Tughluqabad was more or less a detached complex to house the Sultan, his retinue and personal troops; it was, perhaps, never intended to replace 'Old Delhi' as either a commercial or even administrative centre.

Indeed, 'Old Delhi' continued to grow; and this led Muhammad Tughluq (1325–51) to plan an immense length of fortification so as to enclose the entire area between the Qutb Delhi and Siri within its walls, giving to the enclosure the name of Jahanpanah.[50] Thus, now, three settlements, 'Old Delhi', Jahanpanah and Siri arose, linked to each other.

Yazdi said that Jahanpanath exceeded 'Old Delhi' in size; and 'Old Delhi' exceeded Siri. The walls of Jahanpanah had six gates leading out to the north-west, seven to the south, and three into Siri.[51] The north-western wall was skirted by Hauz-i Khas, directly fronting which was a gate.[52] The southern wall of Jahanpanah can be traced easily: the north-western wall appears on maps, but on the ground has virtually disappeared.

As usual, for water supply yet another reservoir was provided. An embankment 850 feet in length with seven arches (and thus called 'Satpula' or 'Satpala') was thrown across a drain near the present village of Khirki, as part of the southern wall of Jahanpanath, to retain a vast sheet of water. The drain still runs in virtually the same channel. The dam towers some 21.3 feet above ground level.[53]

Delhi had thus reached an enormous size—unfortunately, no estimate of its population is possible—when Muhammad Tughluq decided to transfer his capital to Daulatabad in the Deccan. The statement that this was accompanied by a wholesale transfer of population is made by all of our three major authorities, Ibn Battuta, Isami and Barani, with considerable circumstantial detail.[54] It is not intended here to discuss the extent to which Delhi was actually depopulated. Ibn Battuta said that when he arrived in 1334, he could witness the unhappy effects.[55] Barani says that people from the surrounding country came and took the place of those who had been taken to the south.[56] Delhi was subsequently troubled too by

famine, and Muhammad Tughluq was compelled to establish a
camp city on the Ganga river, called Swarga-duari (Gate of
Paradise) where the people of Delhi might go to live on grain
brought up the river.[57]

It is possible that the rebellions in the 1340s further told on the
prosperity of Delhi, and the enormous city began to go partly to ruin.
During the reign of Firuz Tughluq (1351–88) the decline became
perceptible. Firuz Tughluq himself records that the drains flowing
into the Hauz-i Shamsi had been closed by 'people' building dams
across them; and the Hauz-i Alai had silted up, running dry, so that
the 'people of the city' carried on cultivation within it, digging wells
and selling water drawn from them.[58] By Firuz Shah's reign the ruins
of 'Old Delhi' had indeed become a rich source of bricks and Stones
for the new city of Firuzabad.[59]

The ruin of 'Old Delhi' may possibly have become inevitable as a
consequence of the decline of the Sultanate. Enormous settlements
set on the Aravalli rocks, away from the river, must have meant an
extra drain of revenue, to meet the extra cost of water supply and
expense of transporting grain and goods. The revenue must have
perceptibly declined as the Sultanate contracted and the administrative
structure atrophied. There was therefore good reason for a shift to an
economically more suitable position, i.e. along the river, from the
upper rocky grounds. In spite of his valiant effort to repair and rebuild
the older structures and re-excavate the great reservoirs of the older
complex,[60] Firuz Shah was constrained to build his own capital upon
the Yamuna river.

The new capital was Firuzabad. Firuz established it quite early in
his reign, since Barani writing in 1358 mentions its foundation on the
banks of the Yamuna, prophesying that 'in course of time it would be
the envy of the Great Cities'.[61] Afif describes the extent of the new
city in an oft-quoted passage. It was on the Yamuna, 'five *kurohs*'
from (old) Delhi.[62] The total expanse embraced eighteen villages. The
core village (presumably the site of Firuz Shah Kotla) was Kawin or
Gawin. It included lands of the village of Kathiwara, which is
presumably identical with the ford or ferry (*guzar*) of Kath in Barani.[63]
Its exact site is not located; more easily located are Indpat (Indraprastha,
Purana Qila), and the land of the tomb of Sultan Razia (situated in the
Mohalla Bulbuli Khana near Turkman Gate, Shahjahanabad).[64] The
city extended much further northwards across the whole of the later
city of Shahjahanabad up to the base of the Ridge between modern
Sabzi Mandi and the Civil Lines. Afif tells us that:

By the grace of God, the population of Delhi increased so much that the entire space between Indpat and the *Kaushak-i Shikar* had been inhabited, the distance between the limits of Indpat and the *Kaushak-i Shikar* is five *kurohs*.[65]

Kaushak-i Shikar is easy to identify because of the Ashokan pillar which Firuz Shah set up there.[66] This stands on the Ridge between Sabzi Mandi and the Civil Lines. Quite obviously the population extended along the Yamuna river, possibly in a fairly narrow belt. The statement that it extended to Hauz-i Khas is made by Saiyid Ahmad, and is repeated by Carr Stephen, but is without any substance.[67]

It is difficult to the sure about the extent to which the growth of Firuzabad compensated for the decay of 'Old Delhi. Certainly, the settlement was more successful than Kilokhari, which seems, from its exclusion, to have decayed by now. Firuz Shah shifted Delhi to a more suitable terrain; henceforth its settlement were to adjoin the Yamuna rather than the Aravalli ridge. Sher Shah's Delhi, Salim Garh, Humayun's Tomb, Shahjahanabad, even New Delhi, are situated within the alluvial zone. In a geographical sense, as much as historical, Firuzabad set the seal on the decline of the Delhi of the Sultanate with its sites upon and round the rocky wastes, and shifted it compellingly to the lower lands to the north and north-east.

NOTES

1. First ed., 1847. I have used the comprehensive edition by Khalid Nasir Hashmi, Delhi, 1965.

2. Minhaj Siraj, *Tabaqat-i Nasiri*, ed. Abdul Hai Habibi, 2nd. edn, vol. I, Kabul, 1963, p. 400.

3. 'Ali Yazdi, *Zafarnama*, Bib. Ind., Calcutta, 1888, II, p. 125, where the three cities of Delhi are described under the names of Jahanpanah, Siri (to north-east of Jahanpanah), and *Dihli-i Kuhna* (to south west of Jahanpanah).

4. *Tabaqat-i Nasiri*, I, p. 461.

5. Ibid.

6. The earliest reference to this tank seems to be in ibid., I, p. 466.

7. Ziya' Barani, *Tarikh-i Firuz Shahi*, Bib. Ind. edn, Calcutta, 1862, p. 56, where the tank is designated Hauz-i Sultani.

8. *Futuhat-i Firuz Shahi*, ed. S.A. Rashid, Aligarh, 1954, p. 12.

9. Ibn Battuta, *Rehla,* tr. Mehdi Husain, Baroda, 1953, p. 28.

10. See T. Yamamoto, M. Ara, and T. Tsukinowa, *Delhi,* Tokyo, 1970, map. Saiyid Ahmad gives its area as 276 'pucca bighas' or 172.5 acres (*Asaru-s Sanadid,* p. 175).

11. Ibn Battuta, *Rehla,* tr., p.28.

12. Barani, *Tarikh-i Firuz Shahi,* pp. 343–4; Shaikh Nasiruddin, *Khairu-l Majalis,* Aligarh, 1959, p. 126. On p. 325 Barani styles Nizamuddin as Ghayaspuri, i.e. of Ghayaspur.

13. Shaikh Nasiruddin (c.1356) described the *Jama'at Khana* of Nizamuddin as being in Kilokhari and on the bank of the river Jaun (Yamuna) (*Khairu-l Majalis,* p. 283). This statement raises some problems. The Jama'at Khana was in Ghayaspur not Kilokhari, but since the two adjoined each other, Nasiruddin might have spoken loosely here. If the Jama'at Khana's site was the same as of the one now pointed out in Dargah Nizamuddin, we must infer that the Yamuna must then have flowed through the present Zoological park and passed by west of the site of Humayun's tomb. Such a channel, in its southern section, can still be traced: it probably carried only a branch of the river.

14. Barani, p. 175, and passim

15. *Khairu-l Majalis,* p. 126.

16. Barani, p. 175.

17. Ibid. Practically no ruins survive in Kilokhari.

18. Ibid., p. 219.

19. Barani, pp. 254–61, 300. One raid was under Qutlugh Khwaja, followed by another under Targhi. See also Isami, *Futuh-us- Salatin,* ed. A.S. Usha, Madras, 1948, pp. 256–70, 285–6.

20. Barani, pp. 301–2. Is modern Mehrauli a corruption of Mori-Hadhi?

21. Ibid., p. 246; Yazdi's *Zafarnama,* vol. II, 125, gives the direction in relation to 'Old Delhi', i.e. Qutb Delhi.

22. Barani, p. 246.

23. Ibid., p. 254.

24. *Hasan Syzi, Fawaid-ul Fuad,* ed. M. Latif Malik, Lahore, 1966 p. 282 (11 January 1317).

25. Ibid., p. 195 (8 April 1314).

26. Ibid., p. 311 (8 February 1318).

27. Ibn Battuta, *Rehla,* tr, Mehdi Husain, pp. 25, 73–4.

28. Barani, p. 302.

29. Measured from the Survey of India's Delhi Guide Map (1:20,000), 1969 edn.

30. *Zafarnama,* II, vol. p. 125.

31. Carr Stephen, *The Archaeology and Monumental Remains of Delhi,* Ludhiana and Calcutta, 86, pp. 53–4. Alauddin Khalji 'nearly doubled the

length of the Mosque after Altamash's extensions and added about half as much ground to its breadh'(p. 53).

32. *Fawaid-ul Fuad*, p. 282; Barani, p. 299.

33. Barani, pp. 310–12.

34. Ibn Battuta, p. 26.

35. For example, Barani himself, pp. 54, 246, 258, 330.

36. Ibid., pp. 258–66.

37. Ibid., pp. 304ff.

38. Ibn Battuta, p. 26.

39. Amir Khusrau, *Khazainul Futuh*, Aligarh edn, 1927, pp. 31–4. When the water rose in the tank the domed pavilion could only be reached by boat (Ibn Battuta, p. 28). Both structures survive (Carr Stephen, p. 69).

40. *Khazainul Futuh*, pp. 32–3.

41. Sides of the tank measured from map; area from Carr Stephen, p. 83.

42. Ibn Battuta, p. 28.

43. *Zafarnama*, vol. II, pp. 108–9. Because Firuz Shah re-excavated it, Yazdi ascribes its construction to that Sultan.

44. Barani, pp. 417–8.

45. Ibn Battuta, p. 28.

46. Barani, pp. 343–4.

47. Isami, *Futuh-us Salatin*, p. 412; Barani, p. 442; Ibn Battuta, p. 25.

48. Isami, p. 412.

49. Yamamoto, *et al.* vol. III, *Waterworks*, plates 19–22; the textual description is on pp. 46–51.

50. Ibn Battuta, p. 25.

51. *Zafarnama*, vol. II, p. 125.

52. Ibid., p. 116.

53. For description of this work, see Saiyid Ahmad, *Asarus-Sanadid*, pp. 193–4; Carr Stephen, pp. 101–2. There are magnificent photographs in Yamamoto, vol. III, plates 23–4, also a plan opposite p. 56.

54. Ibn Battuta, p. 94; Isami, pp. 446–54; Barani, pp. 473–5.

55. Ibn Battuta, p. 94.

56. Barani, p. 474.

57. Ibid., pp. 485–6. Cf. Ibn Battuta, p. 87.

58. Firuz Shah's inscription, *Futuhat-i Firuz Shahi*, pp. 12–14.

59. Afif, *Tarikh-i Firuz Shahi*, Calcutta, 1890, p. 376.

60. Firuz Shah's building effect in 'old Delhi' is attested by the numerous structures erected or repaired by him; but see Firuz Shah's own *Futuhat-i Firuz Shahi*; Barani, pp. 562–6; and Afif, *passim*.

61. Barani, p. 566.

62. The straight map distance between the Qutb Minar and Firuz Shah Kotla is 13.5 kilometres. Yazdi says it was three *kurohs* from Jahanpanah (*Zafarnama*, vol. II, p. 127).

63. Barani, p. 246. It appears as the village of Kathi in Yazdi, *Zafarnama*, vol. II, p. 85.

64. *Asarus Sanadid*, pp. 179–80.

65. Afif, p. 135. The actual distance is 'six miles as the crow flies' (Carr Stephen, p. 123).

66. Afif, p. 305.

67. *Asarus Sanadid*, p. 92; Carr Stephen, p. 123. Saiyid Ahmad's mistake arose out of a misreading of the text of Yazdi's *Zafarnama* vol. II, pp. 108–9, where it is stated that the tomb of Sultan Firuz Shah (not Firuzabad) was situated near Hauz Khas.

5

The Punjab between the Thirteenth and Fifteenth Centuries

The Punjab has been politically and culturally a very important region of India in all periods of our history; the medieval times being no exception. After all, it was during the medieval period that the Punjab gave Sikhism to the world.

Certain aspects of the history of the Punjab during the period of the Delhi Sultanate, that is during the thirteenth to fifteenth centuries, are of considerable interest. When the Ghorians occupied Punjab, it was broadly divided into three political units: Lahore, Multan and the trans-Sutlej tract centred on Tabarhinda or Bhatinda. Multan had been seized from the Qaramita (Ismailis); Lahore ('Lahor') from the Ghaznavides, AD 1186; and the cis-Sutlej tract from the Chahamanas (1185). These three units remained distinct, except that after the sack of Lahore by the Mongols in 1241, Lahore lost its importance for over two centuries; and Dipalpur (also in the present Bari Doab) became the centre of authority for that area. East of Sutlej, Samana became the headquarters of a large province or iqta replacing Tabarhinda. One may recall that in Balban's reign, the Mongol raids were checked by commanders posted at Multan and Samana.[1] Under Alauddin Khalji, Ghazi Malik was posted at Dipalpur to guard against the Mongols.[2] The importance of the three cities continued into the fourteenth century as well.

The present essay treats these three divisions of the Punjab separately since it would perhaps best contribute to clarity of exposition.

The area inherited from the Ghaznavi kingdom of Lahore comprised the Salt Range or Koh-i Jud, the alluvial plains of the Jech, the upper Rachna and Bari Doabs, and possibly, the present Bet-Jalandhar Doab. Early in the thirteenth century, the Kokhars formed a very important element in the population of the area. They inhabited the area between the Salt Range and Lahore. They harassed Muizuddin of Ghor when he was returning from a campaign against Khusrau Malik and again when in his later days, their presumption led Muizuddin to organize a large campaign against them (1205–6). Iltutmish particularly distinguished himself against them on the banks of the Jhelum river. This proved to be his Muizuddin's campaign. When the Mongols sacked Lahore in 1241, the 'Kokhars and the Hindus' are said to have set about plundering the city.[3]

The Mongol raid on Lahore (1241) presaged a continuous Mongol pressure on the Lahore region. It would seem that the Salt Range virtually passed out of control of the Sultans. This is borne out not only from the fact that Balban once led an expedition into Salt Range as if into a foreign country, but also by place names like Hazara Qarlugh (the present Hazara district), Hazara Gujaran, and Hazara, which we find in the *A'in-i Akbari*.[4] Hazara was the standard Mongol division of a *tuman*; and areas where Hazaras were garrisoned tend to be assigned this name. (Compare the 'Hazarajat' in Afghanistan, whence the Hazara people who claim a Mongol origin.) The Qarlugh were a client Turkish clan, who had come into the Indus region with Jalaluddin, the Khwarizimian prince, and then shifted their loyalty to the Mongols.

As a result, the Kokhars became politically still more important since they occupied the first line of defence of the Sultanate. Towards the end of Balban's reign (1266–86), his eldest son Khan Muhammad, governor of Multan, was killed in an encounter with the Mongols between Lahore and Dipalpur.[5] It is said that his body was recovered from the Mongols by Rai Kalu, a local chief, who was also the father-in-law of the prince.[6] Obviously, the policy of conciliating the local chiefs had begun, to the extent that matrimonial alliances were being contracted to cement the alliance. Rai Kalu's tribe is not stated, but he might well have been a Kokhar.

When under Alauddin Khalji (1296–1316), Ghazi Malik was posted to Dipalpur mainly to check the Mongols, he seems to have looked to establishing local alliances. He married his brother Rajab to the daughter of Rana Mal Bhatti, a chief of Abohar.[7] He seems to have developed friendly relations with the Kokhars as well. In 1321, when he marched against Khusrau Khan, he was joined by Gulchand and Sahaj Rai, two chiefs of that tribe. Gulchand, 'the prince of the Kokhars' distinguished himself in the battle with Khusrau Khan.[8] During the reign of Muhammad Tughluq (1325–51), however, Gulchand along with two (Mongol) officers, Shahu and Halajun, revolted and lost his life when the rebellion was suppressed.[9]

In the latter half of the fourteenth century, the Kokhars seem to have been converted to Islam; but their power remained undiminished.

When Timur invaded India in 1398, Shaikh or Shaikha was the principal Kokhar chief. He had for some time obtained possession of Lahore.[10] His brother Nusrat unsuccessfully contested Timur's passage.[11] Shaikha then offered allegiance to Timur; but he resiled, and was accordingly captured with this family by a detachment of Timur's troops sent to Lahore.[12]

Shaikha was succeeded by his son Jasrath Shaikha or simply Jasrath, a clearly Hindu name. It was under Jasrath that the Kokhars' power seems to have reached its zenith; Jasrath defeated and captured Sultan Ali Shah of Kashmir (1413–20) and even threatened Delhi.[13] But Jasrath seems to have been not only the most powerful but also the last prominent Kokhar chief; after him the Kokhars rapidly diminished in influence, and by the sixteenth century appear only as zamindars in the Bari and Rachna Doabs.[14]

Lahore, in spite of being noticed in the histories from time to time, never regained much importance in the fourteenth century. Two new towns arose in the vicinity, namely Dipalpur, a political centre, and Ajodhan, the seat of the Sufic establishment of Shaikh Fariduddin. Neither place is mentioned in the *Tabqat-i Nasiri*; but Dipalpur, at least, gained clearly from the decay of Lahore. When in the fifteenth century Lahore again began to revive, Dipalpur correspondingly lost it former importance.

The recovery of Lahore was accompanied by an extension of settlement in the Bari Doab region marked by the foundation of townships like Batala, the focal point in the study of urban history being undertaken by J.S. Grewal and Indu Banga. Sujan Rai, writing in 1995, attributed this process of resettlement to the cessation of Mongol invasions,[15] and he seems well justified in this inference. Lahore also apparently gained from a larger demand in Europe for indigo which was linked with Europe's own economic recovery in the fifteenth and sixteenth centuries. This demand was met by the transportation of Bayana indigo to Lahore where caravans assembled for journey to the Levant. When the indigo reached Allepo, the Venetian and other European merchants knew of it as Laor, Lahore, etc. after the name of this major town of the Punjab.

Multan (Mulasthanapura) has a much longer history than Lahore. When Yuan Chwang visited it in the seventh century, it was the capital of the Takka or Takya (Cheh-Kiya).[16] It was known for its celebrated sun-temple, so that at one time it must have been a major place of pilgrimage. Some time later in the seventh century it was annexed to the Kingdom of Sind, becoming the headquarters of its northernmost province. The association with Sind continued after the Arab conquest of that kingdom in 711–14, Multan being described in some detail by the *Chachnama*, the thirteenth-century Persian translation of a very early Arabic narrative of the Arab conquest.[17] The association of Multan with Sind continued well into the fourteenth century (and even till Akbar's time), the city being a capital of a vast region that stretched down to the mouth of the Indus: This was its situation in Qabacha's short-lived Sultanate in the earlier part of the thirteenth century; 'Multan and Sind' formed a single large iqta under the Delhi Sultans;[18] it formed part of the Arghun Kingdom of Sind in the sixteenth century; and late in that century, Akbar's *suba* of Multan included the sub-province of Thatta or Sind.[19] This association with Sind must have reinforced, if not itself been originally responsible, for the influx of a large proportion of Sindhi vocabulary into the Punjabi speech of the Multan area, which is recognized as a separate dialect ('Multani') by philologists. The dialect has given a distinct character to the area as a cultural region.

The river map of the region was different from what it is today. The *Chachnama* for the early eighth century and Yazdi for the close of the fifteenth century show the combined waters of the Chenab and Jhelum flowing to the west of Multan; but the Ravi (Irawa) river flowed to its east. In other words, the Ravi was not flowing in its Sidhnai reach, and Multan lay in the Rachna and not the Bari Doab. The well-known town of Uchh then stood at the junction of all the Punjab rivers, including the Indus, as is stated in the fifteenth-century Palam Baoli inscription. To the east of Multan the Sutlej flowed in two branches, the eastward in its present channels, past Ajodhan (Pakpattan) and the westward in the channel of 'old Bias' still shown in the maps.[20] The presence of rivers in their numerous channels, undrained by large canals taking off from their upper reaches, must have provided a floodland character to agriculture around Multan.

The undoubtedly rich agriculture of the Multan–Uchh area and its strategic position made Multan an ideal mart. The word Multani in the fourteenth century represented a wealthy merchant indulging in large-scale usury (as creditor to potentates) and engaging in long-distance trade. This is the picture that Barani offers of the Multanes in his *Tarikh-i Firuz Shahi*.[21] It is not certain that they were all Hindus, though this is suggested by the connotation of Hindu merchant given to the word in Tek Chand's *Bahar-i Ajam*. Barani speaks of Qazi Abdul Hamid Multani's father as *Malikuttujjar* (prince of merchants).

Multan's significance as commercial centre was enhanced further by the large establishment of the Suhrawardi *silsila*. From the time of Bahauddin Zakariya (thirteenth century), the Suhrawardi saints enjoyed a very high repute; and the tomb of the saint became a pilgrim centre, doing the duty for the city that the sun temple used to perform five or six centuries earlier.

Multan was an important town irrespective of the fortunes of Lahore. But the decline of Lahore after 1241 certainly enhanced its importance. The great trade route between Delhi and the Islamic world passed through Multan. Ajodhan (Pak Pattan) rose in significance not only because of Shaikh Fariduddin Ganj-i Shakar, but also because it lay on the Delhi–Multan route. Sultan Firuz Tughluq's governor of Multan, Ainul Mulk Multani, has left his letters, edited by Professor S.A. Rashid from Lahore, which show the significant position Multan occupied in the traffic with the Islamic countries; there apparently was, among other things, a brisk export of slaves, which Firuz sought to prohibit.

The third segment of medieval Punjab is the cis-Sutlej tract, whose earlier centre seems to have been the town normally spelt Tabarhinda in our texts, which is usually identified by historians with Bhatinda. Climatology dictated that the belt running along the Himalayan foothills could support much cultivation; the seasonal streams running south and south-eastward from this belts disappeared into the Thar Desert at points 150 or 200 miles from the foothills. In its south and south-east the region contained what were oases rather than large compact territories of cultivation, while to the north the cultivation became denser and continuous.

It is, therefore, not surprising that Samana should have enjoyed premier importance in the area with its more northerly position, along with towns like Kaithal and Ghuram. But if the agricultural prosperity belonged to the north, the commercial and military significance attached itself to the south. The Multan–Ajodhan–Abohar–Bhatnair–Hansi–Delhi route was taken by merchants as well as invaders trying to strike at Delhi. (Compare the route recorded by Ibn Battuta with that taken by Timur or, for that matter, by Firuz Tughluq on his march from Sindh to Delhi in 1351.)

Firuz Tughluq's interest in the southern portion of the region must have derived from the area's commercial and strategic importance. The great canal he ran from the Yamuna to Hansi, and beyond, the fort of Hisar Firuza that he founded, and the canal that he seems to have excavated from Sutlej to Sarsuti (Sirsa) are indicators of his close concern with this area.[22]

Timur's invasion ravaged much of the area, and the canals and towns both decayed in the sixteenth century. In the Mughal period, the area to the north-west of Hisar Firuza became strangely unimportant and neglected; the main lines of trade now ran from Delhi to Sirhind and then to Lahore, it being the time of its greatest glory. The high road from Delhi to Multan via Pakpattan was not traversed by any writer known to us in the seventeenth century: it had simply disappeared.[23]

The above, of course, is a very fragmentary picture of the Punjab during the three centuries preceding the establishment of Mughal power in India. The interpretations offered of certain details are mere attempts to stimulate reflection and further research into certain historical phenomena that make up a portion of the known history of medieval Punjab. These should be treated as questions rather than answers, and, still less, solutions.

NOTES

1. Barani, *Tarikh-i Firuz Shahi*, Bib. Ind., p. 81.

2. Ibid., pp. 322–3.

3. All the facts about the Kokhars are from *Tabqat-i Nasiri*,vol. II, ed. Habibi, pp. 398, 403, 433, 166.

4. Hazara Qarlugh and Hazara Gujaran are shown as *mahals* of the Sind Sagar Doab in Abu'l Fazl's *A'in-i Akbari*. Hazara was in the Jech Doab; it is the present Midh Ranjo.

5. Barani, p. 109.

6. Isami, *Futuh-us Salatin*, ed. A.S. Usha, Madras, 1948, p. 180.

7. Afif, *Tarikh-i Firuz Shahi*, Bib. Ind. pp. 37–9.

8. Isami, pp. 378, 384–5.

9. Ibid., p. 471.

10. Yahya Sarhindi, *Tarikh-i Mubarak Shahi*, ed. Hidayat Hosain, Calcutta, 1931, pp. 154–7.

11. Yazdi, *Zafarnama*, vol. II, pp. 56–7.

12. Ibid., pp. 169–72. Apparently, many Kokhars were still Hindus, for Yazdi says that those Hindu who said they were of Shaikha's tribe had been exempted from plunders by Timur during the time that Shaikha remained in the train of Timur. See also Yahya Sirhindi, pp. 166–7.

13.Sirhindi, *Tarikh-i Mubarak Shahi*, pp. 193–4, and ff.

14. *A'in-i Akbari*, statistics for suba Lahore, Column for *bhumi* or zamindars.

15. *Khulasatut-Tawarikh*, ed. Zafar Hasan, Delhi, 1918, pp. 66–7.

16. S. Beal, *Buddhist Records of the Western World*, vol. II, pp. 274–5. Watters doubts the identification of Mu-lo-San-pu-lu with Multan, purely on rigorous philological grounds; he is, however, unconvincing (Watters, *On Yuan Chwang*, II, p. 254).

17. *Chachnama*, text edited by Daudpota; translation (with omissions) in Elliot and Dowson, *History of India as Told by its Own Historians*, vol. I, and by Kalichbeg Fredunbeg.

18. See. e.g., Barani, p. 428.

19. *A'in-i Akbari*, Account of the Twelve *Subas'* in H. Blochmann's ed., Calcutta, 1866–77, vol. I.

20. These remarks are based on the work on historical geography of the region, by Raverty, Ibadur Rahman Khan and Irfan Habib.

21. Barani, pp. 120, 311.

22. The classic account of the West Jamuna Canal is in Afif, *Tarikh-i Firuz Shahi*, pp. 127–31. For the canal from the Sutlej, see *Tarikh-i Mubarak Shahi*, pp. 125–6.

23. See Sheet 4B of Irfan Habib's *Atlas of the Mughal Empire* Delhi, 1982.

FORMATION OF THE EMPIRE

6

Towards an Interpretation of the Mughal Empire

It is nowadays common for Indian history textbooks to treat the various 'empires' that successively occupied the stage of Indian history, with their respective 'administrations', as so many successive repetitions with merely different names for offices and institutions that in substance remained the same: namely the king, the ministers, the provinces, the governors, the taxes, land grants, and so on. But D.D. Kosambi, in his *Introduction to the Study of Indian History* (Bombay, 1975), rightly observed that this repetitive succession cannot be assumed, and that each regime, when subjected to critical study, displays distinct elements that call for analysis in the context of 'relations of production' (as he put it) existing at that particular time.

Of all the 'empires' previous to the British, we know most, of course, about the Mughal empire. And this empire displays so many striking features that it should in fact attract an historical analyst of today as much as it did Bernier. In its large extent and long duration, it had only one precedent, the Mauryan empire, some 1900 years earlier. Havell well might regard it as the fulfilment of the political ambitions embodied in Indian polity for three millennia.

And yet, there is also a temptation to see in the Mughal empire a primitive version of the modern state. Its existence belongs to a period when modern technology had dawned in Europe, some rays of which had also fallen on Asia. Can it then be said, as Barthold[2] implied, that the foundations of the Mughal empire lay in artillery—the most brilliant and dreadful representative of modern technology, as much as did those of the modern absolute monarchies of Europe? Can we say, further, that the Mughal empire, far from being the climax of traditional Indian political endeavour, represented one of the several unsuccessful experiments of History towards that titration which has at last given us the distinct modern civilization of our times?

These questions are unlikely to be answered easily, or perhaps ever, with a simple yes or no. The factors to be considered are too numerous, and often too remote, to be evaluated or assessed with any reasonable assurance of comprehensiveness and accuracy. But is there any student of the period who does not, in his private thoughts, have a predilection for one or the other setting for the Mughal empire, that is for regarding it either as the most successful of the traditional Indian states or as an abortive quasi-modern polity?

The essay attempts to discuss certain matters which may be of interest to a contingent debate on the theme which has been briefly outlined here. Most of the conclusions are naturally tentative; and I can hope for no more than that the aspects touched upon may be found to be deserving of closer scrutiny.

A question that comes to mind regarding the general characterization of the Mughal empire is, what was new—or if not new, then, at any rate, exotic—in the polity of the Mughal empire?

In the view of a number of historians, including Rushbrook Williams[3] and R.P. Tripathi,[4] the institutions and mutual relations of kingship and nobility in the Mughal empire derive essentially from Turko-Mongol traditions, contrasted with the 'Afghan'. The former conferred on the emperor absolute powers over his nobles and subjects, whereas the latter, particularly in the circumstances of the fifteenth century, tended to place the king in no higher a position than of the first among equals. This view has been criticized, first through an analysis of the surviving Turkish and Mongol traditions (for both were not only distinct, but historically different) in the Central Asia of Babur's time, it being shown that these by no means prescribed an absolute despotism.[5] The other criticism is that it is possibly inaccurate to describe the Indo-Afghan or Lodi polity as a mere tribal confederation; for this would underestimate the underlying powers of the monarch that certain tribal forms only barely concealed.[6]

There is still a third factor, to which, perhaps, sufficient attention has not been paid. This is the continuing survival of the framework of the administration of the Delhi Sultanate, established under the Khaljis and Tughluqs, especially the land revenue system. Abul Fazl's statement that Sher Shah sought to copy the administrative measures of Alauddin Khalji which he had read about in Barani's *Tarikh-i Firuz Shahi* would have been effective as a gibe had Sher Shah not proved himself a realist by his success in carrying out these measures. This success testified to the similarity, if not identity, of the administrative system of the early sixteenth century with that of the fourteenth.

The contribution of the Sur regime to the structure of Mughal polity, too, needs to be borne in mind. Sher Shah and Islam Shah created the *zabt* system of land-revenue assessment, the cornerstone of Akbar's land revenue administration. They imposed the *dagh*, or horse branding, an equally basic device for controlling the army. If Abbas Sarwani is to be believed, Sher Shah attempted a conscious centralized despotism; and Islam Shah certainly gave shape to it by bringing the whole of his empire under direct control (*khalisa*), thus anticipating Akbar's measures of 1574.

These achievements were acclaimed by the Afghan historians of the late sixteenth and seventeenth centuries; but they also won wider recognition. There are guarded admissions in Abul Fazl; and a paean of praise for Sher Shah is found in a letter written in 1611 by Mirza Aziz Koka, himself one of 'the old wolves' of the Mughal state.[7] What more could be required as a testimony of the popular admiration of Sher Shah than that Dawar Bakhsh, a claimant to the Mughal throne in 1627, should assume for himself the very same title of Sher Shah?[8]

But, quite obviously, Mughal polity could not have been a simple continuation of the Sultanate and Sur polity. Had it been such, its comparatively greater success would be impossible to explain. What, then, were the new elements of political chemistry out of which Akbar compounded such a large, stable, long-lasting political structure? At the risk of oversimplification, I would say that these were an extreme systematization of administration, a new theoretical basis for sovereignty, and a balanced and stable composition of the ruling class.

In spite of the work done on Akbar's administration, notably by Moreland, Saran and Ibn Hasan, there has not been an adequate appreciation of Akbar's achievement in the realm of systematization of administration. We see such systematization in his creation of *mansab*, classifying all individual officers into definite categories. Whereas before Akbar each appointment, promotion, fixation of pay, and obligation was in the case of higher officers a separate ad hoc arrangement, under Akbar every such action was reduced to a change in the mansab (the number assigned to a man). Increase or diminution of pay and obligation followed a change in the mansab as a matter of course, under set regulations. Much research has gone into discovering the 'decimal system' of military organization under the Delhi Sultans and the Mongols. But mansab has really little kinship with any such system. It has been shown, quite persuasively, that there was no mansab or number-rank in existence before 1574.[9] In fact, no analogous system of numbered ranks can be found in any Central Asian or Middle Eastern state—and certainly not in the Timurid, the Uzbek, the Safavid, and the Ottoman empires. The mansab system was a unique and, as far as centralization went, an unrivalled device for organizing the ruling class.

We get the same sense of systematization in the development of *jagir* as the pure form of land-revenue assignment. It is possible to argue that the jagir fits the definition of iqta' given in the *Siyasatnama* of Nizam-al-Mulk Tusi (twelfth century).[10] But whereas in all earlier states the iqta in practice always became confounded with general administrative charge, the jagir in actual practice exactly fitted the standard definition of iqta'. The maintenance of *jama' dami* (estimated revenue) figures, and the assignment of jagir to a mansab holder, rigidly on the basis of the approved jama' dami equalling the *talab*, or his sanctioned pay, the constant transfer of jagirs, and the restricting of *jagirdar*s' powers to revenue collection alone,[11] are again measures for which precedents and parallels in the Islamic world are not easy to find.

Akbar's division of his empire into *subas*, *sarkars* and *mahalls* and his largely successful attempts to make the entire administrative structure of one suba into an exact replica of the other, with a chain of officers at various levels ultimately controlled by the ministers at the centre, gave identity to Mughal administrative institutions irrespective of the regions where they functioned.

The systematization continued under Akbar's successors. When new administrative categories were created, whether *duaspasihaspa* ranks under Jahangir, or the month scales under Shah Jahan, they too appear, in the ultimate analysis, to substitute general categories for individual exceptions.[12] Even in the sphere of land-revenue administration, where regional differences were inevitable, the zabt system—the characteristic institution of the Mughal revenue administration—was extended to the Deccan by Murshid Quli Khan (1655–8).

Side by side with his immense work of centralization and systematization, we see under Akbar the exposition of a new stress on the absoluteness of sovereignty. The accepted Mughal doctrine of sovereignty was derived from several distinct sources which could by no means be logically interrelated. It partly consisted of an exaltation of the blue blood of the Mughal dynasty. The long history of the Mughals as a ruling dynasty, going back to Timur and Chengiz Khan, rulers not of obscure states but of world empires, was an asset which the Mughals put to skilful use. Abul Fazl's *Akbarnama* offers a superb example of the propaganda carried on for the dynasty on the basis of its past. The Mughals accentuated the consciousness of their exalted status by abstaining from marrying princesses of the dynasty to anyone except a member of the imperial family. On the other hand, the privilege of marrying a daughter to a prince or emperor came to be zealously guarded by a few Iranian, Turanian and Rajput families of high status. The historic halo around the dynasty justified the submission of the chiefs of the proudest clans to its suzerainty.

A second element derived from the earlier Muslim political thinkers. In the chapter, *Rawai-i rozi*, in the *A'in-i Akbari*, Abul Fazl repeats the well-known theory of social contract to justify the sovereign's absolute claims over the individual subject. The strength of this theory lies in its secular character and its foundation on alleged social needs. It has the further merit of being rational.

But rationality was probably not deemed a sufficient incentive to the total obedience that the Mughal sovereign sought. A third element then entered; and that was religious. Ever since the Safavids successfully utilized their past as religious leaders and based their sovereignty on their spiritual authority, the attractions of a similar position for sunni sovereigns were irresistible. The Ottomans ultimately purchased from existing claimants the authority of the Abbasid caliphate; but they were anticipated by Akbar, who, through the *mahzar* of 1579, attempted to assume the position of an interpreter of Islamic law and, in spheres where the existing corpus was silent, of a legislator.[13]

For reasons into which we cannot go here, Akbar's attempt to establish such a position within the framework of Islam proved abortive.[14] Moreover, it did not solve the problem of spiritual authority in relations with his non-Muslim subjects. It therefore gave way to a new attempt in which it was claimed that the emperor enjoyed the position of a spiritual guide and that this position derived not from any particular religion, but directly from God. 'Sovereignty is a ray of light from the Divine Sun', claims Abul Fazl.[15] As such, men of all faiths were beneficiaries of the Divine Light. Thus Aurangzeb would write to Rana Raj Singh when seeking the throne:

Because the persons of the great kings are shadows of God, the attention of this elevated class (of kings), who are the pillars of the great court, is devoted to this, that men belonging to various communities and different religions should live in the vale of peace and pass their days in prosperity, and no one should interfere in the affairs of another. Any one of this sky-glorious group (of kings) who resorted to intolerance, became the cause of dispute and conflict and of harm to the people at large, who are indeed a trust received from God: in reality (such a king) thereby endeavoured to devastate the prosperous creations of God and destroy the foundation of the God-created fabric, which is a habit deserving to be rejected and cast off. God willing, when the true cause (i.e. Aurangzeb's own cause) is successful, and the wishes of the sincerely loyal ones are fulfilled, the benefits of the revered practices and established regulations of my great ancestors, who are so much esteemed by the worshipful ones, will cast lustre on the four-cornered inhabited world.[16]

Akbar initiated the practice of *jharoka darshan*, a striking innovation which nevertheless seemed to be in accordance with Hindu tradition. To a more select circle of disciples, styled the *iradat-gazinan* by Abul Fazl, Akbar was the spiritual guide. Akbar's successors enlarged this circle virtually to include all their nobles; and it became a convention for every high noble, Muslim or Hindu, to address the emperor as *Pir-o murshid*, and designate himself as his *murid*.

It can be seen that, combined with the tolerant religious policy of which Akbar was the author, the basing of political authority on spiritual sanctity was an intelligent device to strengthen the sovereign's position. Its logical implications lay, however, not in secularism, but in an as yet dormant and unelaborated concept of religious equality. Abul Fazl's claims for his master could only be justified by the subsequent theories of Dara Shukoh.

The third important element which Akbar introduced into imperial polity was, as already mentioned, the establishment of certain principles governing the relations between the king and the nobles. That Akbar created a composite nobility has been well recognized since the seventeenth century, when the author of the *Dabistan-i Mazahib* ascribed the prosperity of the Mughal dynasty to the fact that Akbar had succeeded in removing the dependence of the sovereign on the Muslim nobility alone.[17] Though the attribution of the creation of a composite nobility to Akbar is now a part of the established historical dogma, it can be accepted only with much qualification. A composite nobility, in terms of race, existed already under the Khaljis (1290–1320); and a composite nobility, in terms of religion, under Muhammad Tughluq.[18] The latter Sultan too linked his policy towards the nobility with innovations in his religious policy, such as a repressive attitude towards the Muslim orthodoxy, public discourses with yogis (Hindu mendicants) and personal participation in the Holi festival.[19] And yet the effort to give stability to the political structure of the Sultanate by this means had not been successful.

It may be that there were also autonomous causes for the greater success of Akbar in creating a loyal nobility. For instance, the gradual progress of Islamic-Persian court culture among the higher classes of non-Muslims, including the Rajputs, might have generated a common cultural ground for the political alliance between sections of Muslim and non-Muslim aristocracies.

There is also another factor to consider. The rural aristocracy, descendants of the ruling class of the twelfth century, had not only fresh memories in the thirteenth and fourteenth centuries of their past glories, but probably then objected to the imposition of the exotic fiscal system, whereby the bulk of the agricultural surplus was claimed by the Sultan as kharaj (land-tax) to be distributed among his nobles, the muqtis or iqta-holders. By the sixteenth century, the kharaj system could no longer be seen as an innovation, and the rural aristocracy, having been reduced to the status of zamindars, must have largely accommodated themselves to it.[20] It was thus possible to introduce into the Mughal nobility certain zamindar elements (e.g. the Rajput chiefs, Ghakkars, etc.) without endangering its foundations.[21]

Both these factors are easily admitted. But one significant contribution of Akbar that continued to be honoured by his four immediate successors must be given due recognition. This was the enunciation of an essentially humane approach to the individuals constituting the nobility. In this respect, the Mughal empire stood apart from the Sultanate; and it also stood apart from the Safavid and other polities of the contemporary Islamic world.

The official chronicler of Shah Jahan tells us:

In matters of punishments, His Majesty does not regard the nobles as different from ordinary human beings. If per chance mention is made in His Majesty's presence of the cruelty of the Emperors of Constantinople, Iran, and Uzbeks, and of their ferocity in awarding punishments, His Majesty gets so perturbed that the signs of sadness are apparent from his illustrious forehead. His Majesty has often been heard to say that God has given the kings authority and made all men their subjects for the sole purpose that the entire attention of kings be directed towards the maintenance of justice, which is the basis of the functioning of the world and the races of men. Therefore, the king should so award punishments that the cruel cannot oppress their victims, and (the nobles) may treat the poor mildly, and the garden of the world flourish owing to the removal of the thorns of cruelty. Not that in the name of awarding punishments the king should slaughter large numbers of men for a small fault, and on a small suspicion injure fellow beings, who are a trust from God.[22]

The boast for the Mughal empire implicit in this passage was not an empty one. The Mughal emperors shine by contrast with their despotic contemporaries. Taking the *Tarikh-i Alam Ara-i Abbasi*,[23] I compiled a list of the leading nobles executed by Shah Abbas I (1587–1629), the great Safavid emperor. I found that during thirty-one years, he executed no less than forty-eight prominent officers of his, generally upon the slightest suspicion. Some of the executions were on religious grounds.[24] When we turn from this gory record to the annals of the Mughal empire, we find that even dismissals, let alone executions, are very rare. When high officers were dismissed for major faults, they were usually pensioned off with land grants. Confiscation of individual nobles' property, as punishment, was unknown. So also the humiliation of the family of a noble no longer in favour. It was only in the rare cases of rebellions or wars of succession that the nobles met a violent end. Even here an unwritten custom provided that only under exceptional circumstances were nobles of the defeated side to be executed after a battle. In an overwhelmingly large number of cases, nobles who escaped death on the battlefield could be sure of escaping it at their captor's hands. In the wars of succession, it remained indeed usual, until 1713, to offer appointments to the supporters of the defeated claimants. During the war of 1658–9, for example, neither Aurangzeb nor Dara Shukoh executed any noble. It was only the princes of royal blood whose lives remained insecure, ever since Shah Jahan in 1628 established the practice of executing possible rivals.

It was this approach to the nobility, in which loyalty to the throne was assumed from every one, that was perhaps a major factor in enabling the Mughals to avoid a crisis in their relations with the nobles after the aristocratic rebellion of 1580. This approach had a corollary to it. While the Mughal emperor undertook no obligation to maintain an hereditary nobility, and in theory could appoint anyone to any mansab, in actual fact recruitment to the nobility was confined to certain foreign racial elements and indigenous clans which, in spite of their diverse backgrounds, were bound to the Mughal dynasty in grateful obedience. If one collects data about the mansab-holders under the different emperors, one is surprised at the broadly unvarying nature of the proportions shared by the various elements.

Table 1 gives the composition of (a) the 98 mansabdars alive in 1595, and enjoying the mansab of 500 and above; (b) the 100 highest mansabdars in service in 1620; (c) the 100 highest mansabdars in 1656; (d) the 202 mansabdars appointed/promoted to the mansabs of 2,000/ 1,500 and above during the period 1658–78; and (e) 277 mansabdars of the same ranks serving during 1679–1707.[25] It will be seen from the table that the main disturbance in the proportionate strength of the various elements in the Mughal nobility was caused by the entrance of the Marathas and other Dakhinis (the real strength of the latter is concealed in the break-up of the table), who appear in increasing numbers from 1656. This intrusion is, of course, explained by the increasing involvement of the Mughal empire in the Deccan, especially during the reign of Aurangzeb (1659–1707).

Thus we see two opposites reconciled successfully in Mughal polity, namely the absolute despotic power of the emperor, bolstered by immense centralization and a theory of semi-divine sovereignty; and a structure heavily systematized with such conventions governing the relations between the king and his nobles as to deserve even the appellation of 'constitution', with a small if not a capital 'c'. We have seen, further, that in the formation of this policy both the development of institutions, already in existence under the previous regimes, and a deliberate policy on the part of the Mughal emperors, had distinct roles to play. These two causal factors did certainly not have a directly 'modern' origin, even taking that imprecise term in the widest of its possible senses.

And yet it is possible that some of the changes that took place in other parts of the world at the dawn of the modern era did exercise certain influences on the last-stage, but crucial, development of medieval institutions that we have just considered, and on the ideas and intellectual atmosphere in which what was new in the Mughal imperial polity was formulated.

I would begin by taking up a small point: the system of coinage. The Mughal system of coinage was tri-metallic, with coins struck in three metals, gold, silver and copper, with the highest degree of purity achieved anywhere in the world. Such coinage too had its predecessor in the Sultanate coinage of the fourteenth century. But during the fifteenth century coinage had been heavily debased, the main coin being a copper tanka with a progressively declining silver alloy. Sher Shah sought to eliminate the debased coinage, and he minted the first rupee, a coin of 178 grains of virtually pure silver. By the end of the sixteenth century the attempt that had continued under the later Surs and yet more vigorously under Akbar, succeeded in making the rupee the basic unit of currency actually in use.[26] It is pointless to dilate upon the importance of this achievement for successful functioning of commerce and credit, and the importance of the latter, in turn, for the functioning of a highly centralized administration. Yet, it is not to be forgotten that the coming of the rupee was linked to the Spanish discovery of the New World, because that led to a heavy influx of silver, plundered extracted from the newly discovered continents, into the 'Old World', thereby ending the silver famine that had prevailed there since the fourteenth century. Thus what would have been otherwise exceptionally difficult if not impossible—namely the institution of a pure silver currency,

previously limited by conditions of very high silver prices—became possible as an economic byproduct of the Age of Discovery.

There is also the role of the artillery to be considered. It is true that the Mughal army, like the Safavid and Uzbek, and even the Ottoman army, was mainly a cavalry force. It was characteristic that the mansab indicating the size of military contingent its possessor was obliged to maintain was styled *suwar* or 'horseman'. But it would be wrong to think that artillery had no more than a marginal role to play in the Mughal army, especially when we remember that we ought not to be thinking of cannon only, but also, and even particularly, of muskets. After all, if in 1647 there were 200,000 horsemen under the imperial banner, there were also no less than 40,000 infantrymen, consisting of 'matchlock men, gunners, cannoneers and rocketeers'.[27]

It is quite likely that the increasing use of artillery during the hundred years following the battle of Panipat in 1526 gave the Mughal army a decisive weapon against the traditional chiefs with their old-type cavalry retainers (of whom the Rajputs were a characteristic illustration). Moreover, artillery gave to the towns, where alone guns and muskets could be manufactured, a new basis for political and military domination over the countryside. In so far as the Mughal ruling class was mainly urban in character,[28] it must certainly have gained as a result of the new military importance of towns.

We can thus at least identify two new sources of strength and stability that 'modern' developments gave to the Mughal polity—the silver influx, a component of the Price Revolution, and the artillery, an early product of modern technology. It is, moreover, possible that the development in Europe was influencing ideas too, indirectly but powerfully.

Information about the Europeans was available to Akbar and his contemporaries; and this was not confined to knowledge about the Jesuits and Christianity. Abul Fazl was aware that the Europeans had discovered the Americas, which he called *Alam-i Nau*,[29] the New World. The accounts of the time are replete with references to the technological ingenuity of the Firangis, it being mentioned with pride if craftsmen at any place could manufacture articles that might compare with those of European manufacturers. As is well known, by the seventeenth century European physicians and surgeons had established a reputation for western science; and in a notable encounter of the two cultures, Bernier explained the theory of the circulation of blood to Danishmand Khan.[30]

Such information, showing the lead that Europe was attaining in several branches of human activity, could not but engender questioning about the finality of traditional knowledge. This questioning took several forms. On one side was the rational approach of Abul Fazl, who would point out that zinc, as a separate metal (a recent discovery in Asia), was not known to the ancients,[31] or would say that al-Ghazali spoke nonsense when he condemned sciences that were not manifestly based upon the Quran.[32] Then there was Dara Shukoh and men of his stamp, who rejected the traditional sciences, but also rejected rationality, and sought to establish an obscurantist spiritual dogma on the foundations of Comparative Religion.[33] Further to the 'right' still, there were men like Mullah Nasir of Burhanpur who thought that no particular sanctity attached to the classical Islamic jurists, and what they said could be challenged by men of equal or greater learning, like himself.[34] Even Shaykh Ahmad Sirhindi was thought by his critics to be tarnished with similar thoughts of his own superiority over the earlier interpreters.[35]

In the previous (sixteenth) century, the Mahdavi Movement had attained considerable success; and it was certainly a consciously 'revisionist' doctrine.

All these were symptoms of a cleft in the hitherto solid structure of faith in the traditional cultural heritage of Islam. It was this void that was unconsciously sought to be filled by the special position of the Mughal emperor as a spiritual guide, and the self-conscious view of the Mughal empire as a great new polity, essentially just and humane (to the individual members of the ruling class). If this hypothesis is accepted, we can perhaps see a dual ideological role of the Mughal empire. On the one hand, the need of an official theory of sovereignty, and of the specific role of Mughal polity, arose because of the undermining of the traditional ideological structure from tremors originating from the remote and largely unidentified developments of the early modern world; but, in its turn, the theory cemented and strengthened the traditional culture and made the Mughal empire its upholder and protector.

The suggestion that I should like to make is, then, that we should not treat the Mughal empire as simply the last in the line of succession of the traditional Indian empires. It is true that its structure and institutions had deep indigenous roots. Its success also owed not in small measure to the genius of one man, Akbar. But the circumstances and atmosphere in which it was created were shaped by certain other factors as well, that had much to do with the very events that played an important part in the origin and development of modern culture in Europe. A certain intellectual ferment was in the air in India also, stirred in unseen ways by the advance of Europe; and this too contributed to the acceptance of a new ideological basis offered for the Mughal empire.

This does not suggest that these factors converted the Mughal empire into a modern state. If it had some rudiments of an unwritten constitution, it did not yet claim for itself the legislative power and functions that are the hallmarks of a modern state. It was essentially the 'perfection' of a medieval polity, made possible by certain early modern developments. Though this gave it the stability and power denied to its predecessors, it still did not solve the new contradiction inherent in the existence of a medieval polity in a world advancing to modern conditions.

As I see it, this contradiction expressed itself mainly in the contrast between the sense of unity infused in the imperial ruling class, in spite of its heterogeneity, and the absence of the consciousness of such unity among the mass of the imperial subjects. In other words, the subcontinent of India had a centralized quasi-modern state without any developing sense of nationhood. It is true that 'Hindustan', a word so often used, was more than a simple geographical expression. But if it was so, this was not because of any new popular consciousness, but because of its geographical correspondence with the area in which Hindu mythology had been enacted and places of pilgrimage lay scattered. This was not sufficient to overcome divisions of caste and community.

It was for this reason, perhaps, that the Mughal empire proved so vulnerable to the challenges from the Marathas, Jats, Sikhs, and Afghans, who represented not its conventional political opponents, but forces of a new kind, involving the entry of peasant-soldiers. This is not the place to discuss how far these forces were the product of the 'agrarian crisis' of the Mughal empire. What is more significant for the present purpose is that while no serious decision occurred within the Mughal ruling class, in the face of these challenges it still proved incapable of meeting them and failed to invoke any popular support in its struggle. It seemed as if the people at large were indifferent to whether they were under an imperial or a regional regime.

Admittedly, all this is hypothesis, even speculation. But the whole purpose here is simply to suggest a sphere in which speculation may usefully be pursued, in that it may lead to our attaching fresh significance to facts hitherto not noticed, or hardly noticed. Then, one day, perhaps, we may really assign to the Mughal empire its true place in history.

NOTES

1. E.B. Havell, *A History of Aryan Rule in India*, London, n.d., pp. 520–1.

2. V.V. Barthold, 'Iran', tr. G.K. Nariman, in *Posthumous Works of G.K. Nariman*, ed. S.H. Jhabvala, Bombay, 1935, pp. 142–3.

3. 'It will thus be seen that Babur had not merely to conquer a kingdom; he had to create a theory of kingship. He was determined to be no Sultan, hampered by all limitations which had beset the Lodi dynasty; but a *padshah*, looking down upon even his highest *amir*s from the towering eminence upon which the divine right of Timur's blood had placed him' (Rushbrook Williams, *An Empire Builder of the Sixteenth Century*, London, 1918, p. 161).

4. 'The Chaghatain conqueror Babar came to India with ideas (of sovereignty) that were not quite similar to those of either the early Turkish rulers of Delhi or the Afghans' (R.P. Tripathi, *Some Aspects of Muslim Administration*, Allahabad, 1936, pp. 105ff).

5. Iqtidar Alam Khan, 'The Turko-Mongol Theory of Kingship', in *Medieval India: A Miscellany*, II, 1972, pp. 8–18.

6. Iqtidar Husain Siddiqi, *Some Aspects of Afghan Despotism in India*, Aligarh, 1971, pp. 1–60.

7. 'Sher Shah Afghan was not a king (*malik*) but an angel (*malak*). In six years he gave such stability to the structure that the foundations still survive' (B.M. MS. Add. 16859, f. 19a).

8. The curious fact is not mentioned in the Indian chronicles. But it is the title Dawar Bakhsh assumes in his *farman* of 1627 to Raja Jai Singh (Bikaner, old serial no. 176, New S. 021). This is corroborated by the *Tarikh-i Alam Ara-i-Abbasi*, Tehran edn, A.G. 1314, p. 750.

9. A.J. Qaisar, *PIHC*, Delhi session, 1961, pp. 155–7.

10. *Siyasatnama*, ed. C. Scheffer, Paris, 1891–92, p. 28.

11. Cf. Irfan Habib, *Agrarian System of Mughal India, 1556–1707*, Bombay, 1963, pp. 256 ff.

12. Cf. W.H. Moreland, 'Rank (Mansab) in the Mughal State Service', *Journal of Royal Asiatic Society (JRAS)*, 1936, pp. 641–65; Irfan Habib, 'The Mansab System, 1595–1637', *PIHC*, Patiala session, 1968, pp. 221ff.

13. Cf. S. Nurul Hasan, 'The *Mahzar* of Akbar's Reign', *Journal of U.P. History Society*, XVI, 1968, p. 126.

14. Cf. Iqtidar Alam Khan in *JRAS*, 1968, pp. 34–5.

15. *A'in-i Akbari*, III.

16. For the text of the *nishan*, see Kaviraj Shyamaldas, Udaipur, n.d; *Vir Vinod*, II, pp. 419–20 n.

17. *Dabistan-i Mazahib*, ed. Nazar Ashraf, Calcutta, 1809, p. 432.

18. See M. Athar Ali, 'Foundations of Akbar's Organization of the Nobility: An Interpretation', *Medieval India Quarterly,* III (3–4), 1958, pp. 80–7.

19. Isami, *Futuh-us Salatin,* ed. A.S. Usha, Madras, 1948, p. 515.

20. Cf. Irfan Habib, 'Social Distribution of Landed Property in Pre-British India', *Enquiry,* no. 12, pp. 54–6.

21. Dr Ahsan Raza Khan in his unpublished thesis on the chiefs under Akbar has collected interesting data about the chiefs (high zamindars) who were granted mansabs under Akbar.

22. Lahori, *Badshahnama,* I, Bib. Ind., Calcutta, 1866–74, pp. 139–40.

23. Tehran edn, AH 1214.

24. For example in his seventeenth regnal year.

25. These data are based: (a) on the *A'in-i Akbari's* list of mansabdars; (b) on Irfan Habib's list (unpublished) of mansabdars under Jahangir, mainly based on the *Tuzuk-i Jahangiri*; and (c) on Waris, *Badshahnama,* Ethe, 329, for the list of mansabdars in 1656. The racial composition has been established by detailed checking with the biographical information in the chronicles (e.g. Lahori) as well as the *Zakhirat al-Khawanin* and the *Ma'asir al- 'Umara'.* (d) and (e) are based on the list of mansabdars of Aurangzeb's reign given in M. Athar Ali, *The Mughal Nobility under Aurangzeb,* Bombay, 1966.

26. Cf. H.N. Wright, *The Coinage and Metrology of the Sultans of Delhi,* London, 1936, pp. 260–1; Irfan Habib, *Indian Economic and Social History Review (IESHR),* IV, 1967, pp. 217–19.

27. Lahori, *Badshahnama,* II, p. 715.

28. See M. Athar Ali, *Mughal Nobility under Aurangzeb,* pp. 154 ff.

29. *A'in-i Akbari,* III, p. 22.

30. Bernier, *Travels in the Mogul Empire,* Bombay, 1934, pp. 324, 339.

31. *A' in-i Akbari,* I, p. 24.

32. Muhammad Hashim Kishmi, *Zubdat-al-Maqamat,* Mahmud Press, Lucknow, AH 1302, p. 131.

33. Cf. K.R. Qanungo, *Dara Shukoh,* Calcutta, 1935, pp. 78ff.

34. Muhammad Baqa, *Mirut al alam,* MS Aligarh; Abd al-Salam, 84/314, Pairaish III.

35. S.A. Rizvi, *Muslim Revivalist Movements in Northern India in the 16th and 17th Centuries,* Agra, 1965, pp. 268–70.

7

The Pre-colonial Social Structure and the Polity of the Mughal Empire

India for at least the last three millennia has been an agrarian society, and, for much of that period, land revenue has been at the core of its polities. The transformation of this society under the pressure of a colonial industrial power is one of the major facts of modern history; but that transformation—destructive, regenerative, or neither—can be understood adequately only when we have been able to define the contours of the earlier order. For this there is the evidence of documents and statistics; and these have to be analysed—a task for which we are so greatly tempted to use the great theoretical frameworks of Marx and Weber. The Imperialists and Nationalists too have left us with some basic notions, but which we have to check and test with evidence with the greatest integrity of purpose.

I have just spoken of the previous 'order'; there can immediately be a question whether we are justified in speaking of such an order in the singular—why not a multiplicity of systems? Could there be an agrarian regime common to Rajasthan and Kerala, to Bengal and the Punjab? Or did the Lodi Kingdom and Vijayanagar have similar polities? Are we not assuming a unity or uniformity where none existed? There is considerable insistence at the present time on the regional focus; and this is not unreasonable. The agriculture pursued in regions of over 80 inches of annual rainfall has its own implications for the organization of agrarian life, different from those of a region on the fringe of the desert; and India has both the extremes. Added to this are the cultural specificities expressing themselves in divergent traditions; and the variations must be immense.

But these were variations largely of detail, not of essence. No analysis can ignore these variations; but an analysis which concerns itself with these alone would surely ignore the wood for the trees. The elements of uniformity, on the other hand, affect the very heart of the Indian social system.

For one thing, there is the universality of individual peasant cultivation. This, of course, is not saying much; this economic form was a feature of all civilized societies until the British landowners proved in the eighteenth century that there could be a lordship without a peasantry. But it is the social organization of the Indian peasantry which gave it a distinctive feature, a universality within India, a specificity in relation to the world. This, of course, lay in the caste system. The caste defined who could be a peasant; it created hereditary menial labourers to sustain peasant agriculture (the present Scheduled Castes); and it provided for the village artisans and servants to serve the material and social needs of the peasant. This function of the caste system furnishes the general basis of Indian agrarian society. Its influence on the formation of the superior agrarian classes (e.g. zamindars) is not always so well marked, but in their exercise of superior rights the Nairs in Kerala might still have had something in common with the Rajputs of northern India.

The second common feature is represented by the land-tax. James Mill was not the first to be excited by the curious fact that rent in India should take the form of land-revenue.[1] Cornwallis had fixed the land-revenue at 10/11 of the rent, to begin with; and Thomas Munro had sought to fix the land-revenue at a third of the produce, as a kind of fair rent. Sovereignty in India thus seemed to be equivalent to the right to rent and this was surely the reason why from the sixteenth century European travellers had spoken of the king as the sole proprietor of the land. This had been said with equal impartiality of the Mughal empire as of rulers in south India.[2] No claim to landownership for the king was laid by Indian writers until the eighteenth century. They seemed unaware that the only form in which surplus could be legally extracted must be the landowner's 'rent'. Yet, the concept that the land-tax embraced all produce above that required for the peasant's subsistence for continuing the cycle of agricultural production was deeply rooted. Bhimsen's explanation for the massive temples of the south, built out of the rulers' revenue which were enormous owing to the low costs of subsistence, is an excellent illustration of this concept of the land-tax.[3] And from the fact of the land-tax approximating to rent, Qazi Muhammad A'la declared the king to be the possessor of the soil, if not its proprietor.[4] Why and how Indian agrarian society developed the system of tax-rent instead of landowners' rent is certainly an important subject for comparative history; but there can be little doubt as to its universality in seventeenth-and eighteenth-century India, north as well as south.

Between these two poles, the peasant and the king (and his bureaucrats or nobles, who collected the revenue on his behalf and largely retained it) stood a series of intermediate classes. Their existence too was universal. The simple two-tier structure of the ruler and ruled (*ra'iyyat*, hence 'ryot', peasants), though accepted as an original relation by Moreland,[5] could not really have existed anywhere in that form. A triangular relationship, for example king/nobility–zamindar–peasant, was a truer approximation to reality; and this lies at the root of the remarkable discussion of the Indian agrarian conditions in Qazi Muhammad Ala's *Risala Ahkam Arazi* (early eighteenth century).[6] But even this was only a rough approximation to reality; the intermediate classes had a complex composition and structure everywhere, though with some important common features.

Almost everywhere the intermediary classes were divisible into two clear categories, which, from the point of view of the ruling class, might be defined respectively as the dependent and the accessary classes. The dependent classes included the Brahman landholders of *brahmadeya* villages and the Muslim holders of *aimma* or *madad-i ma'ash* grants: these were generally granted the revenue owing to the sovereign from certain lands. They received grants from their patrons out of the same motives as induced European lords to part with lands for the Church in the Middle Ages, that is expectation of benefits in afterlife.

Of a different nature altogether were the classes which I have called accessary—accessary, that is, to the main business of surplus extraction. If the sovereign wished to realize 'rent', he had to associate with this process persons who had some local power or position; for this service, they had to be remunerated by a share of the revenue they collected. Such would be the zamindars, or hereditary potentates, and village headmen (muqaddams), each class remunerated by a share of the tax, traditionally 10 per cent (*nankar*) in northern India for the zamindars, 2½ per cent for village headmen, and so on. The remuneration might be made in allowance of tax-free lands, but these were a mere form of commission, and not an outright revenue grant as in the case of madad-i ma'ash lands.

The structure of these accessary classes coincided with the traditional structure of privilege, which cannot exactly be called a hierarchy because there was not necessarily any chain of command and obligation. It seemed as if each class had some privilege, to distinguish it from others. Thus beginning with the menial castes or outcastes, who could not hold any land, but had merely some customary privileges of garbage collecting or skinning dead animals; the *paikasht* or non-resident peasants who were permitted to cultivate the land of a village under certain terms and conditions;[7] the *khudkasht* or *palti*s or resident cultivators, who had an absolute right to cultivate within the village; the privileged higher castes, who paid revenue at lower rates,[8] and who in the Deccan and south India came to bear the designation of *mirasdar*. Above or often from amongst these, were the headmen (muqaddams, *mahtauns, patels*, etc.), who laid claims to certain customary dues. These in turn tended to merge with the zamindars (*bhumias, wanthyas*, etc.), who laid claims to perquisites and exactions realized from villagers in cash and kind on a hereditary basis.[9] Every hereditary privilege was actually or potentially a saleable right, and thus the structure of privilege tended to appear at its apex as a system of property relationships. A market—not in land as such—but in zamindari, and even headmen's rights, therefore long preceded the British conquests, and was almost a universal feature of agrarian life in India around the middle of the eighteenth century.[10]

In the foregoing sketch I have tended to describe the agrarian conditions in a static framework. One may recall Marx's assessment of the Indian society (as a characteristic form of the 'Asiatic') that it was 'unchanging' and 'stagnatory'.[11] This judgement is, perhaps, both right and wrong. Right, to the extent that it contrasts the rapidity of social transformation in Europe from the close of the fifteenth century with the inability of the Indian society similarly to generate capitalism. But this, at best, would be stating the obvious: the question is whether there was any social and economic change at all which may or may not have been in the direction of capitalism.

I would suggest that built into the agrarian structure that I have described, there were three possible factors which compelled change and created at least a recurring instability in the entire system.

First, the internal strains in the political structure. I know that with all the dedicated attention being now paid to the 'subaltern classes', a person who like me wallows in the study of the nobility, should feel extremely obsolete. However, surely there would be no 'subaltern classes' if there was not a ruling class. How sufficiently the latter performed the functions necessary for the perpetuation of their own dominance, is an essential element of the medieval historical situation. At the core of this was the degree of unity and stability the ruling class could attain. That the twin phenomena had essentially contradictory prerequisites was well stressed by Barani in the fourteenth century. Unity required an absolute despotic sovereign; stability needed limitations on his powers. The principal achievement of Akbar was the securing of a workable compromise under what may be regarded as an unwritten 'constitution' of the Mughal empire. A theoretically absolute king, had to function within a fairly firm framework of the mansab and jagir system, and recognized conventions. A composite nobility, a religious policy of tolerance (*Sulh-i Kul* under Akbar), a continuous recruitment of immigrants, were all facets of the compromise. The seventeenth century showed that the strains could be reconciled or subordinated to the larger interests of the empire. But already by Aurangzeb's time, the early signs of breakdown became noticeable. It may be that once the natural geographical limits of expansion were reached, the interests of the divergent sections of the nobility could no longer be subsumed within a fulfilment (always limited) of the interests of all. Aurangzeb's religious policy may be one reflection of the new dissensions; the unprecedented bloodthirsty bitterness of the war of succession of 1713, their final general expression.

Thus the empire collapsed, partly at least from its own internal fissures and imbalances. Indian statesmanship could not create a successor, whether under Maratha leadership, or, what would have been far less plausible, under Afghan tutelage. There is no reason to ignore or overlook this political breakdown, although by itself it is only part of the story.

Second, the land-tax: its magnitude and mode of realization had inevitably to lead to a subversion of relationships previously established. It has been argued that it was retrogressive (the same standard share of the crop irrespective of the size of holding of the revenue-payer), and, therefore if rigorously assessed, would pauperize the poorer peasant and intensify differentiation. On the other hand, its collection involved collaboration of the accessary classes. If agriculture was adversely affected by heavy demand, the customary claims of these privileged groups would be affected as well. Thus inevitably the collaboration would be replaced by conflict. Part of the history of the Mughal Empire and even the Maratha regimes has indeed been explained in terms of this analysis.[12]

I would, however, enter a word of caution here. While the land-tax might impose an intolerable burden on a segment of the agrarian population, it is not necessary to believe that the ruined population was always a high proportion of the total rural population. The ruin of one village might be simultaneous with the relative prosperity of ten. I have therefore some doubt about the stagnation which is sometimes assumed for the few centuries before the British conquests. In this respect the demographic data are of some interest. Moreland estimated India's population at 100 million for 1605;[13] by 1800 it was nearly 200 million.[14] Could a doubling of population be regarded as consonant with absolute economic stagnation? The picture would not substantially alter even if

Moreland's figure is revised to 125 million[15] or even 140–150 million.[16]

Clearly, the land-tax did leave a share of the surplus sticking to the fingers of the accessory classes and even the higher privileged strata, and this could not only create an agrarian market, but perhaps even go back as agricultural inputs (cattle, seed, etc.) to expand agricultural production.[17] One need not surely be totally converted by Sir John Shore's criticism of the zamindars.[18]

The third possible source of change was monetization. The prevalence of the cash nexus has already been stressed frequently enough to require any further elaboration.[19] Whether the peasant put a part of his produce on the market to pay land-tax or buy goods for his own use, has no direct relevance to the effects of market relations on agriculture. It could only determine whether the goods produced in return went to the town (where the tax collections would be mainly disbursed) or to the village. Market conditions must lead, through the usual routine, to usury and differentiation. A moneyed rural class must come to exist; and we may recall Tavernier's remark that a village must be small indeed if it has no shroff.[20] The sale of rights and privileges of which I have spoken above must have kept pace with the process of monetization. It is also very likely that the influx of New World silver from c. 1550 to c. 1750 greatly expanded money circulation not only in the absolute terms of metal but, more important, in terms of transactions.

There must, therefore, have been an expansion of trade. This, I think, is in conformity with the force of early English evidence about the considerable size of merchant wealth in India whether in the seventeenth or eighteenth century. But why such monetization should subvert any existing political and economic relationships is difficult to understand.

It is difficult to designate the economy on the eve of the British conquest as in crisis. What was in crisis was the political apparatus. What happened, probably, was that the British were able to utilize the political crisis to assume dominance, while being able to derive full advantage from controlling a fairly well functioning economy. According to Sir John Shore's estimate made in 1789, out of a total agricultural production of Rs 8.51 crore in Bengal, the land revenue claimed by the Company accounted for about Rs 2.50 crore.[21] Such a high share for revenue out of the gross agricultural product shows the enormous size of the fiscal claims which the English not only inherited but enforced with full vigour. It was, perhaps, unfortunate for India that this was so; for this all the more cleared the way for the tribute or drain of wealth to England which both Shore and Cornwallis mourned but accepted as a law of nature.[22] It is not only the ways in which the Company revised the mode of assessment and collection through the Permanent, Ryotwari and Mahalwari Settlements that are important, but also how the revenues so collected were spent. The drain broke the 'circuit' underlying the functioning of the Indian agrarian economy; and serious consequences were bound to flow from this critical disruption. They demand a much closer analysis especially for the latter half of the eighteenth century than has been applied to them so far.[23]

There is a further related point to be considered as well. If the land-tax inherited by the East India Company was akin to rent, rather than a tax to meet the needs of government, inputs for further expansion of agricultural production ought to have come out of the land revenue collections, at least in areas such as the Ryotwari regions where the land revenue retained its inherited character until the middle of the nineteenth century. And yet government expenditure (notably salaries of Company officials as well as the payments to Britain, of Company dividends, etc.) expanded to eat up the entire revenues, with hardly any expenditure on public works worth the name. This might or might not have posed a noticeable contrast to the practice of previous governments; but the total waste of the rental resources was an enormous drag on the agrarian economy. The difference of the Permanent Settlement zamindars to the situation of their ryots was strongly criticized by shore and others; but criticism could hardly be convincing when it came from a government which made virtually no return to agriculture from its own resources when it itself drew the bulk of the rent. This was surely tantamount to continuing the medieval legacy in the wrong age.

NOTES

1. One can hardly improve upon the discussion of this theme in the late Eric Stokes, *The English Utilitarians and India*, Oxford, 1959, pp. 81ff.

2. The statements with regard to the Mughal Empire are well known, especially through the pages of Bernier. For the Golkunda kingdom, see Methwold in *Relations of Golkunda*, ed. W.H. Moreland, Hakluyt Society, London, 1932, pp. 10–11.

3. Bhim Sen, *Nuskha-i Dilkhusha*, Br. Mus. or 23, ff. 112b–113b.

4. *Risala-i Ahkam-i Arazi*, Maulana Azad Library (Aligarh) MSS Abdus Salam, 331–10, ff. 616–62a.

5. W.H. Moreland, *Agrarian System of Moslem India*, Cambridge 1929, p. 2, but see also pp. 67ff.

6. Maulana Azad Library (Aligarh) MSS Abdus Salam. Arabiya 331–10ff. 43b–65a.

7. Cf. Satish Chandra, 'Some Aspects of Indian Village Society in Northern India during the 18th century', *IHR*, I, 1974, pp. 51–64.

8. See Dilbagh Singh, *IHR* II(2), pp. 299–311; S.P. Gupta, *PIHC*, Aligarh, 1975, pp. 235–7; R.P. Rana, *IESHR*, XVIII(3–4), pp. 292–326.

9. Cf. S. Moosvi, *IESHR*, XI (3), pp. 359–74 for the size of zamindar's income.

10. Cf. Irfan Habib, *Agrarian System of Mughal India*, Bombay, 1963, pp. 129–31, 157–59.

11. K. Marx and F. Engels, *On Colonialism*, Moscow, 1976, pp. 35–41.

12. See Irfan Habib, *Agrarian System of Mughal India*, esp. ch. IX.

13. W.H. Moreland, *India at the Death of Akbar*, London, 1920, pp. 19–20.

14. Morris D. Morris, *IESHR*, XI(2–3), p. 311.

15. Kingsley Davis, *Population of India and Pakistan*, Princeton, 1951, p. 24.

16. Irfan Habib, in *Cambridge Economic History of India*, I, Cambridge, 1980, p. 166.

17. Cf. Satish Chandra, 'Some Institutional Factors in Providing Capital Inputs for the Improvement and Extension of Cultivation in Medieval India', *IHR*, III(1), 1976, pp. 83–98.

18. Minutes of 18 June 1789; Appendix I to the *Fifth Report*, London, 1812, p. 169.

19. For example, Irfan Habib, *Agrarian System of Mughal India*, Bombay, 1963, pp. 236–40.

20. J.B. Tavernier, *Travels*, tr. V. Ball, ed. Crooke, London, 1925, I, p. 24.

21. Shore's Minute, *Fifth Report*, p. 181.

22. *Fifth Report*, 1812, pp. 183, 493.

23. H. Furber's *John Company at Work*, Cambridge, 1951, still remains the major work on the subject of the eighteenth-century drain, despite its very strong bias against the Indian nationalists' critique of the drain.

8

The Mughal Polity
A Critique of 'Revisionist' Approaches

The nature of the pre-colonial Indian state, especially as one could see it in similarity or opposition to the state in Europe, has exercised a particular fascination since the seventeenth century, when François Bernier spelled out his theory about Oriental monarchies, with special reference to the Mughal Empire and Turkey. It may be recalled that he saw eastern states as different from the European in two major particulars: (1) The king here was the owner of the soil, in other words, the exactor of rent; and (2) those who actually collected the tax-rent held only temporary tenures, as holders of jagirs or *timars*, unlike the hereditary European lords. The temporary tenures, which were a necessary reflex of state ownership of land led to over-exploitation of the peasantry, and, therefore, a progressive decline of the economy and polity. This was in contrast to western Europe, where the limitation of state right of sovereignty and the dominance of private property over the land under its protection, were the surest means to progress and prosperity. Already in Bernier we have the articulation of the contrast between the Oriental despotic state and the occidental laissez-faire state.[1]

The colonial conquest did not, by inducing greater familiarity, force an alteration of Bernier's basic thesis. It could at once be seen that over much of India, there was little that could be identified as European landlord's rent, whereas the most visible claimant to a comparable position in size was the tax collected by, or in the name of, the ruler. The theory was wholly taken over by James Mill in his *History of British India*, and in his later arguments at East India House, that the Indians were the most lightly taxed people in the world, since what the state took from them under the designation of land revenue was the landlords' rent and not tax.[2] In 1839, John Crawfurd would speak of his objection to an 'Asiatic land-tax' as 'a tax which aims at the entire absorption by the state of all it can seize of the rent of the country, nearly the whole industry of which is rural'.[3] Though Mill and Crawfurd were on the opposite sides in the revenue controversy, their perceptions of the pre-colonial Indian state and its rights to rent were identical.

The tradition continued till W.H. Moreland (1929) who in his pioneer essay on the medieval Indian agrarian system recognized

The fact that in the Mogul period the state disposed of from a third to a half of the gross produce of the land constituted *by far the most* potent factor in the distribution of the national income;... [and] that next only to the weather, the administration was the *dominant fact in the economic life* of the country. (italics ours.)[4]

This naturally assigned to the pre-colonial state an economic role which distinguished it crucially from its European counterpart. If one emphasized the selfish nature of the king and the ruling class of the pre-colonial times, exhibited in a lack of reasonable restraint in taxation, one would call it 'despotic'. Where one wished to consider the exaction of rent as a necessary device for extending disinterested protection, as the British thought was true in their case, a word like 'paternalistic' was thought more to suit such a state, which, created in pre-colonial times, continued in its essential fiscal aspect into the colonial. The great difference in intent, not substance, of the state is well put by Macaulay when he presented William Bentinck as having 'infused into Oriental despotism the Spirit of British freedom'.[5]

It was inevitable that this portraiture of the pre-colonial state should receive reconsideration from historians having a standpoint different from the masters of the Raj. R.P. Tripathi in a thesis submitted in 1926, argued that there were limits to despotism in 'the Muslim theory of sovereignty'.[6] Ibn Hasan (1933), while disavowing any attempt to comment or condemn the Mughal polity from the standpoint of 'modern institutions', insisted that the 'military form' of the state and the institution of monarchy were derived from the geography and social institutions of the country.[7] In other words, it did not have an independent, self-propelled tendency towards total authority. P. Saran (1941), more directly responding to the Bernier-generated theories, asserted that 'our modern [read: colonial] institutions are not in all respects necessarily an advance over their predecessors'; he denied that the king in India had been the owner of the soil, and insisted that 'the peasants who cultivated the land were the de facto as well as de jure owners of their respective plots'.[8] Saran was also definite that there was little room for over-taxation in the Mughal system. In all there seemed to be a tendency to look at the Mughal empire as essentially similar to contemporary European polities, institutionally committed to a self-limiting sovereignty and charged with the role of a benevolent protector of society rather than its principal slave-driver.

New questions came to be posed once the colonial ban on Marxist literature was lifted, and Marxist ideas began increasingly to influence historians after 1947. As is well known, Marx took over the concept of the Asiatic rent-exacting state 'Oriental Despotism' or, but modified it heavily by ascribing to it a concern for 'public works', chiefly irrigation, and by integrating with it the institution of village communities.[9] At the same time, he put forward the concept of the state as the protector (and, therefore, the instrument) of the principal exploiting class in society, and indicated that the specific relationship of the state with society would vary, within this basic area, from one 'mode of production' to another, the series comprising 'the Asiatic, the ancient, the feudal and the modern bourgeois mode of production'.[10] The major interpretation of pre-colonial history under Marxian influence was that of D.D. Kosambi (1956). He saw in the Mauryan state of late fourth and third centuries BC a reflex of the Asiatic state, but argued that there was a decline in both state power and urbanism during the first millennium. In the evolution of 'Indian feudalism', he saw a weak state, its authority weakened constantly by the rise of local potentates ('from below') or by the installation of king's officials as territorial potentates ('from above').[11] However, it was not clear how the weak, feudal polity continued in the Delhi Sultanate (thirteenth and fourteenth centuries) and the Mughal Empire (sixteenth and seventeenth centuries). Kosambi was obviously on rather unsure ground when he took the very statements made by Marx for his concept of Oriental Despotism, as evidence of a 'feudal system'.[12]

A different approach was adopted by scholars who, while largely seeking a conformity with the Marxist framework, wished first to describe Mughal polity before classifying it. Satish Chandra (1959) offered an excellent synthesis of the work already done on sources of Mughal political history and administration in the introduction to his work on the Mughal Empire during the first half of the eighteenth century.[13] In his work on the agrarian system of the Mughal Empire,[14] Irfan Habib (1963) broadly accepted and underlined the centralized nature of Mughal polity and the large share of the surplus that the Mughal land-tax represented. On this he presented an impressive amount of documentary evidence. At the same time he insisted that the centralized ruling class of the Mughal Empire coexisted, in a relationship of collaboration and antagonism, with another scattered, localized hereditary 'junior' ruling class, that of the zamindars, who were smaller co-sharers in the surplus. This assertion was based on a fresh scrutiny of Mughal historical works and official records supplemented by an extensive study of local 'private' documents.[15] The view of the Mughal agrarian system as a relationship between just two sides, the state and the peasantry, was thus replaced with the conception of a three-tiered structure, the tiers being the imperial ruling class, the zamindars and the peasants. Irfan Habib asserted that 'the peculiar feature of the state in Mughal India was that it served not merely as the protective arm of the exploiting classes, but was itself the principal instrument of exploitation'.[16] This brought him, of course, very close to the concept of 'Oriental Despotism' (or to the 'Tributary Mode' of Samir Amin). But implicit in his entire work was also the view that the state was wider than the formal framework of the Mughal Empire, and the zamindars constituted a centrifugal force. S. Nurul Hasan (1973) with his classification of 'primary', 'intermediary' and 'tributary' zamindars was subsequently particularly to reinforce these conclusions.[17] One could almost say that these views presumed an 'Oriental Despotism' superimposed over a 'feudal' substratum to create the state of seventeenth-century India. However, while accepting the force of much of the evidence presented on the concentration of authority in the Mughal Empire, I argued (1972) that the very systematization of the polity represented a control on its arbitrariness, and one could even see in the Empire a 'quasi-modern', rather than an 'Asiatic state'.[18]

While in India these conclusions received considerable acceptance, and have received continuing confirmation from studies of documentary material from all parts of India, these views have been subjected to increasing suspicion by an ever larger set of western scholars.

The starting point of the objections seems to be the rejection of a view that India could really have developed centralized or systematized state institutions in view of its cultural and social circumstances. Burton Stein (1980) raised this objection in a challenging form, when he argued that the model of the state in south India was that of the 'segmentary state' located in African tribal society by Aidan Southal.[19] The new discovery was that caste, religion and ethnicity were now the forming social institutions which occupied much of the space assigned by modern theory to the state, while the formal state tended to be weak in the same ratio as distance from the capital, to be unsystematized and accommodative of local autonomies. It would have been too much to expect that having found the concept so useful for a particular period, Burton Stein and others would not assume that it was also applicable to the rest of India. In the enthusiasm for the new doctrine one could easily forget that Stein's imposition of the Segmentary State on south India itself has not found unanimous acceptance; R. Champakalakshmi (1981) and D.N. Jha (1982) have recorded important caveats and rebuttals.[20]

The 'revisionist' approach to the analysis of Mughal polity arrived at by 'Mughal-centred' historians (Frank Perlin's expression) has now taken a number of forms. The first was initiated in asides, rather than in substance, by C.A. Bayly (1983).[21] He acknowledged that 'the key note of Mughal rule had been size and centralization'.[22] Yet he also suggested that 'the previous writing (on the Mughal Empire) has been too preoccupied with the state at the expense of the corporate groups which constituted it'; in other words, that unlike post-Reformation Europe, the state in India was not 'the unchallenged political form'. He saw in the decline of the Mughal Empire a positive element, where these 'corporate groups' or 'social classes' played their role through the 'commercialization' and 'decentralization' of Mughal polity in the eighteenth century, in extending agriculture and intensifying commerce, and then shifted their loyalties to the British, as the most—for them— beneficial power. The British conquest was thus an Indo-British affair— the culmination of Bayly's 'continuity' thesis.[23] Implicit in this thesis was a favourable assessment of the performance of the regional elite, forming the eighteenth-century transition states, as if decentralization and regionalization were the historical objectives of the Mughal Empire: there was, therefore, no real decline.[24]

Bayly's thesis was supported by Muzaffar Alam (1986), who took over the glorification of the permanent jagir and revenue farming (*ijara*) as indices not of collapse of government and equity, but of regionalization and commercialization—and, therefore, of 'growth'.[25] He has now made the gratifying supplementary discovery that, but for the work of western scholars from Bernard Cohn (1962) to Bayly and André Wink (1986), there would be no emphasis laid on eighteenth-century regional economy and the 'local social context of politics'.[26]

A second line of approach has been adopted by André Wink (1986), which in its conclusions loosely meshes with the Bayly argument. Wink has had access only to material in Marathi (and not apparently even to the extensive Persian records of the Marathas), but he starts with the assumption that 'Mughal sources' consist of only a few chronicles which 'merely hide behind a façade of moralistic or religious condemnation'. Once he has so easily wished away the mass of Persian and Rajasthani documentation that 'Mughal historians' have been using, he has no difficulty in first assuming a universalist Islamic theory of sovereignty, which allegedly applied to the Mughal Empire, then emphasizing the actuality of the power of 'the intermediary gentry or zamindari stratum', and finally seeing the constant reconciliation of the two by means of the process of *fitna*, an Arabic word meaning sedition, to which Wink gave so wide a range of meanings (all his own) to make it virtually an equivalent of policy or adjustment. He was so led away by his own theory that to him the centralization and systematization of the Mughal Empire became virtually illusory, its expansion achieved by fitna, its 'decline' (to be always put within inverted commas) the consummation of its expansion. 'The Mughal Empire' merely 'represented a form of sovereignty, a balancing system of continually shifting rivalries and alliances—At no stage did it transcend fitna'.[27] One begins to ask why Wink did not put the words 'empire' and 'expansion' also within inverted commas, and have done with it.

If there were any peaks of mystification left unscaled by Wink, these have been ascended by Frank Perlin (1985). Like Wink, Perlin's main documentary base is Marathi (not inclusive of Persian records of the Marathas); Wink's cult of fitna is here paralleled by that of *watan* (another Arabic word) seen by Perlin as the basic factor behind state formation.[28] The picture of the Mughal Empire, its centralization and systematization, drawn by 'Mughal-centred' historians is dismissed in a few sentences and footnotes as being the work of those who cannot relate text to context, and 'fish' out data from different areas of individual complexity to create an illusory uniformity.[29] The contradictions in the Mughal agrarian system, derived by Irfan Habib from a large mass of documents, are described without further ado as contradictions not of fact but 'of our organization of knowledge about the state'.[30] All this, in spite of Perlin not himself caring to present any evidence about the polity, economy and society of the Mughal empire.

If one blows away the smoke of the 'revisionist' verbiage, there remains precious little fact that can take us anywhere beyond the three-tier relationship of the Empire–zamindar–peasantry, which since the early 1960s has been the cornerstone of conventional Mughal historiography. Bayly's 'corporate groups', Wink's fitna and Perlin's watan are all different ways of defining and describing the position of the intermediate class in this triangular relationship. On the Mughal state itself no new light has been shed, no illumination gained. This may justify the recent bitter observation of Burton Stein that the history of 'the mightiest of the pre-colonial kingdoms of India has not been substantially revised... and there appears to be no disposition on the part of most Mughalists to do so'. In the manner of one finding a useful scapegoat he locates the cause of this stultification in 'the inertia induced by the siege mentality of Aligarh'![31] The reason, of course, is not in anyone's mentality, but in the fact that fresh explorations of documentary evidence have only tended to confirm and underline the standard propositions about the elements of centralization and systematization in the Mughal polity and the position of the zamindar class. There may be new readings of village communities or monetization or legal systems; but nothing has come up even remotely to challenge the basic perceptions about mansab and jagir.

The controversy about the nature of the pre-colonial Indian state may be of some value, if it enables us to elucidate better the basic features of the Mughal Empire, especially in comparison to its eighteenth-century successors. Here it may be well to remind ourselves that there are two separate problems to consider. The question of centralization must be kept distinct from that of the plenitude of state power. On the one hand, a state with a low quantum of power within society may be extensive and centralized. On the other, a small decentralized state may enjoy unchallenged supremacy over society within its constricted borders. It is obviously an elementary error to suppose that a historian who finds that the Mughal Empire was centralized and had a high degree of administrative unity must also be assumed to assert that the Mughal Empire was to be put in the same class as a Post-Reformation European Enlightened Despotism. And yet this accusation is implicit in Bayly as well as all the succeeding 'revisionists'.

On the issue of centralization, two objections to its actuality within the Mughal Empire have been put forward. The first raised by Gerard Fussman (1982/1990) relates to the problem of communications. He presents a map based on speeds of relay-couriers in the Mughal Empire, and then infers from this the necessary 'existence of local representatives of the king, who had at their disposal a large amount of power'.[32] The inference is drawn in respect of the Mauryan Empire, but it would be most directly relevant to the Mughals. One could most easily retort that speed of communications did not increase between Akbar's time and the installation of the telegraph in about the middle of the nineteenth century, and yet it would be hard to argue that the East India Company's government in India in Lord William Bentinck's time was decentralized in any recognizable sense of the word. As far as the Mughal Empire is concerned, it is enough to see documents, such as letters from governors (notably, Aurangzeb's letters as viceroy of the Deccan, in *Adab-i Alamgiri*), the reports of the proceedings at the governor's headquarters (e.g. *Akhbarat* of Prince Azam's headquarters at Ahmadabad), and the news reports (e.g. the *waqai* of the Deccan and of Ajmer) that have survived to show the plenitude of power that the emperor reserved for himself and for central ministers. The discussion on the degree of Mughal centralization must surely rest on a scrutiny of such documentation.

The only declared support for the revisionist approach by looking at details of seventeenth-century Mughal documentation that I know of has come from Chetan Singh (1988).[33] Basically his argument is to challenge the view that 'on account of frequent transfers the Mughal bureaucracy was unable to develop regional moorings'.[34] He asserts that officials appointed as governors of Punjab 'belonged to areas lying within it', and mentions the names of Ghazi Beg Tarkhan, Dilawar Khan Kakar, and Khwaja Main (*sic*).[35] Of these, however, Ghazi Beg Tarkhan 'belonged' to Sind, not Punjab, and was governor of Thatta at the beginning of Jahangir's reign; he then held successively governorship of Qandahar (1606–7, and he died there in 1612–13). He was governor of Multan for only a short while in Jahangir's second regnal year. Dilawar Khan (Ibrahim Khan) Kakar was an Afghan. After a brief term in Lahore, he is not known to have been posted in Punjab at all. In 1617–18 he was appointed governor of Kashmir, where he died in 1619–20. 'Khwaja Main'(by this must be meant Khwaja Muin Khan) was simply deputy governor of Lahore in 1656–7, when this appointment ceased. Nothing else is known about him.[36] How Chetan Singh assumed that all the three 'belonged' to Punjab is a mystery. Moreover, he thinks that Lahore and Multan provinces constituted one region (Multan then included northern Sind as well); they might for him, but there is no reason to believe that the Mughals thought so. For them, the two were distinct provinces, with totally different sets of officials. They could not have known that Ranjit Singh and the British would one day make Lahore and Multan (minus upper Sind) into one unit. This disposes of most 'appointments' in the same region that Chetan Singh pinpoints.[37] As for those to whom he ascribes regional affiliations, one can easily see that this has been done by ignoring other postings received by these very officials.

Najabat Khan Mirza Shuja in fact not only twice held the governorship of Multan, but also twice held the *faujdari* of Koil (Aligarh) in Agra suba and died in 1663–4 as subedar of Malwa![38] Qulij Khan, twice subedar of Multan, served also as subedar of Delhi, Allahabad, Qandahar, Lahore and Kabul. Said Khan Bahadur, twice subedar of Lahore, also served twice as subedar of Kabul and once of Qandahar and Bihar. Lashkar Khan, twice subedar of Multan, also served as subedar of Kashmir, Thatta and Bihar. Murshid Quli Khan, whose appointments in Lahore and Multan Chetan Singh refers to, served as *mir atish* (artillery commander) at the court and from 1652 to his death in 1658, was the diwan first of Balaghat and of the whole of the Mughal

Deccan.[39] Any regional attachment of these officers, once we examine their whole careers, is hard to discern. Rather, what strikes one is the ease with which they would be shifted to distant areas, from Kabul to Bihar, or from the Punjab to the Deccan.

If one can construct 'regionalization of the administrative functionaries'[40] in the face of such contrary evidence, and in the absence of any positive one worth the name, we can only imagine that one is working to a brief and not going to the sources with an open mind.

The second question relates to the degree of power of the state (and not just of the centre) over society. This, as we have seen, is about what power the state, centralized or not, exercised within a given territory. It may not matter for this purpose whether the given territory, say Gujarat, was administered from Ahmadabad or Agra. We are here concerned with how much of the rural surplus was taken by the state, how much did it interfere in commerce or community life, and so on. In the economic sphere the central question is the nature and size of the land-tax.[41] That the modes of assessment of land-tax and customary shares of the zamindars varied from area to area was well recognized in conventional historiography (as well as, richly enough, in Mughal documentation). The key issue is whether there was any substantial region in the Mughal Empire, where the land-tax was not seen as the major claim on peasants' surplus. On this matter, the 'revisionists' have been strangely silent. For here the Persian, the Rajasthani, the Marathi and the English documentation is universally in agreement: the 'text' is at peace with the 'context'. A state which claimed such a heavy share out of agricultural produce, as Moreland saw, could not just be a marginal social institution, or one among many, as we are now being told to suppose.

As for other limiting features, such as that the Mughal Empire was not a legislating state, that is creating its own law independent of and suspending customary and religious laws, nor a state committed to economic growth beyond measures designed to lead to future tax growth, these limitations have never been doubted by historians. In fact, this was implicit in the traditional view that full sovereignty in the sense of complete legislative control over society is the produce of modern European history and cannot be looked for in non-European pre-modern states.[42] No historian had ever laid claim that Mughal polity was in these aspects the equal of the European post-Reformation state. And if the 'revisionists' have this in mind only, there should be no ground for disagreement with anyone. But the picture of the Mughal Empire in its classic phase, as a centralized polity, geared to systematization and the creation of an all-imperial bureaucracy, would still remain unshaken.

NOTES

1. François Bernier, *Travels in the Mughal Empire* AD *1656–1668*, tr. A. Constable, 2nd edn revised by V.A. Smith, Oxford, 1916, pp. 223–38.

2. James Mill, *History of British India*, 2nd edn, London, 1820, vol. I, pp. 277–8; and his evidence before the Commons Select Committee in 1831, quoted by E. Stokes, *The English Utilitarians and India*, Oxford, 1959, p. 91.

3. Quoted by Stokes, ibid., p. 62.

4. W.H. Moreland, *Agrarian System of Moslem India*, Allahabad reprint, n.d., p. XII.

5. Obituary of William Bentinck quoted by V.A. Smith in *Oxford History of India*, Oxford, 1918, p. 657.

6. *Some Aspects of Muslim Administration*, 2nd rev. edn, Allahabad, 1956, pp. 1–6.

7. Ibn Hasan, *Central Structure of the Mughal Empire*, New Delhi, 1970, pp. 5, 35, 37.

8. P. Saran, *The Provincial Government of the Mughals*, Allahabad, 1941, pp. xx, 333.

9. Marx first spelt out his ideas on the pre-colonial Indian state and society in 'British Rule in India', article published in *New York Tribune*, 1853 (Marx and Engels, *On Colonialism*, Moscow, 1976, pp. 35–41).

10. See F. Engels, *The Origin of the Family, Private Property and the State*, Moscow, 1948, esp. ch. IX. The list of the successive mode first appears in Marx's Preface to his contribution to the *Critique of Political Economy*, orig. pub. 1859.

11. D.D. Kosambi, *An Introduction to the Study of Indian History*, Bombay, 1956.

12. Ibid., p. 362.

13. Satish Chandra, *Parties and Politics at the Mughal Court, 1707–1740*, Aligarh, 1959, pp. XV–L.

14. Irfan Habib, *The Agrarian System of Mughal India*, Bombay, 1963.

15. See specially ibid., pp. 136–89.

16. Ibid., p. 257.

17. Saiyid Nurul Hasan, *Thoughts on Agrarian Relations in Mughal India*, New Delhi, 1973, pp. 18–40.

18. Presidential Address, Medieval India Section, *PIHC*, Muzaffarpur session, 1972; rev. version, *JRAS*, London, 1978, no. 1, pp. 38–49.

19. Burton Stein, *Peasant, State and Society of Medieval South India*, Delhi, 1980, p. 23.

20. R. Champakalakshmi, *IESHR*, xviii(3–4), pp. 411–26; D.N. Jha, *IHR*, viii(1–2), pp. 74–94.

21. C.A. Bayly, *Rulers, Townsmen and Bazaars: North Indian Society in the Age of British Expansion, 1770–1870*, Cambridge, 1983.

22. Ibid., p. 465.

23. Ibid., p. 5.

24. Bayly sums up his arguments conveniently in his conclusion (ibid., pp. 458–72).

25. Muzaffar Alam, *The Crisis of Empire in Mughal North India: Awadh and the Punjab, 1707–48*, Delhi, 1986, esp. p. 318.

26. *IESHR*, xxviii(i) (1991), p. 43 and n. It sheds interesting light on consciously 'todate' historiography that Muzaffar Alam in his list of eight authors should have overlooked all works of Indian scholars in the same genre, such as N.K. Sinha (on Bengal), Asok Sen and Nikhiles Guha (Mysore), Raghubir Sinh (Malwa), Ashin Das Gupta (Surat), S.P. Gupta and G.D. Sharma (Rajasthan), V.V. Diwekar (Maharashtra) and Indu Banga (Punjab), to name a few only.

27. André Wink, *Land and Sovereignty in India. Agrarian Society and Politics under the Eighteenth Century Maratha Svarjya*, Cambridge, 1986, p. 34.

28. Frank Perlin, 'State Formation Reconsidered', *Modern Asian Studies*, xix (3), pp. 415–80.

29. Ibid., pp. 418ff., esp. pp. 419 and n, 420 and n, 423 and n.

30. Ibid., p. 427 and n.

31. *South Asia Research*, x(2), November 1990, p. 125–6.

32. Gerard Fussman, 'Central and Provincial Administration in Ancient India', *IHR*, xiv (1–2), pp. 54–6, 67 (map). Fussman's article originally appeared in *Annales, économies, sociétés, civilisations* (1982).

33. Chetan Singh, 'Centre and Periphery in the Mughal State: The Case of Seventeenth Century Panjab', *Modern Asian Studies* 22(2) (1988), pp. 299–318.

34. Ibid., p. 304.

35. Ibid., p. 305.

36. No authorities for statements made here are separately cited, because the references can be traced by looking up the names in the index to my *Apparatus of Empire. Award of Ranks, Offices and Titles of the Mughal Nobility*

(1574–1658), Delhi, 1985. Curiously, Chetan Singh makes no mention of the lists of Governors of Lahore and Multan as well as other subas worked out by Irfan Habib (*Medieval India*, I, pp. 91–4) and by me (ibid., pp. 96–133; and *Medieval India*, III, pp. 80–112).

37. Chetan Singh, 'Centre and Periphery', pp. 306–7.

38. For his last appointment, *Alamgirnama*, Bib. Ind., p. 873, for the other details *Apparatus of Empire* (indexed refs).

39. For the careers of all these officials, whose cases Chetan Singh, pp. 306–7, cites as indicators of regional affiliations, see *Apparatus of Empire* (indexed refs).

40. Chetan Singh, 'Centre and Periphery', p. 317.

41. 'At the heart of the Indian administration lay the land revenue system' (Eric Stokes, *The English Utilitarians and India*, Delhi, 1959/1982, p. 81).

42. I may here quote my own remark on these limitations of the Mughal state, in *JRAS*, 1978, no. I, p. 47; 'If it [the Mughal Empire] had some rudiments of an unwritten constitution, it yet did not claim for itself the legislative power and functions that are the hall-marks of a modern state.'

9
Political Structures of the Islamic Orient in the Sixteenth and Seventeenth Centuries

It is possible to place the four major empires of Asia, apart from China, during the sixteenth and seventeenth centuries into a single category according to three distinct and separate modes of classification. First of all, the Ottomans (West Asia), the Safavids (Iran), the Uzbeks (Central Asia), and the Mughals (India) can be seen as belonging to the category of Islamic states; and Islam (and the law, polity and culture historically associated with it) can be regarded as one of the distinguishing features of this class of states. Second, one may adopt, with François Bernier, the frankly Eurocentric view that these states shared among themselves a negative characteristic, namely they lacked the merits of European law and politics, especially full-scale private property in land. Finally, there is the classification which flows from the question asked by Marx: Was there something common to these state systems that inhibited their societies from growing into capitalism? So stated, these classifications appear simplistic, even banal; I propose to show, however, that studies on the lines opened by these simple questions can nevertheless give us insights, just as they also compel us to offer many qualifications and even reservations to the standard theories.

I

The Islamic associations of the four empires are so obvious that one need not labour the point. The crucial question is whether Islam was a substratum or only a veneer. It must be admitted that these states set out to enforce the sharia as it was understood by the school that carried official sanction—any of the four schools of jurists among Sunnis in three of the four empires, while Safavid Iran followed the sharia as interpreted by the Shi'ite theologians. By and large, it gave a universal civil and criminal law (with only minor shades of differences) to all these countries. The qazi, however corrupt and however frequently the butt of ridicule, yet represented a unique legal universality over a region extending from the Bay of Bengal to the Atlantic. Conversely, this universality meant that, however absolute, the state lacked the power to legislate. The Tudor monarchy, with its control over Parliament and its legislation, was thus surely far more absolute or despotic than any Great Mughal.

The sharia not only delimited the sovereignty of the state in this crucial manner; it also tended to define more positively how this could be constituted. During the first two centuries after the death of the Prophet (AD 632), the concept of the *khilafat* (caliphate) had taken shape, based not on the Quran,[1] but on the political history of Islam during the period. The institution of the caliphate, as it decayed after the ninth century, became more and more the object of theological or scholarly definition (as in Mawardi): who could be a caliph and what the caliph could or could not do would be rigorously laid down. As the caliph's place came to be taken increasingly by kings (sultans), the latter could be visualized as deputies of the caliphs, so to speak; if so, they could not have any powers which the caliph did not enjoy. At best, Muslim rulers could begin claiming to be caliphs themselves as was done by the Ottomans and, more indifferently, by the Mughals. Only the Safavids claimed a distinctly higher position—that of the representative of the *imam*. But when Akbar, the Mughal emperor, in 1579 obtained from his doctors a declaration (mahzar) that he could sit in judgement over various interpretations of Muslim law, this created much indignation among the devout and helped to bring about a revolt which almost shook his throne.

None the less, it is true that political tradition within Islam too was of historical growth, and the powers and pretensions—and not only the nominal titles of the sultans—grew with time. Other traditions like the ancient Iranian, the Turkic and Mongol were either invoked or absorbed, and it is possible to say that the sultans after Timur took the Mongol Khans rather than the Samanids for their models. This brings me to the consideration of another important strand in the political and social history of the Islamic world—the conflict between nomadism and civilization.

If one looks at the physical map of the Old World, one finds starting from China north of the Great Wall, a huge band of steppe and desert generally heading west, while tending slightly to the south. The Gobi and Takla Makan deserts turn into the arid grasslands of Central Asia and southern Russia, after the band crosses the Tienan Shan range.

Sweeping across Iran with its waterless plateau, it encompasses the Arabian desert; and, then, across the Red Sea and the Nile, it forms the great Sahara, dividing Africa into two. In this brief description we have not been able to list the many smaller deserts and steppes identified and named by geographers. Suffice it to say that this vast waterless band with deserts and grasslands has been the largest known reservoir of nomadic peoples. As it cut right across the Islamic world it made it consist essentially of deserts and oases, the biggest of the latter being the Fertile Cresent (Egypt, Syria, and Iraq), followed closely by Mavraunnahar (itself divided into the three 'Oases' of Ferghana, the Zarafshan valley and Khwarizm or Khiva).

The two regions which offer exceptions to this infestation of steppe and desert are India and the Balkans, both of which were brought under the ambit of Islam in the secondary phase of its expansion (after the twelfth century); their populations also remained non-Muslim in the larger part. For the history of the core area of the Islamic world, in general, the nomad-city syndrome seems to set the red thread; and it is the particular virtue of Ibn Khaldun, the great historian of the fourteenth century, to have perceived this fact and to have built a theory of historical development on its basis.[2]

Historians often see the steppe element as a dynamic source of much of Islamic polity. The Arabs themselves were, after all, desert nomads. Founders of all the dynasties of the four empires we are concerned with here, the Ottomans (from Seljuqs), the Uzbeks (from Mongols of the Golden Horde) and the Mughals (from the Chaghtai Horde) had steppe ancestors; and Isma'il, the founder of the Safavid dynasty, had his following initially among the Turkoman nomads, so that Turkish remained for long the language of the Safavid court. It is easy, as we look closer, to drill holes in this generalization. Paul Wittek[3] has already shown that the impulse behind the rise of the Ottoman state even in its earliest phase was not of nomadic origin, but lay in a combination of the Ghazi tradition with the conditions of government associated with Higher Islam. The Mughal Empire in India certainly displayed no feature that could be identified as direct importations from nomadism.

Going beyond this, even the widespread attribution of the origins of Islam and its success as one of great nomadic movements needs qualification. The Prophet himself was not a nomad but a merchant of the Quraish tribe, which was a settled community of the Arabian peninsula's biggest town, Mecca. The Quran, in a well-known passage, doubts the bedouin's genuineness of belief.[4] Clearly, Islam both subdued and utilized the nomad; its own urbanism[5] saved it from the fate of other nomadic traditions, that of a total absorption among the conquered civilized societies.

Yet, the fact remains that the bedouin formed the bulk of Arab soldiers who demolished the Iranian and (in part) the Byzantine Empire. So also the fact that the successive nomadic conquests by the Seljuqs, the Qara Khitai, and the Mongols, all originated from the nomadic reservoir of the Asian steppes. The infiltration of nomadic notions and institutions was thus bound continuously to modify the political tradition and 'applied' law in the Islamic world.

It is possible to see the influence of nomadism in the evolution of the concept of an implicit state property in land. As Kovalevsky noticed long ago, Islamic law has a fairly well-developed concept of private property in land (as behoves an urban tradition codified so largely in Iran).[6] The nomads, on the other hand, could only have a concept of tribal possession of a territory; and individual possession of a particular strip of land had no meaning for the bedouin or other nomadic peoples.[7] A conquered territory belonged to the tribe, and was not divisible among its individuals. The personal iqta of early Islam was thus contrasted to territory belonging to the entire Islamic (or rather Arab-Islamic) community, of which the caliph was the head. Thus the iqta now came to mean merely a temporary assignment of the claims to surplus from the land which were thought to vest in the caliph. The doctrine of state property could seldom be distinctly enunciated, in view of the lack of its reconcilability with Islamic law; but it came to arise in practice nevertheless.

This implicit concept was nomadic; in itself it could have little significance but for its being combined with the purely sedentary notion of land-tax. The classic Islamic concept of kharaj (land-tax on non-Muslims ranging from a fifth to half of the produce) and 'ushr (tithe on Muslims), seems quite alien to the later development of the land-tax. 'Ushr disappeared, except as a concessionary arrangement with favoured elements; and Muslim peasants too had normally to pay kharaj. Finally, the kharaj approached or exceeded half of the produce wherever this could be realized. In other words, it tended to approximate to the surplus, or potential rent. This enlargement of the state demand could take place only by a corresponding destruction of private property; and it is extremely tempting to see in this process the evolution of an idea initially germinated by tribal nomads: the tribal possession over land converted into state property. This development was crucial for what may be regarded as the common fiscal feature of all the four states we are considering, an identification, which so far as we can see, grew within the fold of Islam under repeated nomadic tribal impulses.[8]

But if the Islamic background provided such a unifying factor in the fiscal system of all these four states, we must remember that the Ottoman Empire and, still more, the Mughal Empire, had large non-Muslim populations. Even if one were to attribute the Ottoman control over the Balkans to simple military subjugation through an outward expansion of Islam (though this too is questionable, since the Ottomans conquered the Balkans first, and the Islamic lands outside Anatolia only later), it is difficult to say the same about the Mughal Empire, which did not have any Islamic hinterland at all. The successful implantation in India, and possibly in the Balkans, of forms of political organization developed in the Islamic world, must then be regarded as a singular historic achievement. Once formed, the institutions of 'Islamic' polity offered immense advantages to those at the head of power. In this sense it is even possible to say that the Rajput states of north India in the fifteenth and sixteenth centuries or the contemporary Vijayanagar Empire of the south were 'Islamic' polities though they did not accept the Islamic faith, while accepting its tradition in crucial matters like taxation and state property.[9] The advantage of these Islamic institutions to a Hindu ruling class was just as great as was that of the caste system among its Hindu subjects for the Muslim ruling class, which thereby derived cheap artisan labour for its own use.

II

With such features as we have touched upon, how far were these Islamic states different from those that developed with the absolute monarchies in Europe during the sixteenth and seventeenth centuries? The question was asked and sought to be answered by François Bernier in his remarkable description of Oriental states and societies on the basis of personal observations in the East during the twelve years from 1656–68.[10]

Bernier came to India after visiting Constantinople, Syria and Egypt and was familiar with the conditions of the Ottoman Empire. Thereafter he spent nine years in India. He was, therefore, no bird of passage, no superficial sightseer. What gives additional weight to his interpretation of the Orient is his scientific background and his association with the new philosophical school of which Pierre Gassendi was a notable representative. Earlier European travellers of the sixteenth century, like Bernier's own fellow-countryman, Pyrard de Laval, had based their assumption of European superiority on the well-known fact that Christianity was a superior religion; otherwise, in commerce and crafts the people in India were similar to them or even more skilled.[11] In Bernier's eyes, on the other hand, European superiority lay essentially in its science, arts, technology, property laws and social system. Furthermore, not only was Europe ahead, but the Orient was receding. Bernier located the major difference between the West and East, in the nature of the state. European states recognized private property and so created all the stability, security and public welfare that private property generates. It was otherwise with oriental states like those of the Ottomans and the Mughals. Their indifference to private property was causing a steady devastation of the economies and societies of these empires: 'I have carefully compared the condition of European States, where that right [of private property] is recognized, with the condition of those countries where it is not known, and am persuaded that the absence of it among the people is injurious to the best interest of the Sovereign himself.'[12]

Specifically speaking, the absence of private property, according to Bernier, affected the oriental states in the following manner. The king, being the owner of the soil, distributed the right to collect taxes over particular territories to assignees or tax-farmers who had temporary tenures. These assignments were known in the Ottoman Empire as timar, and in the Mughal Empire as jagir. Being temporary, the attitude of the assignees to the land under their jurisdiction could be summed up as follows:

The Timariots, Governors, and Revenue Contractors on their part reason in this manner: Why should the neglected state of this land create uneasiness in our minds? And why should we expend our own money and time to render it fruitful? We may be deprived of it in a single moment, and our exertions would benefit neither ourselves nor our children. Let us draw from the soil all the money we can, though the peasants should starve or abscond, and we should leave it, when commanded to quit, a dreary wilderness.[13]

This, said Bernier, was at the root of the visible ruin of eastern states. Bernier's theory has received much attention from historians of the Mughal Empire, notably because he gave a fairly accurate depiction of the jagir system. The Empire was indeed divided up into the jagirs or assignments held by nobles in lieu of pay under their mansabs, or numerical ranks, that also defined the size and composition of the military contingents they were to maintain. In a sense the lands reserved for the king's own revenues, called khalisa, could be termed his jagirs. The jagirs, including the khalisa, were constantly transferred, each period of assignment on average barely exceeding two or three years.[14] There has, therefore, been a strongly held view that the jagir system brought about the collapse of the Mughal Empire as a viable economic system, just as Bernier had suggested.[15]

But to generalize this view for all the Islamic empires would overlook the fact that the other three empires of our period did not have a system of assignment-transfers working as rigorously as in the Mughal Empire. Take, for instance, the Ottoman timar. The timar, or 'military fief', was transferable only in name; a timariot was not removed so long as he brought troops; and the son usually succeeded his father. Centralization of the grant of timars in the sixteenth century had the result only of creating large estates at the cost of the small ones, leading to disaffection among the timariots, which made some small timariots leaders of peasant uprisings in Anatolia.[16] There would be little here to support the Bernier thesis of devastation of peasant by 'temporary' timariots.

If we turn to the Safavid Empire the picture is almost the same. The counterpart of jagir in that empire was the *tuyul*. Bernier's contemporary, Chardin, reported that the tuyuls were virtually the property of those to whom they were assigned; and wherever the holder expected to hold the land in his lifetime and transfer it to his son, the peasants were correspondingly better treated.[17] Rapid transfers of tuyuls appear, in fact, to have been very rare.

As far as the Uzbek Empire is concerned, the Mughal jagir system was so alien to its organization that when in the 1640s Nazar (Nadir) Muhammad, the Khan of Bokhara, tried to imitate the Mughals and transfer his governors and commanders from their territories, he brought about a rebellion against himself, which ultimately resulted in his expulsion from the Khanate.[18]

It seems, then, fairly clear that the rigorous system of temporary assignments was a characteristic feature of the Mughal Empire alone, but of not of the other three empires, where transfer and resumption of fiefs was in the nature of an ultimate weapon and only occasionally exercised.

This would remove much of the universality in Bernier's explanation of the decline of oriental empires. What he says, then, was at best true of India alone as far as the jagir system is concerned; as to its consequences even in India there remains some room for doubt.[19]

While the agrarian aspect of Bernier's theory has excited the most interest, it must be remembered that he extended the ill-effects of

'Oriental Despotism' to trade and industry as well. Merchants' wealth was subject to usurpation and confiscation; so they had to hide their wealth and hoard treasure (and so were not about to use seek it capital). The craftsmen were unable to apply themselves because they could always be forced to work at low wages.[20] Thus the contempt for private property led to a constriction of commerce and crafts as well.

While abuses of the kind Bernier mentions can be illustrated from individual instances of oppression and injustice, there seems to be no reason to believe that the merchants were not allowed to have private property or that the artisans were semi-servile. Halil Inalcik has shown how commerce expanded in the Ottoman Empire, and Irfan Habib has referred to the growth of merchant capital in India aided by institutions like deposit banking and insurance.[21] It can hardly be said that the oriental despots throttled commerce by continuous confiscation of merchant property, or that such confiscations were a characteristic feature of the Asian empires we are studying.

In other words, Bernier has given us brilliant answers to a cogent question; but the answers tend to become less and less convincing as we look closer into the evidence.

III

Bernier's work won considerable readership in Europe and much of European writing on 'Oriental Despotism' down to the nineteenth century bore marks of his influence.[22] Karl Marx read him in 1853 and was certainly impressed by the acuteness of his observations. Yet, Marx's own perception of the oriental state was intrinsically different; with all its imperfections it may be said to make a fundamental break with the earlier traditions, though Marx had little before him except for some information directly or indirectly derived from reports of British administrators in India.

The essential question asked by Marx was whether there were any social and political obstacles to growth (particularly, growth into capitalism) in oriental societies, as a result of which their civilization seemed to have atrophied. Marx found the answer in a combination of two institutions, the village community and 'Oriental Despotism'. The village community, a primitive 'republic', was based on a hereditary division of labour (e.g. caste), and by its stable but pliant nature enabled the surplus it produced to be extracted by the external power, the despotic ruling class. Land-tax and rent, therefore, coincided. The tax-rent was usually taken in kind; it was then sold by the state, since money economy and commerce existed only outside the village communities. The 'economic' basis of the extra-economic coercion by the despot lay in the irrigation works that the state provided to the village communities.[23]

The cycle of production and re-production was here completed without any need of capitalistic intervention. More, since the villages remained autonomous and almost amoebic units, the emergence and fall of individual dynasties or empires had no significance for the system, which expanded or contracted, but never grew.

Marx's model of the oriental state has an inner logical consistency that is most persuasive; it is accordingly open to extreme oversimplification as in the hands of Karl A. Wittfogel (*Oriental Despotism*, 1957). But there are a number of factual weaknesses in the theory. The 'village community' of Marx is largely an ideal reconstructed by British administrators who tended to ignore the realities of internal stratification within the village just as they tended partly to overlook the universality of individual landholding existing within it. Furthermore the village community model of Marx could hardly apply to the Ottoman Empire and Iran which has no caste system to supply a hereditary, fixed division of labour.[24] In most parts of India, moreover, the peasants normally paid rent in money and only partly or occasionally in grain, so that grain-rent cannot be taken to be as universal a basis for the fiscal systems of oriental states as Marx had thought. As for the state structures proper, Marx wrote too little about them to enable one to argue with him over this crucial aspect of oriental polities. It may, however, be said that irrigation works were not very important sectors of state activity in the four empires that we are discussing, with the possible exception of Safavid Iran. In the north Indian plains, at any rate, irrigation was largely looked after by the peasants themselves, mainly though the digging of wells, though the state too laid out canals.

If many of the perceptions that Marx obtained must now be rejected or heavily qualified, three essential features of his 'Asiatic mode' seem still valid in relation to the four empires with which we are concerned: first, the practical identity of tax with rent; second, the identity of the rent-appropriators and the bureaucracy (this point is implicit rather than explicit in Marx's writings); and, finally, the parasitic nature of the urban economy based on the expenditure of the state's tax-income.

Are these features sufficient to set the oriental states apart from the European absolutist states of the sixteenth and seventeenth centuries? In the absolutist European states we have the rent in more or less pure form, it being appropriated by individual landowners and not by the state; hence follows a separation of state bureaucracy and the landowning aristocracy; a standing army paid directly by the state replaces landowners' retainers; and an urban economy arises marked by the growing importance of the middle classes. The oriental states by their structures appear to have inhibited such developments within the societies they controlled; but whether this led to a total absence of such features is another question.[25]

I have discussed successively the three types of major analytical framework in which the western, central and South Asian states of the sixteenth and seventeenth centuries can be studied. Their unities and specificities must be set by the side of contemporary systems in other parts of the world to understand them better. In other words, there has to be an inward as well as outward comparison of the structures of their polities. What has been offered above represents merely preliminary suggestions towards developing a suitable basis for classifying (or trying to classify) pre-modern states, with the four empires of the Islamic Orient seen as a possible single category. No sure success can be claimed for such an enterprise; it is only claimed that an attempt to explore the possibility can yet yield a number of important new perceptions of the general or individual characteristics of the polities of these empires.

NOTES

1. Except for one verse asking the faithful to 'obey God, His Prophet and those in authority among you', the Quran has almost nothing to offer on the nature and functions of sovereignty.

2. Cf. Muhsin Mahdi, *Ibn Khaldun's Philosophy of History*, Chicago, 1964, pp. 193ff.

3. *The Rise of the Ottoman Empire*, Royal Asiatic Society, London, 1971.

4. Quran, Sura IX, 98.

5. See F. Lokkegaard's description of Islam as 'a religion for townspeople' (*Islamic Taxation in the Classic Period*, Copenhagen, 1950, p. 32).

6. *Communal Landholding* (in Russian), 1879, cited by Rosa Luxemburg, *The Accumulation of Capital*, tr. A. Schwarzchild, London, 1951, pp. 372–3n.

104   *Mughal India*

7. Lokkegaard, *Islamic Taxation*, p. 20.

8. One recalls that in 1853 Marx attributed to Muslims the creation of state property in land in Asia under the principle of 'no property in land' (letter of 14 June 1853 in *Selected Correspondence*, ed. Dona Torr, Calcutta, 1945, p. 62).

9. I may mention in passing that I consider Burton Stein's application of the segmentary state thesis to the Vijayanagar Empire in *Cambridge Economic History of India*, ed. T. Raychaudhuri and I. Habib, 1982, rather unconvincing.

10. Bernier, *Travels in the Mughal Empire, AD 1656–68*, tr. A. Constable, 2nd edn revised by V.A. Smith, Oxford, 1916.

11. Pyrard de Laval (1607–10) says of Indians: 'They are all cunning folk, and owe nothing to the people of the West, themselves endowed with a keener intelligence than is usual with us, and hands as subtle as ours' (*The Voyages of François Pyrard de Laval to the East Indies, the Maldives, the Moluccas and Brazil*, tr. and ed. A. Grey, assisted by H.C.P. Bell, ii, part i, Hakluyt Society, London, 1888).

12. Bernier, *Travels*, p. 226.

13. Ibid., p. 227.

14. See Irfan Habib, *Agrarian System of Mughal India*, Bombay, 1963, ch. vii. The only non-transferable jagirs were the watan jagirs, which did not cover a relatively significant area.

15. Ibid., ch. ix.

16. Cf. Fernand Braudel, *The Mediterranean and the Mediterranean World in the Age of Philip II*, Eng. tr., Fontana edn, 1975, ii, pp. 718–24.

17. Cf. Ann K.S. Lambton, *Landlord and Peasant in Persia*, London, 1953, p. 110.

18. Abdul Hamid Lahori, *Badshah Nama*, Bib. Ind., Calcutta, 1867–68, pp. 295, 401–2.

19. See Athar Ali, 'The Passing of Empire: The Mughal Case', *Modern Asian Studies*, Cambridge, 1975, ix, part 3, pp. 385–96.

20. Bernier, *Travels*, pp. 225–9.

21. See both writers' contributions in *The Journal of Economic History*, xxix(1), March 1969.

22. Cf. Perry Anderson, *Lineages of the Absolutist State*, London, 1974, pp. 462ff.

23. Marx formulated his views on India initially in 1853, and articles in the *New York Daily Tribune* of that year (conveniently collected by Shlomo Avineri in *Karl Marx on Colonialism and Modernization*, Anchor

Books, New York, 1969) are a particularly important source of his views. His classic statement on the village community occurs in *Capital*, I, Eng. tr., ed. Dona Torr, London, 1938, p. 35. For tax and rent coinciding, see *Capital*, III, Moscow, 1959, pp. 771–2.

24. Conversely, because of the other identities in these civilizations, this may be treated as a refutation of the thesis popularized by Louis Dumont in *Homo Hierarchicus*, Paladin edn, London, 1972, that the caste system made India into a totally different civilization from any other.

25. Here attention may be drawn to a strong body of opinion among scholars in India which holds that the Mughal Empire did help create a middle class. The first salvo was fired by W.C. Smith, 'The Mughal Empire and the Middle Classes', *Islamic Culture*, Hyderabad, 1944, pp. 349–63. See also Iqtidar Alam Khan, 'The Middle Classes in the Mughal Empire', Presidential Address, Medieval India section, *PIHC*, Aligarh session, 1975.

POLITICAL THOUGHT

10

The Evolution of the Perception of India

Akbar and Abul Fazl

For more than a century, the status of India as a concept has repeatedly been under discussion. Is it really anything more than a 'geographical expression', its ring of mountain ranges in a rough semi-circle in the north, and that of the ocean in the form of an inverted cone in the south, making its geographical entity far more distinct than that of many other countries? Its limits formed the ideal 'scientific frontiers' for the British Indian Empire and suggested a continued tradition of ambitions of supremacy over land enclosed by them, which the Raj claimed consciously to be its inheritance. Whether there was still anything beyond a territory imagined for political convenience in cultural terms was something on which spokesmen of British imperialism allowed themselves to be of two minds. V.A. Smith would assert,[1] while the Simon Commission would deny,[2] a 'unity in diversity'. More recently, partly under the influence of works like Anderson's *Imagined Communities*[3], there has been criticism among subaltern and/or post-modern circles of the concept of the Indian nation. As Partha Chatterjee tells us, 'the very singularity of the idea of a national history of India' tends to divide 'Indians' even further[4] — though one wonders where the 'Indians' as a pre-divided lot have arisen from, if there was no India.

There should be no two opinions, therefore, that the case for the study of a history of the concept of India is strong, both for those who assert its present or past reality, as did the spokesmen of the National Movement, and for those who deny it in the footsteps of Lord Simon. To this study, the present chapter, touching on the perception of India in the minds of Akbar and his advisors—admittedly a most elite group—is a modest contribution.

One has then to begin with the Arabic–Persian tradition in which Akbar's background especially lay and in which India had two names, the Arabic 'Hind' from ancient Iranian 'Hindu' (the Avestan variant of Vedic Sindhu), whence the Greek 'India' also came; and the late Iranian 'Hindustan', created by the Iranian tendency of adding 'stan' as suffix to territorial names (Tukharistan, Sijistan, Gurjistan, etc.). As outsiders, the Iranians were prone to consider India to cover all territory east of the Indus, whence the two names. In the eleventh century, the scientist Abu Raihan al-Biruni, in his celebrated *Kitab al-Hind* (1035) was able to offer a precise geographical definition of the country of Hind as being 'limited in the south by the above mentioned Indian ocean, and on all three other sides by the lofty mountains, the waters of which flow down to it'.[5] By his study of Sanskrit scientific and sacred texts, Alberuni was also made aware of a problem in the perception of the territory too. The inhabitable world extending southward from Himavant was Bharata-varsha, which was the centre of Jambu-dvipa. Alberuni says that there was an assumption that Bharata-varsha comprised the entire inhabitable world, whereas, the parts named and ascribed to it were located in Hind alone.[6] To Alberuni 'Hindus', as inhabitants of this country, had an identifiable single higher culture, with Sanskrit as its language, which he made it his business to study and interpret, critically and without bias. He thus saw a firm cultural unity, reflected in an arrogant insularity on the part of the Hindus, which he regretted characteristically on account of the obstruction it raised to the study of their culture by an outsider.[7]

Once the Ghorian conquest and the establishment of the Sultanate had implanted over a large part of India another higher culture in parallel existence with the brahmanical, the clear-cut all-exclusive identification of the brahmanical culture and India, so natural for Alberuni, could no longer be sustained. Yet, the concept of Hindustan for the same limits as in Alberuni survived, sometimes with culturally neutral qualities. This is most visible in Isami's ode to India (1350), which begins:

> Blessed the splendour of the country of Hindustan,
> For Heaven itself is envious of this scented garden.

What is acclaimed is its climate, its rivers, its fertility, its life-strengthening environment, attracting all immigrants to settle here. Cultural specifity plays no part here.[8]

But already in 1318 Amir Khusrau in his metrical work *Nuh Sipihr* found other more profound qualities beyond these purely natural or physical ones, to attribute to India. He stridently proclaimed his patriotism: 'Hind' was the land (*zamin*) 'of his birth, where he lived, his native place'; 'the love of one's native land (watan) is part of one's faith (*iman*)'.[9] He too thought that India (for which he uses the name Hind throughout) was paradise-like in the fertility of its soil and pleasant climate.[10] To this he adds the achievements of Hindu learning and beliefs. Like Greece (*Rum*), the Hindus had sciences, and their higher minds believed in one God.[11] This is an echo of Alberuni. But then Amir Khusrau begins to speak in the first person plural. 'We', Indians, are able to speak foreign languages; but the Chinese, Mongols, Turks and Arabs are unable to speak 'our Hindi tongue'.[12] Indians do not go to other countries to seek knowledge; others have to come here.[13] India has given the world the numerals, the *Panchatantra* tales, and chess.[14] He goes on to associate India with certain languages from outside that now had currency within it. 'The Ghorians and Turks' had brought with them Persian, which was now learnt by all levels of people; then there were the regional languages (Hindawi's), of which Khusrau lists twelve (including Tamil and Kannada) and, finally, Sanskrit, the language of the learned Brahmans.[15] He takes special pride in this wealth of languages. Clearly, with Khusrau, India has an entity that is not defined merely by brahmanical high culture, though it is an essential part of it. Already, we see a tendency to envision India as a country with a composite culture specific to itself, to which a member of the Turkish Muslim immigrant family like Amir Khusrau can proudly proclaim his allegiance, and which had adopted Persian as one of its own languages.

A noteworthy development which was bound to affect the perception of India as a country with cultural and social institutions of its own, was the growth of a Muslim community within India, distinct from the Muslim communities of other countries. The orthodox theologian and historian Abdul Qadir Badauni, in his work on ethics written in 1590–1 acknowledges that marriages for limited periods and divorce (by the husband) are permitted by Muslim law and sanctified by precedent, but then comments, 'What good custom have the people of India that they shun this practice and regard it [divorce] as the worst word of abuse, so much so that if someone is called *talaqi* [divorcer], he, out of folly, would be ready to fight to death.'[16] Clearly, Badauni thought that Muslims in India had a way of life different from Muslims of other countries, for example in thinking very ill of divorcing one's wife. Whether this outlook was influenced by the absolute permanence of marriage in Hindu law cannot be said for certain: but the recognized existence of a distinct Indian Muslim custom is unmistakable here.

Almost simultaneously came the recognition of India as an entity
for historical purposes. It began with Badauni's friend, Nizamuddin
Ahmad, who in 1593–4 completed his *Tabaqat-i Akbari*, designed to
give the annals separately for nine regions of India (Delhi, Deccan,
Gujarat, Malwa, Bengal, Jaunpur, Kashmir, Sind, and Multan). Such
a departure from dynastic history in favour of a general history of
India is something for which Nizamuddin has surely not received
adequate credit. He inspired a series of works, including Firishta's
celebrated *Gulshan-l Ibrahimi* (1609–10), where the attempt is
extended to reconstruct even the pre-Islamic history of the country.
Even if the conception of history is rather narrow here, a little more
than a grouping of separate dynastic histories (laboriously compiled),
the constant underlying assumption of the historical unity of India is
remarkable.[17]

The concept of India had thus gone much beyond a purely territorial
one in the Indo-Muslim tradition with which Akbar had been in the
main familiar. Though born in India (1542), Akbar's boyhood was
spent in Afghanistan, until 1555, and he himself spoke later of his
arrival in India ('Hind').[18] He developed an increasing interest in the
language and customs of his subjects. In 1563, confronting Adham
Khan, he used a Hindi word of abuse still current.[19] He composed
verses in Hindi, containing, in the words of his official biographer,
'colourful conceits'.[20] Imitating 'the loyal Indians', he let grow his
hair, rather than cut it short:[21] and he never kept a beard. His love for
Indian tales made him commission the translation of *Singhasan Battisi*
even before 1571–2.[22] But it is in October 1578 that, for the first time,
we find him referring with affection and pride to the people of India
('Hind'). When in an assembly at the court, Akbar 'praised the truth-
based nature of the people of India, whose women, however hard the
life they might have lived (with their husbands) show the greatest
affection and love for their husbands once they are dead', and went
on to refer to the self-sacrifice offered by Indian women as sati. At
the same time, Akbar condemned the pusillanimity of men of
'Hindustan' who allowed or encouraged such acts by their women.[23]
Since Muslims did not practise anything remotely resembling sati, the
identification of Indians and India with Hindus and Hinduism both in
the friendly and critical aspects is unmistakable.

A similar identification tended to occur when Akbar began to
acquire familiarity with the religious beliefs of the various schools of
Hinduism. In 1578, again, two Brahmans, Purushuttam and Devi (?),
introduced him to these complexities leading him to believe that

transmigration of souls was an essential element of Hinduism.[24] In his sayings, as reported by Abul Fazl, Akbar shows a grasp of the doctrine of transmigration of souls, and the consequence which such a belief led to in India: divine incarnation not prophethood. Thus he observed: 'In India ('Hind'), no one set forth a claim to Prophethood: this is because the claim to Divinity has had precedence here'.[25]

We see in these statements a pride in India tempered with a critical spirit. If India is to be identified by the currency of certain customs and beliefs, it is not necessary that these should be accepted. Akbar thus adds a new component to the vision of India, that of reform. His prohibition of forced sati and of pre-puberty marriage, his demand for equal inheritance for the daughter, his condemnation of slavery and slave trade,[26] all suggest the rejection of some of the burdens of the past. From India seen as a cultural unity, and then as a cultural diversity undergoing synthesis, we have with Akbar the first vision of India undergoing change. It was linked to a bold rejection of traditionalism:

The pursuit of reason ('*aql*) and rejection of traditionalism (*taqlid*) are so brilliantly patent as to be above the need of argument. If traditionalism was proper, the prophets would merely have followed their own elders [and not come with new messages].[27]

One could almost say that with Akbar we begin to have in a rudimentary form a pre-modern vision of a modernized India, a patriotism without revivalism. But to understand in greater detail and depth, what India meant to Akbar and his circle we have to go to his principal spokesman, Abul Fazl.

There is no doubt that Abul Fazl was more conscious of the geography of India than any previous writer. In the north he considered the great mountain ranges to separate India from Turan (Central Asia) and Iran an one side and China ('Chin and Machin') on the other.[28] The following passage from his pen was long an aid to the arguments of those British strategists who would place the 'scientific frontier' of the Raj across the heart of Afghanistan:

Intelligent men of the past have considered Kabul and Qandahar as the twin gates of Hindustan, one (Qandahar) for the passage to Iran, and the other for that to Turan. By guarding these two places, Hindustan obtains peace from the alien (raider), and global traffic by these two routes can prosper.[29]

It is significant that Abul Fazl considers India to be a peninsula, for he says that the sea borders Hindustan 'on the east, west and south'.

He claims, however, that Hindustan also included 'Sarandip (Sri Lanka), Achin (in Sumatra), Maluk (Malaya), Malagha (Malacca) and many islands', so that 'the sea cannot really demarcate its limits'.[30] This too is a rather expansive concept of India—anticipating the 'Greater India' of later days—which one can hardly endorse. But probably Abul Fazl meant no more than that the sea could not prevent Indian cultural influences from reaching these countries; and this in itself was an interesting statement for him to make.

Abul Fazl displays his patriotism by showering unqualified praise on the people of India:

The people of this country are God-seeking, generous-hearted, friendly to strangers, pleasant-faced, of broad forehead, patrons of learning, lovers of asceticism, inclined to justice, contented, hard working and efficient, true to salt, truth-seeing and attached to loyalty.[31]

These qualities, it is worth noting, are assigned to inhabitants of the territory, not to the followers of any religious persuasion. But since the majority of Indians were Hindus, Abul Fazl claims that 'all' (that is, including the Hindus) 'acclaim the oneness of God'. Though some of them revere images, he argues, this is not really idol worship, since images are used merely to assist in the worship of God.[32] We are not concerned here with the veracity of this defence, but with the fact that Abul Fazl needs to make it, since his praise of Indians as God-seekers would cover the Hindus as well.

The recognition of India as the birthplace of an important culture, which found its major expression in the Indian ('Hindi') languages, becomes the starting-point of a long and accurate survey of it in the latter portion of the *A'in-i Akbari*, entitled 'Account of Hindustan' (*Ahwal-i Hindustan*). There is no indication in Abul Fazl that he intended the culture to be considered in a sectarian colour: It is characteristic of modern biases that when he begins by stating his intention 'to describe a little of the conditions of this country and survey the opinions of the Indian (Hindi-*nazad*) sages',[33] the translator renders the last phrase as 'the opinion professed by the majority of the learned among the Hindus'.[34] Indeed, Abul Fazl does not begin with religion at all, but with Indian beliefs in the spheres of astronomy and geography. His attitude in this respect is very similar to that of Alberuni, who too was concerned with the entire range of Indian learning. At the conclusion of his survey, Abul Fazl regrets that he did not have time to compare the opinions of the learned of India with those of Greece and Persia.[35] This again suggests, beyond regret, at not having proceeded as Alberuni had done, the harbouring of an essentially secular or non-sectarian perception of Indian culture.

There is no doubt that Abul Fazl's description of Indian culture running to about 150 pages of the large folio edition in Persian is an outstanding achievement in detail and accuracy, covering secular learning, religion, ritual and ethnography. The account is totally independent of Alberuni and from the point of view purely of information adds much to Alberuni. Abul Fazl professedly derived his knowledge from a large number of Indian texts, through the medium of numerous learned interpreters and translators,[36] but the care and precision he exercised in setting out the information is very greatly to his credit. The survey needs to be analysed, despite Sarkar's rather disparaging remarks,[37] since it tells us how, with what points of emphasis, various beliefs and opinions were held or expressed at the time (*c*. 1595).

Abul Fazl has a particular interest in presenting to the Persian-knowing reader the essentials of Indian culture, which is seen, despite its diversities, as a unity. He looks forward to a larger unity, so that 'the inner and external conflict should turn into amity, the thorn-bush of enmity and hostility into the garden of friendship and the sounds of reasoned argument should come forth and an informed assemblage be arranged'.[38] He is too scientific and too scornful of 'tradition-bound imitators'[39] to approve of the various Indian beliefs and opinions he surveys. He says, on one occasion, in obvious deprecation of the Indian and Greek views on the habitable world, that 'today the truth-inclined learned consider the south to be inhabited just like the north'.[40]

In other words, Abul Fazl was looking to much beyond a parallel coexistence of cultures or to a composite traditional Indian culture, a mere synthesis of traditions. He made his own bow to the cultural coexistence when after a survey of the traditional culture of India, he goes on to give us notices of foreigners arriving in India ('Hindustan') from Adam to Humayun,[41] and then of Muslim divines and saints of India,[42] as if these constituted streams that too belonged to India. But such streams had to join together, purified by reason, before the higher unity could be achieved. For this higher ground to be reached, Abul Fazl saw an essential role to lie with the sovereign.

Humayun's arrival in India after so many travails was to be celebrated, because it led to Akbar's accession, and it was under the aegis of Akbar's justice and judgement of men that 'Hindustan has become the concourse of good men of the seven climes and every one in different ways attains his object'.[43] The key instrument of the sovereign was Sulh-i Kul, absolute peace, a means of relief for individuals like Abul Fazl himself,[44] as well as peoples. For the sovereign is 'father of humanity. All kinds of people seek comfort from him, and no dust of duality rises forth from the variety of religions believed in by men'. At the same time, the sovereign 'should not seek popularity among people through opposing Reason'.[45] In other words, tolerance of existing beliefs is only one part of the sovereign's duty; persuasion to follow reason, and so reject traditionalism is a necessary and complementary one.

We can now see that Abul Fazl reaches a conclusion which justifies Akbar's promotion of both rationalism and social reform, in order to construct a 'Hindustan' that could stand out in the world. Is this view still so 'singular' that it must be summarily thrown out of court as some are now suggesting?

NOTES

1. *Oxford History of India*, London, 1919, pp. ix–x.

2. See the critique of its views in R.P. Dutt, *India Today*, Bombay, 1947, pp. 237–9.

3. Benedict Anderson, *Imagined Communities: Reflections on the Origin and Spread of Nationalism*, London, 1983.

4. *Subaltern Studies*, VIII, New Delhi, 1994, p. 49.

5. Edward C. Sachau (tr.), *Alberuni's India*, London, 1910, I, p. 198.

6. Ibid., pp. 294–8.

7. Ibid., pp. 22–4.

8. Isami, *Futuh-us Salatin*, ed. A.S. Usha, Madras, 1948, pp. 404–5. Isami was writing at Daulatabad in the Deccan and his 'Hindustan' thus included the whole of India.

9. *Nuh Sipihr*, ed. Mohammad Wahid Mirza, London, 1950, p. 150.

10. Ibid., pp. 151–61.

11. Ibid., pp. 162–6.

12. Ibid., pp. 166–7.

13. Ibid., pp. 167–8.

14. Ibid., pp. 168–70.

15. Ibid., pp. 178–181.

16. *Nijat al-Rashid*, ed. Sayyid Muinu'l Haqq, Lahore, 1972, p. 437.

17. There is a faint earlier glimmer of it, though, in Isami, who says that

Alauddin Khalji enriched, while Muhammad Tughluq ravaged, 'Hindustan' (*Futuh-us Salatin*, p. 605).

18. Abul Fazl, *A'in-i Akbari*, Naval Kishore, Lucknow, 1892, III, p. 118: 'When we arrived in India our heart was attracted to the elephants'.

19. Bayazid Bayat, *Tazkara-i Humayun wa Akbar*, ed. M. Hidayat Hosain, Calcutta, 1941, pp. 251–2.

20. Abul Fazl, *Akbarnama*, ed. Ahmad Ali, Calcutta, 1873–87, I, pp. 270–1.

21. First version of *Akbarnama*, B.L. Add. 27, 247, f.294a.

22. Badauni, *Muntakhab'ut Tawarikh*, Calcutta, 1865–9, II, pp. 177–8.

23. *Akbarnama*, first version, B.L. Add. 27, 247, ff. 295b–296a. A stronger condemnation of the men's behaviour by Akbar is quoted by Abul Fazl among the sayings of Akbar towards the end of *A'in-i Akbar*, III, p. 190.

24. Badauni, *Muntakhab ut-Tawarikh*, II, pp. 398–400.

25. *A'in-i Akbari*, III, p. 185.

26. Cf. Irfan Habib, 'Akbar and Social Inequities: A Study of the Evolution of his Ideas', *PIHC*, Warangal session, Delhi, 1993, pp. 300–10, who sees in Akbar, 'the early flickers of that critique of traditional India, which would later turn into flame in the 19th Century Indian Renaissance'.

27. Akbar's sayings in *A'in-i Akbari*, III, p. 179.

28. Ibid., II, p. 192. See the citation of this passage in V.A. Smith, *Oxford History of India*, p. 755 in a discussion of the scientific frontier.

29. *A'in-i Akbari*, Naval Kishore, III, p. 4.

30. Ibid.

31. Ibid., p. 5.

32. Ibid.

33. Ibid., p. 2.

34. *A'in-i Akbari*, III, tr. H.S. Jarrett, ed. Jadunath Sarkar, Calcutta, 1948, p. 1. It is also not clear where Jarrett gets his 'majority' from. With similar inaccuracy, though less unjustly, Jarrett and Sarkar render 'Hindi' (Indian) language as Sanskrit.

35. *A'in-i Akbari*, Naval Kishore, III, p. 177. In respect of astronomy and geography, Abul Fazl does indeed make extensive references to Greek views and findings.

36. Ibid., p. 2.

37. *A'in-i Akbari*, III, tr. Jarrett, ed. Sarkar, p. IV.

38. *A'in-i Akbari*, Naval Kishore, III, p. 2.

39. Ibid., p. 30.

40. Ibid., p. 22.

41. Ibid., pp. 152–63.
42. Ibid., pp. 163–77. In this Abul Fazl had a very orthodox scholar preceding him by a few years. Abdul Haqq of Delhi completed in 1591 the *Akbar ul-Akhyar*, a collection of biographical notices of 255 Indian Muslim saints.
43. *A'in-i Akbari*, Naval Kishore, III, p. 163.
44. Ibid., pp. 177–8.
45. Ibid., I, p. 3.

11

The State in Islamic Thought in India

Islamic justifications of sovereignty usually take as their starting-point the Quranic injunction, 'Obey God and His Prophet and those in authority among you'. It is best to remember, however, the context in which this Revelation came. The Prophet was trying to establish his authority from his seat at Medina over the various parts of the Arabian Peninsula. The tribal chiefs (shaykhs, saiyids) were persuaded, by force, by inducements or by sincere conversion, to accept the hegemony of the Medina republic; and it was important, not only that the entire tribe should follow its chiefs in their conversion to Islam, but should accept them as conduits of authority emanating from the Prophet. Traditional sources of authority were thus put to the use of the new religious community; and it is easy to understand, then, the meaning which the Prophet's contemporaries must have given to the celebrated Revelation quoted above. They were not being asked to shed their chiefs or their tribal system of political organization. They were to continue obeying the chiefs and conform to the tribal system, since these had now been subordinated to the Prophet's control, fiscal, military and religious; and the chiefs' continued strength was important for the success of Islam as a political force.

With the death of the Prophet in AD 632 a totally new significance devolved upon that brief Divine injunction. So long as the Prophet lived, religious and political authority was combined in him without much distinction. Revelations to him were the source of legislation which changed established tribal customs; they also could justify some apparently transitory measures of policy or some particular acts or decisions of the Prophet. With his death, all Revelations would cease; the direct source of legislation would dry up. His successor (*khalifa*) could not directly invoke God to justify any measures; he could only invoke a known revelation in the Quran, or the known tradition (*hadis*) of the practice and opinion of the Prophet (*Sunna*). In effect, not only were the caliphs or khalifas the mere successors to the temporal or political power of the Prophet; they lacked an essential element of sovereignty, namely the capacity to make law. If they were to extract obedience at all, it became all the more necessary to cite the authority of the Quranic verse enjoining submission to 'those in authority'.

The practice of the four 'Pious' Caliphs (AD 632–61), especially their modest conception of their own role, led to a denigration of sovereignty in orthodox Islamic tradition. The imam (the leader, the caliph) was only a *shari'*, 'enforcer of law'. Even where in practice the caliphs promulgated measures, which were of a legislative character, or set precedents for future lawyers (Caliph Umar was particularly notable for this), the claim still remained that these were only secondary extensions of the decisions made by the Prophet himself, or applications of the traditional practices or sentiments of the Arabs that the Prophet had either countenanced or approved.

There were many reasons for the collapse of the Pious Caliphate. The absence of an established norm of determining succession was one: The claims of companionship to the Prophet, the traditional Quraiyshite loyalties, the blood-ties with the Prophet, all stood in mutual contradiction. But beyond these complex difficulties faced by the Pious Caliphate, there was the further one of Islam becoming a power outside Arabia: First, because the Arabs under the Pious Caliphs had conquered vast non-Arab lands, which they plundered and exploited, but had also to administer. Second, because there would be a stream of non-Arabs (mawwali) from the conquered lands of the Byzantine and Sassanid Empires bringing their own traditions into Islam, and even converting their masters over to these traditions.

It was manifestly impossible to administer the complex societies of Byzantium and Persia on the basis of a system forged in the tribal mores of Arabia. Even with the growing manufacture of the Prophet's traditions to justify one measure or another, the process remained a difficult one. Moreover, the unending forgeries of hadis (Prophet's sayings) tended to shake popular confidence in the Sunna: and thus there soon started a splendid scholarly exercise to weed out the 'weak' traditions, and build up a body of authoritative traditions, which, though containing much posthumous matter, still became, after a passage of time, so well established that further forgeries or additions became nearly impossible.

It was, therefore, inevitable that the caliphs looked increasingly to the imperial traditions of the conquered countries to reinforce their authority. Mu'awiya (AD 661–80), who was so adept at using Islamic theology as well as Arab tribal traditions to bolster his position, was yet regarded by later Arabs as the first Caesar (*Qaisar*) in Islam. His capital, Damascus, became the site of infusion of a whole body of Byzantine court traditions into Islamic polity. Similarly, under the Abbasid caliphs (AD 750–847), with their seat of authority in Iraq, Sassanid traditions became an important element not only determining court ceremonial, and influencing the creation of such offices as of the vizier, but also ascribing to caliph a position and power quite outside the framework of orthodox Islam, a framework which the theologians and jurists were almost simultaneously forging (in theory) into a rigid structure.

As the Abbasid caliphate declined, the Persian tradition become even more important for the provincial governors who began to set up their local independent dynasties. It was no accident that at the Sassanid court (tenth century) Bil'ami should prepare a Persian version of Tabari's celebrated History, in which the history and traditions of the Sassanid Empire would be added in a very long and important section. In the next century came Firdausi's *Shahnama*, with its glorification of the Sassanid emperors, their court, their sense of justice, their immense power, and a belittling (by implication, but on occasion in explicit terms) of the Arab intrusion. Out of this revival of a past imperial tradition arose the concept of the sultan. The word sultan was an old Arabic one: the sense now given to it, however, was quite new.

The sultan, a temporal sovereign, stood in contrast to the caliph, a temporal successor of the Prophet. If the former did not enjoy the religious halo of the latter, he also did not labour under the disadvantage of being bound by the limitations that the religious tradition placed upon the authority of the caliph. Mahmud of Ghaznin (AD 999–30) came to be regarded as the first sultan, the epitome of the new sovereign. Not for nothing would tradition also say that Firdausi dedicated his *Shahnama* to Sultan Mahmud, in spite of Mahmud being a Turk, and so hardly likely to be favourably inclined to the biased version of the great ancient conflicts between the Persians and Turks that Firdausi presented.

If the institutions of the Abbasid caliphate, representing a transition from the Islamic to the imperial tradition, were subjected to an analysis by the great Muslim jurist Mawardi (AD 972–1058), the institutions of the sultanate received their classic description in the *Siyasatnama* of Nizam-al-Mulk Tusi, a minister in the Siljuqid Empire (eleventh and twelfth centuries).

This particular development of the sultanate as a form of state was made possible by the perfection of three institutions which gave it its characteristic strength. The fiscal system, which had taken shape breaking through or distorting the restrictions of Muslim law, had now as its basis a single land-tax (kharaj) that was so determined as to appropriate the bulk of the peasants' surplus. The sultan determined, too, how this surplus would be distributed by having the absolute right to appoint its appropriators—nobles, commanders, governors, etc—and transferring their territorial revenue assignments (iqta') at will. Finally, a system of 'king's justice' and means of terror developed, by which the sultan and his officers could judge and award punishments without reference to the Shariat (Muslim Law).

The new sovereignty dominated the thought of Ziauddin Barani, the famous Indian historian of the fourteenth century. An acute thinker, Barani did not write history as a simple narration, but within a cause-and-effect framework and often to illustrate his basic ideas. He completed his famous History (*Tarikh-i Firuz Shahi*) in 1357 near the end of a long life during which he had served as an adviser to a great sultan of Delhi (Muhammad Tughluq).

Barani's basic preoccupation is with maintaining social stability. This derived from his devoted attachment to the principle of inherited qualities. He shared enthusiastically the view often espoused in Sa'di's *Gulistan* and *Bostan*, composed in the previous century, that a man's character was determined by his station at birth. Only those born in aristocratic families had the right to belong to the ruling class; the infusion of any upstarts would be a terrible disaster. Barani was not directly pleading for a caste system on Indian lines; these views of his, as I have just suggested, were derived from an established sentiment in the Islamic world. But, in essence, he came very near to justifying a rigid system of inherited class structure almost akin to the caste system. In both the *Tarikh-i Firuz Shahi* and in his *Fatawa-i Jahandari*, a collection of anecdotes and dialogues on the problem of sovereignty, he reverts again and again to the misfortune that society faces when the established families are destroyed and those born in inferior classes become rich and powerful.

The primary justification that Barani saw in the new embodiment of sovereignty, the sultanate, as distinct from the caliphate, was its ability to prevent a social upheaval of this kind. Unlike the caliphs this was the sultans' sole reason for existence: For where the caliphs held their power by deserts (*istihqaq*), the Muslim kings obtained it by sheer force (*taghallub*). Barani says plainly in the *Fatawa-i*

Jahandari that the humble and modest ways of the Pious Caliphs, with their action and conduct restricted by a strict observance of God's word and the Prophet's precedents, were not suited to the ways of his own time. The Muslim community, in his view, had so degenerated in morals and discipline that it was no longer possible for it to be controlled by the Shariat alone. Indeed, if the Shariat itself was to be saved, that is if its rules were to be enforced, extra-Shariat engines of terror and punishment were necessary. Barani approvingly attributes this particular statement to Balban, the famous sultan of Delhi, 1266–86. It was the sultan who was the fountainhead of this entire penal system. Barani also conceived that while it was the duty of the sultan to enforce the Shariat, he must also have the discretion to modify or relax the strict instruments of the Shariat. He could modify the enforcement of the law against drinking, gambling, usury or prostitution. A too rigid enforcement of the law might unnecessarily provoke disorder. For this view, too, Barani sets Balban as his model. In other words, Barani recognizes that the sultanate was an institution that had no place within the Shariat; and that it necessarily limits the operation of the Shariat; but he urges that it was still necessary for the continued survival of the Shariat even within its narrowed sphere. Without the sultan's authority and terror all ties binding society would collapse, because, as Barani often remarks in his *Tarikh*, the Muslims would tend to turn immoral and the Hindus rebellious.

Barani, therefore, considers the despotic power of the sultan as necessary, in spite of its imperfections and horrors. He is not blind to the suffering and torture that the unbridled authority of the sultan might inflict on large sections of his subjects; and he describes the punishments inflicted by Balban or Alauddin Khalji or Muhammad Tughluq with considerable pity for the victims.

Barani is also sceptical of any divine origin of the sultan's power. In his chapter on Balban, it is true, he approvingly quotes Balban for saying that while 'monarchy is the embodiment of despotism', there is a reflection (*mazhar*) of the divine in the heart of the sovereign. Barani might be correct or incorrect in his ascription of the latter view to Balban, whom he admired for his resolutely espoused theory of birth. But it is best to remember that Barani himself tells us of Jalaluddin Khalji's discovery upon becoming sultan (AD 1290) that there was nothing to be found in the internal fabric of sovereignty: it was 'all empty'. That is, the sovereign was after all a man, with all the human weaknesses and imperfections, and had no extra-human guidance to resort to. At such protestations of the old Khalji sultan,

Barani makes the younger Khalji nobles mutter among themselves, 'Sovereignty is (after all) nothing but terror, power and title to unshared authority.' It was the ability of the sultan to destroy and reward — that set him up over and above his fellow beings. That was all.

But Barani is conscious throughout of a contradiction that cannot be resolved, and whose development in various forms runs like a red thread through his *Tarikh*. His justification for the sultan's power is that it protects social stability; but, in practice, the sultan finds it necessary to overthrow the established nobility and replace it with upstarts. Thus the sultans themselves become the source of continuous social disturbance. Barani attributes the rise of the slave nobles at the cost of the free-born in the thirteenth century to the weakness of the sultan's authority under Iltutmish's successors. But what of Alauddin Khalji's recruitment of the people of 'low birth', and of Muhammad Tughluq's measures of the same kind on a vaster scale? These were despotic rulers, by no means weak or incompetent in any sense. Barani tells us, moreover, that Muhammad Tughluq always decried men of 'low birth' in his conversations; yet, he says, he gave them the highest offices. Barani therefore wonders at the 'contradictory qualities' of that sultan. But we can, perhaps, answer Barani by suggesting that the contradiction lay within the situation. Despotic monarchy could not pull on with a rigidly hereditary nobility. The tendency of despotism was to convert an aristocracy into a bureaucracy. This could not be done without the influx of external elements, and thus just as the sultan, while enforcing the Shariat, must restrict its scope, so too, while protecting social stability, he must make exceptions to protect his own despotism.

Barani's entire theory of the sultanate, brilliant as it was, thus led to a dilemma to which he had no solution.

If Barani was the great political thinker of the Delhi Sultanate, Abul Fazl was the great spokesman for the Mughal Empire. Abul Fazl offers a sharp contrast to Barani, in that with Abul Fazl, the anxiety about the contradiction between the sultan and the Shariat disappears. The latter excites in him little interest as far as his theory of sovereignty is concerned. His only common ground with Barani is his concern with social stability; but he handles the whole question in a completely different manner.

In a chapter of his great work *A'in-i Akbari*, titled *Rawai-i Rozi*, or the maintenance of livelihood, Abul Fazl offers a justification for sovereignty based on the simple fact of social contract. In words which make us recall Hobbes, he describes the contradiction of society before the emergence of the sovereign. There was complete instability, a veritable anarchy: No man was safe from another. Property, life, honour—none were safe. Indeed, property could not emerge, life was short, honour non-existent. In desperation men went to someone, who was able and strong, and solicited him to protect them. For this the protector employed soldiers, for whose pay he needed resources. These were provided by the protected people. Out of this arrangement arose the sovereign, taxes and subjects. If, then, at the beginning of the history of sovereignty there was only an act of contract, did this place any limitations on the sovereign? None, says Abul Fazl. It is the moral duty of the subject to submit to the will of the sovereign in respect of his property as well as life, since the sovereign protects the greatest thing of all, the subject's honour. If in practice, there are limitations on the share of subjects' property taken away in taxation, this limitation is no part of the contract, but is a mere matter of discretion on the part of the sovereign, who restrains himself out of compassion for his subjects.

But Abul Fazl has another theory of sovereignty, with which the social contract theory cannot be fully reconciled. His father Shaikh Mubarak had often pleaded for a special position for the king within the juridical world of Islam. In 1579 in the controversial Mahzar, the leading theologians at Akbar's court had sought to give Akbar as much authority to interpret law or even legislate, as had been conceded to the great Muslim jurists (Imam Abu Hanifa, Hambal, and others). But Akbar was not apparently satisfied with this limited position, and very soon he was no longer anxious to have any position at all as a 'king of Islam'. He now sought a wider religious justification and Abul Fazl, as his major intellectual-courtier, set out to provide him with one.

Sovereignty, said Abul Fazl, was in nature a divine light (*farr-i izadi*). With this statement he seems to dismiss as inadequate the traditional reference to the king as the shadow of God (*zill-i Ilahi*). At Akbar's court, Light was often regarded as the greatest Divine blessing and, indeed, a symbol of God. Since sovereignty was a Divine Ray of Light, the sovereign, though himself not divine, was called upon to work as an Agent of God, and thus partook of the authority and burdens that were fashioned, as it were, 'in the image of God'. Just as God's favours (sunlight, rain, etc.) fell on all irrespective of religious beliefs, so too the sovereign could not discriminate, in dispensing his favours, between the votaries of the different faiths. This became a doctrine for justifying the tolerant religious policy initiated by Akbar, and it was invoked by Jahangir and indeed even by Aurangzeb (in his *nishan* to Rana Raj Singh) to a similar purpose.

Being derived directly from God, sovereignty need not be restricted by association with any particular sect or faith. It came to be a fashionable dogma at Akbar's court that all religions are in essence the same; only the forms varied. Abul Fazl carries this to its logical conclusion by detaching sovereignty from the forms of any particular religion or its law, notably from Islam and Shariat. It follows then that unlike Barani, Abul Fazl can see no justification for sovereignty to be assigned the function of enforcing any particular religious system law. Here then was a complete break from the traditional Muslim outlook, including that of Barani.

Abul Fazl was astute enough to underline the relevance of his theory of sovereignty for a multi-religious country like India. Here the sovereign should not be tarnished with association with any one sect or religion alone. As sovereign, he must be above all religions. It can be seen that his views were not fully secular; he thought that the sovereign, being God's agent, had certain spiritual obligations, namely to promote certain religious beliefs, for example in God, in the Light as His symbol, and in inter-sectarian peace (Sulh-i Kul), and so on. The quasi-divine status of the sovereign had to be sustained by an appropriate religious status assumed by the sovereign and kept up through a ceremonial carved out of borrowings from different faiths.

Abul Fazl is undoubtedly one of the greatest thinkers and scholars that India has produced. One may pick holes in his theory of social contract and still more in his theory of divine origin of sovereignty, particularly since the two theories are not logically compatible with each other. Indeed, he may be said to have tried to ride two horses, and combined (in anticipation) the views of Hobbes and James I (and he went much beyond James I in his claim for the sovereign). Yet the essential bedrock of rationality in Abul Fazl's thought commands respect, even admiration. Certainly no one after him in India debated the issues of sovereignty at the same high level of reason and abstraction.

A thinker who wrote during the declining phase of the Mughal Empire, Shah Waliullah (1704–62) offers a third theory of polity which, though not as incisive as Barani's nor as brilliant as Abul Fazl's, nevertheless has claims to be considered as a serious contribution to medieval political thought.

Shah Waliullah was a theologian, and he wrote his famous work *Hujatullah il Baligha* as a treatise on Muslim law, ritual and ethics.

But in an important portion early in his work, he discourses on the universality of certain human needs, economic activities, social customs, and ethical values. He argues that the organization of society which results from these phenomena is in many respects equally universal, 'from east to west'. He urges that the foundations of *all* social organization lie in the universality of inborn inequality. Some are by nature (*tab'an*) born to dominate over others, some, says he with supreme *naivety*, are by nature inclined to obey others and love to be slaves. Women are inferior to men and must be subservient to the latter.

These natural divisions happily suit our convenience. The son of an ironsmith finds it more convenient to follow the profession of his father. Society acts on basis of cooperation of, and adjustment between, these various classes and groups of men. The cooperation takes place under the aegis of rulers (*muluk*). Waliullah follows early Muslim jurists in taking muluk as a universal category of sovereigns, whereas the khalifas are specifically Muslim. But unlike Barani and other more careful historians, Waliullah subsequently fails to distinguish between the khalifas and ordinary Muslim rulers.

Waliullah does not postulate an original social contract, though he does emphasize the role of the sovereigns in keeping the various parts of society together. At the same time, he departs from Abul Fazl in arguing that there are limits to the sovereign's impositions upon his subjects. He says that in his own time the decline of the contemporary states was caused by two factors:

(i) a large number of persons who ought to have rendered service to the state became simple parasites living as useless burdens on the treasury; and

(ii) the sovereign imposed heavy taxation on the peasants and artisans, which caused them to rise in rebellion.

Obviously Shah Waliullah's perception was influenced by the contemporary problems of the Mughal Empire, in which there had been a breakdown of agrarian administration.

It is a remarkable feature in Shah Waliullah's thought that such insights (limited as they are) are left behind when he enters the realm of Islamic law and theology. Forgetting his own admonitions to sovereigns to avoid oppressive measures, he now recommends that the infidels should be treated as hewers of wood and drawers of water, and as no better than beasts of burden.

This, then, was the ultimate contradiction which could not be resolved so long as political thought remained shackled to the constraints of orthodoxy. Shah Waliullah was not perhaps an unintelligent man, he perceived the decline of the polity to which his class was tied; and he was acute enough to place its decline partly at least in an economic perspective. But he was not acute enough to suggest an alternative basis for political practice; his actual solution, obedience to the Shariat, was only a means of solace for depressed spirits; it could offer no light to practical men.

12

Elements of Social Justice in
Medieval Islamic Thought

I

Before we can analyse the perception of social justice in an earlier age, we should first have some clarification as to what we mean by this term. I would, therefore, begin with what the term connotes to a modern theorist of some repute, John Rawls. Rawls tells us that 'justice is the first virtue of social institutions, as truth is of systems of thought.'[1] Justice must, therefore, be sought in the thought and beliefs of mankind, even in prehistoric times, whenever and wherever 'social institutions', like family, clan, occupations, etc. arose. But 'social justice' is of later growth, for, according to Rawls: 'A conception of social justice, then, is to be regarded as providing in the first instance a standard whereby the distributive aspects of the basic structure of society are to be assessed.'[2]

Clearly, distributive problems with human societies arose only after man began to produce surpluses; and this sets a much later period for the emergence of any ideas of social justice other than simple justice, which latter would be merely concerned with obedience to custom.

But, in fact, the two principles of justice (or, as perhaps, he should have better said, social justice) that Rawls frames are such as could not possibly have been invoked before very recent times. He gives the following description of the two principles:

First: each person is to have an equal right to the most extensive basic liberty compatible with a similar liberty for others. Second: social and economic inequalities are to be arranged so that they are both (a) reasonably expected to be to every one's advantage, and (b) attached to positions and offices open to all.[3]

It will be seen that these two principles invoke the three ideals of liberty, equality and fraternity, which were central to the political thought generating and sustaining the French Revolution of 1789. In other words, social justice, as conceived by modern theorists, is barely two hundred years old. When, therefore, we turn to earlier periods, our study can only be that of attitudes towards these ideals, or some concessions made to them, rather than that of attempts to do away with imperfections in the professed pursuit of them.

For convenience, I would limit my study to the medieval Indian political regimes and writers of a professedly Islamic complexion and focus on their perception of justice in the fields of social hierarchy, slavery and women. The realm of social justice, doubtless extends much beyond these fields, but I believe that a scrutiny of beliefs and practice in this limited area would still be adequately illustrative, if not fully, exhaustive.

II

One may begin by raising the question of concept of social justice in the Islamic tradition to the point (or points) that it was received in India or began to interact with the Indian reality. Contrary to the express or implicit assertion in many modern apologetic or fundamentalist writing, it is not possible to identify any religion, including Islam, with an ideal social order. This is because by its very definition, religion, in its own consciousness, is primarily concerned not with this, but with the other world. This explains the point in an early Islamic tradition traced to 'Umar, later to be the second caliph of Islam. 'Umar remonstrated with the Prophet that the Persians and Byzantines had all the affluence given to them by God when they did not believe in Him. The Prophet replied, '(But) in this world (only).' 'Umar thereupon begged God's forgiveness.[4] The requirements of the present world were, therefore, after all, secondary; worldly life had to be organized by the believers only in so far as this was necessary for obedience to the dictates of God, in turn necessary for salvation in the world beyond. Serious Muslim thinkers agreed that worldly practice formed a realm, namely that of ethics, which was not exclusively the preserve of one religion. The very orthodox theologians Abdul Qadir Badauni in his own work on ethics (1591–2) recognized that 'not only Islamic scholars, but also sages of every religion (*millat*) like Christians, Jews, Zoroastrians and Hindus have books on the subject of ethics (*ikhlaq*)', and explicitly commended the Indian *Kalila wa Dimna* (the Perso-Arabic version of the *Panchatantra*) and the Iranian *Marzban-nama* and *Javedan*.[5]

It is, therefore, unhistorical to assume that Islam could represent a conscious social revolution at any stage, despite the fact that, in the eyes of its believers, its aim was to win the world for God. The universality of its appeal (and, therefore, in a sense equality of all in common humility before God) was inherent in the Prophet's message from the beginning. 'Men were once one community', God had decreed; He had sent 'the prophets as messengers' to them all.[6] And so God told the Prophet of Islam: 'Say, O men, I am the Messenger of Allah to you all from Him who rules over earth and sky.'[7] But the universality of the message was at the heart of the faith alone; it was by no means the core of the prescribed practice of worldly life, of the realms of law and justice. In treating of the Quranic canons of social conduct one must recall that pagan communities in the Arabian peninsula with their various customs already coexisted with Jewish and Christian communities following a mixture of biblical and Roman law. If the Islamic umma was to be a single community, it had to have practices of its own, which in a large part would still draw from the pool of varied social customs existing within the peninsula. The reforms that the Quranic injunctions made might also, therefore, look to us as compromises between uniformity and existing custom. The famous Quranic injunction to obey God, His Prophet and 'those in authority among you'[8] could be taken to mean that, subject to the commands of God and His Prophet, the hereditary rulers and tribal chiefs (shaykhs and saiyids) could still claim the allegiance of the faithful.[9] Other aspects of social inequality are also implied in the Quran. A Quranic verse is protective about trading (*al-bai*);[10] and there is, on the other hand, the well-known verse holding 'the Arab nomad' in scorn as being hostile to the Faith.[11] Here is then a visible reflection of the high position of the mercantile Quraysh above the bedouin tribes, a circumstance which early Islamic polity inherited, consolidated and hugely enlarged.[12]

In respect of women, the duality is similarly present. The Quran recognizes that women have rights similar to those of men, a recognition given partial reflection in the Islamic law of inheritance.[13] The principle derived almost certainly from Islam's insistence on individual obligation in respect of fidelity to God borne by both men and women; but equally certainly it came from the social milieu of pagan Mecca where the Prophet's wife Khadija had been a merchant in her own right. Yet, the reality of a patriarchal environment is not forgotten. 'Men are in a degree above them (women)', and, for men the women are like a field to sow; 'so go to your tilth as you will'.[14]

Islam admits both slavery and concubinage, the latter explicit in a Quranic verse.[15] Both institutions were strongly entrenched in pagan society. On the other hand, among the virtues of the righteous is the ability 'to set slaves (*fi al-riqabo*) free'.[16] Manumitting one's slaves was thus at par with giving up part of one's wealth, in order to give relief to the needy. But manumission of individual slaves no more dispensed with slavery than did charity dispense with concentrations of wealth in early Islamic society.

I would again like to repeat that the Quranic concern with these matters of social distinctions is secondary; to someone less familiar with the Quran's principal concern with the individual's complete submission (*islam*) to God, these may, indeed, appear as compromises between the perceived equality before God and the existing inequality among believers. But I would argue that the spiritual principle and practical adjustments are on two different planes altogether; and equality in worldly society was never a part of the aspirations of original Islam.

The history of early Islamic polity, as analysed classically by Wellhausen in *The Arab Kingdom and its Fall*,[17] brings out the transformation in the concepts of social hierarchy, as the Arabs dramatically expanded their hegemony, destroying the Sassanid empire and much of the Byzantine within the seventh century. Tribes jostled for position within the new hegemony; and under the acknowledged Qurayshite supremacy, two great tribal federations emerged, the northern or Muzar (comprising mainly the Qais and Tamim) and the southern or Yemenite (mainly Kalb and Azad) to contest each other's pre-eminence. There was the tribal Arab's dislike of the non-tribal Hellenized Syrian Arabs (*Shamis*) manifest in the hostility of the tribes settled in Iraq towards them. But with increasing severity there grew the scorn and contempt for the non-Arab converts, called mawwali or clients, because, characteristically, it was thought unacceptable if a non-Arab claimed to be a Muslim without having at the same time been allowed to become a client (*mawla*) of an Arab tribe. As these converts, especially Iranians, became more and more important as soldiers and secretaries and, then, as scholars, theologians and literati, the suppression of the mawwali became one of the pillars of the policies of the Ummayyad caliphate (660–750), notably under Hajjaj ibn Yusuf, the Ummayyad viceroy of Iraq and the eastern regions of the caliphate.[18]

This hierarchical structure began to fall, with the forces let loose by the so-called Abbasid revolution. Without going into the objections raised by historians of the Arabist school like Shaban[19] to Wellhausen's thesis of the overthrow of Arabism involved in the installation of the Abbasid dynasty in 750, the long-term results can hardly be disputed.[20] With the 'emancipation' of the mawwali, Islam lost its exclusive identification with Arab tradition, and Arabic became for two centuries the literary language of Iran. The universality of Islam was invoked to rule out racialism and tribalism from the social ethics of Islam. This was done by a long process of reconstruction (with much unconscious creative forgery of the prophetic traditions, the hadis), a process which has been given its classical analysis by Sahacht.[21] Thus, a scattered unsystematic assemblage of Quranic injunction and Arab tribal spirit and customs was now sought to be converted in the eighth and ninth centuries into a system of law by one of the greatest intellectual efforts in the history of Islam. The effort was 'to systematize ... and by the tendency to "Islamicize", to impregnate the sphere of law with religious and ethical ideas, to subject it to Islamic norms'.[22] The effort was not only reflected in giving an absolute multi-racial universality to Islam; it was also expressed in the emergence of new ethical ideas, which impelled bans that did not exist in the Quran. Temporary contractual marriages (*mut'a*) which destroyed the woman's stable place in the family, had undoubtedly been a part of Arab social practice both during pagan days and under early Islam. Traditions, accepted by all schools, except the Shi'ite, now became current asserting that the Prophet disapproved of mut'a.[23] Similarly, a more humane spirit could be discerned in the treatment of slavery. A woman slave made into a concubine to give him a child could not then be sold away by the master—a new legal doctrine without any historical proof of such protection extended to the *Umm al-walad* concubines in the Prophet's time or even under the Pious Caliphs.[24] We see, then, that with the change in the territorial and civilizational context of Islam, new ethical perceptions began to modify and, in some respects, transform social outlook, in what today may seem to be a movement towards a more benign 'social justice'.

It is, however, necessary to remember that while this movement was emancipatory in some respects, in relation, for example, to the mawwali, and to certain categories of women and female slaves, it was not a conscious movement towards equality. For one thing, there was no attempt to deny the inferior status of women (however much protection might be extended to them) or to question the legality and legitimacy of slavery (increasingly humane though were the injunctions for treatment of the slaves).[25] For another, as the Arab tribal customs and jealousies were given less and less accommodation, the protection of property and inheritance and the honouring of contracts became more and more central to Islamic law. Where in an earlier age, constant war and booty seemed to be in accordance with God's insistent decree, now stability was seen as the great virtue of properly arranged societies. It was, therefore, not an accident that the ideal regime to many Islamic thinkers, notably Ibn Khaldun (fourteenth century) began to be identified with the pre-Islamic Sassanid Empire of Iran, where the rulers ruled for the common good, that is, for the continuing stability of established hierarchy.[26] The craving for society where birth should determine one's position in the apparatus of power that one finds in the Indian historian Ziauddin Barani (1357) is, therefore, fully in accordance with the main thrust of Islamic thought as it had developed by that time.[27]

Barani's ideas on hierarchy, then, had a blue-blooded Islamic ancestry, immersed as he himself was in Islamic history and theology. With due respect to a scholar of the calibre of the late Professor Mohammed Habib, it is difficult to see in his ideas any influence of 'the traditions of the Hindu caste system'.[28] It is noticeable that Barani never invokes the caste system as an acceptable hierarchical order. More precisely, in his vision of the ideal social order, there is no hint of a ban on occupational mobility or of a hereditary priesthood, nor any concept of inherited purity or pollution. All the essentials of the caste system are, therefore, lacking.

III

Given the nature and development of Islamic theology and thought, as I have sketched above, it is easy to see that with the coming of Islam to India, there resulted no encounter between a religion of social equality and the classical order of *homo hierarchicus*, to borrow from the title of Dumont's book.[29] Rather, two systems of hierarchy of different sorts met and interacted.

This dimension of the reality perhaps best explains why the attitude of Muslim statesmen and thinkers towards the caste system was so accommodating. With regard to the rulers, one can cite a very early example, Muhammad ibn Qasim. After his seizure of the capital of Sind (712), he virtually took over the entire Brahman bureaucracy of the fallen regime, and allowed his Brahman advisers and officials to determine how the outcastes should be treated:

The minister (the Brahman Siyakar) said, in the presence of Moka of Basaya, that during the reign of Rai Chach, the (Jatts of) Lohana, that is, Lakha and Summa, were not allowed to wear soft garments, or put satin (caps) on their head, but could only wear black woollen cloth above and below, and throw a coarse sheet over the shoulder, and had to go about bare-headed and bare-footed. Whoever wore a soft garment was fined. When they came out of their house, they had to take a dog with them so that their identity be known to all. It was decreed that no high person from amongst them might ride a horse. ... They have no high and low among them and are of a savage temperament.... (Thereupon) Muhammad-i Qasim said: 'What disgusting people are these! They are like the steppe nomads of Fars and Koh Paya (in Iran). The same regulations (as before) should continue in regard to them.' Muhammad-i Qasim kept them subject to that prescribed mode and manner of conduct.[30]

There is little that needs to be added to this. The Arab conquest did not signify any emancipation of the low castes, since the older social regime was left undisturbed. There was no recognition of any violation of any Islamic principles of 'social justice' in the retention of the old constraints.

There centuries later, Alberuni set himself to study the Indian civilization in all its aspects. No greater intellect than he could be produced by the world of Islam in the realms with which he concerned himself. He shows a remarkable tolerance for the caste system, though he admits that such an institution is not permitted in Islam. He argues that the caste system arose out of the rulers' concern for their subjects' welfare. 'The kings of antiquity, who were industriously devoted to the duties of their office, spent most of their care on the division of their subjects into different classes and orders, which they tried to preserve from intermixture and disorder'. He recalled, in this connection, 'the history of the ancient Chosroes (Sassanid emperors), for they had created great institutions, which could not be broken through by the special merits of any individual, nor by bribery'.[31] We here have once again the admiration for the stable hierarchy of pre-Islamic Iran, which Alberuni invokes to explain (and, perhaps, justify) the caste system for his Muslim readers.

Alberuni was an objective, and often sympathetic, observer of Hinduism. But even among Muslims who held an obvious religious bias, one looks in vain for a critique or denunciation of the caste system throughout medieval times.[32] Indeed, later descriptions of the caste system, such as those of Abul Fazl (*c.* 1595), delineate it with almost clinical neutrality.[33] It is possible, indeed, that some prejudices from the Indian caste system entered popular Muslim ethos quite early. Thus Barani tells us of Iltutmish's officers discovering that his minister Nizamul Mulk Junaidi was of lowly origin, being the descendant of a weaver;[34] and this reminds us of the especially low position allowed to the weaver in the caste system, as reported by Alberuni.[35] Or again Barani's own use of an abusive epithet for an officer of Muhammad Tughluq, which might then have been in use for sweepers.[36] Only on some rare occasions does a spirit different from that of the Brahmanical appear in the treatment of the lowest castes, as in Akbar's treatment of the khidmatiyas, a *Chandala* caste.[37]

While the caste system was thus tolerated among the Hindus, yet, despite some transferred prejudices, it never established itself among Muslims in a significant measure. Part of the reason lay in the fact that Muslim law, which was created outside the environment of the caste system, steadily expanded at the expense of inherited custom within Muslim communities. Another reason was the fact that Muslim perceptions of purity and pollution were so different from the caste perceptions that the latter could not be adopted. One illustration may serve: When the Arabs invaded Sind early in the eighth century, they were denounced by their opponents as 'beef-eating *Chandalas*'.[38] Badauni (1590–1) cites a saying of the Prophet (given in Arabic) that God curses the slaughterer of the cow, the tree-feller and the slave-seller. Badauni found this quotation in books on ethics though he agreed that it was of questionable authenticity. Nevertheless, he saw that there was reason behind the condemnation of the three actions which were legitimate only under necessity. Yet, he says 'the belief of the common people (among Muslims) is that unless they eat beef, their faith cannot be true'. He goes on ironically to add, 'Praise be to God, and wonderful it is, what Islam has come to.'[39] The observation underlines the continuous process of the undermining of the caste sense of 'purity' in converted communities by a kind of aggressive popular Muslim assertion of a counter-custom or ritual, even when there was no provision for the latter in orthodox theology.

IV

We have seen that the Quran has a dual perception of woman: she has a person of her own, with rights to property, and is not the slave, in any sense, of her father or her husband.[40] On the other hand, she is deemed inferior to man, an inferiority reflected in the daughter's share to inheritance being half that of son;[41] also, no evidence is acceptable if all witnesses are women, and the evidence of two women counts as that of one man.[42] This duality of approach is to be found almost universally in the thought and practice of medieval Islam.

There is no doubt that the distinct individual rights of women continued to be preserved in Muslim jurisprudence. The illustrative evidence for this comes from documents relating to marriage contracts and divorce settlements from the port of Surat to which Moosvi has drawn attention.[43] Here we find the wife ensuring through conditions in the marriage contract that the husband be bound to pay her a fixed dower, abstain from taking another wife or having liaison with a concubine, to not physically injure the contracting wife, to provide for her specific subsistence needs and not to be absent for more than a fixed period. The marriage was to be deemed terminated if any of these conditions were not fulfilled by the husband. On the other hand, one women simply bought a divorce from her husband by paying him a particular amount.[44]

The tendency of Muslim ethical and legal authorities was to criticize the availability of 'easy divorce' by which husbands might dispose of their wives, who were thus bound to have an insecure position all the time. This position is well represented by Badauni who, while acknowledging the actual occurrence of temporary, even one-night, marriages in the Prophet's time,[45] says that 'since divorce is the least liked of permissible things, resort to divorce is far from manliness'. He then goes on to commend the Indians' distaste of divorce: 'What good custom the people of India have that they shun this practice, and consider its attribution to them the worst of abuse.'[46]

Yet, if the woman's right to look to the welfare of her person and property was conceded, on one side, quite a contrary spirit prevailed, on the other.

Thus, it was held that man had a right to sexual appetite, which could not be allowed to woman. Jahangir's contemporary, Shaikh Ahmad Sirhindi, commended God for having shown such consideration for men's appetites as to allow man to have four wives, and enjoy any number of concubines and use the device of divorce to change wives at will;[47] women, on the contrary, were to be condemned as mischievous and sinful for having similar urges towards men, as may be seen in the verses of the fourteenth century poets, Amir Khusrau and Isami.[48] Badauni too waxes eloquent on the theme.[49] Shaikh Ahmad Sirhindi, taking things to the extreme, as usual, asserted that women were primarily to blame for adulterous acts, so that God held adulteresses to be more reprehensible than their male partners.[50]

Such statements provided the rationale for prescribing the strictest seclusion for women. Amir Khusrau had exhorted the woman to keep her face to the wall and her back to the door, and not to pass through the door to leave the inside of the house.[51] Badauni, invoking a supposed prohibition on women riding horses attributed to the Prophet, makes the demand that a woman should not come out of the four walls of the house and should treat the wall as her covering garment (*chadar*). He even says that the best place for a woman is the purdah or the grave.[52]

This is virtually halfway to the statement that the grave is one's best son-in-law, a saying attributed to the Prophet by the historian Afif (*c.* 1400),[53] but actually found in pre-Islamic Arabic poetry.[54]

The dual attitude is responsible for the attitude towards sati in Indo-Muslim writing. Amir Khusrau recognized that the self-destruction of the woman upon the death of her husband was not permitted 'in Islam'.[55] And we may well believe Ibn Battuta when he speaks of his shock when he first witnessed widow-burning in India.[56] There was a jurists' opinion spoken of in Badauni's time that if a Hindu woman resolved to burn herself (and so commit an illegal act), she became a 'booty for Muslims', and whoever could, might seize and enslave her. Badauni to his credit doubted the existence of such an opinion. On the other hand, he was full of admiration for the Hindu women who so sacrificed themselves for their husbands and contrasted their devotion to 'the (lack of) manliness of us weak-willed people' in the path of devotion to the Divine Beloved.[57] He duly quotes a verse in his support, but he might better have quoted Amir Khusrau's famous couplet:

> The world has no manly lover like the Hindu wife.
> Not every insect is equal to burning itself out over a dead candle.[58]

Indeed, Amir Khusrau had been an outspoken admirer of the fortitude and devotion of the Hindu widow offering herself as sati.[59]

A change in the attitude towards women came with Akbar; and it is possible that in some respects contacts with Christianity played a role in the framing of his ideas. His preference for monogamy was first expressed in 1578 in a conversation with a Christian layman.[60] There were then discussions on monogamy with the first Jesuit mission in 1580.[61] Badauni reports a firm order enforcing it in 1587,[62] and Abul Fazl (*c.* 1595) reports Akbar's opinion that a second marriage was justified only if the first wife had proved barren or sonless.[63] Such advice on restraint was naturally opposed to the traditional view. So also was Akbar's dislike of marriage between minors, first expressed in 1582.[64] This, too, could be of Christian inspiration. Akbar's criticism of sati could also perhaps have been engendered by the protest of Jesuit fathers in 1580 at his appearance at widow-burnings.[65] It was in 1583 that Akbar first acted personally to prevent the burning of a non-consenting widow of a Rajput officer.[66] Badauni reports a prohibition of forced satis in 1591;[67] and the *A'in-i Akbari* (*c.* 1595) treats it as a standing regulation.[68]

But it is not possible to attribute Akbar's concern for increasing Muslim women's share in inheritance to any Christian influence. Akbar's explicit criticism of Muslim law, that it allowed a smaller share to the daughter, while as the weaker person she should have a larger share (than her brother),[69] suggests a perceptive vision of justice that, perhaps, owed more to Akbar's growing humanistic concerns than any new religious influence. Indeed, Akbar's sentiments of increasing protectiveness towards women's interests and his refusal to join the chorus over women's innate inferiority, deserve a special tribute which has so far been rarely extended to him.[70]

V

Slavery in India long pre-dated Islam, as Dev Raj Chanana's study has well shown.[71] Its actual harshness is apparent from the texts of thirteenth-century documents on female slaves in the *Lekhapadhati*.[72] As we have seen, Islam too accepted the institution of slavery it had inherited from pagan society; and captives in war, including civil population seized as booty, were an important source of the burgeoning slave population in early Islamic society. It has, indeed, been argued that in a similar fashion, there was a considerable enhancement of slave population in the north Indian towns as a result of the Ghorian invasions and the long process of subjugation of the countryside in the thirteenth and fourteenth centuries.[73] Whether this view can be quantitatively established is another matter, for comparative data for the preceding period are simply not available.

The view on slavery, as one can see in Indo-Muslim thought, tends to begin from two propositions: One is that the master's right over the slave's person is proprietary in nature, so that the slave cannot, of his own, terminate the relationship. This not only imposed the duty on civil authorities to recover the fugitive slave, as they were obliged to recover any stolen property; it was quite also in form for sufis like Nizamuddin Auliya (d. 1324) to pray for the recapture of such a slave.[74] The second proposition was that the slave was, in the religious sphere, a full human being in the eyes of the Lord. Thus, observed the same Nizamuddin Auliya in a conversation recorded in 1308, 'in this (spiritual) path, the question of who is master and who slave does not arise.'[75] From this proposition derived a number of inferences. While it was deemed legitimate to take a slave-girl for a concubine, her will being of no moment,[76] it was not at all legitimate for the master to let his female slaves be similarly used by other men.[77] I do not know on what authority Badauni, who condemned the latter practice, noted that 'this practice has survived among the Hindus of India till this day in some places.'[78] But a slave sent out to earn income for himself, could legitimately be required to part with a share of it by his master.[79]

The view further developed that the relationship between the master and slave was personal in nature, and a sale of slaves, though lawful was not ethical. We have seen that Badauni (1591–2) quotes a saying attributed to the Prophet that a slave-seller is a person, with two others, whom God curses.[80] Although a flourishing slave trade existed between Delhi and Ghaznin in the thirteenth and fourteenth centuries, there are two passages in Nizamuddin Auliya's conversations which suggest at least a mild disapproval of those who participated in the trade.[81] Akbar's prohibition of slave trade, first issued in 1562–3 and strengthened later,[82] was thus in line with an ethical doctrine developing within Muslim thought.

The disapproval of slave trade naturally led to the questioning of whether free persons (hurr, pl. *ahrar*) could be made into slaves. That non-Muslims could be enslaved in military raids was accepted for a fact of life in the thirteenth and fourteenth centuries even in sufic literature.[83] But even this became a matter of controversy in the fifteenth century. It is reported by Badauni that in an assembly of a hundred and twenty jurists convened before Sultan Mahmud Sharqi, Samauddin argued that non-Muslims of hostile territory could not be enslaved, though Qazi A'zam of Lakhnauti presented the opposite case. Badauni felt that the latter had had the better of the argument;[84] yet the fact of there having been such a controversy itself is significant.

Another aspect of the debate was whether distressed parents could sell their children. Apparently, under the pressure of slave-purchasers, certain scholars of Agra, like Mufti Bahauddin, issued an opinion during the famine of 1556–7, permitting such a practice; others like Shaikh Mubarak (the father of Abul Fazl) and the orthodox theologian, Mian Hatim, refused to endorse it.[85] Badauni's own sympathies were with the latter view, and in his *Nijatur Rashid* (1590–1) he held that one of the evil practices found among the Muslims much more than the followers of other religions, and especially in India, was the selling away of the freeborn as slaves. Yet he praised God that in more recent times 'this practice has been abandoned to some degree.'[86]

There was good Quranic sanction, as noted earlier, for considering the liberation of a slave a most praiseworthy act. This view coincided with the growing recognition that slavery was a most unnatural state for a free-born man, the recognition extended, as we have seen, to cover non-Muslims as well. But once a non-Muslim was enslaved, and became a convert to Islam, freeing such a slave in circumstances where manumission would lead to apostasy by the slave, compelled weighing of the merit of manumission against the dire sin of colluding in apostasy. Nevertheless, the grant of freedom to a slave had become so meritorious in Muslim ethics that Nizamuddin Auliya had no hesitation (though with tears in his eyes) to approve of such manumission.[87] Here, again, Akbar followed the logic of an established trend in Islamic tradition when during the famine of 1594, he ordered that parents who sold their children under compulsion could recover them by returning the amount they had received, though, as one has to presume from the context, this might involve a return to the children's original religion.[88] In 1680, in the time of Aurangzeb, it could be successfully argued that the return of a child in such cases involved no sin, because the reversion of a child to the religion of his parents involved no act of apostasy on his part, he being a minor.[89]

The foregoing discussion of certain elements in medieval Indo-Muslim attitude towards what appear to us as gross violation of any credible system of social justice shows that we are not dealing here with any closed system. Nor was thought so much bound with theology that growing ethical perceptions had no effect on it. It is true that there were few spirits bold enough like Abul Fazl to claim that if Imam Abu Hanifa had been alive in his day, he would have written a different interpretation of law (*fiqh*).[90] But the change, however constricted by original premises, is nonetheless perceptible over time in the attitudes to hierarchy, women and slaves. The conditions of India, rather than Hindu thought directly, exerted their influence too, as Islam had to come to terms with a long-term coexistence with Hinduism. Sympathies tended to cross religious boundaries, at least at the level of ethical conduct, even in a man so orthodox as Abdul Qadir Badauni. If, for the reason I set out at the beginning of this essay, no vision of social justice, as we understand it today, could be expected from medieval thought, we still have gropings towards such social justice. And these are especially precious, because each represented an expansion of the human spirit. It is precisely the presence of such human spirit that, in the final analysis, enables us to judge the historical level of each civilization.

NOTES

1. John Rawls, *A Theory of Justice*, Cambridge, Mass. 1971, p. 3.
2. Ibid., p. 9.

3. Ibid., p. 60.

4. Quoted from Bukhari, *Sahih*, by Maxime Rodinson, *Mohammad*, Eng. tr., Penguin Books, 1973, p. 282.

5. Badauni, *Nijatur Rashid*, ed. S. Moinul Haq, Lahore, 1972, pp. 21–2.

6. Quran, II, 209.

7. Quran, III, 155–8.

8. Quran, IV, 62.

9. For the rather unconvincing view of commentators that the persons in authority referred to were the Prophet's own appointees alone, see Reuben Levy, *The Social Structure of Islam*, Cambridge, 1957, p. 276.

10. Quran, II, 275.

11. Quran, IX, 97.

12. 'He (Muhammad) had conquered an empire for those who had rejected him, the Quraysh. A not uncommon outcome of revolutions' (Rodinson, *Muhammad*, p. 295).

13. Quran, II, 228.

14. Ibid., II, 223, 228.

15. Quran, IV, 3.

16. Quran, II, 177.

17. Julius Wellhausen, *The Arab Kingdom and its Fall*, Eng. tr., London, 1927/1973. Wellhausen's German text came out in 1902; but the pioneering work had been done in the field by Ignaz Goldziher in two essays, 'The Arabic Tribes and Islam' and 'Arab and Ajam', published in his *Muslim Studies*, Eng. tr., I, London, 1967, pp. 45–136, the studies having been published in German (*Muhammadanische studien*) in 1889–90.

18. Apart from his well-known measures against the mawwali discussed by Wellhausen, pp. 243–57, 496–500, one may recall his reprimand to Muhammad ibn Qasim, the conqueror of Sind, for praising the heroism of a *mawla* in the same breath as Arab warriors. The *mawla*, he declared, must be deemed 'a wretch', 'a hypocrite', not deserving to be mentioned in despatches (*Chachnama*, ed. Umar Daudpota, Hyderabad-Deccan, 1939, p. 192).

19. *The Abbasid Revolution*, Cambridge, 1970.

20. See Wellhausen's insightful passage on these results, *The Arab Kingdom*, pp. 556ff.

21. Joseph Schacht, *The Origins of Muhammadan Jurisprudence*, Oxford, 1950. Schacht acknowledges his debt to the previous work of Goldziher and Margoliouth.

22. Ibid., p. 283.

23. Ibid., pp. 266–7. It is interesting to find Badauni giving evidence for *mut'a* sanctioned by the Prophet and then giving contradictory traditions about who abolished the practice (*Nijatu'r Rashid*, pp. 434–8).

24. Schacht, ibid., pp. 264–6.

25. 'It cannot be denied ... that the Islamic spirit helped to make good treatment of slaves a duty and inner duty, and to encourage an attitude which had its roots in the oldest documents of Islam' (Goldziher, *Muslim Studies*, I, p. 117).

26. Cf. Muhsin Mahdi, *Ibn Khaldun's Philosophy of History*, Chicago, 1964, pp. 248–51.

27. Barani's main ideas in this respect are found scattered throughout his *Tarikh-i Firuz Shahi*, ed. Saiyid Ahmad Khan, W. Nassau Lees and Maulavi Kabiruddin, Bib. Ind., Calcutta, 1860–2, but especially in its introduction, and in Advice XXII in the same author's *Fatawa-i Jahandari* (tr. M. Habib and Afsar Begum, *Medieval India Quarterly*, III (3–4), 1958, pp. 181–8).

28. *Medieval India Quarterly*, ibid., p. 224.

29. Louis Dumont, *Homo Hierarchicus*, Paladin edn, London, 1972. Without accepting Dumont's interpretation of the caste system (cf. Irfan Habib's critique in *Essays in Indian History*, New Delhi, 1995, pp. 161ff), I find it still useful as a standard 'brahmanical' exposition, a kind of 'ideal' to which reality may be counterposed.

30. *Chachnama*, pp. 214–15.

31. Edward C. Sachau (tr.), *Alberuni's India*, London, 1910, I, pp. 99–100.

32. Cf. Irfan Habib, *Essays in Indian History*, pp. 172–3.

33. *A'in-i Akbari*, Nawal Kishore ed., Lucknow, 1892, pp. 42–5.

34. Barani, *Tarikh-i Firuz Shahi*, p. 39.

35. Sachau, I, p. 101.

36. *Bhangri Bhangi Khurafati* (*Tarikh-i Firuz Shahi*, p. 487).

37. Abul Fazl, *Akbarnama*, ed. Ahmad Ali and Abdur Rahim, Bib. Ind., Calcutta, 1873–87, III, p. 604.

38. *Chachnama*, p. 195.

39. *Nijatur Rashid*, p. 264.

40. Reuben Levy, *The Social Structure of Islam*, Cambridge, 1957, pp. 97–8.

41. Quran, V, p. 12.

42. Quran, II, p. 282.

43. Shireen Moosvi, 'Travails of a Mercantile Community in Surat', *PIHC*, 52nd session. (1991–2), Delhi, 1992, pp. 401–9.

44. See translations of the relevant documents in ibid., pp. 404–9. The original texts are in *Bibliothique Nationale (Bib. Nat.)*, Blochet, Suppl. Pers. 482, a collection compiled *c.* 1650.

45. *Nijatur Rashid*, pp. 434–5.

46. Ibid., p. 437.

47. Letter to Abdur Rahim Khan-i Khanan (*Maktubat-i Imam Rabbani*, Nawal Kishore, Lucknow, 1889, I, pp. 190–1).

48. Amir Khusrau, *Hasht Bihisht*, ed. Sulaiman Ashraf, Aligarh, 1336/ 1918, pp. 26-9; Isami, *Futuh-us Salatin*, ed. A.S. Usha, Madras, 1948, pp. 134–5.

49. *Nijatur Rashid*, p. 460.

50. *Maktubat-i Imam Rabbani*, III, p. 69.

51. *Hasht Bihisht*, pp. 28–9.

52. *Nijatu-r Rashid*, p. 460.

53. Shams Siraj Afif, *Tarikh-i Firuz Shahi*, ed. Vilayat Husain, Bib. Ind., Calcutta, 1888–91, p. 352.

54. Quoted in Levy, *Social Structure of Islam*, p. 92.

55. *Nuh Sipihr*, ed. Wahid Mirza, London, 1950, pp. 194–5.

56. *The Travels of Ibn Battuta* (AD *1325–1354*), tr. H.R.A. Gibb, London, Indian reprint, New Delhi, 1993, III, p. 616.

57. *Nijatu-r Rashid*, p. 412.

58. *Hamchu Hindu zan jahan ra*, etc.

59. Cf. *Nuh Sipihr*, pp. 194–5.

60. Abul Fazl, *Akbarnama*, first version, B. L. Add. 27, 247, f.296a.

61. A. Monserrate, *Commentary on his Journey to the Court of Akbar*, tr. J.S. Hoyland and S.N. Banerjee, Calcutta, 1922, pp. 43–8.

62. Badauni, *Muntakhabu-t Tawarikh*, ed. Ali, Ahmad and Less, Bib. Ind., Calcutta, 1864–9, II, pp. 355–6.

63. *A'in-i Akbari*, ed. H. Blochmann, Bib. Ind., Calcutta, 1866–7, II, p. 243.

64. *Akbarnama*, first version, B. L. Add. 27, 247, f. 327b. Cf. II, pp. 306, 338, 355–6.

65. Monserrate, *Commentary*, pp. 61–2.

66. *Akbarnama*, III, pp. 402–3.

67. *Muntakhab-ut Tawarikh*, II, p. 376.

68. *A'in-i Akbari*, ed. Blochmann, I, p. 284.

69. Ibid., II, p. 235.

70. See, however, Irfan Habib in *PIHC*, 53rd session, 1992–3, pp. 303–5.

71. Dev Raj Chanana, *Slavery in Ancient India as depicted in Pali and Sanskrit Texts*, New Delhi, 1960.

72. Cf. Pushpa Prasad, 'Female Slavery in the 13th-century Gujarat Documents in the *Lekhapadhati*', *IHR,* xv (1–2), 1988–9, pp. 269–75.

73. Tapan Raychaudhuri and Irfan Habib (eds), *Cambridge Economic History of India*, I, Cambridge, 1982, pp. 89–93.

74. Both these aspects are brought out very well in the anecdote of the recovery of Khwaja Khujandi's slave by the prayers of Shaikh Nizamuddin Auliya (*Khairul Majalis*, ed. Khaliq Ahmad Nizami, Aligarh, 1959, p. 184).

75. Amir Hasan Sijzi, *Fawaid-u'l Fawad*, ed. M. Latif Malik, Lahore, 1966, p. 5.

76. For this see Abul Fath Gilani (1581), *Ruq'at*, ed. M. Bashir Husain, Lahore, 1968, p. 22.

77. *Nijatur Rashid*, pp. 242–3.

78. Ibid., p. 243.

79. Cf. Nur Turk and his slave working as cotton carder, anecdote in *Fawaid-ul Fawad*, pp. 334–5.

80. *Nijatur Rashid*, p. 264.

81. *Fawaid-u'l Fawad*, pp. 14–15, 192–3.

82. See Irfan Habib, *PIHC,* 53rd session, 1992–3, pp. 300–1, for an adequate discussion. It is interesting, however, that Rafiuddin Ibrahim Shirazi attributed Akbar's action in his early years to a young Brahman woman then receiving his favour (*Tazkarat-ul Muluk*, B. L. Add. 23833, ff. 231b–232a).

83. *Fawaidu-l Fawad*, pp. 278, 379; *Khairu-l Majalis*, 236–8.

84. *Nijatu-r Rashid*, p. 240.

85. *Muntakhab-ut Tawarikh*, III, pp. 66–89.

86. *Nijatu-r Rashid*, pp. 239–40.

87. *Fawaid-u'l Fawad*, pp. 278–9, 339–40. Nizamuddin conceded, however, that the conventional theologians (*Ulama-i Zahiri*) would forbid such action.

88. *Muntakhab-ut Tawarikh*, II, p. 390.

89. *Waqa'i 'Sarkar Ranthambhor wa Suba Ajmer*, transcript in Library of CAS in History, Aligarh, II, p. 578.

90. *Muntakhabu-t Tawarikh*, III, p. 79.

THE RELIGIOUS WORLD

AKBAR'S PROGRESS
FROM AJMER TO THE SALT RANGE
1577-78

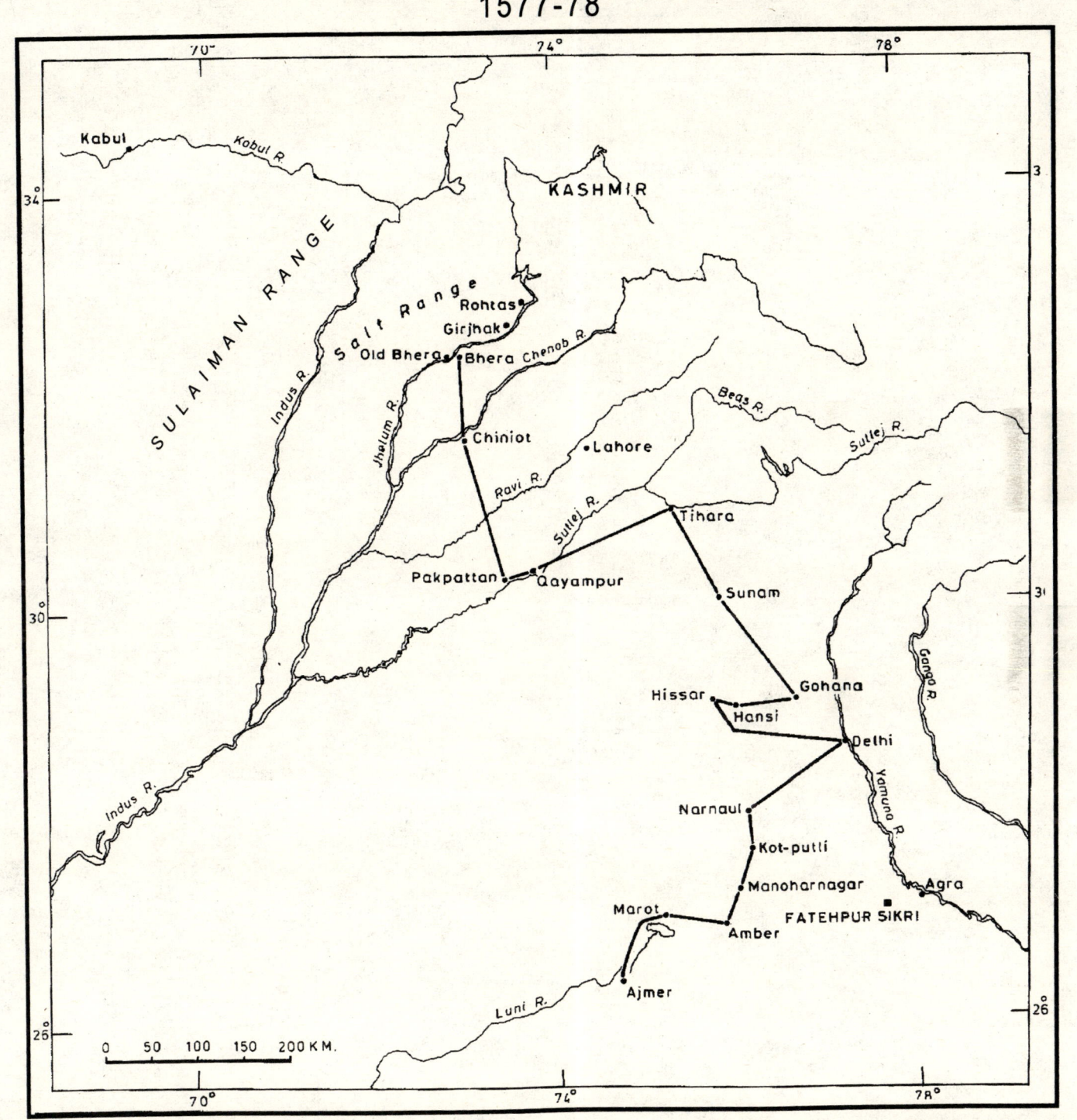

13

The 'Vision' in the Salt Range, 1578

An Interpretation

The development of Akbar's religious ideas, all historians would agree, reached a critical point in the late 1570s. Why this crisis arrived could be attributed to several factors. Badauni attributes it to Akbar's increasing irritation with the theologians, the influence upon him of his Rajput queens and of Birbal, and the pantheistic and heterodox ideas insinuated into his mind by Shaikh Mubarak, his son Abul Fazl and others. But there was a special, psychological dimension to this crisis as well, which cannot be lost sight of. This was a factor too that made the crisis especially severe for Akbar.

While describing the construction of the famous 'Ibadat Khana at Fatehpur Sikri in 983/1575–6, Badauni tells us that since Akbar had won so many victories and the empire had so greatly expanded, he was increasingly affected by a sense of gratitude to God:

Respect for the Real Benefactor established itself in his heart, and in order to render thanks to those acts of assistance, by way of humility and sincerity, he used to sit in early mornings on an old stone in an old cell, near the Imperial Palaces, but away on one side from habitation, when he used to become engrossed in meditation.[1]

It was natural that in such condition, he should turn particularly to mysticism, which seemed to offer to the votary an intense personal relationship with God. Again, Badauni, who was a direct witness of what took place in those days at Fatehpur Sikri, tells us of Akbar's introduction to Ibn al-Arabi's extreme mystical and semi-pantheistic concepts as something that had come about before 986/1578–9:

For some time Shaikh Tajuddin, son of Shaikh Zakariya Ajodhani Dehlawi, who was called 'Tajul Arifin' by many notables, was the principal disciple of Shaikh Zaman Panipati, author of *Sharh-i Lawaih* and many learned works. In the science of mysticism and of Divine Unity he was a second Ibn al-'Arabi and had written a long commentary on *Nuzhatu- l Arwah*. In the manner described, His majesty summoning him for several nights, heard from him the ecstatic ravings and futilities of the mystic. He was not constrained by any obligation to the demands of orthodox law, and so laid (before the king) the doctrine of Unity of Existence (*Wahdat-i Wujud*), which the false mystics believe in, and which ultimately leads to libertarianism and heresy....[2]

One of the mystic (sufic) practices that began to attract Akbar now was abstention from meat. Abul Fazl aptly gives to meat-less diet the name *sufiana* in the *A'in-i Akbari*.[3] Badauni was later to attribute this to the influence of Birbal and Akbar's Hindu queens, who argued against beef-eating,[4] but here the abstention was from all meat, and the source of inspiration was clearly the sufic tradition, based originally perhaps more on ascetic intent than on love of animal life which Akbar deliberately read into it. Certainly, the latter reading was much in accord with the logic of Ibn al-'Arabi's pantheism. It may be recalled that contacts with Jains were established only at a later date.

Consistent with Akbar's internal striving for spiritual solace was his great devotion, exhibited at this time, to the Ajmer shrine (the *dargah* of Muinuddin Chishti), which amounted to sheer addiction. He went there repeatedly; and the height was reached when in March 1576, he traversed the last stage of the journey on foot 'making externalia a means of increasing internal illumination'.[5] He returned to Ajmer the same year in September, and was so swayed by holy inspiration that he even expressed a desire to go on the Haj pilgrimage; in lieu of this, a splendid Haj-party on the emperor's behalf was sent off from Ajmer, with presents of Rs 6 lakh, and no less than 12,000 robes of honour to be distributed.[6] If one were to disregard the element of vanity behind this display of splendour, it can hardly be denied that when Akbar left Ajmer in October 1577 his personal religious affiliations, however deepened and spiritualized, were within the framework of Islam.

Akbar had been turning to Ajmer not for religious reasons alone. The pacification and administration of Gujarat and Mewar needed his attention; and he left Ajmer to make a tour of Gogunda and Udaipur, and then returned. But when he left it on 15 October, it was not to march back to his capital Fatehpur Sikri, but to make his way to the Punjab.[7]

One reason why Akbar took this decision is stated by Abul Fazl to lie in his secret thoughts 'for hastening to Kabul'.[8] It may be safely assumed that it had much to do with affairs in Kabul, where Akbar's younger brother, Mirza Hakim, had long been ruling as an independent ruler. He had previously tried his luck against Akbar by invading the Punjab in 1566, and was to do so again in 1580. But it is possible that this time Akbar had certain intentions of his own. Shah Tahmasp died in May 1576; and reports must have arrived of the subsequent happenings in Iran under his successor Shah Ismail, who killed a number of his brothers and relatives and was soon to be done to death himself.[9] This might have been regarded by Akbar and his advisers as an opportune moment to secure Kabul, or at least clip Mirza Hakim's wings.

There, then, began a march, seemingly leisurely, but presumably intended to gather reinforcements as Akbar proceeded north and north-westwards. Passing through Amber, Manoharnagar (a fortress whose foundations he now laid), Kotputli and Narnaul, Akbar reached Delhi, on 27 Azar (8 November).[10] But he left it on 26 Dai (7 December), to go hunting, proceeding first to Hissar, then to Hansi and Gohana, and thence turning back towards Delhi. From here he wheeled back to Sunam, then going to Shadiwal and Tihara on the Sutlej. Here again, a sharp change in direction brought him to Qayampur. Crossing the Sutlej on a bridge of boats, he came to Patan or Pakpatan, which he reached on 12 Isfandarmuz (23 February 1578). Proceeding from here, the Ravi was crossed at Khanpur (not identified) on 3 Farwardin (14 March), and the Chenab at Chiniot on 31 Farwardin (10 April).[11] Akbar then proceeded towards Bhera, in the vicinity of which a great hunt for wild animals was to be organized.

If we draw this itinerary on the map, a curious indecisive mode of progress appears there. There are inexplicable turn-abouts at Hissar, Gohana and Tihara. Lahore is totally bypassed. It is possible that Akbar was trying to conceal his intentions by avoiding a march in the straight direction of Kabul, a device to put Mirza Hakim and his counsellors off their guard. This would be quite in character with a master tactician like Akbar.

Yet, what is interesting in the routes adopted is also the religious or rather mystic dimension. An event to be borne in mind is the appearance of the comet, which passed its perihelion on 26 October, just after Akbar had left Ajmer. Contemporaries attached an ominous significance to the appearance of comets, and Abul Fazl is not above offering a detailed 'scientific' expositions of its ill effects, reinforced by historical experience.[12] The recent events in Iran showed, to Abul Fazl's consternation, that the comet of 1577 was no less malevolent.[13] One must assume that Akbar, though not an easy prey to superstition, was not immune from one that could be so reasonably argued and so closely illustrated from facts. One must suppose, given his acutely activated spiritual senses, that anxiety for divine protection and gratification of having been protected so far made him especially vulnerable to mystic invocations and ritual. This tended to give a *rationale* to the turns and twists in Akbar's marches.

We are fortunate that we can supplement here the more courtly and diplomatic version of events in the final text of the *Akbarnama* by an earlier text of the work, preserved in a unique copy of the British Library (Add. 27247).[14] At Narnaul on 21 November, Akbar especially went to the house of Shaikh Nizam who, says Abul Fazl patronizingly enough, had opened a spiritual 'shop' there. Yet, in spite of Abul Fazl's later belittling of what the mystics could offer to a spiritually rich person like Akbar, it is apparent that he felt himself called upon to explain why the emperor should have gone to Shaikh Nizam seeking instruction on things divine.[15] In December, Akbar made a point of going to Hansi to pray at the shrine of Shaikh Jamal, a disciple of the famous Chishti mystic, Fariduddin Ganj Shakar (thirteenth century).[16] He was still so respectful towards religious divines that when one noted theologian, Muhammad Yazdi, arrived at his camp about the time (about 31 January 1578), he sent him to Shaikh Abdun Nabi, the orthodox theologian and minister for revenue grants, accompanied by his own son, Sultan Murad.[17]

A little later at Shadiwal, when Akbar apparently decided to make a journey to Pakpattan, the place of the tomb and shrine of Farid Ganj Shakar, he decided not to eat meat on Fridays till he reached that place, as an act of ascetic devotion to that saint. Clearly, it was in his mind, as Abul Fazl explicitly proclaims here, that killing and eating an animal and so making one's stomach 'a graveyard of animals' was unethical in itself.[18] Arriving at Pakpattan Akbar performed all the rituals that a devotee was expected to perform and met two notable Sufis.[19] When at Chiniot on 10 April, Akbar issued an order banning bird-catching and fishing, while speaking 'many truths' about these 'improper acts'.[20]

We can see here how Akbar's mind was gravitating towards Sufism, and how, what was an ascetic practice in Sufism appeared to him an act of ethical conduct. It created the background for the dramatic incident in the Salt Range in May 1578. The incident is described by Arif Qandahari, writing in 1580–1, without his being conscious of Akbar formulating any new religious ideas. He is followed by Abul Fazl (two versions), Shaikh Nizamuddin Ahmad and Badauni. We could do best by combining the facts as they give them.

Having reached Bhera, Akbar crossed the Jhelam on 22 April. From Girjhak to Old Bhera, both on the right bank of the river, a distance of 25 *kurohs* (or some 60 miles) intervened. A line of beaters was established with these as terminal points and with the river as the natural barrier. Wild animals were to be collected and then herded together in what, perhaps, could be one of the largest *qamargha* hunts ever organized. Troops were deployed to make it a success. On 25 April, Mirza Yusuf Khan, Naurang Khan and Asaf Khan were despatched to take charge of the arrangements. All the nobles and other mansabdars, 'troop by troop, army by army' (i.e. their contingents) were sent to take up their positions. On 27 April, the Baluch chiefs from across the Indus, recently subjugated (Haji Khan, Jatta Khan, etc.), arrived to render obeisance, and they too were sent off to take part in the enterprise.[21] Clearly, the aim Akbar had in mind was to organize an enormous military exercise.

All the mansabdars' contingents could now be seen in operation, and tested for numerical strength and efficiency. Conducted almost in sight of what was Akbar's great border fort at this time, namely Rohtas, the exercise would be a show of strength for Mirza Hakim and others at Kabul to take full cognizance of. If the qamargha is seen in this light, the actual slaughter of animals when herded into one mass by the beaters comes out as only a very secondary object of the 'hunt'.

It was on 4 May, when the time for the slaughter of the wild herd driven into the designated ground was near, that, as Akbar was sitting under a tree, he suddenly had an inner 'illumination from divine light'; a 'strange condition' (*halate 'ajib*) came over him; a 'strong emotion' (*jazba-i qawi*) took possession of him, so three historians have told us.[22] It was a public change of heart, a scene for later court painters to paint in *Akbarnama* illustrations. As Akbar came out of his reverie, he ordered the lines to be withdrawn and the hemmed-in beasts, 'some thousands' to be left free. Fast messengers were dispatched to put the order into effect.[23]

We can see now that Akbar's spiritual inclinations shown in periodic abstention from meat and prohibition of bird-killing and fishing were leading up to such a denouement. A slaughter of animals on this scale would have been totally opposed to his developing inclinations towards the protection of animal life.

Akbar took, however, another step which showed his own religious, perhaps partly superstitious, anxieties. He had let his hair grow like the Hindus ('the truth-following Hindus'), contrary to the Muslim practice—'the practice of my ancestors'. He now decided to cut his hair short, and so revert to the practice previously abandoned.[24] This decision to revert to this 'approved practice' (*sunnat-i sunnia*) was noted with gratification by Arif Qandahri, writing within two years or so of the event.[25] Was Akbar here sincerely contrite at this deviation from the rites of his own faith, or was it a gesture made for the consumption of the overwhelming Muslim population across the Indus? The latter, though not impossible, is unlikely; and one must suppose that Akbar at this point of time had come heavily under the influence of Muslim mysticism.

This is further confirmed by his other steps. Greatly trying to establish the spiritual significance of the vision he had received, he built a large pavilion and laid out an extensive garden;[26] but, most significantly, he named the place the 'Little Mecca' (*Makka-i Khurd*).[27] His vision then was altogether within the Islamic framework.

Akbar's spiritual experience and the calling off of the qamargha had no diplomatic and military sequel. A great military exercise had taken place. A line extending for much over 60 miles had been formed: if there was one person for every two yards more than 50,000 troops must have been deployed. The message that such an assemblage of armed men ready for action would get to those for whom it was intended.

If there was no sequel, much was perhaps due to the intervention of Akbar's mother, Hamida Banu Mariyam Zamani. The movement of her son westward with an increasing rally of troops could not conceal from her what Akbar's intentions were. It was clearly this, not her anxiety about Akbar's health[28]—for she could hardly have learnt of the old Bhera vision and responded to it so fast—that brought her to Bhera from Fatehpur Sikri in pursuit of her son. She wished to avoid, one must suppose, an open strife in the family. A compromise was effected. Mirza Hakim's full sister, Sakina Banu, was now sent as envoy to Mirza Hakim, for an offer of marriage of Salim (who was then nine years) to Mirza Hakim's daughter. The kingdom of Kabul could then be claimed for Salim in inheritance.[29] At the same time, a mission was sent to Badakhshan to accept Shah Rukh Mirza's mother's apologies for her son's conduct.[30] A kind of paramountcy over the two Timurid states still surviving on the border could possibly have been in contemplation. For the moment, however, the military campaign was abandoned, and Akbar began his journey back to Fatehpur Sikri by the more conventional route.

The entire episode suggests that in the first phase of his spiritual crisis, Akbar's effort was to turn heavily to the Islamic mystical sources. One can then see how this would logically lead in 1579 to his reading the *Khutba* or Friday sermon in the Fatehpur Sikri mosque and to the mahzar or statement of eminent theologians recognizing his special position as interpreter of Muslim law.[31]

Why this path, involving a certain amount of Muslim orthodoxy with religious tolerance, could not be continued by Akbar, cannot, perhaps be answered from the point of view of political exigencies alone, much though, and quite rightly, Iqtidar Alam Khan has stressed the relationship between the two in an important essay.[32] One must give due weight to the fact that Akbar, in his spiritual anxieties, demanded a kind of solace, a degree of internal peace that Islam or, for that matter, any religion could not provide him with. Already, late in 1578 at Fatehpur Sikri, in an answer to Mirza Aziz Koka, Akbar would cast doubt on men's claims to divine incarnation in India and prophethood elsewhere.[33] The doubts would grow apace, and create that stormy mental crisis of 1579–80, out of which a cogent perception of Divine omnipotence and the equal illusoriness of World and Religion would be grasped and the principle of Sulh-i Kul, Absolute Peace, crafted to create for Akbar his own world of spirit.[34] It was essentially the work of a reasoner, if not fully of a rationalist; and we may be belittling the earnestness of the intellectual and moral endeavour if we suppose either that it was a chance synthesis of several religions or a mere religious rationalization of political expediency. The incident of 1578 that we have analysed shows clearly enough that politics and religion ran for him a parallel, rather than an intermixing, course.

NOTES

1. Badauni, *Muntakhab'ul Lubab*, ed. W.N. Lees and Ahmad Ali, Calcutta, 1865, II, p. 200. This personal need for solace on Akbar's side is lost sight of in Abul Fazl's long passage on the *Ibadat Khana*.

2. Badauni, II, p. 258.

3. *A'in-i Akbari*, I, ed. H. Blochmann, Calcutta, 1866–7, I, p. 59.

4. Badauni, II, pp. 302–3.

5. *Akbarnama*, Bib. Ind. ed. II, p. 164.

6. Ibid., pp. 191–2, 217.

7. *Akbarnama*, III, p. 220.

8. Ibid., p. 244.

9. These events are described in *Akbarnama*, III, pp. 224–7.

10. Ibid., p. 227.

11. Ibid., p. 239.

12. Ibid., pp. 221–4.

13. Ibid., pp. 224–7.

14. This was used occasionally by Henry Beveridge in his translation of the *Akbarnama*; it is surprising that he did not appreciate its full historical value.

15. The explanation is longer in Add. 27247, f. 291a than in *Akbarnama*, III, p. 227.

16. *Akbarnama*, III, p. 232.

17. Add. 27247, ff. 292b–293a; *Akbarnama*, III, pp. 232–3.

18. Add. 27247, f. 293a. In his final version, Abul Fazl omits here all references to Shaikh Farid's shrine; but this is a misleading omission.

19. *Akbarnama*, III, p. 236.

20. Add. 27247, f. 293(a). No reference in final version.

21. All these details are from Add. 27247, f. 294a., Cf. *Akbarnama*, III, p. 241, which has shortened the narrative somewhat.

22. *Akbarnama*, version of Add. 27247, f. 294a and the published edn, pp. 241–2 (the first statements); Nizamuddin Ahmad, *Tabaqat-i Akbari*, ed. B. De., Calcutta, 1931, II, p. 337, and Badauni, II, pp. 243–54 (the third statement).

23. *Akbarnama*, both versions.

24. *Akbarnama*, III, p. 242 (Add. 27247, f. 294a, has a clear text.

25. *Arif Qandahari,Tarikh-i Akbari*, ed. Muinuddin Nadvi *et al.*, Rampur, 1962, p. 254.

26. Nizamuddin Ahmad, II, p. 338; Badauni, II, p. 254.

27. Arif Qandahari, p. 236. Being the earliest source, with no axe to grind, there is no reason to disbelieve the information he gives. Abul Fazl and the other historians, who seem to follow him here, omit all references to the name.

28. As supposed by V.A. Smith, *Akbar the Great Mogul*, 2nd edn, Indian reprint, Delhi, 1962, p. 114.

29. *Akbarnama*, III, pp. 243.

30. Ibid., p. 243.

31. See *Akbarnama*, Add. 27247, ff. 298b–299a, ed. pp. 268–73; Nizamuddin Ahmad, II, pp. 343–16; Badauni, II, pp. 270–2.

32. 'Nobility under Akbar and the Development of his Religious Policy', *JRAS* (1968), pp. 29–36.

33. I would continue to urge that for Akbar's own final ideas, an accurate understanding of Abul Fazl's chapter *A'in-i Rahnamuni* in *A'in-i Akbari*, ed. H. Blockmann, I, pp. 158–61, is indispensable.

34. Ibid.

14

Sulh-i Kul and the Religious Ideas of Akbar

That Akbar formulated a religious policy for the Mughal Empire that can in some ways claim to be a forerunner of the secular aspects of modern Indian polity, is now almost a historical cliche; that he founded a new religion is a school textbook dogma that serious historians have long been trying to eradicate without much success.

My present endeavour is not so much as to concentrate on Akbar's religious policy, but to treat of Akbar's religious philosophy, beliefs or ideas (whatever word be the most appropriate) that he came to entertain during the last twenty-five years or so of his life. These cannot be separated from his positive practical measures; and this will be clear, I hope, from my own exposition. But ideas will form my starting-point, and the measures will serve only to illustrate.

Much can be written on the evolution of Akbar's religious ideas. It became part of the imperial legend that one of the miraculous powers of Akbar was that, though he remained formally illiterate (ummi) like the Arabian Prophet, he could understand and appreciate the highest thoughts, principles and works of art and literature.[1] It is almost certain that, though encouraged by Akbar himself, as his Happy Sayings reproduced in the *A'in-i Akbari* show, his illiteracy was more or less a myth. The basis was probably no more than this that as a child Akbar had paid more attention to playing games than to learning the alphabet. Quite possibly, the habit of reading directly never grew because of the custom of officials reading out documents and books to princes. But a man who had such an eye for calligraphy and book illustration, and built up a splendid library, could not have been illiterate by any standard. It does seem probable, however, that Akbar did not obtain formal education in the theological and legal sciences that formed the core of all knowledge in the eyes of the orthodox. This may be because his tutor Abdul Latif was liberal, as suggested by Badauni,[2] or because Akbar had little inclination towards the dull details of theology.

It is possible that Akbar's later liberation from theology owed a little at least to the absence of his personal commitment to this or that school, forged in the process of early education. But while Akbar's knowledge of Muslim theology probably never became profound, like many 'laymen', he stood, in his youth, in considerable awe of the prowess of religious men. This awe amounted often to superstition, as exhibited by his self-deprecation before Mulla Abdullah Sultanpuri,[3] his excessive adulation of the dargah of Ajmer,[4] and his faith in the prayers of Shaikh Salim Chishti.[5] It must be remembered that by his time the mystics were as much a part of the Muslim religious establishment as any mullas or conventional theologians.

As Iqtidar Alam Khan has shown, Akbar's early measures of tolerance, and the abolition of the pilgrimage tax and jizya in the early 1560s were episodic and of little immediate significance.[6] Writing later, Abul Fazl probably exaggerates their importance. On the other hand, Akbar soon initiated a vigorous 'Islamic' policy, illustrated by the *Fathnama-i Chittor*, the proclamation on the fall of Chittor in 1568, where the infidels are reviled; the reimposition of jizya in 1575 is also symbolic of this policy. Indeed, Akbar, bolstered by his success against the Rajputs, was looking forward to widespread acclamation as a great conqueror of Islam.

It was probably here, in the realm of relations between political sovereignty and theological Law, that the contradiction germinated, which later on led to a complete reformulation of Akbar's religious views. There is no doubt that Safavid Iran exercised considerable influence on the minds and manners of Akbar's court. The Safavid Shah was also a religious figure, a representative of the imam, and thus superior to all religious divines of the country. It was not unnatural that Akbar should aspire to such a status within the Sunni framework. It was obviously with this view that Ibadat Khana consultations or discussions of theologians were initiated. Akbar hoped to implement what theologians told him, and, in return, secure from the latter a recognition of his own supreme position.

But, as Badauni lamented, the theologians could not agree on any thing,[7] while, to their credit, on some matters like the number of lawful wives, they could not reconcile Akbar's own practice with any reading of the Quranic injunctions. In 1579, they were at last persuaded to sign a statement of testimony (mahzar) recognizing that Akbar possessed a particular religious status. The text has fortunately been preserved for us in the *Tabaqat-i Akbari* of Nizamuddin Ahmad[8] and the *Muntakhabut Tawarikh* of Abdul Qadir Badauni.[9] The statement admits that the position of a just king (*Sultan-i 'Adil*) is above that of a *mujtahid* (interpreter of law); that Akbar was such a Sultan-i 'Adil;

and that Akbar, therefore, could (a) accept any of the existing divergent authoritative interpretations of mujtahids, (b) give his own opinion on any matter, provided it did not violate the *nas* (Holy Quran). All the leading theologians at the court signed (i.e. affixed their seals), but we can see now that the mahzar did not ultimately meet Akbar's ambitions: Abul Fazl in his *Akbarnama* passes it by very casually.[10] Akbar's immediate attempt to take it seriously, and to abide by his newly gained religious status among Muslims by giving a Friday sermon, failed to enthuse either himself, or, apparently his audience.[11] The authority assigned to him was of marginal import, and yet a novelty considered dangerous in its implications by traditionalist Muslims.

Akbar had already begun looking towards other religions, first out of curiosity, and after the mahzar, out of an increasing desire to put his own position beyond the narrow framework of traditional Islam. Acquaviva's Jesuit mission came soon after the mahzar. The 1580–1 rebellion set a seal on the alienation of Akbar from Islamic orthodoxy; and the phase opened in which Akbar defined his own views more and more sharply. It is with a restatement of these views that I shall henceforth be chiefly concerned.

It may be argued by the sceptic that so much has been written on Akbar's religious views that a fresh exposition can only be superfluous. And yet there is need, first of all, to establish accurately what views Akbar held or developed after the failure of his appeasement of the Muslim orthodoxy that had culminated in the mahzar of 1579, that is during the period 1580–1605, when, according to popular textbook writers, he created a religion, the *Din-i Ilahi*, to absorb all religions.

Our primary source for Akbar's ideas of this final phase of his life are Abul Fazl's *Akbarnama* and *A'in-i Akbari*. These works were read out to Akbar and personally approved by him.[12] They were, therefore, no mere official works by a hack. Nor did they necessarily contain only the ideas which Abul Fazl himself held. They contained the ideas and reflected the ideology of the patron, though the draftsman himself was a master of style and a scholar of no mean learning. In the urge to endorse or reject the contentions of the critic Badauni or the narratives of the Jesuit fathers, these two works have been strangely undervalued as the source of Akbar's belief and practice in religious matters. The effort here is to set matters right in this respect.

On reading the *Akbarnama* and the *A'in-i Akbari*, one realizes immediately that Akbar wished to assert his very strong belief in God; but his concept of the way God is to be worshipped was independent of either orthodox Islam or Hinduism. As the 'Happy Sayings' set out in the *A'in* show, he believed, as did the Sufis, that God is to be grasped and worshipped by different men according to the limitations of their knowledge. God was formless (*be-surat*) and could not be grasped in any form except by the greatest effort of the mind (*chira-dasti-i khyal*).[13] To worship such a one, physical action in prayer (*Suri-paristish*) was suitable only for the unawakened ones.[14] Otherwise, worship could only be an act of the heart. Elsewhere, Akbar is said to have held that the real act of God worship is to have 'an illuminated heart that loves Light' (*Raushan-dil-i nur dosti*).[15] Akbar, therefore, deprecated both the image-worship of the Hindus and the prayer-ritual of the Muslims. His deprecation of image-worship is particularly borne upon us when the author of the *Akbarnama* styles Todar Mal a 'simple one' (*sada-lauh*), because he mourned the loss of the idols he used to worship; it goes on to call him 'a blind follower of custom and narrow-mindedness.'[16] For the benefit of this famous revenue minister, Akbar also sermonized to the effect that no worship of God is superior to looking after the weak.[17]

The importance Akbar gave to Light might well be due to the fact that it is formless; and there was, therefore, a natural tendency to exalt the Sun, the source of Light, as is indicated in the *A'in*'s chapters, *A'in-i Rahnamuni* and *A'in-i Iradat Gazinan*.[18] Akbar said that 'the exalted Sun is of great benefit for rulers; and so they direct words of praise to it and count it God-worship, though the narrow-minded ones suspect them (of sun worship).'[19] Akbar obviously had in mind the Nauroz festivities of the Sassanid tradition, in which the Parsi worship of Sun and Light had a role. Akbar was thus attempting to reconcile that ancient royal tradition with his own theory of divine light.

The *A'in-i Rahnamuni* further reveals that Akbar's idea of God was heavily influenced by pantheism: God creates visible differences whereas the Reality is the same. 'One heart-ensnaring Beauty lights up thousands of curtains (*pardah*).' Akbar, indeed, protests that to ascribe evil to Satan (as is done by conventional Muslims) is really to limit the absoluteness of God. The evil of Satan too comes from God.[20] At the same time, he is no believer in divine incarnations. He makes a wry dig at this belief of popular Hinduism, when he says that in India no one claimed to be a prophet because all would-be prophets claimed to be 'God'.[21] Akbar thus expressed a positive disbelief in any visual appearance of the Creator in any form whatsoever.

Akbar saw a close relationship between the Divine Sovereign and the temporal sovereign. To see sovereigns (*farman dahan*) is considered to be worship of God;[22] and for sovereigns, in return, the dispensing of justice and administering the world, is the real mode of worship.[23]

The *A'in* accordingly styles sovereignty, in a well-known phrase, as farr-i izadi, divine light.[24]

As a sovereign, who is indeed 'the elect of God', Akbar saw himself in a direct relationship with God, independent of any religion. Predisposed to pantheism, he saw *din* (religion) itself to be as illusory as *dunya* (*A'in-i Rahnamuni*). To continue to follow the ritual of one's faith was a mere reflex or imitation (*taqlid*). In this respect, he exalted *aql* (reason) and condemned taqlid, arguing that if taqlid was desirable, all prophets would have merely followed old customs (and not brought forth new laws).[25] In this respect Akbar was thus following a tradition, once strong in classical antiquity, as against orthodox Islam, that of aql or Reason opposed to *naql* or imitation. But he used it to subject even Islam to a rational questioning.

He saw in Islam (as well as in other religions of his time), an illusory separateness from other religions, based on a differentiation in ritual and belief brought about by taqlid or imitation. It is significant that throughout the *Akbarnama* and the *A'in-i Akbari*, a very neutral terminology is adopted in references to Islam. Islam is not styled as such at all. It is usually called *Ahmadi-Kesh*, that is the Muhammadan doctrine, as one may say in English. *Ahmadi-Kesh* is clearly a term coined by Akbar or by Abul Fazl with his approval. No other work in Persian ever uses such a designation for Islam. Was it that the word Islam, implying submission to God as the characteristic element of the faith, was thought by Akbar to be too value-loaded, to be used for it?

Akbar not only felt free of any restraint of Islamic law; he could also freely criticize it. It is interesting to read his criticism of how daughters are treated in Islamic law. 'In the *Ahmadi-Kesh*, the daughter receives a smaller share in inheritance although it is better that the weaker should receive the larger share.'[26] He had as little patience with Hindu customs and practices, and condemned child marriage in no uncertain terms, describing it as an act that displeases God.[27]

Akbar's view of himself as a repository of enlightened ideas did not imply a missionary or propagandist motive. On the contrary, he had an extremely elitist view of the people to whom such knowledge — or any knowledge, for the matter — must be confined. He approvingly cited an anecdote of Shah Tahmasp in which he punished a personal servant for displaying erudition. 'Whenever servants take to knowledge (*ilm*), various affairs would become disordered'.[28] As to divine knowledge, it had to be even more restricted: 'The enhancement of wisdom cannot encompass every house, and recognition cannot be received by every heart. If one does reach the stage of recognition, one has to take to silence out of the fear of life-taking men. If such a full-hearted one speaks out, good-natured simple ones, accusing him of infidelity and heresy, deprive him of his life' (*A'in-i Rahnamuni*). He held no divine message for ordinary men: 'Let the artisans (*peshawar*) be more skilled at their work. That is divine worship for them.'[29] Quite clearly, if Akbar had any spiritual integration in mind, it was solely at an aristocratic level. In any case to talk of, or expect, ideas of 'national integration', when the idea of nation itself did not exist or was at best dormant, can only be an anachronism.

It is this essentially elitist view of Akbar about the possessors of religious truth that must be basic to any interpretation of the organization and ritual he instituted for its propagation. S.R. Sharma has already cogently argued that Akbar aimed at initiating no religion, and certainly did not coin and did not use the word *Din-i Ilahi*.[30] But such is the force of a preconceived notion that Blochmann, one of the ablest of translators, fell consistently into such error. He rendered *A'in-i Iradat Gazinan*, literally, regulations for those privileged to be (His Majesty's) disciples, as 'Ordinances of the Divine-Faith'. Even when translating Badauni, in his notes for his translation of the *A'in*, Blochmann translated *halqa-i iradat* and *silsilah-i muridan*, literally circle of disciples, as 'Divine Faith' and 'the new religion', in two passages.[31]

The very fact that Akbar was employing the terminology of the Sufi silsilahs, especially calling his spiritual followers iradat-gazinan or murids, disciples, suggests that Akbar was here aspiring to a position analogous to a murshid, or spiritual guide of an elite set of disciples. Abul Fazl bears this out: 'Whoever desires to be enrolled as a disciple finds great difficulty in his plea being accepted.'[32] Only when the integrity of such a candidate was established to Akbar's satisfaction would he admit him to the *silsilah-i iradat*.

Another mistranslation, here again by Blochmann, has completely altered the whole sense of the original. Abul Fazl says that 'in spite of the difficulties that lie (in the path of admission) and the strictness in choosing the candidate, thousands upon thousands of men of all classes have worn the mantle of trust (in His Majesty) and hold (entry into) the circle of discipleship as a means of attaining every good fortune.'[33] In other words, a few were accepted out of thousands—a pardonable exaggeration from a courtier. Blochmann converts all these unknown unaccepted candidates as 'converts' to 'the New Faith'.[34]

One may pass over the principal injunctions and petty ritual that Akbar provided for the accepted disciples.[35] The content of his teaching is, however, summed up most intelligently by his son Jahangir, when soon after his own accession in 1605, he followed his father in enrolling his own murids:

Let the disciples never make their own time dark and disturbed by the hostility against any religious community (*millat*) from amongst the religions; with men of all faiths, let them follow the path of *Sulh-i Kul* (Absolute Peace). Let them not kill any living being with their own hands or carry arms, except in war and hunt.[36]

The key principle to be communicated was Absolute Peace or Sulh-i Kul, a term favoured too by Abul Fazl.

There is no evidence to suggest that Akbar intended his circle of disciples to be anything more than a limited circle of sincere admirers. It was not even to be a ginger-group propagating the principles of a new ideology.

And yet, Akbar was not averse to establishing for himself a holy position in the eyes of the multitude. So far as we know, no Hindu ruler had employed the ceremony of jharoka darshan, where the sovereign appeared at dawn to be seen at the latticed window by those believing that a sight of him was auspicious. Clearly, the ceremony suggested that the sovereign was himself either semi-divine or, at least, of such sacred substance that catching sight of him was a greater religious gain than immersion in holy water.[37] It was a most intelligent use of a widely held Hindu belief in early morning immersion to bolster the sovereign's claim to not only being a guru (the equivalent of pir), but to possibly something more in the spiritual world.

It is also clear that Akbar did not simply look for the devotion of the multitude obtained by claims to sanctity. He did imply that his religious ideas had to be reflected in his own practice. While the real doctrine of pantheism was to be prudently conveyed to a select group of 'disciples', the principles of Sulh-i Kul that flowed from it were of general import for imperial policy in all spheres.

The author of the seventeenth-century encyclopaedic work on religions, the *Dabistan-i Mazahib*, made a striking observation when he traced Akbar's policy of religious toleration to the need of keeping within his nobility men of all creeds and faiths.[38] This needs no substantiation today; the fact is too obvious. One may remember only that the need extended not only to tolerating Hindus, but Shias as well. From my own study of grants of mansabs,[39] the relative position of the Hindus and Iranis (who were mostly Shias) in the higher and medium ranks of Akbar's nobility in the year 1595 appear as given in Table 1.

TABLE 1

Mansabdars Excluding
Sons and Grandsons of the Emperor, Alive in 1595

	Total	Hindus	Iranis
5,000 and above	8	1	4
3,000 to 4,500	13	3	5
1,000 to 2,500	37	6	6
500 to 900	61	12	12
200 to 450	160	25	48
	279	47	75

The figures reflect the truly composite character that Akbar imparted to the Mughal ruling class. The Hindus claiming a share of 16.8 per cent in the nobility may be thought to have yet obtained only a small foothold; and yet this was to grow in size in the seventeenth century under the next three successors of Akbar. For this I have set out the evidence in my book *The Mughal Nobility under Aurangzeb*.[40]

A noteworthy element of Akbar's policy during his last twenty-five years was not only general toleration for men of all faiths, about which so much has already been said, but also his tolerance of Shias and prohibition of Sunni–Shia conflict. With pride Jahangir could say that while elsewhere Shias persecuted Sunnis and vice versa, in his father's empire, 'the Sunnis and Shias prayed in one mosque'.[41] The policy was clearly set forth in Abul Fazl's account of the execution of Mirza Faulad, who had killed a Shia theologian, Ahmad Thattawi: every religious group was free to worship God freely in its own way, but not to quarrel with others. Mulla Ahmad 'was very firm and free of tongue is support of the Imamite (Shia) faith and constantly raised the Sunni–Shia question.' But Akbar would show no mercy to his murderer, who was executed in spite of pleas by the highest officers.[42]

Abul Fazl's language here and elsewhere implies no special esteem for Shiaism, either on his part or Akbar's. The implicit but repeated suggestions by Dr Athar Abbas Rizvi in his recent work that Akbar was hostile only to Sunni orthodoxy, has little basis.[43] Shia theologians were by no means more liberal than the Sunnis in their attitude to non-Muslims; and it is difficult to locate in Akbar's religious ideas any particular trace of Shiite influence. Certainly, there was no exaltation anywhere of the person or status of Ali in any of the Happy Sayings of Akbar or in Abul Fazl's works.

In one way, then, Akbar made the Mughal Empire into a neutral force as far as the internal controversies of Islam were concerned. This by itself may have been a matter of consternation to the Sunni ulama, who till now had been in the ascendant, and one of frustration for the Shiite scholars, who saw that the path of dominance could only be the difficult one of persuasion and not the shorter one of persecution of their opponents. But all this cannot explain the suggestions in our sources that Islam as a whole suffered during Akbar's last years.

The historian Badauni's effective rhetoric against Akbar and his plaintive and repeated statements about the hard days for Islam have been dismissed or deprecated as the exaggerations of a narrow-minded theologian, who inflated the decline of the ulama's influence into a decline of Islam. The Jesuit fathers' statements supporting Badauni's general statements about the ruin of mosques[44] have been ascribed to their excessive readiness to believe that Akbar was abandoning the faith of his forefathers. Criticism of these two sources on these lines may be read in S.R. Sharma's *Religious Policy of the Mughal Emperors*.[45]

But it is important to remember that statements about the declining fortunes of Islam as a practised religion during Akbar's later years are not confined to these two sources alone.

One important work of Jahangir's reign is the *Tarikh-i Khan Jahani*, written in 1613 by Niamatullah, a protégé of Jahangir's favourite Afghan noble, Khan Jahan Lodi. The author is no bigot and praises Khan Jahan Lodi for constantly speaking out before Jahangir in praise of the bravery and loyalty of the Rajputs at a time when the Emperor was greatly annoyed with them.[46] Yet, the same writer offers this passage for the conditions prevailing at Akbar's death, and the change which took place with Jahangir's accession:

The Prophet's *Shariat*, which like the red flower withered by the autumn wind, blossomed afresh with the vernal wind, with the accession of the King of Islam (Jahangir); and the mosques, *khanqahs* and *madrasas* that had become for the last thirty years the abode of birds and beasts, while the call to Muslim prayer was heard by no one, were cleared (of them) and became clean once again.[47]

One may then take it that the Jesuits were not wrong when they found mosques seized and used for other purposes; and that though Badauni might have been guilty of exhaling much smoke, there was at least some fire behind the smoke of his rhetoric.

The question arises whether Islam suffered from some positive persecution during the reign of Akbar. Another contemporary divine, Shaikh Ahmad Sirhindi, in a letter apparently written soon after Jahangir's accession, indeed asserts that this was so. According to him, the greatest misfortune that had befallen Islam in times of weakness was that the Muslims had been allowed to practise their religion and the infidels theirs (normally, implies the mystic-theologian, the latter should not have been so allowed). But what had happened in the period immediately past was that the infidels openly practised their rites, while the Muslims were prevented from so doing; and if they did so, they were killed, so says the divine with the usual smug exaggeration of which the self-righteous are so capable.[48]

The allegation of persecution stated in such terms, takes us necessarily to the matter of martyrs which every persecution of a religion with faithful followers must produce. Here, admittedly, the evidence becomes weak; for an account of specific punishments meted out to theologians or others who stood up for the open practice of their religion is difficult to find.

An interesting work in this connection is Muhammad Sadiq's *Tabaqat-i Shah Jahani*, written in 1636–7, which gives biographies of Muslim theologians reign by reign. The author alleges that towards the end of his reign 'Akbar Badshah deviated from the Faith (of Islam) and summoned mystics and theologians from all parts and inflicted punishments on them.'[49] But the only case of an execution he records is that of Haji Sultan Thansesari, who in fact was a revenue collector appointed, curiously enough, on Abul Fazl's recommendation. He was executed on the complaint of Hindus 'for justice', in 1600. Since even Muhammad Sadiq refrains from calling him a *shahid* (martyr), it is not clear if any religious issue was at all involved. In another anecdote, the same author records that Shaikh

Abul Fath, when summoned to Akbar's court, went post-haste
expecting to be punished, but was immediately permitted to return
home by Akbar.[50]

We are, therefore, left with general statements about persecution
and punishments but hardly any particulars. The roll of martyrs is a
disappointingly short one, if indeed it at all exists.

Moreover, there are contradictions in our evidence that are not
easy to explain. Thus mosques continued to be built during Akbar's
last years. The most outstanding example is the exceptionally large
mosque built by Man Singh at Raj Mahal in Bengal, in 1592. The
local tradition presents a curious picture of Akbar as an orthodox
Muslim sovereign. The Archaeological Survey reports that the
mosque 'was originally intended for a temple, but was afterwards
turned into the Jama Masjid for fear of the Emperor'.[51]

It is therefore unlikely that Muslim rites of public prayer were
suppressed. True, cow slaughter was prohibited at least in the Punjab,
and this prohibition was continued by Jahangir.[52] But this does not
amount to suppression of any Islamic ritual.

One, then, has to look for an explanation of why the cause of
Islam seemed to suffer during Akbar's last years without there being
any perceptible sign of persecution. Partly, it is possible that once
the Emperor's own neutral views were known, Muslim nobles too
might have refrained from a too conspicuous patronage of Islamic
ritual and the theologians. The implications of Akbar's espousal of
pantheism and references to Islam simply as *Ahmadi-Kesh* would
have been lost only on a very dull-witted courtier. In this respect
Aziz Koka's letter to Akbar from Mecca, written in 1594 is of great
interest. From the safety of his temporary sojourn in the holy city of
Islam, this leading noble at Akbar's court virtually accused Akbar
of 'claiming to be a Prophet and abolishing the faith of Muhammad'.
He warned him against the insincere nobles, who 'prefer the infidels
to the Muslims' and so were encouraging him in his policies.[53] Such
nobles would have thought it generally prudent to exhibit agreement
with their sovereign and be lukewarm in extending grants and
charities on which Muslim theologians and institutions so largely
subsisted.[54]

The drying up of nobles' patronage must have paralleled a
reduction in the flow of imperial financial patronage, which used to
sustain a large number of mosques, madrasas and khanqahs. The
main channel of state patronage was the grant of *suyurghal*, or
revenue grants. Badauni has described how successive measures

curtailed the grants made to Muslim theologians.[55] Abul Fazl in his own chapter on suyurghal justifies such measures of curtailment as essential to prevent fraud. All lands previously held in grant were transferred to specified villages. Later, all grants of above 500 bighas were held forfeit unless approved afresh by the Emperor. Then, of all grants of above 100 bighas, three-fifths of the area was to be resumed, except in the case of grants held by Irani and Turani women. If anyone asked for a transfer of land for convenience, he was to lose a fourth. A number of qazis, 'those turban wearers of evil heart and long-sleeved ones of little minds', as Abul Fazl styled them, were forthwith deprived of their lands. Upon the death of a grantee holding land exceeding 15 bighas, the land was to be resumed until the heirs proved their deserts before the Emperor—an expensive procedure under any circumstances. Finally, even those grants which were less than 100 bighas were to be rechecked by the *sadr* (central minister in charge of the grants) and Abul Fazl himself was to see if they had not been obtained by the undeserving.[56] The effect of these successive measures on the grantees can be imagined. Since they constituted the core of the class of professional theologians it was probably no longer possible to maintain mosques and madrasas in the old prosperity; and, perhaps, many such institutions might have been left without support and eventually abandoned. No positive persecution was needed to bring about this situation.

The conclusions that emerge, then, are that Akbar, in pursuit of Empire and under the light of an exceptionally brilliant mind, evolved a set of mutually consistent religious ideas derived from a multiplicity of sources but processed and refined by a considerable application of reason. The sincerity with which the beliefs once evolved came to be held, was accompanied by an anxiety to provide them with practical application to which we may apply the term Sulh-i Kul. In this application, there was an extension in the opening of doors to the Hindus and to Shias, as far as the ranks of the nobility were concerned; and there was a withdrawal of patronage to a class particularly hostile to Akbar's own views and policies, the Muslim orthodoxy. Critics of Sulh-i Kul were naturally prone to denounce the new policy which certainly had other sources of justification. Given India's variegated culture and multiplicity of religious beliefs, what Akbar was attempting to secure was an integrated ruling class. That he also thereby took a step which could later on be invoked by India's modern nation-builders is not only a tribute to the breadth of his vision, but also an illustration of the way in which historical processes occur achieving ends which in earlier times would have been only dimly grasped, or would perhaps have remained totally undiscerned.

NOTES

1. Abul Fazl, *Akbarnama*, Bib. Ind., Calcutta, 1873–87, pp. 256, 270–1.

2. Abdul Qadir Badauni, *Muntakhab-ut Tawarikh*, ed. Ahmad Ali and Lees, Bib. Ind., Calcutta, 1864–69, II, p. 30.

3. Ibid., II, p. 203.

4. *Akbarnama*, II, pp. 154–8.

5. *Tuzuk-i Jahangiri*, ed. Syed Ahmad Khan, 1863–64, p. 1.

6. Iqtidar Alam Khan, 'The Nobility under Akbar and the Development of His Religious Policy, 1560–80, *JRAS*, 1968, no. 1, pp. 29–36.

7. Badauni, II, pp. 210–11, 259–60.

8. *Tabaqat-i Akbari*, Bib. Ind., vol. II, pp. 344–6.

9. Badauni, II, p. 270.

10. *Akbarnama*, III, pp. 269–70.

11. *Tabaqat-i Akbari*, II, p. 344; Badauni, II, p. 268; *Akbarnama*, III, p. 270.

12. *Akbarnama*, I, p. 10; *A'in-i Akbari*, ed. Blochmann, Calcutta, 1867–77, III, pp. 277–44.

13. *A'in-i Akbari*, III, p. 228.

14. Ibid.

15. Ibid., I, p. 43.

16. *Akbarnama*, III, p. 221.

17. Ibid, p. 567.

18. *A'in-i Akbari*, I, pp. 158, 160.

19. Ibid., III, p. 235. Akbar correctly anticipated the reaction of the narrow-minded ones of the twentieth, as well as the sixteenth century. Maulana Abul Hasan Ali Nadvi in his *Tarikh-i Da'wat o' Azimat*, IV, Lucknow, 1980, p. 199, reproducing this passage blatantly mistranslates *niyayashgari* as 'worship', and presents this passage as evidence of Akbar's religious heresy.

20. *A'in-i Akbari*, III, p. 158.

21. Ibid., p. 236.

22. Ibid., p. 243.

23. Ibid., p. 220.

24. Ibid., I, p. 159.

25. Ibid., III, p. 229.

26. Ibid., p. 235.

27. Ibid., p. 242.

28. Ibid., p. 244,

29. Ibid., I, pp. 158–60.

30. S.R. Sharma, *The Religious Policy of the Mughal Emperors*, 2nd edn, Bombay, 1962, p. 42.

31. *A'in-i Akbari*, tr. Blochmann, 2nd edn, rev. by Phillott, Royal Asiatic Society of Bengal, Calcutta, 1939, I, p. 175.

32. Ibid., p. 159.

33. Ibid., pp. 158–60 (*Ain-i Rahnamuni*).

34. Ibid., p. 174.

35. Ibid., I, pp. 158–60.

36. *Tuzuk-i Jahangiri*, ed. Saiyid Aligarh, 1863–4, p. 29.

37. *A'in-i Akbari*, tr. Blochmann, 2nd edn, revised by Phillot, I, p. 217.

38. *Dabistan-i Mazahib*, ed. Nazar Ashraf, Calcutta, 1809, I, p. 314.

39. *The Apparatus of Empire*, New Delhi, 1985.

40. M. Athar Ali, *The Mughal Nobility under Aurangzeb,* Bombay, 1966.

41. *Tuzuk*, p. 16.

42. *Akbarnama*, III, p. 527.

43. S.A.A. Rizvi, *Religious and Intellectual History of the Muslims in Akbar's Reign*, (*1556–1605*), New Delhi, 1975.

44. C.H. Payne, *Akbar and the Jesuits*, London, 1926, p. 67.

45. S.R. Sharma, *The Religious Policy of the Mughal Emperors*, p. 46.

46. Khwaja Niamat Ullah, *Tarikh-i Khan-i Jahani*, ed. Saiyid Muhammad Imamuddin, Dacca, 1960, pp. 670–1.

47. Ibid, p. 668.

48. *Maktubat-i Imam Rabbani*, I, Letter no. 47.

49. *Tabaqat-i Shah Jahani*, f. 451 (AMU Collection, no. 226).

50. Ibid., f. 421.

51. *List of Ancient Monuments in Bengal*, revised and corrected up to August 1898. Issued by Government of Bengal: Public Works Department, Calcutta, 1896, pp. 460–1.

52. *Tazkira-i Pir Hassu Taili*, f. 36b, Dept. of History, AMU, Aligarh.

53. This letter is preserved in the Cambridge University Library, King's College Collection, MS 194, ff. 5b–8b.

54. There were, of course, exceptions: Akbar's favourite noble, Shaikh

Farid Bukhari, the *mir bakhshi,* had a great reputation for patronizing theologians through grants from his jagirs (Farid Bhakkari, *Zakhirat-ul Khawanin,* ed. Syed Moinul Haq, Karachi, 1961, I, pp. 139–41).

55. Badauni, II, pp. 204–5, 274, 315, 343.
56. *A'in-i Akbari,* I, p. 198.

15

Translations of Sanskrit Works
at Akbar's Court

The concluding portion of Abul Fazl's *A'in-i Akbari* contains an extensive account of the thought and customs of India. No previous effort of this nature and scale was made after that 'great moment in World History' when one of the most outstanding scientists of the Islamic civilization, Alberuni, set himself to study, expound and analyse the religion and sciences of India in the eleventh century. Abul Fazl's own English translator, Jarrett, tells us how much Alberuni's work is superior to Abul Fazl's. Without contesting the essence of this judgement one could still argue that (a) while Abul Fazl has derived and 'processed' some material from Alberuni, the bulk of his information comes from newly tapped independent sources, and (b) the purpose of the two works is different: Alberuni's to elaborate, understand and criticize, Abul Fazl's to describe and summarize the Indian sciences. What is important for us is to consider the first of these two factual statements. If Abul Fazl had sources of information independent of Alberuni, what were these?

It is clear from Abul Fazl's account that a considerable part of his information comes from oral testimony of the learned among the Brahmans and Jains. We know from Jain accounts that Abul Fazl was throughout in close touch with them just as he was with the Jesuit Fathers.

But another part of the information came from fresh material translated from Sanskrit. The project of translating Sanskrit works at Akbar's court has been commented upon by such a large number of modern scholars that I claim no discovery here.[1] What I propose doing here is to go over the Persian evidence for this remarkable endeavour once again and present it here, throughout in fresh narration and, hopefully, with a few new additional data.

The first indication of Akbar's interest in translating Indian works in reported by Badauni: Khwaja Hasan Marwi had been asked by Akbar to translate the *Singhasan Battisi*, but he had left for Kabul in AH 979/1572, leaving the work incomplete.[2] When, therefore, Akbar

met Badauni at Kanauj in July–August 1574, he desired him to translate
the '*Singhasan Battisi*, which consists of 32 tales of Raja Bikramajit
of Malwa'. A learned Brahman was assigned the task of interpreting
the work (in Hindi presumably) for him. Badauni presented the first
sheet of his Persian translation to Akbar 'the very same day'; but it
took him eight years to complete the translation. When completed
Badauni gave it the title of *Nama-i khirad afza*, 'the Wisdom-enhancing
Book', the title being also a chronogram (AH 989/1581). To Badauni's
personal gratification a copy of the work was placed in the imperial
library.[3] While many other manuscripts of the Persian version of this
work are known, none seems to have been definitely identified with
Badauni's translation.

The effort at translating ancient Indian works received further
impetus with the arrival of Shaikh Bhawan, a Brahman newly
converted to Islam, at Akbar's court in AH 983/1575–6. Badauni is
again our authority for this first enterprise, namely, the translation of
the *Atharva-Veda*.

In this year Shaikh Bhawan, who was a Brahman scholar, came from the
countries of Deccan to take service at Court. Having voluntarily obtained
the honour of accepting Islam, he joined the circle of the personal attendants
(*khasa-khailan*) of His Majesty. His Majesty ordered that the *Atharva-
Veda* ('Bed Atharban'), which is the fourth one out of the four celebrated
books of the Indians, and some of whose injunctions are like those of the
Muslim Community, should be explained, and I should render it from the
Indian language into Persian. Since there were many obscurities in the
text, and the interpreter (Shaikh Bhawan) was unable to explain them, and
the intention could not be understood, I reported this to the Emperor.
(Thereupon) first, Shaikh Faizi and then Haji Ibrahim Sirhindi was ordered
to translate it. He did not render it in a satisfactory manner, and no trace of
the work for this reason survives.[4]

One reason the translation did not give satisfaction to Akbar was,
perhaps, that with the zeal of a convert, Shaikh Bhawan sought to
give to the *Atharva-Veda* text meanings which might please his co-
religionists. For Badauni goes on to tell us of the curious ways in
which Bhawan interpreted the text.

One of the many injunctions of that work is this that until they recite a
text that has several *la* letters and sounds like the Muslim confession of
faith *la ilaha il l'allah* (There is no god but God), they could not receive
salvation. Secondly, beef is permitted upon certain conditions. Further
the dead are to be buried, not burnt. Shaikh Bhawan used to come out
victorious in debate with the Brahmans of all India; and out of this

motive had accepted the True Faith. God be praised.⁵

On this it is fitting to record a rival, though later, tradition recorded about 1653 in the *Dabistan-i mazahib*.

Nain Jot says: I said (to Shaikh Bawan, name so spelt). 'Translate this passage.' When he translated it, its meaning appeared to be wholly contrary and opposite to the meaning of *la ilaha il l'allah*. More, those conditions of beef-eating were contrary to the way of the Muslims. Further, the way of burial was in a different fashion, which is not permitted among the Muslims. His Majesty and all those present laughed at the Brahman (convert), and His Majesty said: 'Look at the Muslims and Hindus, that during such a long argument, no one asked, what the meaning of this text is'. He praised me considerably.⁶

The date when the translation was completed cannot be precisely established, but Shaikh Ibrahim Sirhindi died in 1583; and so the work must have been finished before this year.⁷ It must, therefore, have been the second known work of translation to be completed, from Sanskrit into Persian. Owing to the difficulties posed by its archaic language, its choice was, perhaps, not a fortunate one, being dictated more by Shaikh Bhawan's assertiveness, in the beginning, than by any independent indication of its contents.

Badauni is not fully right in saying that the translation was so unsatisfactory as to be forgotten. Abul Fazl indeed records in the *A'in-i Akbari* (*c*. 1591) that among the important works translated upon Akbar's orders was 'the book *Atharban*, which, according to the beliefs of these people, is one of the four Divine Books, (and which) was translated by Haji Ibrahim Sirhindi into Persian'.⁸ No manuscript of this translation is, however, known to exist; so, in the larger range of time, Badauni has been proved right.

The next major work to be translated was the immensely long and rich compilation, the Mahabharata. The work started in AH 990/1582, and Badauni, again, is our main informant about how it began. Writing in AH 990/1582, he says:

Collecting together the learned men of India, His Majesty directed that the book *Mahabharata* should be translated. For some nights His Majesty personally (had it) explained to Naqib Khan, who wrote out the resultant text in Persian. On the third night His Majesty summoned me and ordered me to translate it in collaboration with Naqib Khan. In three or four months out of the eighteen chapters (*fan*) of that stock of useless fables, at which the world may remain in wonderment, I wrote out two chapters. And what censures I did not hear (from Akbar), so that the

accusations that I am an 'unlawful earner' or 'a turnip eater' (apparently
expressions used by Akbar) meant as if my destiny from those books
was just this. Destiny is destiny. Thereafter Mulla Shiri and Naqib Khan
completed that section, and one section Sultan Haji Thanesari 'Munfarid'
brought to completion. Shaikh Faizi was then appointed to write it in
verse and prose, but he too did not complete more than two chapters
(*fan*). Again, the said Haji wrote out two sections and rectified the errors
which were committed in the first round, and fitting one part with another,
compiled a hundred fasciculi. The direction was to establish exactitude
in a minute manner so that nothing of the original should be lost. In the
end upon some fault, His Majesty ordered him (Haji Thanesari) to be
dismissed and sent away to Bhakkar, his native city, where he still is.
Most of the interpreters and translators are in Hell along with the Korus
and Pandavs, and as for the remaining ones, may God save them, and
mercifully destine them to repent.... His Majesty named the work *Razm-
nama* (Epic), and had it illustrated and transcribed in many copies, and
the nobles too were ordered to have it transcribed by way of obtaining
blessings. Shaikh Abul Fazl, contrary to the dictates of the commentary
on the Quranic *ayat al-kursi* that he had composed, wrote a preface of
the length of two quires (*juzv*) for that work.[9]

Badauni's passage ought to be read with the afterword in the British
Museum MS of the *Razm-nama* of Akbar's library, transcribed in AH
1007/1598–99, containing chapters (*fan*) XIV–XVIII, i.e. the last
portion.[10] The concluding chapter XVIII is very short and the afterword
which comes at the end is unfortunately damaged, and some portions
cannot be restored. It tells us that the work was commissioned by
Akbar on Monday, 9 *Ramzan* (year lost). If the year was AH 990/1582
as stated by Badauni, the date would be 27 September 1582. The
writer of the afterword is Naqib Khan himself ('Naqib Khan, son of
'Abdul Latif al Hasani')'.

He translated it from Sanskrit into the Persian language in the space of one
and a half years. Some Brahmans, namely, Rana, Sita, Rani, Madas, Nahar,
Chitrabhoj Sen, and Shaikh Bhawan, who, with His Majesty's attention,
has become honoured by having accepted Islam, read that book and
explained it to this sinful author in Hindi, and the author wrote it down in
Persian.[11]

This has the merit of telling us of the way translation was carried
out, Sanskrit being rendered into Hindi by a set of pundits, and the
Hindi then rendered into Persian. Unfortunately, the afterword is not
dated; but assuming that the translation began in 1582, the work should
have finished in 1584.

The second is the brief reference in the *A'in-i Akbari:*

The book *Mahabharat*, one of the ancient books of Hindustan, was translated from Hindi into Persian by Naqib Khan, Maulana Abdul Qadir Badauni, and Shaikh Sultan Thanesari. It comprises some one lakh couplets. His Majesty named this ancient epic *Razm–nama*.[12]

A little later, the *A'in* puts the *Razm-nama* among those works which were illustrated by Akbar's painters.[13]

The work was certainly complete by 1591, when Akbar sent Prince Murad a copy of the *Razm-nama*.[14] It seems, however, that portions went on being read aloud to Akbar, and it was through this that an embarrassing situation arose for Badauni in 1595. On the occasion of Nauroz (20 March 1595), Akbar complained to Abul Fazl that Badauni, whom he had thought to be of mystical bent, was really a 'fanatical theologian' (*faqih-i muta 'assib*). He had let his orthodoxy lead him to insert into the portion of the *Razm-nama* rendered by him, the concept of the Day of Judgement, which was alien to the Indians who believed in transmigration of souls (*tanasukh*). Badauni had much to do to explain that he had not deviated from the duty of translator and that Indians did believe that heaven and hell existed as intermediate stages in soul-transmigrations.[15] Many manuscripts of the *Razm-nama* exist.[16]

Abul Fazl says that 'the same persons (who had translated the *Razm-nama*) also rendered into Persian the Ramayana, which is one of the ancient compilations of India. It contains the detailed narrative of the life of Ramchandar, and records many unique points of wisdom'.[17] Badauni suggests, however, that he alone was the translator, and that the work began in AH 992/1584.

At this time, His Majesty ordered me to translate the book *Ramayan*, which is older than the *Mahabharat*. It has 25,000 *shloks*, and every *shlok* is a sentence of 65 letters. It is the tale of Ramchandar, *raja* of Awadh (Ayodhya), who is also called Ram, and Hindus worshipped him as an Incarnation of God.[18]

Badauni claims he was able to translate the work in four years; but there is, perhaps, some error in his counting because he was able to present his translation to Akbar only in early 1591. We have the following characteristic passage:

In the month of Jumada 999 (February–March 1591) having translated the book *Ramayan* in the space of four years and made a copy of the whole, I submitted it to His Majesty. Since in the end I had written (the couplet):

We wrote a tale to the Sultan who fulfils (our wishes).
We burnt up our life for him who gives lives.

His Majesty was very pleased, and asked, 'How many quires (*juzv*) it has come to?' I replied, 'In the first instance in summary, nearly seventy quires, then, in the detailed translation, 120 quires'. His Majesty said, 'Write a preface after the fashion of authors'. Since it had hardly anything worthwhile and I would have to write a preface without any prefatory praise of the Prophet (*na't*), I dissimulated. From that black test, as destructive as my life, I seek refuge with God. (But) copying infidelity is not infidelity ... .[19]

Manuscripts of this translation also survive, one with 176 full-page paintings (from Akbar's atelier?) in the Jaipur Palace.[20] Abul Fazl, indeed, records that the Ramayana too was illustrated for Akbar's library.[21]

The Yogavasishtha is an appendix to the Ramayana dealing with 'all manners of topics including final release'.[22] It is possible that Abul Fazl had this text in mind when he referred to 'the many unique points of wisdom' in connection with the Ramayana.[23] But otherwise he does not seem to refer to this text. But manuscripts exist of a translation by Nizam Panipati, prepared with the help of two pundits, and dedicated to Prince Salim.[24] It must, therefore, have been prepared before 1605. Whether this was received at Akbar's court is, however, uncertain.

Abul Fazl informs us in the *A'in-i Akbari* that 'The *Haribans* (*Harivamsa*) which consists of an account of Kishan (*Krishna*), Mulla Shiri translated into Persian.'[25] We know that Mulla Shiri was a poet of some repute, though not a scholar, at Akbar's court.[26] But unluckily no manuscript of this translation appears to have survived.

The work of translation was extended to non-religious literature as well:

The *Lilavati*, which from amongst the works from the pen of the learned of India in Arithmetic (*hisab*), (my) elder brother Shaikh Abul Faiz Faizi transferred from a Hindi to a Persian garb; the book *Tajik*, which on the science of astronomy is a reliable authority, was translated into Persian by Muhammad Khan Gujarati, at His Majesty's instance.[27]

The first of these was Bhaskaracharya's celebrated work *Lilavati* on Arithmetic (1150). Faizi's translation is extant in several manuscript copies, and two editions (1827, 1854–55) exist. The year (AH 995/ 1587) when the translation was completed is given in the preface, which begins with the praise of Akbar. Faizi also claims in the preface that Akbar directed him to translate the work.[28]

Of the second translated work, the so-called *Tajik* on astronomy, no extant manuscript appears to be recorded. It could be a translation of the Sanskrit work the astronomer Nilkantha wrote on Jyotish at Akbar's court, the *Tajikanilkanti* in Saka 1509/1587.[29]

Abul Fazl also mentions the translation of Kalhana's *Rajatarangini*, the celebrated history of Kashmir. 'The History of Kashmir, which contains the annals of four thousand years of that country Maulana Shah Muhammad Shahabadi rendered from the language of Kashmir (*sic*: Sanskrit) into Persian.'[30]

When Badauni in 1595 saved himself from imperial wrath over a suspected inaccuracy in his translation of the Mahabharata, he had hoped that he would get a suitable post elsewhere and leave the court with its heretical ways; but Akbar had other ideas:

His Majesty (in Ramazan 1003/May–June 1595) told Shaikh Abul Fazl in my presence, 'Although he (Badauni) would also have served well at the post in Ajmer, yet whenever we give him something to translate, he does it very well and to our satisfaction. We do not wish that he should be separated from us.' Shaikh and others confirmed this. The same day, it was ordered that of the Hindi annals, which Sultan Zainul Abidin had translated in past and given the name of *Bahr ul Asmar*, I should translate the remaining part and complete it. I was to complete the task in five months, since the latter portion of that work comprised 60 quires. Soon afterwards I was called at night to the throne in the Palace, and asked about the stories in each chapter till dawn. His Majesty said: Since in Part one which Sultan Zainul Abidin had translated, the Persian is quite unidiomatic, you should write this out afresh in idiomatic language.[31]

Badauni was given 10,000 copper *tanka*s and a horse in reward, and hoped to finish his task quickly in two or three months.[32] But he finished his *Tarikh* apparently before he finished his translation.

The work is the same as *Rajatarangini*. It is curious that Badauni does not refer to the translation by Shah Muhammad Shahabadi at all. The surviving manuscripts of the Persian *Rajatarangini*, defective as they are, do not seem to elucidate the matter.[33] One possibility is that Shah Muhammad Shahabadi was the translator of the work under Zainul Abidin, and the work was merely transcribed for Akbar's library; in that case a slip on the part of Abul Fazl must be assumed. The task of a fresh rendering was assigned to Badauni, after the *A'in-i Akbari* had been completed so that the new translation would not be mentioned by Abul Fazl at all.

If Akbar's effort at translating Sanskrit texts began with one set of famous tales, the *Singhasan Battisi*, it ended with another, still more famous. An early version of the Indian 'animal tales', the *Panchatantra* had received an old Persian garb as early as the sixth century. By 750 it had appeared in Arabic under the tittle *Kalila wa Damna*, whence it dispersed in Europe through a series of translations. In the twelfth century it was rendered into Persian under the title *Anwar-i Suhaili*. This latter work, on Akbar's wishes, Abul Fazl rendered into simplified Persian prose as *Iyar-i Danish* in 1588, becoming a fairly popular text, with more than one printed edition in the last century.[34] But it was borne upon Akbar that the *Iyar-i danish* had, by the natural process of descent from translations into various languages, diverged greatly from the Indian *Panchatantra*, which itself was greatly enriched by the additions of further stories. So Akbar ordered Mustafa Khaliqdad Abbasi to make a translation directly from an original copy of *Panchatantra* in 'Hindui' (Sanskrit) in the imperial library. This turned out to be Purnabhadra's version, the *Panchakhyana*, compiled in 1199. Haqdad's translation, which is both very idiomatic and literal cannot be dated very precisely, but his preface shows that it was written after the composition of *Iyar-i Danish* but before Abul Fazl's death, that is between 1588 and 1602, probably *c*. 1600.[35]

I may mention that I exclude Faizi's *Nal Daman* from consideration here because it is not really a translation but a retelling in Persian of the Indian tale.

When one looks at Akbar's translation project, one realizes that its centre-piece is the Mahabharata; and it should therefore be of little surprise to us that the Vaishnavite facet of Hinduism was more prominent at Akbar's court than the Saivite. The Upanishads and Shankaracharya are not represented. It was left to Akbar's great grandson, Dara Shukoh, to add the Upanishads to the Brahmanical literature available in Persian, through a splendid translation, the *Sirr-i Akbar*. The scientific texts translated were rather few, though the two Sanskrit sets of tales brought into Persian were culturally important.[35] In any case, it would be churlish to stress the limitations of the extent and coverage of Akbar's translation project. What stands out, when, —to use Abul Fazl's favourite phrase — 'the veil is lifted' behind the achievement, is the lofty vision and grandiose design of a shared, unified intellectual heritage belonging to all mankind.

NOTES

1. See, esp. Syed Athar Abbas Rizvi, *Religious and Intellectual History of the Muslims in Akbar's Reign*, New Delhi, 1975, pp. 202–22.

2. Abdul Qadir Badauni, *Muntakhab al-Tawarikh*, ed. Ali Ahmad and Lees, Bib. Ind., Calcutta, 1864–69, III, pp. 177–8.

3. Ibid., II, pp. 183–4. Badauni's statements in vol. I, p. 67, suggest that he carried out a revision in AH 1003/1594–95.

4. Ibid., II, pp. 212–13.

5. Ibid., II, p. 213.

6. Anonymous, *Dabistan-i- Mazahib* (Bombay edn), p. 265. I have not been able to identify Nain Jot, apparently a Brahman divine or scholar at Akbar's court.

7. Abul Fazl, *Akbar-nama*, Bib. Ind., Calcutta, 1873–87 edn, III, pp. 408–9.

8. *A'in-i Akbari*, ed., Blochmann, Calcutta, 1866–77, I, pp. 115–16.

9. *Muntakhab al-Tawarikh*, II, pp. 319–21.

10. British Museum Or. 12076. This MS is illustrated by Akbar's painters. The date of transcription is given at the end of Chapter (*fan*) XVII on f. 136a.

11. British Museum Or. 12,076, f. 138b. It is interesting to find Shaikh Bhawan reappearing as a translator despite his misadventures with the *Atharva-veda*.

12. *A'in-i Akbari*, I, p. 115.

13. Ibid., pp. 117–18.

14. See an early version of the *Akbarnama*, cited by Iqtidar Alam Khan, 'Akbar's Personality Traits and World Outlook', in: *Akbar and his India*, ed. Irfan Habib, New Delhi, 1997, p. 89 & n., 95.

15. *Muntakhab al-Tawarikh*, II, pp. 398–400.

16. See list in D.N. Marshall, *Mughals in India: A Bibliographical Survey*, Bombay, 1967, pp. 18–19.

17. *A'in-i Akbari*, I, p. 115.

18. *Muntakhab al-Tawarikh*, II, pp. 336–7.

19. Ibid., p. 366.

20. Marshall, *Mughals in India*, p. 19.

21. *A'in-i Akbari*, I, p. 117.

22. A.B. Keith, *History of Sanskrit Literature*, Oxford, 1920, p. 480.

23. *A'in-i Akbari*, I, p. 115.

24. Marshall, *Mughals in India*, p. 377.

25. *A'in-i Akbari*, II, p. 116.

26. Nizamuddin Ahmad, *Tabaqat-i Akbari*, ed. B. De, Calcutta, 1931, II, pp. 409–1.

27. *A'in-i Akbari*, I, p. 116.

28. C.A. Storey, *Persian Literature: A Bio-bibliographical Survey*, vol. II (1), London, 1972, pp. 4–5. I have read the Preface in a photocopy of

a MS in the Rajasthan Oriental Research Institute Library, Tonk (lent to me by Professor R.S. Sarma).

29. See Marshall, *Mughals in India*, p. 374.

30. *A'in-i Akbari*, I, p. 116.

31. *Muntakhab al-Tawarikh*, II, pp. 401–2.

32. Ibid., p. 402.

33. Storey, *Persian Literature*, vol. II (3), London, 939, p. 679, where, however, the year of Badauni's translation is wrongly given as AH 999/1590–91.

34. See Marshall, *Mughals in India*, p. 35.

35. See Mustafa Khaliqdad 'Abbasi, *Panchakhyana* (Persian *Panchakyana*), Persian text, ed. Tara Chand and S.A.H. Abbasi, Aligarh, 1973, a critical edition with a very informative introduction from the editors.

16

The Religious World of Jahangir

I

Jahangir in succeeding Akbar has been at a disadvantage. The brilliant father has so much outshone the son that the latter's personality and reign tend to fall under a kind of a rain-shadow despite the acknowledged charm of Jahangir's memoirs and his reputation as a naturalist and patron of the arts. One aspect to which adequate attention has not been paid is his religious policy. This received only limited attention in Beni Prasad's biography of the emperor;[1] and the chapter in S.R. Sharma's work, *Religious Policy of the Mughal Emperors* has obviously a case to argue, namely that the Muslim reaction to Akbar's liberal policy led Jahangir to make departures from it.[2]

One major argument for a change in Jahangir's religious policy has been linked to the accession crisis. It has been said that Jahangir in order to obtain the throne placated the Muslim nobility by offering, through Shaikh Farid Bukhari, a leading Indian Muslim noble and the Mir Bakhshi, to reverse or modify his father's policy of tolerance and give up the Din-i Ilahi allegedly established by Akbar.[3] This view has already been contested.[4] In actual fact there is no contemporary evidence to this effect, except that of the Jesuit fathers, who reported that though up to his accession Jahangir 'had been looked upon almost as a Christian', he had now 'sworn an oath to the Moors to uphold the law of Mafamede'. As evidence of this they cited three acts: (a) Orders for cleansing of mosques; (b) restoration of Muslim fasts and prayers; and (c) the assumption of the title Nuruddin Muhammad Jahangir, which they interpreted to mean 'The Splendour of the Law of Mafamede, Conqueror of the World'.[5]

Before we discuss (a) and (b), let us consider (c), for on this Jahangir himself has written in explicit terms:

It struck me that the work of sovereigns is World-seizing (*Jahangiri*), I should style myself Jahangir, and, since my accession took place at the rising of the (holy) presence of the Great Luminary (the sun) and the illumination of the world (by its rays), I took the title Nuruddin; and since I had also heard in the days of my princehood from the Indian sages that after the expiry of the reign of Jalaluddin Akbar Padshah, a person named Nuruddin would become the manager of the affairs of the Empire, this too was in my mind. So I took the style and title of Nuruddin Jahangir.[6]

It can be seen that Jahangir here omits the name Muhammad altogether from the titles and styles of both his father and himself,[7] and the two reasons he gives for the title Nuruddin are both unconnected with Islam. Indeed, the first clearly affirms his respect for the sun — an important feature of Akbar's religious beliefs — and the second exhibits an anxiety to have a title similar in meaning to his father's: *Nur* (light, illumination) to follow *Jalal* (splendour, glory); a suggestion, moreover, that he ascribes not to Muslim theologians, but to 'Indian sages', which rather hints at Hindu astrologers and the like. Jahangir cannot here be accused of having these as his private reasons, while he let the world at large share the views that the Jesuit fathers espoused. We know that Jahangir wrote his memoirs for the public eye. As early as 1613, the author of the *Tarikh-i Khan Jahani* wrote that he was abstaining from writing in detail on Jahangir's reign, 'since His Majesty with his own hand has been recording the events and happenings of His Majesty's reign by way of diary'.[8] Apparently, the earlier portion of the memoirs was already issued for circulation before 1613. Thus, there was no concealing of Jahangir's reasons for adopting the title Nuruddin Jahangir. The Jesuits were as wrong in seeing in it an assurance to Muslim theologians as they were in believing that Jahangir had previously been on the point of becoming Christian.

As for the statements (a) and (b), no orders of the kind mentioned by the Jesuits at Agra are recorded in his memoirs by Jahangir. These seem to be mere inferences from two references to mosques in the Twelve Edicts that Jahangir says he issued after his accession. Edict 2 enjoins that

wherever on the routes there occur cases of theft and robbery, and the place is at some distance from inhabited sites, let the *jagirdars* of the area lay out a *serai* and mosque and dig a well, so that people settle there; if the spot is near *khalisa* territory, let its officers do the same.

According to Edict 3, all property of persons dying intestate was to be spent 'on purposes authorized by the Sharia, namely, construction of mosques and *serais*, the repair of broken bridges and the excavation of tanks and wells'.[9] Edict 2 is obviously designed to establish settlements on roads, and the mosque and wells there come as naturally paired to serais, since serais usually contained within a mosque and a well. Edict 3 relates only to the use of money on structures of public use in which mosques were included. Neither orders suggest an alteration of policy since no one has seriously argued that mosques were destroyed or their building prohibited under Akbar; indeed, Raja Man Singh built the great mosque at Raj Mahal in the later years of Akbar's reign (1592).[10] He must have thought that the act would be approved at the court.

This much can still be stated in the good fathers' defence: they were not alone in the inference that a new dawn had come for Islam. Ni'matullah (1613) in a passage on Jahangir's accession says:

The Prophet's Law (*Shari'at-i Nabawi*) which had withered like a red flower by the winter wind, obtained renewal at the accession of the king of Islam and mosques, hospices and *madrasas* which for thirty years had become the homes of beasts and birds, and from which no calls for prayer were heard by any one, (became) clean and cleansed, and the Prophetic call to prayer reached the sky; moreover all directions and prohibitions and the Rules of Islam as current among the people are enforced.[11]

Shaikh Ahmad Sirhindi had also received a similar impression, but he was soon undeceived.[12]

There was, however, not much reason for any great apprehension on the part of the Jesuits or expectations on that of the orthodox. In the course of his account of the very same twelve Edicts, Jahangir says in respect of Edict 10:

Like my esteemed father I ordered that every year beginning with 18 Rabi I, which is my birthday, for a period of days equal to the years of my life, no animals should be slaughtered; and a prohibition of animal slaughter was likewise made for two days in every week: Thursday, the day of my accession and sunday which is the day of my father's birth, and he greatly esteemed this day for the further reason that it is dedicated to the holy presence of the Great Luminary (the Sun) and is the first day of the Creation and so auspicious; and of the days that he had prohibited animal slaughter this was one.[13]

That this order was in fact issued and enforced is well documented. The copy of its text as sent to suba Gujarat is preserved, from which it appears that on the days in question hunting and fishing were also prohibited.[14] In his fifth regnal year Jahangir repeated the order,[15] and he was so strict about it that when in 1612 the Id-i Qurban (or Iduz

Zuha) occurred on a Thursday, he did not allow the ritual slaughter to take place on that day, but only on the next.[16] He again notes his own abstention from meat on these days in the twelfth regnal year.[17] In 1626 Pelsaert noted that the order was being enforced, though 'extremely inconvenient for ordinary people'. He thought, however, that the order or rather enforcement was secured 'by bribery' from the king or governors.[18] This was in obvious conformity with Akbar's particular concern about animal killing for purposes of human food, a concern which repeatedly occurs in his 'august sayings' recorded by Abul Fazl.[19]

That Jahangir had not the least intention of disavowing his father's religious beliefs and policies is not only indicated by the enthusiastic way in which he praises them in his memoirs, but also by his public decision to continue with what is now popularly, but inaccurately, known as Din-i Ilahi. The passage from his memoirs, which we quote here, in fact, is a very accurate statement of Akbar's instructions to his disciples, as set out in the *A'in-i Akbari*. [20]

I appointed Shaikh Ahmed Lahori, who during the time of my princehood stood in relation to me as a servant, son of a servant (*khanazad*) and disciple, to the office of Mir Adl (officer in charge of justice). The disciples (*muridan*) and sincere ones (*arbab-i ikhlas*) are presented through him; and the *shast* [girdle] and *shabih* [portrait on medallion] were given to those recommended by him. At the time of the disciples being received into discipleship (*iradat*), they are given a few words of instruction by me: They are not to darken and disturb their time by enmity to any of the religious communities (*millat-a*), and with all persons of the various creeds they should pursue the path of Absolute Peace (*sulh-i kul*). They should kill no living being with their own hand, nor should they skin anything except in war and chase:

> Do not render lifeless a thing of life,
> Except in chase or the field of strife.

The luminaries, which are the reflectors of God's light, must be shown respect according to their ranks. At all times and in all circumstances they must remain aware that God is the real causer and Creator, nay they should so meditate on him that whether in private or in company their heart should not for a moment be without thought or attention in respect of Him:

> The lame, the ignorant, the sleepy-looking, the unmannerly;
> You (too) should go on looking at Him and calling for Him.

My father had obtained mastery over these truths, and few were the times when he was free from such thoughts.[21]

If Jahangir's text is compared with the two chapters in the *A'in-i Akbari* relating to what Blochmann misreads as Divine Faith,[22] it will be found that Jahangir uses exactly the same terminology as Abul Fazl for the spiritual followers of the emperor, namely, 'disciples' (iradat-gazinan/muridan).

As for the grant of *shast* and *shabih*, these two were parts of the ritual of discipleship instituted by Akbar. The shast was a girdle carrying the shabih or medallion bearing the emperor's portrait with the formula *Allahu Akbar* (God is Great), these being put upon the headgear of the disciples.[23] S.H. Hodiwala in his usual thorough fashion has investigated the matter and pointed out that the so-called 'portrait *mohurs*' of Jahangir are precisely these medallions.[24] He draws our attention to the unique medallion in H. Nelson Wright's Collection, bearing the bust of Akbar, with the invocation *Allahu Akbar*. Yet the year given is 1 Regnal Year and 1014 (= AD 1605–6), which means that it was made immediately after Jahangir's accession. On the reverse is a radiated sun, characteristically symbolic of the respect for the sun, which Jahangir recognizes as an important component of Akbar's religious views inherited by him. Hodiwala holds that this medallion shows Jahangir's anxiety to 'attract the sympathy or enlist the support of his father's amirs and other influential members of the Ilahi Faith'.[25] This does not, however, exclude the fact that Jahangir did sincerely believe in those principles. Indeed, Hodiwala himself quotes Sir Thomas Roe, who in 1616 reported that 'falling upon his father's concept, (Jahangir) hath dared to enter farther in ... and hath formed to himself a New law, mingled of all, which many have accepted'.[26] The fact that he continued to have medallions made, substituting his own portrait for that of his father, in all later issues, and presenting them to favoured courtiers (including Roe himself) shows that his acceptance of Akbar's religious views was no passing fancy or diplomatic manoeuvre, but a conviction sincerely held.

II

When two individuals hold similar views, they may yet act differently in response to similar circumstances. It would, therefore, not be surprising if Jahangir's conduct were to depart from what one would have expected from Akbar in certain situations. There are also the variations necessarily imposed by contexts and audiences. Jahangir in his memoirs addresses what is largely a Persian-reading Muslim audience. It is therefore, inescapable that at times he seeks to establish an identity with them. This comes out very well from the argument he advances for the coexistence of Hindus and Muslims in his empire, in the first version of his memoirs:

I ordered that, with this exception (prohibition of forcible *sati*), they (the Hindus) may follow whatever is their prescribed custom, and none should exercise force or compulsion or oppression over another. Since God the Almighty has made me shadow of God, and just as God's grace is extended to all creatures, God's shadow too must also do the same. It is impossible to carry out a general slaughter. Five-sixths of the people of Hindustan are idol-worshipping Hindus. Most of the work of agriculture, cloth-weaving and crafts is in their hands. If we try to make all of them Muslims that is not possible except by killing them, which too is impossible. God the Almighty will judge at the Day of Judgement. What have I to do with the religious practices of the world.[27]

It will be seen that the first portion of this passage is in consonance with the official doctrine under Akbar: the sovereign, as God's representative, treats all as equal claimants to his attention, just as God makes nature's bounty available to all irrespective of faith. But in the second part the impracticality of intolerance is stressed as an argument that may more easily persuade a Muslim audience. It is interesting, however, that in the standard version of his memoirs, Jahangir omits this passage altogether.

A similar inclination to appeal to the sentiments of his readers is clearly discernible in what Jahangir says about Guru Arjan and his death in 1606:

In Gobindwal, which is on the bank of Beas river, there was a Hindu named Arjan, who by assuming the garb of a (religious) guide and instructor (*Pir-o Shaikhi*) had made a large number of simple Hindus and even of ignorant and foolish Muslims into followers of his own ways and practices and had trumpeted abroad his position as (religious) guide and saint (*pir-o-wilayat*). They called him *guru*, and from all sides fools and fraud-believers came to him and expressed their absolute faith in him. For three or four generations this shop had been kept warm. Several times it crossed my mind that either this false shop should be overthrown or he should be brought into the fold of the people of Islam. (Nothing came of this) until Khusrau passed that way (during his rebellion). This obscure mannequin determined to wait on him. At the place, where he resided, Khusrau too set camp. He went and saw him (Khusrau), conveyed to his ear irrelevant matters and with his finger put the saffron mark on his forehead which the Hindus call *qashqa* (i.e. *tika*) and consider auspicious. When this incident was reported to my elevated court, and I very well knew his falsehood, I ordered that he should be brought to me, and handed over his habitations, houses and children to Murtaza Khan. Having brought his possessions under confiscation (*qaid-i zabt*), I ordered that he be capitally punished.[28]

This account of Guru Arjan's tragic end is inaccurate both with regard to motive (in so far as the idea of a preconceived object of furthering Islam and suppressing Sikhism is introduced) and to the actual circumstances of the punishment.

As for the first, the motive, Shaikh Ahmad Sirhindi wrote a letter to Shaikh Farid (Murtaza Khan) immediately after receiving the news of Guru Arjan's death, in which with much jubilation he says:

At this time, the killing of the accursed *kafir* of Gobindwal, has been a very happy event. It is a matter of great defeat of the reprobated Hindus. *For whatever reason he has been killed, and for whatever motive he has been put to death*, the humiliation of *kafirs* is the very life of Islam.[29]

Since Murtaza Khan was himself concerned in the enforcement of the punishment (as stated by Jahangir himself), it is inconceivable that Shaikh Ahmad would have suggested that the action was taken on grounds other than religious persecution, had this not been the case.

There is then the equally contemporary account of the Jesuits accompanying the Court. They attribute the action against Guru Arjan solely to the circumstance that when Khusrau was fleeing to Lahore, 'the Guru congratulated him and placed his tiara (*sic*) on his head'. The Guru was apprehended, and upon the intercession of 'certain Gentiles', a fine of 'a hundred thousand crusadoes' (Rs 250,000) was imposed on him. For this a 'wealthy Gentile' became his surety. The Guru, however, declined to pay it; failing which the unnamed surety proceeded to seize his worldly possessions including furniture and cloths. When this proved insufficient, the Guru was subjected 'to every kind of ill-usage' to force him to produce the money. 'At last, the poor man died, overcome by the miseries imposed upon him by those who had formerly paid him reverence.' Failing to secure the amount, the surety himself had to face confiscation of his own possessions and imprisonment, during which he died.[30] Thus there was no order for the execution of Guru Arjan from Jahangir himself.

Nearly fifty years later (1653), the author of the *Dabistan-i Mazahib*, who was on very good personal terms with Guru Arjan's son and successor Guru Har Gobind, and was otherwise very familiar with Sikh tradition, describes the event as follows:

For the reason that Arjan Mal had given blessings to Prince Khusrau, son of His Majesty, who had rebelled against his father, His Majesty Nuruddin Muhammad Jahangir Padshah ordered that he be called to account and mulcted. A very large amount was demanded from him. The Guru was unable to pay it. He was therefore tied up in the desert (in the environs) of Lahore, and he died from the fierceness of the sun, heat of summer, and torture by the levy collectors. This happened in 1015 (= AD 1606–7).[31]

In essential particulars the account is identical with that of the Jesuits. It is around the circumstances as detailed in these two narratives, though independently of these narratives, of course, that later Sikh traditions developed, which in full richness, are reproduced by Macauliffe.

These traditions say that it was Guru Arjan's taking pity on Khusrau during his flight that enabled his rival Prithia to rouse the Emperor's ire against the Guru. When summoned, the Guru justified his action in assisting Khusrau, and a fine of Rs 200,000 was imposed on him. The Guru declined to pay the fine, nor would he allow his followers to pay it. He was therefore placed under the surveillance of his previous follower Chandu, and was subjected to severe torture by pouring upon him burning sand, etc. After five days, the Guru passed away when he was allowed to bathe in the Ravi.[32]

From all this independent evidence it is surely clear that Jahangir's action against Guru Arjan had as its cause political despotism, not religious persecution, and that Jahangir ordered the imposition of a heavy fine on Guru Arjan and not his execution. The contrary statements he himself makes are clearly made with a view to his audience. This does not absolve him of opportunism; but that is a sin different from the one he owns himself, trying to win glory for Islam by force.

One reaches similar conclusions when one reads Jahangir's passage on the banishment of Jain monks, though here the basic fault seems to be a weakness for vainglory.

Jahangir says that in his father's time the two sects of 'Hindu heretics', the Seorahs (Jain monks), namely, the Tapa and Karthal, were respectively represented at his father's court by Balchand and Mansingh. The latter held himself to be a master of astrology and geomancy; so when upon Akbar's death, Rai Singh Bhurtiya of Bikaner asked him about Jahangir's prospects as emperor, Mansingh advised him that Jahangir would only last for two years. As a result Rai Singh retired from the capital to his home seat, and only later returned to his allegiance 'shame-faced and downcast'. That Rai Singh was a patron of Jainism, we know otherwise, for there survive two Jaina works written under his patronage.[33] Less convincing is Jahangir's assertion that he suddenly recalled Mansingh's offence in 1617 while in Gujarat and summoned him to court some twelve years after the committing of the offence. Mansingh in the meantime had been struck with leprosy and took poison on the journey to Gujarat. So, according to Jahangir, he met his deserts.

But then he adds:

The *seorahs* are found in all parts or India, but mostly in Gujarat. Since the entire commerce, purchase and sale is carried on by the Banyas, the *seorahs* (patronized by them) are found here in large numbers. They have built for them, besides idol-temples, houses for their residence and worship which are truly homes of mischief. They send their wives and daughters to these *seorahs*, and there is little sense of honour and shame in the matter, and various kinds of mischief and imprudence are committed by them. For this reason, I ordered that the *seorahs* be banished, and *farmans* were sent to all parts that wherever there be *seorahs*, they should be expelled from my empire.[34]

Jahangir attributes his *farman* to reports of scandal, and the episode of Mansingh is not given as the reason of the order, which also does not distinguish between the two Jain sects. But what he omits to tell us anywhere is that the farman was actually withdrawn, for which the evidence is furnished by the Jain work *Vijayatilaka Suri Rasa*, written by Darshanavijaya in 1622–40.[35]

In fact, evidence showing that Jahangir was not hostile to the Jains, and that the order of banishment of the monks, even if not withdrawn, was never put into effect, is overwhelming. M.S. Commissariat has already drawn attention to the evidence of the Jain literature and Mughal farmans bearing on the point as early as 1935.[36] To supplement him there is the Jain literature which Marshall's important bibliographical work, *Mughals in India* lists. It tells us that as early as Akbar's reign (1589) there were two Jain monks, Vinayadeva and Vijayadeva at Jahangir's (Salim's) princely court.[37] Bhanuchandra Gani and other Jain monks attended Akbar's court as well as Jahangir's;[38] Kalyanasagara Suri was granted interviews by

Jahangir at his court;[39] a Jain master had a disputed Jain work referred to him by Jahangir for decision;[40] and a Jain *savant*, Siddhichandra Upadhyaya was granted the title of *Khush Fahm* (Of Good Understanding) by Jahangir.[41] An order survives of Jahangir, prohibiting animal slaughter in Gujarat during days sacred to the Jains.[42]

The epigraphic evidence is no less conclusive. The order of ban on Jain monks was supposed to have been issued in 1617; Yet Jain temple inscriptions on the sacred Shetrunja hill, dated 1618 and 1626, extol Jahangir. As many as seven of these, dated Samvat 1675/AD 1618, begin with references to Surtan Nurdi Jahangir Sawai, and three go on to mention both Prince Khusrau and the *sobai* (governor of the suba or province) Sahiyan Surtan Khurram (Shah Jahan, Sultan Khurram).[43] So far were Jahangir and Khurram from being seen as hostile by the Jains that Jain records contain 'faithful portraits of Jahangir and Khurram'.[44] This could hardly have been the case had they been persecutors of the Jains.

Moreover, there is no indication in any other source independent of Jahangir's memoirs that any Jain monk actually suffered banishment. Muhammad Ali Khan's detailed history of Gujarat, *Mirat-i Ahmadi*, makes no reference at all to the event. The English and the Portuguese too do not seem to have heard of it. Why, then, did Jahangir make the critical statements about the Jains and boast of having banished their monks? There seems to be no other explanation than that he thought that in the eyes of many of his readers this would exalt his status as powerful Sultan who could suppress an infidel sect, doubly condemned for heresy and scandal. Facts were, therefore, suitably modified for the purpose.

How the memoirs omit reference to facts which Jahangir thought might not appeal to the Muslim reader, though in line with his concept of Sulh-i Kul, was the conversion of three sons of his brother Daniyal to Christianity. For this we have eyewitness accounts from Hawkins and William Finch, the event occuring in July–September 1610 at Agra and the princes obtaining Portuguese names.[45] The princes' subsequent renunciation of their new faith does not deprive the event of its uniqueness in the annals of the Mughal dynasty, more so since it took place which full encouragement from Jahangir. Yet neither the princes' conversion to Christianity nor their apostasy from it find mention in the memoirs. This, again, shows that the memoirs in themselves, though the basic text for our knowledge about Jahangir's views, are not a sufficient source.

III

It has been our argument that Jahangir's own religious views were largely identical with those of Akbar, and his practice tended to conform to them. Where what he writes in the memoirs suggests a deviation, this is, in two or three major cases, found to be a partial misrepresentation of actuality to suit the sentiments of his readers. Nevertheless, the memoirs contain enough material to show his continuance of his father's religious policy, notably in relation to Hinduism.

In Jahangir's approach to Hinduism, as in Akbar's, two elements should be distinguished: his tolerance of beliefs and practices associated with it, and his own views about their truth or correctness.

With regard to the first, Jahangir spells out his approach fairly well in the passage we have already referred to, given in the first version of his memoirs. Except for forcible sati, the Hindus were to be left free to follow their beliefs and customs.[46] The author of the *Dabistan-i Mazahib* goes further and tells us that Jahangir even appointed a judicial authority to deal with disputes among Hindus. Sri Kant of Kashmir, appointed to this post, says the author, was a scholar of repute in all the branches of Indian learning (*shastra*), *smriti* (law), *kavi* (poet), *tark* (dialectics), *vaidya* (medicine), *jyotish* (astrology), *patanjal* (breath-control) and *vedant* (pantheism). 'His Majesty Nuruddin Muhammad Jahangir appointed Sri Kant to the office of *Qazi* (judge) of the Hindus so that they might be at ease and be in no need to seek favour from a Muslim'.[47] In allowing Hindu practices Jahangir even imposed bans on cow slaughter, which was distinct from, and in addition to, the prohibition of animal slaughter on certain days. There was a ban on cow-slaughter (presumably in the Punjab) which Akbar had imposed. Jahangir continued this for 'he continued his father's ways (*suluk*) in the world of religion and made no difference of any degree in that path.' Shah Jahan, however, rescinded the ban.[48] The ban was in force also in parts of Gujarat, for the English at Surat could not be allowed to buy 'bullocks and kine' for meat in 1614 since 'the king had granted his *firman* to the Banians for a mightie summe yearly to save their lives'.[49] The ban seems to have been enforced more strictly in 1622 when Raja Bikramajit was sent by Shah Jahan to govern Gujarat on his behalf.[50] Pietro della Valle found the ban in force at Cambay in 1623.[51]

Jahangir continued and extended Akbar's practice of gifts and grants to Brahmans and temples. In his first regnal year (1605–6) while marching against Khusrau, he notes that he gave large amounts of money to Shaikh Fazlullah and Raja Dhirdhar to distribute among the *faqir*s (needy Muslim religious men) and Brahmans.[52] In 1621, Jahangir diverged from his way to visit Hardwar, 'one of the established important places of worship of the Hindus, where Brahmans and recluses retire in lonely places to worship God in their own way.' There he distributed gifts in cash and kind to each of them according to their deserts.[53] The documents in possession of the Vrindayan temples of the Chaitanya sect show how Jahangir went on adding to the grants of both the temples and their votaries. He converted Todar Mal's temporary grant of 89 *bigha*s 9 *biswa*s to Madan Mohan temple into a permanent imperial grant in 1613. He added at least two more temples to the list of temple-recipients in Akbar's farman of 1598, giving ten and fifteen bighas (1613 and 1614). During the period 1612–15, he made at least five new grants to Chaitanya-divines, aggregating 121 bighas.[54] It would later be said in criticism of Jahangir that during his reign a very large number of temples in Banaras (Varanasi) were erected, some of them incomplete when he died.[55]

The same policy was reflected in Jahangir's continuing the same access of non-muslims to mansabs in the Mughal imperial service. Out of a total of 172 known holders of high mansabs in 1621, 30 or 17.4 per cent were Rajputs and other Hindus; this was virtually the same proportion as in 1595 when out of 123 holders of high mansabs, 22 or 17.9 per cent were Hindus.[56] This is not, however, the place to discuss his attitude towards the various factions of the nobility and particular clans of Rajputs, which changed with altered political situations.

Jahangir had, however, distinct views on matters of religion, and these, being largely similar to those of Akbar, did not fit in with popular Hinduism. Like Akbar he was critical of the theory of incarnation (*hulul*) and of image-worship. Describing a discussion with Pandits ('Hindu sages'), in conformity with his father's custom, he argued that God, who is infinite, cannot be limited to particular space ('length, width and depth'), of physical bodies; nor, if His presence is seen as that of divine light, can it be made specific to just ten bodies (presumably, Vishnu's incarnations); nor can this be the exposure of divine attributes in some frames only, for miraculous powers have been possessed by men in every religion. The Brahmans responded that they held them to be divine incarnations so that meditating on them they could reach God. Jahangir could not, however, agree that such bodies and images could assist in the devotee's union with God.[57]

These two reservations are reflected in his aversion to the boar avatar of Vishnu and insistence that the boar-image be thrown out of the temple built by his favourite noble Rana Shankar at Pushkar.[58] His hostility to image worship is reflected also in his uncomplimentary comments on the temples of Vrindavan which he visited in 1619, though as we have seen, he had given and confirmed grants to these very temples.[59]

Jahangir's major area of interest in religion was, clearly, pantheism. It was this interest which made him seek the company of Mian Mir, the famous Qadri Sufi and friend of Guru Arjan, and hear from him 'truths and matters of knowledge of God'; he says charmingly that Mian Mir was too spiritual a personage to be offered money.[60] On the other hand, he did not find much satisfaction in an interview with a purely juridical scholar like Qazi Nasir Burhanpuri.[61] To Shaikh Ahmad Sirhindi, who made great claims for himself in the spiritual path, while insisting on a close, fanatical enforcement of the Shariat, he was positively hostile.[62] It is, therefore, by no means surprising that among Hindu divines, Jahangir should seek first and foremost votaries of the Vedanta ('Bedant'), 'the science of *tasawwuf* (mysticism).[63]

In this search Jahangir came across the man whom he has praised above all others (except perhaps Akbar) and to whose mode of life he devotes an enthusiastic description. The man was the ascetic Jadrup Gosain. Jahangir met him in Ujjain in 1617 on his way to Gujarat, recalling that Akbar too had greatly commended him.[64] On his return journey (1618) he went and saw him twice ('without exaggeration to be in his company is real riches').[65] He met him twice again next year in Mathura.[66] When Hakim Beg, brother-in-law of Jahangir's famous wife, Nur Jahan, while holding the charge of Mathura, ill-treated Jadrup, Jahangir dismissed him forthwith from service.[67] It is, unfortunately, not clear what Jadrup discoursed on besides the general principles of Vedanta, for Jahangir speaks in general terms of 'elevated statements' received from him and of his 'high understanding, elevated nature and sharp capacity of comprehension united with God-given knowledge'.[68] Jahangir also visited an unnamed *sanyasi* at Ahmadabad when he praises highly for enlightenment and grasp of reason, and knowledge of sufistic matters, according to his own faith.'[69]

Jahangir also seems to have been impressed by *yoga*, and he speaks admiringly of sanyasi Moti, who had obtained the art of complete immovability by his own volition.[70] He is also said to have greatly esteemed Gusain Chitrupa, a yogi ascetic of great ability, devoted to 'God-worship'.[71]

As we close this essay, we should stress that Jahangir's religious views and his religious policy had other facets too which we have not discussed or have passed over cursorily, such as his relations with Muslim divines and with Christians. An inclusion of these would certainly have given us a more rounded picture. But our object has been more limited, namely to enquire whether Jahangir altered or tried to alter the religious approach of his father, as has often been argued. Our findings have been contrary to this argument. We have found that there is no indication that he made any pledge of change upon his accession; that he continued to publicly espouse Akbar's policy. His own statements on the two or three occasions where they seem to suggest modification in this statement, ought to be viewed with some scepticism owing to the influence of his readership upon Jahangir as a writer. Finally, that his actual approach to Hindus and Hinduism was fairly closely in line with that of his father. For all this Jahangir seems to deserve far more credit than has usually been assigned to him by historians.

NOTES

1. Beni Prasad, *History of Jahangir*, 5th edn, Allahabad, 1962, pp. 409–10.

2. 3rd rev. and enlarged edn, Bombay, 1972, pp. 81–103.

3. Beni Prasad, *History of Jahangir*, p. 409; R.P. Tripathi, *Rise and Fall of the Mughal Empire*, Allahabad, 1963, p. 356; M. Yasin, *Social History of Islamic India*, Lucknow, 1958, p. 151.

4. Irfan Habib, *PIHC*, 23rd Session Aligarh 1960, Part I, Calcutta, 1961, pp. 212–3.

5. Relations of Fernao Guerreiro, tr. C.H. Payne, *Jahangir and the Jesuits*, London, 1930, p. 3.

6. *Tuzuk-i Jahangiri*, ed. Saiyid Ahmad, Ghazipur and Aligarh, 1863–4, pp. 1–2.

7. It is significant that Nurul Haq, a very orthodox writer, in his *Zubdatut Tawarikh*, British Library, Or. 1650, f.270b, after describing in detail the circumstances leading to Jahangir's accession, says that he took the title Abul Muzaffar Nuruddin Jahangir Padshah Ghazi. In actual fact Muhammad was a part of the title, as may be seen from Jahangir's seals on his farmans; the point is simply that, it had no special significance on this occasion. It was also a part of Akbar's imperial style and title.

8. Ni'matullah, *Tarikh-i Khan Jahani*, ed. S.M. Imam al-Din, Dacca, 1962, pp. 704–5.

9. *Tuzuk-i Jahangiri*, p. 4.

10. *Ancient Monuments of Bengal*, Calcutta, 1986, pp. 460–1. On a lofty corner minar of the Jama Masjid at Burhanpur, Akbar has left an inscription dated AH 1009/AD 1600–1 (A. Cunningham in *Archaeological Survey Reports*, IX. p. 117).

11. *Tarikh-i Khan Jahani*, II, p. 668.

12. *Maktubat-i Imam Rabbani*, I, Letter no. 65 (There being more than four editions, reference to Shaikh Ahmad's letters is best made by volume and number of letter). Cf. Irfan Habib, *PIHC*, (1960), p. 213.

13. *Tuzuk-i Jahangiri*, p. 4.

14. MS in Bibliotheque Nationale, Paris, Blochet, Suppl. Pers. 482, f. 20a–b.

15. *Tuzuk-i-Jahangiri*, p. 89.

16. Ibid., p. 91.

17. Ibid., p. 207–8.

18. Franciso Pelsaert, 'Remonstrantie', tr. W.H. Moreland and P. Goyl, *Jahangir's India*, p. 49. Such order against animal slaughter should be distinguished from the ban on cow-slaughter, which was also promulgated in certain regions.

19. *A'in-i Akbari*, II, pp. 240–1.

20. Ibid., I, pp. 158–61. Blochmann's transl. of this portion (vol. I, 2nd edn revised by D.C. Phillott, Calcutta, 1939, pp. 170–6) is very inaccurate and should not be used. The words 'Divine faith' or 'New Faith' are throughout unwarranted by the text.

21. *Tuzuk-i Jahangiri*, p. 28.

22. *A'in-i Akbari*, I, pp. 158–61.

23. Ibid., I, p. 160, to be read with Badauni, *Muntakhabut-Tawarikh*, ed. Ali Ahmad and Lees, Calcutta, 1864–9, II, p. 338.

24. S.H. Hodiwala, *Historical Studies in Mughal Numismatics*, Bombay 1923, reprint 1976, pp. 147–70.

25. Ibid., pp. 152–3.

26. *Embassy of Sir Thomas Roe*, ed. W. Foster, London, 1926, p. 314; quoted by Hodiwala, p. 150 n.

27. Riza Library, Rampur, MS 175, *Tarikh-i Farsi*, CAS (History) Library Transcript, p. 22.

28. *Tuzuk-i Jahangiri*, p. 34.

29. *Maktubat-i Imam Rabbani*, I, Letter no. 193.

30. *Jahangir and the Jesuits*, pp. 11–12. For the value of crusades, see ibid., p. 37, where 200,000 crusados = 500,000 rupees.

31. *Dabistan-i Mazahib*, Bombay edn. p. 187.

32. M.A. Macauliffe, *The Sikh Religion, its Gurus, Sacred Writings and Authors*, Oxford, 1909, III, pp. 84–100. Macauliffe's own comments, say on p. 100, should be distinguished from the facts described in his sources.

33. Jahanvimal Gani's *Shabdabhedaprakashtika*, composed in 1598 (Marshall, *Mughals in India*, Bombay, 1967, p. 235, no. 825) and Hanuman's *Khandprashasti* (Marshall, p. 174, no. 591).

34. *Tuzuk-i Jahangiri*, p. 217.

35. For the work, see Marshall, p. 130, no. 406. S.R. Sharma, *Religious Policy of the Mughal Emperors*, 3rd edn, pp. 88–9, disbelieves this fact simply because Beni Prasad (*History of Jahangir*, 5th edn, p. 408) cities no authority for the statement that the order was withdrawn after some time. Beni Prasad must have this or some other Jaina work in mind.

36. M.S. Commissariat, *Studies in the History of Gujarat*, Bombay 1935/photo reprint, Ahmedabad, 1987. Commissariat discusses the matter again in his *History of Gujarat*, II, Bombay, 1957.

37. Manjirishi, *Vinayadeva Suri Rasa* (Marshall, p. 285, no. 1029).

38. Siddhichandra Upadhaya, *Bhanuchandra Charita* (Marshall, pp. 449–50, no. 1721(ii).

39. Udayasagara Suri, *Kalyansagara Charita rasa* (Marshall, p. 469, no. 1804).

40. Karipasagara, *Nemivijaya Nirvana rasa*, composed 1617 (Marshall, p. 265, no. 938).

41. Siddhi Chandra Upadhyaya, *Vasavadatta Vivarana* (Marshall, p. 449, no. 1721, (i).

42. H. Sastri (ed.), *Ancient Vijnaptipatras*, Baroda, 1942, cited by Marshall, p. 221, no. 777.

43. G. Buhler, 'The Jaina Inscriptions from Satrumjaya', *Epigraphia Indica*, II, pp. 34–5, 60–3, 68.

44. Marshall, p. 221, no. 777; S.R. Sharma, p. 89, suggests that Khurram out of his 'orthodoxy' might have been behind the order issued against the Jain monks.

45. *Early Travels in India*, ed. W. Foster, London, 1921, pp. 86, 116, 147–8. Finch's account is the most detailed and circumstantial.

46. CAS in History (Aligarh) transcript of Riza Library, Rampur, MS, p. 22.

47. *Dabistan-i Mazahib*, Bombay edn, pp. 153–4. The author goes on to say that this decision was in accordance with Akbar's Law (*Namus–i Akbari*) by which all people, whatever their differences of faith, were to be extended royal favour and protected in their mode of worship and conduct.

48. Surat Singh, *Tazkira Pir Hassu Teli*, composed in verse in 1647, autograph (?) in CAS in History, Aligarh, f. 36b.

49. Downton in *Purchas his Pilgrimes*, Mclehose ed. IV, Glasgow, 1906, pp. 219–20.

50. *English Factories in India, 1622–23*, ed. W. Foster, p. 110.

51. *Travels of Pietro della Valle in India*, tr. Edward Grey, London, 1892, I, p. 11.

52. *Tuzuk-i Jahangiri*, p. 27.

53. Ibid., p. 337.

54. Tarapada Mukherjee and Irfan Habib, 'The Mughal Administration and the Temples of Vrindavan during the Reigns of Jahangir and Shah Jahan', *PIHC,* Dharwad 49th session (1988), pp. 288–9.

55. Abdul Hamid Lahori, *Padshahnama,* Bib. Ind., I (a), pp. 451–2.

56. M. Athar Ali, *Apparatus of Empire,* Oxford, 1985, pp. xx–xxi. The figures for 'medium' mansabs for 1621 are incomplete, but give a better proportion for Hindus than in 1595. The 'high' mansabs here include both the categories of 'highest' and 'high' in *Apparatus.*

57. *Tuzuk-i Jahangiri,* p. 14. Akbar's criticism of the divine incarnation theory is reflected in his 'august saying' that in India no one set a claim to prophethood, because the claim to being God is so much acceptable here. (*A'in-i Akbari,* II, p. 236). But he seems to have been more favourable to the theory of transmigration of souls (*tanasukh*): 'The fact that children fall severely ill points towards *tanasukh.*' Jahangir was equally unable to accept the divinity of Christ (*Jahangir and the Jesuits,* pp. 58–63).

58. *Tuzuk-i-Jahangiri,* p. 124.

59. Ibid., p. 279.

60. Ibid., pp. 286–7.

61. Ibid., p. 333. On the circumstances leading to this interview, see a very interesting account in Shaikh Muhammad Baqa 'Baqa', *Miratu-l 'Alam,* Aligarh MS Abdus Salam Coll. 84/314, f. 225a.

62. *Tuzuk-i Jahangiri,* pp. 272–3, 308, Cf. Friedmann, *Shaikh Ahmad Sirhindi,* Montreal, 1917, pp. 83–4.

63. *Tuzuk-i Jahangiri,* p. 176. By tasawwuf Jahangir must have more presisely meant the seeking of communion with God.

64. Ibid., pp. 175–7.

65. Ibid., pp. 250–3.

66. Ibid., pp. 279–81.

67. Shaikh Farid Bhakkari, *Zakhirat-ul Khwanin,* Aligarh Habib Ganj Coll. 32/74, ff. 96b–97a.

68. *Tuzuk-i Jahangiri,* pp. 279–80; on his mastery of Vedanta, see p. 176.

69. Ibid., p. 237.

70. Ibid., pp. 341–2.

71. *Dabistan-i Mazahib,* Bombay, 1575, pp. 146–7. But this could be the same as Jadrup (= Chitrarupa), whose mode of life was that of an ascetic; and Yoga might therefore be used here in a loose sense. For the identification of Chitrarupa with Jadrup, see Chapter 19).

17

The Religious Environment
under Shah Jahan and Aurangzeb

Today we are apt to think—and such thinking is an essential part of the legacy of the National Movement—that state and religion are two separate entities; and that the basis of the modern state is the nation, which is independent of all religions. In the world contemporaneous with Akbar, such a concept would have seemed strange and utterly unacceptable. The 'nation' existed nowhere though proto-nations were just emerging into historical light in post-Renaissance Europe. In China, one may argue, religion did not exist in the form known in the Semitic and Indo-European worlds; but still, such as it was, it was seen as a function of the state, a subordinate arm of a polity presided over by the Son of Heaven. In the rest of the Old World, in theory at least, religion laid down the functions of the ruler, who could be the Protector of the Cows and the Brahman, the Commander of the Faithful or the Defender of the Faith, depending on the religious tradition to which the ruler happened to be affiliated. It followed from this that the suppression of religions other than the dominant one and of heresy, was the basic acceptable reason of existence of the state. Monserrate, the Jesuit missionary at Akbar's court, remarked very justly that rejection of all other religions was the essence of every religion; and, of course no one who believed in tolerance could be the guardian of the true faith.

From these beginnings it took Europe a long, tortuous path to traverse from the time of Reformation in the sixteenth century, when there were the bitterest of wars of religion, to the French Revolution, when at last the dogma of supremacy of the Church over the state was abolished and the Cult of Reason was proclaimed. Even then, the loosening of the stranglehold of the Church on state was slow in coming, and the old bastions were the last to fall in the Catholic world, and in some parts of the Islamic world they have yet to fall. It has been through this long conflict that the modern secular state has emerged.

The Mughal Empire did not contribute to the creation of the modern secular state. And yet, if one looks at the world in and about 1600, it constituted the most interesting exception among the important and political structures of the world, in that tolerance, rather than intolerance, was seen by it as its vital function, its basic obligation to God and Man.

This crucial reversal of the accepted role of the state was the work of the great Akbar. It either stemmed from, or was the rationalization of, very strong religious concepts that he came to develop.

On reading the *Akbarnama* and the *A'in-i Akbari*, one realizes immediately that Akbar wished to assert his very strong belief in God; but his concept of the way God is to be worshipped was independent of either orthodox Islam or Hinduism. As the 'Happy Sayings' set out in the *A'in* show, he believed, as did the Sufis, that God is to be grasped and worshipped by different men according to the limitations of their knowledge. God was formless (be-surat) and could not be grasped in any form except by the greatest effort of the mind (chira-dasti-i khyal). To worship such a one, physical action in prayer (Suri paristish) was suitable only for the unawakened ones. Otherwise worship could only be an act of the heart. Elsewhere, Akbar is said to have held that the real act of God-worship is to have 'an illuminated heart that loves Light' (*Raushan-dil-i nur dosti*). Akbar, therefore, deprecated both the image worship of the Hindus and the prayer ritual of the Muslims. His deprecation of image worship is particularly borne upon us when the author of the *Akbarnama* styles Todar Mal a 'simple one' (sada-lauh), because he mourned the loss of the idols he used to worship; it goes on to call him 'a blind follower of custom' and narrow-minded. For the benefit of this celebrated Minister, Akbar also sermonized to the effect that no worship of God is superior to looking after the weak.

The importance Akbar gave to Light might well be due to the fact that it is formless; and there was, therefore, a natural tendency to exalt the Sun, the source of Light, as is indicated in the *A'in*-s chapters, *A'in-i Rahnamuni* and *A'in-i Iradat Gazinan*. Akbar said that 'the exalted Sun is a great benefit for rulers; and so they direct words of praise to it and count it God worship, though the narrow-minded ones suspect them (of sun worship).' Akbar obviously had in mind the Nauroz festivities of the Sassanid tradition, in which the Parsi worship of Sun and Light had a role. Akbar was thus attempting to reconcile that ancient royal tradition with his own theory of divine Light.

The textbooks often present the picture of Shah Jahan as an

orthodox Muslim king and indeed Shah Jahan did take some pride in calling himself a king of Islam. But he continued in all its basic aspects the tolerant policy of his grandfather Akbar and father Jahangir. In the thirty years of his reign, from 1628 to 1658, he continued to appoint and promote Rajputs to high ranks. In 1637, out of a total of 194 known holders of high mansabs, 35 or 18 per cent were Hindus; this was the same proportion as in 1621. It is not relevant here to discuss his attitude towards particular clans of the Rajputs which changed with changing political situations.

Much of the belief that Shah Jahan reversed or modified the religious policy of his grandfather rests on his order of the sixth regnal year (1633–4), in which he is said to have ordered the destruction of temples whose construction had not been completed. But the documents of that very period from Vrindavan show a different attitude altogether. Not only were the grants of Madan Mohan temple and sister-temples renewed during the period, but some local official's obstruction to the ringing of the bell at the Madan Mohan temple was condemned by an imperial farman of 24 November 1634 in the most stringent terms. The worship of the deity is here described as 'divine worship' (*'ibadat-i ilahi*), a strange slip for an emperor of Islam. The grants for the other great temple of Vrindavan, the Govind-Dev temple, were not only confirmed, but the management of the temple itself was handed over to the Amber rulers. From these particulars it is clear that Shah Jahan never intended, even in the early years of his reign, any departure from the traditional policy. It is worth remembering that he also patronized Hindi poetry, the poet Sundar Kavi Rai being one of his favourite courtiers.

But beyond this, the period of Shah Jahan reminds one of the time of Akbar, in that there was once again a movement to bridge the great gap between Hinduism and Islam and evolve a common language for both religions.

The most celebrated spokesman of this trend was Prince Dara Shukoh, the eldest son of Shah Jahan and heir-apparent. Dara Shukoh had immense interest in religious matters from an early age, and he was an admirer of the famous Qadri mystic, Miyan Mir and a disciple of Miyan Mir's spiritual successor (khalifa) Mulla Shah Badakhshi. Miyan Mir was known for his extreme friendliness with non-Muslim religious leaders; and he prescribed respect for all faiths for his disciples. Dara Shukoh's interest under his influence extended from Muslim mysticism to Vedantic philosophy. His study led him to the conclusion that the difference between Islam and Hinduism was merely verbal (*lafzi*); and to prove this he wrote a tract called *Majmu'-al Bahrain*, the Meeting of two Oceans. In this he gave an exposition of the Vedantic view of Universe and Truth, giving Sanskrit terms and explanations of their meanings. To him the Muslim mystics as well as Hindu saints were haqshanas or discerners of the truth. Though the book shows Dara's considerable familiarity with Sanskrit, it is also clear that he must have derived considerable help from *pundit*s in preparing the book.

From this small tract, Dara Shukoh went on to attempt a more ambitious enterprise—a translation into Persian of the Upanishads. This was completed in 1657 under the title *Sirr-i-Akbar*, the Great Secret. Dara translated 52 of the Upanishads with extreme faithfulness. He was so carried away by the Upanishads that he asserted that these were 'the hidden book' spoken of in the Quran. The modern interest in the Upanishads in a sense goes back to Dara Shukoh, because it was his Persian translation of these philosophical texts which first introduced them to the outside world.

Dara came in touch with the *bhakt*s as well. Chandrabhan Brahman has left a record of his conversations with Baba Lal, a Vaishnavite saint, who seems also to have had some links with the Kabir *Panth*. The conversations took place in 1653, and relate to sundry questions on Hindu religious and philosophical concepts.

Unlike Akbar, Dara found no harm in even image worship. Under every image (*but*), he said, 'Faith (iman) lies hidden.' He constructed a stone railing at the temple of Keshav Rai at Mathura.

Dara Shukoh pursued his cause unmindful of the deprecations of the orthodox. He showed his own scorn for the orthodox in verses like the following:

> Heaven is a place where there is no *Mulla*,
> Where there is no noise and disturbance (*ghugha*) from the *Mulla*!

The prince had a tragic end when, defeated in the war of succession, he was killed by orders of Aurangzeb in August 1659. Aurangzeb's official history accuses him of practising heresy in the name of mysticism; of seeking the company of Brahmans, jogis and sanyasis; of considering the Vedas (read Upanishads) to be divine scriptures; of wearing a ring with *Prabhu* inscribed on it, and so on. The accusations were intended to tarnish his reputation. These now look as the best certificate that Dara could ever hope to have obtained to win him credit and good name in the eyes of right-thinking people.

Dara had a very liberal and upright contemporary in Muhibullah Ilahabadi, a scholar of great erudition. Muhibullah declared that the Prophet of Islam was sent as a 'mercy' by God to all creatures, and not to Muslims alone. How could then any sovereign distinguish between Muslims and non-Muslims? He argued strongly in defence of the pantheistic views of Ibn-al Arabi, which formed the bedrock of his own tolerance of the traditions of other religions.

A man of a completely different background was Sarmad. A Jewish rabbi in Iran, he became a Muslim and then a complete panthiest. He came to India as a merchant, but gave up his trade to become a mystic. His favourite disciple was Abhai Chand, to whom he even taught Hebrew, and who translated a portion of the Old Testament in Persian for the author of the *Dabistan-i Mazahib*.

Abhai Chand wrote:

> I obey the Quran; I also have the same faith as the temple priests.
> I am a Jewish rabbi; at the same time I am a *kafir* as well as Musalman.

Sarmad and Abhai Chand belonged thus to all faiths, since God was everything. Sarmad says:

> He (God) became stone and wood in both the *Kaaba* and the image-temple (*but khana*);
> At one place he became black stone (*hijr al aswad*) of the *Kaaba*; at another a Hindu idol.

Contrary to common belief propagated in even scholarly texts, Sarmad was not on close terms with Dara Shukoh. Once Dara wrote to him, but he excused himself from answering the prince's queries because of his own ignorance.

Sarmad was arrested at Delhi in the early years of Aurangzeb's reign and executed for his scandalous views. The French traveller Bernier approved of his execution; but the defiant spirit carved its own niche in the heart of the people of Delhi who still consider him a *shahid*, a martyr.

At the intellectual level, a very important creation of Shah Jahan's time was the book *Dabistan-i Mazahib*, the greatest book ever written in India on comparative religion. Its author was not Mohsin Fani as is widely believed, but a Parsi, who omits to name himself. The author is clearly at home in ancient Persian, Arabic and even

Sanskrit. He seems deliberately to have trained himself for the task and travelled widely to collect material on religions and religious sects. His book, completed some time between 1653 and 1658, sets out to give an impartial and detailed account of all religions and religious sects derived from their own books and followers. A long section on Parsis is followed by a long one on Hindus and the various sects of India. He devotes a chapter to Judaism and another to Christianity; both are accurately depicted. At the end there are descriptions of the various Islamic sects, ending with the beliefs of the Sufis. The author of the *Dabistan-i Mazahib* professes to be doing no more than 'interpreting' the various religions for the reader; but it is obvious that his own sympathies lie with the pantheists and the liberal and tolerant schools. He seems to regard the various religions as so many endeavours to find the Universal Truth though he does not on that account omit to describe their mutual contradictions and inconsistencies. The author may be expected to have naturally gravitated towards Dara Shukoh, whom he mentions once only but not in terms that would suggest that he had obtained any patronage from that prince.

Shah Jahan's reign thus saw a considerable flowering of the tolerant spirit, for which the Mughal State, by its refusal to be censorious of such thought, if not by more positive support (which too came from Dara Shukoh, the crown prince), could reasonably claim credit.

How far then can Shah Jahan's deposition in 1658 be considered a terminal point for this policy?

The war of succession among Shah Jahan's sons has been considered a decisive turning-point by historians who choose to view the whole history of medieval India as largely a struggle between two communities, and it has been held that the war was a struggle between two opposite policies: Dara stood for religious tolerance and Aurangzeb for Muslim orthodoxy. I have elsewhere argued that the religious issue was not involved in the war of succession. There is a very interesting document which was brought to light by Shyamaldas from the Udaipur records. This is a *nishan* which Aurangzeb sent to Rana Raj Singh. It bore the impression of the palm of Aurangzeb and it is obvious that he attached very great importance to its contents. Here Aurangzeb makes the following declaration:

Because the persons of the great kings are shadows of God, the attention of this elevated class [of kings] who are the pillars of the great court is devoted to this, that men belonging to various communities and different religions should live in the vale of peace and pass their days in prosperity, and no one should interfere in the affairs of another. Anyone of this sky-glorious group [of kings] who resorted to intolerance, became the cause of dispute and conflict and of harm to the people at large, who were indeed a trust received from God: In reality [such a king] thereby endeavoured to devastate the prosperous creations of God and destroy the foundations of the God-created fabric, which is a habit deserving to be rejected and cast off. God willing, when the true cause [i.e. Aurangzeb's own cause] is successful, and the wishes of the sincerely loyal ones are fulfilled, the benefits of the revered practices and established regulations of my great ancestors, who are so much esteemed by the worshipful ones, will cast lustre on the four-cornered inhabited world.

Would a man who was raising a religious war-cry at the time, have condemned in such strong terms any attempt at intolerance or religious discrimination? What is significant is that rather than stress the religious issue, he was anxious to avoid it by declaring himself on the side of the established imperial policy.

After his accession Aurangzeb sought to justify the imprisonment of his father and the execution of his brothers by successes in the military sphere and a vigorous policy of expansion. It began in 1659 but for reasons that lie outside our present scope of discussion, it was followed by a spate of rebellions. The Jats rebelled under Gokla in the mid-1660s, the Satnamis rebelled in 1672; in 1667 the Yusufzais revolted near Peshawar and in 1672 the Afridis rose. In 1670, Shivaji again opened war against the Mughals and sacked Surat for the second time. With all these setbacks, Aurangzeb was clearly in need of new *ex post facto* justification for his coup of 1658–59. Consistent with his orthodox temperament, which he had been developing, the justification for his unpopular action was provided by an emphasis on the Islamic character of the empire, and a new religious policy was inaugurated to create a religious halo around the imperial crown. A discriminatory policy against the Hindus followed, of which the imposition of jizya in 1679 was the culminating point. This was coupled with an attempt to associate the Muslim orthodoxy as closely as possible with the empire. In the 1670s, the emperor's attempt to appeal to Muslim religious divines for support in respect of every political action even provoked a protest from some of the nobles. In a letter written to the emperor in the late 1670s, Mahabat Khan expressed his surprise at the emperor's policy that had made 'fowlers into captives and sparrows into huntsmen'. 'The experienced and able officers of the state are deprived of all trust and confidence while full reliance is placed on hypocritical mystics (*mashikhan-riya kosh*) and empty-headed scholars (*ulmayan-i tahi hosh*).'

That Aurangzeb's policy was wrong-headed was not seen by Mahabat Khan alone. We know from the Akhbarat as well as Manucci that the influential princess, Jahan Ara made known her views against his measures. The imposition of jiziya was opposed by many, and a representation, ascribed (perhaps wrongly) to Shivaji circulated widely.

But while there cannot be two opinions about the unwisdom of Aurangzeb's policy, from the point of view of the Mughal empire itself certain essential facts may not be overlooked. As I showed in my book, *The Mughal Nobility Under Aurangzeb*, Hindus constituted 21.6 per cent of Mughal nobles of the rank of 1000 and above during 1658–79, but 31.6 per cent of such nobles during 1679–1707, his last phase, where one would have expected the percentage to decline. The reverse development was, of course, due to the influx of the Marathas who in 1679–1707 comprised one-sixth of all Mughal nobles of 1000 *zat* and above. Whatever the reason, the Hindus' presence had increased.

The picture that emerges of Aurangzeb from the Akhbarat is also not one of a uniformly religious tyrant. He gratefully acknowledges Rajput valour and loyalty; and, at one place, commends Brahman officers for their courage generally. At lower levels of administration the traditional policy often prevailed, without anyone looking over the shoulder in fear of imperial reprimand. Jhan Chandra has published many cases of grants to Hindus by Aurangzeb and his officials. I introduce here a yet unpublished document from Vrindavan.

On 7 February 1704, Mukhtar Khan, Governor of suba Agra issued a *parwana* declaring that the Chaitanya *gosain*s had founded Vrindavan and established pilgrimages in Braj Bhum. Therefore the followers of the sect under Brajanand deserved a fee of one rupee per annum from each village in as many as eighteen *pargana*s of Mathura and the vicinity, half a rupee at each harvest. This fee was to be paid to Brajanand and was allowed as an impost on account of *Kharj Sadir o warid*, expenses on guests and travellers from each village. Thus, in essence, it was a government levy for the benefit of Brajanand Gosain and his Vaishnavite followers.

Aurangzeb's policy was, therefore, a partial aberration and cannot cloud the immense achievement of the Mughal empire, not only in applying a practical policy of tolerance but also fashioning a theoretical justification of it. That justification was itself not sectarian; but, whether as stated by Abul Fazl in a largely rational framework, or by Dara

Shukoh, in an absolutely mystical one, was a firmly religious one.
God was at its centre, and the state, in the shape of the sovereign,
was his vicegerent. Such a state was thus not a secular state; but for
the very reason that the God–State relationship could be set beyond
the frontiers of individual religions, and the State had a divinely-ordained
duty to be tolerant. This is the sum and substance of even Aurangzeb's
own nishan to Rana Raj Singh.

It is of some interest to speculate whether the theoretical justification
had some inherent weaknesses. So long as successes continued, the
sovereign could be projected as God's representative without need
for any further props. As successes dried up the need for props
would appear; and a sectarian policy would have its attractions. I
have suggested this as a factor which explains Aurangzeb's religious
policy though without justifying it.

Whatever its theoretical and practical weaknesses it is possible
that the Mughal view of Indian culture as a composite one and of the
state as a supra-religious state has contributed much to our own ways
of thought. Often it seems to have greater appeal to us than the concept
of a coldly secular state. But it is also possible that political and
economic difficulties now deflect us from the secular path, by making
a religious colouring a better protection for holding on to power. Since
such a situation presently looms before us, should we not learn from
the failure of Aurangzeb?

18

Sidelights into Ideological and Religious Attitudes in the Punjab during the Seventeenth Century

A few years ago the Department of History, Aligarh Muslim University, acquired from a dealer in Amritsar a unique manuscript entitled *Tazkira-i Pir Hassu Taili* (hereafter *TPHT*). It is a metrical work, comprising some 7000 verses, all in the same metre, except the chapter headings which have a separate metre of their own. The manuscript is written on good paper in excellent hand, carefully revised and corrected, and has all the marks of an autograph of the author. While the author is obviously a versifier, rather than a poet (no poet would write 7000 verses in the same metre), he has a scholar's knowledge of Persian and his spellings are impeccable.

But the very prosaic character of the work contributes to its real historical value. It is the work of a minor revenue official of the Punjab, a Brahman himself; and it is about a Muslim oilman and porter who became a minor local saint. It not only gives us a glimpse into the religious stirrings and petty obscurantism that were generated among the educated and ordinary people at this time, but also furnishes us with an excellent view of the ethical concept of the Mughal-period 'petty-bourgeoisie', the small officials and traders.

Before analysing the interesting historical material contained in this work, it would be obviously convenient to offer, in a short compass, some information about the saint, his disciples, and the author and his family, as we can glean it from this work.

Hassu Taili, 'Hassu, the oilman', or to give his proper Arabicized name Hasan 'Assar, was born on an unknown date, sometime in the sixteenth century, at Makhiwal, on the bank of the Chenab. His father bore the name Shaikh Chandu Taili and his mother, Maili. He had an elder brother Shaikh Taru; and a sister named Piyari is also mentioned (*TPHT*, ff. 68a–b, 89a–b). It may be mentioned in passing that in the old Punjab, the Tailis or oilmen were a wholly Muslim caste.[1]

A critical change in Hassu's life came when he was twelve. His brother gave him twelve rupees to go to a village to buy sesame. On the way he met one of the (living) 'nine *naths* of Gorakhnath'. The latter recognized in him his sixty-first disciple, the premier of all, who had spent eighty-two years in severe austerities before his birth in the Taili's house (*TPHI*, ff. 89a–90b). Hassu now embarked on his career as a saint. He went to Lahore where he worked as a porter (*hammal*); ff. 90b, 99a). Subsequently, the saint became a grain merchant, and opened a grain store at 'Lohari mandi' (f. 47b). His devout admirer paints him as a merchant of a curious type: knowing everything about future prices, yet buying dear and selling cheap (f. 12a–6). He died at Lahore in AH 1011/1603 at the alleged age of 120 years (f. 100b).[2] His tomb still survives, an object of some veneration; and so too is the spot remembered where he used to sell his grain.[3]

Till his death Hassu Taili appears to have remained formally a Muslim, though he did not follow the five basic observances of Islam. For this latter, our author has ready explanations: He prayed all the time, so why should he have prayed in public? Why should he have paid *zakat*, or kept daily fasts when he never had anything stored up, or never broke his fast? Why should he have gone to Hajj, to go round the Kaaba, when he went round the Kaaba of his heart a hundred times in one breath (f. 12b). His chief disciple, Shaikh Kamal, used the term *malamatiya* to designate his master's school (f. 102a). This was apt since the malamatiyas were a group of Muslim Sufis, who in order not to appear pious, used to avoid all the observable attributes of piety. Like many Sufis, he ate no meat (f. 36a).

But it is obvious that Hassu Taili's sights were set farther than the malamatiyas. While not disowning his Islamic connections, his freedom from Islamic observances was fully in accord with the claim, made at least on his behalf by his disciples, that he had similar connections with non-Muslim sects. We have already seen that he was supposed to be in the line of the Naths of Gorakhnath (ff. 89a–90b; see also f. 178a). For the benefit of such followers of his as had faith in Guru Nanak, he could be held to be an incarnation of Nanak himself (f. 159a–b).

With these credentials, Pir Hassu Taili could claim allegiance from men of various sects. In his court all the eighty-four *Siddha*s were present; 'Gorakhnath's teacher, Tirathnath' had come as a servant before the *Pir* (ff. 69a–b). Or again, the Brahmans could not recite the eighteen Puranas and four Vedas without his leave, and the jogis had become his followers. As for Muslims, the Saiyids had given the reins of their faith into his hands. In short, Muslims and Hindus had all accepted his bondage, and recited his name day and night (*TPHI*, ff. 456–46a, 70a–71a, 75a–b). The landed aristocrats, the *rais*, *ranas* and zamindars owed allegiance to Pir Hassu and he was respected by them (f. 75a).

Quoting such exaggerated claims is relevant here only in so far as it indicates the diversity of composition of Hassu's disciples. This diversity will become still more apparent if we have a look at the principal disciples that he left behind.

His chief disciple was Shaikh Kamal. His original name was Ayyub Qureshi (Surat Singh's explanation of this name is that since Abu Bakr was know as Siddiq, so Ayyub was Kamal!). He belonged to Darbela in Sind (ff. 72b–74b). The profession of his father is not stated, but he had apparently an educated background. Among other prominent disciples was Shaikh Dula, an indigo merchant; Abdul Karim, a sweeper; Shaikh Isa and Shaikh Hamid (ff. 23a–b, 24b–25a, 93a–b, 94b, 68a–b,).

Among his Hindu disciples were Asa Karan, Ganpat Das, Ram Rangi, and Bayagdas 'Ramayya' (a title given to him by Hassu), both the last named being Brahmans; and Chajju Bhagat, a trader (ff. 159a, 44a, 43a–b). A similarly mixed composition is seen in the list of disciples of Shaikh Kamal: Fateh Muhammad, Hassan Hafiz, Shah Mir, Haji Muhammad Lohar, Shaikh Husain, Khwaja Sodanand, Kalyan Mana, Jagga, Bhagwati, Sarichand (*qanungo*), Nihal Chand, Jethmal (a goldsmith), Raghunath, Ganesh, Bhakt Gawali Rai, Gopal Brahman, Nand Rai, Rai Basant, Khwaja Hari Chand, Bayagdas Puri, Girdhar Pandit, etc (ff. 173–4).

The allegiance of the family of the author, Surat Singh, was to Shaikh Kamal, and through him to Hassu Taili (ff. 54b, 173–4).

Surat Singh was born at the town of Natesar in the pargana of Patti Hibatpur (now Patti in District Amritsar). All the men of the town were merchants and belonged to the Kamboj sect (*firqa*) (of the Brahman caste?). Surat Singh too belonged to this sect. His father was Duni Chand, son of Jogidas; and he had an elder brother Khwaja Ganga Ram. Both Ganga Ram and Surat Singh took to the bureaucratic profession (ff. 181, 182a; see also ff. 121–2 and 254). Ganga Ram served as *amil* of Jahangirpur (ff. 122–3), and subsequently was appointed as *Khan-i Saman* in the sarkar of Saf Shikan Khan but resigned that post (f. 162–b). Later on he was appointed as Khan-i Saman in the sarkar of Aqil Khan (ff. 163–4). Surat Singh was appointed as *Karkun* in Bhatinda and remained there till the time of the writing of his work (AH 1054–57/1644–47; ff. 155a, 182b).

Surat Singh's interest in Persian poetry was more than casual, for he refers to a poetical session at Agra where he was present with some other notable poets of the time — including Chandrabhan Brahman and Shaida (f. 86b). It was Ganga Ram who was obviously the more religiously inclined of the two brothers, for he left home and joined the Bairagis; but he later took allegiance to Shaikh Kamal (*TPHI*, ff. 54b, 122b–123), and Surat Singh followed suit.

As we have said in the beginning, Surat Singh's work is of value not as a great exposition of spiritual experience but as a window into the mind of a man of his class in seventeenth-century Punjab. Here was a Brahman, with a mercantile and bureaucratic background, by his caste familiar with the orthodox creed of his faith, but by his Persian education familiar equally with the Islamic tradition. He is at once a supporter of Hindu–Muslim unity and of the separation of the two traditions. It is quite natural for him to begin with the praise of God and then of Prophet Muhammad, in terms that any Muslim would find acceptable. He wants Hindus and Muslims to live together in amity, but he insists that they should keep to their own customs. Indeed, he is suspicious of Hindus behaving like Muslims. He praises Shah Jahan for his justice and the protection extended by him to Muslims and Hindus alike. That emperor found the Hindus and Muslims 'mixed' (*makhalut*; f. 101a) and not following their own separate paths. Shah Jahan, however, remedied this by putting them in their respective ways. In this connection the author himself decries those Hindus who secretly do the sinful things that Muslims do, while they put on the *tika* and sacred thread in public (f. 108b).

There is also no explicit rejection of the caste system, though it does seem remarkable that a man of Surat Singh's stamp should, without any inhibition, state the low castes and lowly professions of his favourite saint and some of his principal followers. For this, perhaps, the traditional Indian view that religious men ought to be poor (popularized in particular by the Nath Jogis to whom Surat Singh appears attached), and also the general atmosphere created by the Bhakti and Sufi movements of the fifteenth and sixteenth centuries, ought to be held responsible. However, there is never any suggestion of interdining among Hassu Taili's disciples. Thus, in Surat Singh's mind there seems to be little wrong in the caste system and its separatist customs. Here his attitude is quite different from that of Guru Nanak and his followers who sprang from the same soil.

Surat Singh obviously continues to have many of the customary inhibitions of the community. Thus he had a great horror of cow-slaughter and applauds Akbar and Jahangir for prohibiting it (presumably, in the Punjab; *TPHI*, f. 36b). He thus furnishes us with a fact not previously known to us. It is difficult to second him in similarly applauding Hassu Taili's curse, when an Afghan admirer served him beef, for this curse is alleged to have brought about a general famine (ff. 36a–b).

The human sympathies of Surat Singh and his saint are also rather limited. To him the *khalq* (creatures of God) to be saved are either those who owe allegiance to his saint or belong to his class or community. Thus he records among the miracles of Hassu, one in which the saint, having accepted a very petty *nazar* (offering) from a Hindu banker who had squandered the deposit left with him by a 'Mughal', and who expected the Mughal to come any day with a farman to secure repayment, protected the defalcator by invoking divine aid in getting the Mughal robbed of that precious document (f. 17). Or, when a corrupt revenue official was expecting dismissal and punishment, after having shown indifference to Shaikh Kamal, Surat Singh came forward to help him, once he had offered his allegiance to that saint, in getting the tell-tale village papers burnt and replaced with others (f. 22a).

It is also interesting that a number of the miracles of Hassu Taili are concerned not with feeding and helping the utter destitute, but assisting nobles and merchants. It is obvious that to Surat Singh, Hassu Taili appears in the best light when by his prayers, Abdur Rahim Khan Khanan conquers Sind or succeeds in the Deccan (ff. 13a–b, 14b–15a, 23b–33a, 91b), or Abul Fazl is saved from an illness, or Akbar and Jahangir are reconciled (ff. 23b–24a, 41a–b, 49b), etc. A number of other miracles concern merchants—how Hassu Taili causes one boat of merchants to flounder and saves another (ff. 43a–b); how, invoked in time he saves a caravan from fire (ff. 22a–b); how, again, he enables Lahore merchants in the Deccan to earn high profits when they go to him (or rather his apparition) there (ff. 42a–b, 43a).

His own view of Hassu Taili is not that of an essentially kindly saint; but kindly now, and fearful in his punishment the next moment. A *kotwal*, when asked for a nazar, sends a very petty amount, and so loses his life (ff. 18b–19a).

The nazar is a very important vehicle of saintly protection. Once accepted, even the criminal is sure of protection. The nazar has value as index of the sincerity of the devotee, for the saint himself has no need of nazar (f. 22a).

Besides being of value in itself for telling us of a minor religious movement in the Punjab, and indicating the ideological outlook to which it appealed, Surat Singh's work contains some important historical information as well.

For one thing, it shows beyond doubt that Guru Nanak's religious status was widely accepted in the Punjab, even by Hindus and Muslims who were not followers of the contemporary Guru. Surat Singh describes how Nanak when he died was claimed by men of both religions; and in order to satisfy them, he left behind two bodies. His other references to Nanak also show his own deep feeling for him as a teacher. He refers to his great verses (*TPHI*,ff. 122a–123a). But it would be obvious from the foregoing that his own ideas were far too orthodox: he would prefer the obscurantism of Hassu Taili to the liberating message of Nanak.

An interesting piece of information in the present work relates to the prohibition of tobacco. Pir Hassu appeared in a dream to Abdul Karim to warn him against the use of tobacco (f. 134a). Since tobacco smoking became common in India during Jahangir's reign, the ban on it in the religious sects of the seventeenth century seems to have come almost spontaneously. The ban came in Sikhism and the Kabirpanthis and was present in the Satnami sect when it arose in Narnaul in the middle of the seventeenth century. By the mechanism of a dream it also percolated among the followers of Hassu Taili. It is noteworthy that the more orthodox Muslims did not consider tobacco smoking a religious vice.

The work contains certain details about Mughal administration. I have already elsewhere referred to the interesting material it contains about the officials and the mode of procedure in the establishment of nobles.[4] From the long passage concerning the revenue collector of Jahangirpur, it appears that the amin used to check the records of the amil by a direct examination of the village patwaris' papers.

Not to be overlooked is a valuable reference to the famine of 1574–75, so far only dimly mentioned in Persian sources (ff. 36a–b). Known as the *Battisiya* (from Samwat 1632), it was very severely felt in the entire region from Burhanpur and Gujarat to Lahore, Multan and Kashmir.[5]

Surat Singh's work is thus an important historical document. To the modern reader Surat Singh's intellectual horizons and human sympathies may appear rather limited, and his favourite saint and spiritual guide very sectarian, more concerned with allegiance to himself than with merit and works. Yet, we ought not to ignore the importance of a religious sect so prominently drawing its disciples from amongst both Hindus and Muslims, and declaring its connection with ascetic and mystic predecessors in both religions. Our irritation at the obscurantist elements in Pir Hassu Taili and other 'saints' may be tempered further by consideration of their working-class origins which they made no attempt to hide.

NOTES

1. Ibbetson, *Punjab Castes*, Lahore, 1916, p. 324.

2. Latif says that Pir Hassn Taili 'died in 1002 AH (AD 1593), four years after the death of Aurangzeb'. (Latif, *Lahore*, Lahore, 1892, 202–3). This last statement of Latif is palpably wrong.

3. Ibid. Latif says his shop 'still exits in Chowk Jhanda'.

4. See my book, *The Mughal Nobility under Aurangzeb*, Bombay, 1996, p. 162.

5. These sources refer to a severe famine in Gujarat, but only an expected drought in northern India, the danger being, however, averted by timely showers. (Cf. Irfan Habib, *Agrarian System of Mughal India*, Bombay, 1963, p. 101 & n).

19

Pursuing an Elusive Seeker of Universal Truth

The Identity and Environment of the Author of the *Dabistan-i Mazahib*

In or soon after AH 1063/AD 1653, an anonymous author completed and issued in Persian a work on the religions of the world called the *Dabistan,* now popularly known as *Dabistan-i Mazahib*[1] (*Dabistan-i Mazahib,* published Ibrahim ibn Nur Muhammad, Bombay, 1292/ 1875, hereafter cited as *DM*). Given its large canvas, the detailed research it embodied, the number of texts consulted, the number of votaries of all religions approached for information, and the absolute impartiality with which all beliefs were presented make the book unique in all literature of its time.

The book is divided into twelve *ta'lim*s or chapters on the beliefs of (1) Parsis, (2) Hindus, (3) Tibetans, (4) Jews, (5) Christians, (6) Muslims, (7) *Sadiqi*s, (8) Monotheists, (9) Raushanyas, (10) *Ilahi*s (Pure monotheists), (11) Rationalists and (12) Sufis. The account of each religion or sect is derived, as far as possible, from its own votaries, often directly by the author himself. The book begins with a very short, ten-line preface; but at the end the author sums up what his method of proceeding has been throughout the book:

It is generally spread about that [all people] belong to [one of] five communities: Hindus, Jews, Magians, Christians and Muslims. Each of these five sects claims that its Law is superior over all others, and in support of their Law they bring forth scriptures giving their beliefs. After the completion of this book it may once again be stated that some excellent persons have said that among the sects and religions, in the ordinary persons' descriptions of faiths and beliefs, there is to be found much partiality, so that truth has remained concealed, especially (now) that besides the [five religions], the number of sects has [reputedly] reached thirty. With this desire [to write impartially] the author engaged himself in writing this book. In this record of the faiths of one's ancestors, and the beliefs of the different sects, whatever has been recorded has been received from the lips of persons possessed of those beliefs and from their own books. In the account of individuals of all faiths, these are referred to in the same terms of respect as are extended to them by their disciples and sincere followers, so that there should be no trace left of intolerance and partiality. The author has no ambition other than that of fulfilling the office of interpreter. (*DM,* p. 327)

The entire text of the work bears out very well the claims made for lack of bias by the author. Moreover, the author shows a remarkable capacity for comprehension of diverse, and often complex beliefs, and lays them out in an orderly fashion, with an eye to the essentials. So far as possible, he is careful to identify his sources, whether persons or texts.

The last date and place we have of him in the book are 1063/1652–3, and Srikakul (modern. Srikakulam, Andhra Pradesh) in the Qutbshahi kingdom on the borders of Orissa (*DM,* p. 105). But whenever and wherever the author issued the book, the work became popular enough to be preserved in a large number of manuscript copies.[1] Under the patronage of W.B. Bayley, it was printed by Nazar Ashraf in a very accurate edition in movable type at Calcutta in 1809.[2] A lithographed edition was brought out by Ibrahim bin Nur Muhammad from Bombay, 1292/1875; and this is the edition I have used. Two years later Munshi Nawal Kishore published a lithographed edition from Lucknow.[3] Initial 'Orientalist' interest in the work was kindled by its preservation of much information about the Parsis and some other sects, such as the Raushanyas, of whom little was then known to the European scholarly world. F. Gladwin translated the section on the Parsis and published it from Calcutta in 1789; a German version by E. Dalburg from Wurzburg followed in 1809. The chapter on the Raushanyas was similarly translated into English by J. Leyden for the *Asiatic Researches*, XI, Calcutta.[4] The whole work was translated into English by D. Shea and A. Troyer, *The Dabistan or School of Manners*, in three volumes (London, 1843). The translation rendered good service for the time, despite its inaccuracies, some of which were serious enough.[5] A Gujarati translation by Mobed Fardunji Murzbanji was published from Bombay still earlier (1815, with a second edition in 1845).[6] The very important subsection on the Sikhs has been edited and translated by Ganda Singh (Madras, 1942).[7]

As modern scholarship has come into possession of most of the older texts used by the author of the *Dabistan*, its importance as a source for those religions has undoubtedly receded. Yet, its significance as a primary source for understanding the religious environment of India at the time of the author, the actual meaning given to older terms and beliefs by people contemporaneous with the author, the customs practised, etc. has probably not been fully appreciated. The more one reads the book, the more one has the sense of a quarry crying to be worked.

How little has been explored of this book is shown by how little has been done to explore the identity and life of the author himself. For long, a false identity was accepted—the identification with Muhsin Fani of Kashmir, who, according to Lachchmi Narain Shafiq's *Gul-i Rana*, died in 1670.[8] There is no basis for this identification; since the facts given by the author about himself and his work cannot possibly fit Muhsin Fani.[9] There is also the possibility that Muhsin is referred to in the *Dabistan* itself as 'a scholar (*fazil*), Muhammad Muhsin by name' who gave the author information of what he had heard from Mobad Sarosh (*DM*, p. 33), whom the author himself had met twice in Kashmir (pp. 33, 35). There is still less basis for the attribution of the work to one Muhammad Amin in two late-eighteenth-century manuscripts.[10]

One thing clear from the texts of the *Dabistan* itself is that the author had the poetic name or *takhallus* of 'Mobad'. The work, in fact, begins with five couplets addressed to God, and the poet's 'signature' in the fifth verse reads 'Mobad'. Mobad's verses are also quoted elsewhere in the work, but the introductory verses show that they were composed with the title of *Dabistan* in mind (*ai nam-i tu sar-i daftar-i itfal-i dabistan*), making it almost certain that the author was himself the poet quoted. 'Mobad' means a Parsi priest as well as 'the head of wine-sellers',[11] and so is an apt style for a poet in Persian to adopt. Rieu, drawing the same inference, points out that 'Mobad Shah' is given as the takhallus of the author in the subscription of the original manuscript the British Museum of (Add. 25,849), the original having itself been transcribed in 1209/1794–5. The full name of the author there is stated to be 'Mir Zulfiqar Ali al-Husaini, with the poetic title of Mobad Shah'.[12] But we have a much earlier testimony to the same effect from Azad Bilgrami, writing in 1762–3, when he refers to 'the *Dabistan*, the work of Mirza Zulfiqar with the poetic title of (*mutkhallis bi*) Mobad'.[13] The addition of 'Ali al-Husaini' to the personal name and 'Shah' to the poetic title might then well be later accretions.

The curious fact remains that while, indirectly, the author reveals his poetic title 'Mobad' which, in its turn, suggests, but does not prove, some Parsi affinity, he throughout abstains from divulging his personal name, as well as his religion. And yet the facts he gives about his own life are numerous enough. On the basis of these, Troyer in his 'Preliminary Discourse' to the Shea–Troyer translation has reconstructed the main facts of the author's life;[14] and Rieu too has given a summary notice of his life.[15] Shea's reconstruction is, however, full of errors, not least being his confusion between the town of Gujarat of the Punjab (as carefully indicated by the author of the *Dabistan*) and the region of Gujarat.

It has, therefore, seemed desirable to set out in a largely chronological form, some of the autobiographical data that our author provides in his work, and see, with an open mind, the picture of the author which emerges therefrom.

When we construct the author's life from the numerous references to himself in the work, his original Parsi background becomes obvious. The very first recorded event in his life belongs to 1028/1619, when according to what Mobad Hoshyar told him later in life, he took him to Balak Nath Tapshri, a yogi of great powers, who predicted that the author would be a 'man of God' (*Khuda-shanas*; *DM*, p. 144).[16] Clearly, the author was so small at the time that he could not be expected to remember the event on his own. We may infer, then, that he was no more than three years old, and was, therefore, born *c.* 1616. He was still so young five years later (1033/1623–4) that, while being taken from Patna to Agra, he was carried by Mobad Hoshyar 'in his arms' to another yogi, Gosain Chatrupa (the celebrated Jadrup/Chadrup of Jahangir's memoirs), who blessed the author, taught him the *surya mantra* and asked one of his disciples, Ganesh Man, to remain with him, instructing him till he attained his age of majority (*DM*, p. 147).[17]

Here we need to pause a little: In 1619 an infant, he is taken to a seer who predicts a future for him as a mystic; in 1623–4, the famous Jadrup makes much of him and assigns a disciple of his to be with him. We shall see that in 1642–3, when he was still a young man of less than thirty, Guru Hargobind was to address him as 'Nanak'. These references could not possibly have been made because of the author's own spiritual attainments. We must rather suppose that he had been born in a family of high spiritual reputation, perhaps, in the direct line of descent of the heads of a priestly order. But let us return to the story of his life.

While recalling his being taken to Chatrupa by Mobad Hoshyar, the author refers to his earlier account of Mobad Hoshyar. He must then be the highly praised Mobad Hoshyar (I), who was a descendant of Rustam, and who was born at Surat and died in 1050/1640–1 at Agra (*DM*, pp. 32–3).[18] He must be distinguished from Mobad Hoshyar (II), a descendant of the sage Jamasp, whom the author met first of all in Kashmir in 1036/1626–7 (p. 33), and from another Mobad Hoshyar (III), son of Khurshid, who was born in Patna and met the author in Kashmir only in 1049/1639–40 (pp. 36–7). It would seem that Mobad Hoshyar (I) was a kind of guardian of the author during the latter's minority, the author's own parents being not at all mentioned. Till 1048/1638–9, he kept company with the author, who in 1048/1638–9 went with him to see a Parsi priest, with Kochik Bahram (p. 36).

From 1036/1626 to 1040/1630–1 the author appears to have sojourned in Kashmir, where his recorded intellectual or religious contacts were exclusively with Parsi priests. In 1036/1626–7, as we have seen, he met the second Mobad Hoshyar, as well as Mobad Sarosh, son of Kaiwan (*DM*, p. 34); and in 1040/1630–1, Mobad Sarosh again (p. 35); Pil Azar, a merchant belonging to the Shidrangi sect of the Parsis (p. 41); Raham of the Paikari sect, and Andariman, belonging to the Alari sect, both of whom he met 'in the house of Shadosh' (p. 62); and Shaidab of the Akhshi sect (p. 63)[19]. The only exception is his meeting with Ishar Kar, a yogi in 1036/1627, also in Kashmir (p. 148).

The remarkable fact is that till 1630–1, when he must have reached the age of eighteen, he records his coming into any kind of contact with thirteen religious men (including Shaidosh), of whom ten were Parsis, and three Hindus. The first recorded encounter with a Muslim divine occurred only in 1046/1636–7, when, journeying out of Kashmir, he met Arif Subhani in Bangash-i Bala (upper Kurrun Valley in Pakistan's NWFP); and Arif Subhani was a Sufi, who was not tied to the rites of any one religion (*DM*, p. 323). His next encounter with a Muslim was with Mahmud Fal Hasiri in Kashmir in 1047/1637–8, but Mahmud is merely quoted for a story about a Parsi divine Mahrab, a disciple of Farshad (pp. 42–3).

The dominance of Parsis in the author's intellectual life continues in 1048/1638–9. With the guardian of his childhood, Mobad Hoshyar I, he meets Kochik Bahram at Lahore (*DM*, p. 36), and also Jawan Sher of the Parsi Shidabiya sect (p. 63). The author journeyed from Lahore to Kashmir, in this year in the company of Khaki, a merchant who belonged to the same sect (pp. 62–3). In Kashmir the same year he met Ashur Beg Qaramanlu, a Sufi again, who gave him a report about his personal experience of the Parsi divine Farzana Bahram (p. 40).

But it is during these two years that the author for the first time reports meeting Muslim scholars and divines, free from any Parsi context. In 1048\1639–40 he meets Mulla Adil Kashghari at Lahore, the Mulla being the source for a statement on Sunni belief in the absoluteness of God (*DM*, p. 211). The next year in Kashmir he met Mulla Ismail Sufi, a disciple of the mystic Miyan Mir (p. 321). He met the Vedantic seer Gyani Rina, once in the company of 'the famous poet and master of eloquence, Mulla Shaida, the Indian' (p. 135). He continued to meet other Hindu divines as well; Sarur Nath Tapashri in Lahore in 1048/1638–9 (p. 144), and Srikant in Kashmir the next year.

In 1050/1640–1, Mobad Hoshyar I died at Agra, having presumably left the author's company (*DM*, p. 33). From this year inclusive there is no record of the author meeting any Parsi divine except for one occasion to be mentioned below. It seems as if from 1640–1 the author no longer lived among the Parsis, and shifted to a life mainly among Muslims and Hindus. It is difficult to say that this was either because he took service with some Mughal officer, of which he makes no mention; or because of a formal conversion to Islam, of which, again, there is not the slightest suggestion in his text. It is clear, however, that not only did he detach himself from his hitherto dominant Parsi environment, but he also took to extensive travel. In 1050/1640–1, leaving Kashmir, he visited Gujarat (Punjab) (p. 162) and the nearby town of Wazirabad (p. 162). He was at Lahore in 1052/1643–4 (p. 161), staying on there till the next year (pp. 218, 254), when he travelled to Kiratpur in the Punjab Hills (pp. 147, 190), and, then, the same year (1053/1644–5), to Kabul (p. 299) onwards to Meshed in Iran (p. 241) On his way back he visited Multan, in 1054/1644–5 (p. 231) from where he went to Gujarat (Punjab) in 1055/1645–6 (p. 152); in the latter year he was also at Peshawar (p. 144). In 1056/1641–7, he began his journey across India. We find him at Dunara near Jodhpur (p. 167), on the way to which he had passed through Merta (p. 167). His object seems to have been Surat, the great port where he reports himself in the next year (p. 202).[20] The same year (1057/1647) he travelled to Haidarabad (p. 194). From there he made his way back to Gujarat in the Punjab which, from his repeated periods of stay there, seems to have become his family seat after he left Kashmir. He was staying at this place in 1059/1649 where, significantly, he met, for the only reported occasion after

1639–0, two Parsis (p. 62).[21] But the same year we find him travelling to Srikakul on the borders of Orissa, the place being then in Qutbshahi control (p. 125). He fell ill there in 1061/1651 (p. 15), and was still there in 1063/1652–3, the last year mentioned in the book (p. 105). Everywhere he seems to have been meeting persons of all religions and persuasions, giving him information about their beliefs, scriptures and traditions.

It would seem then that a fundamental change in the author's life took place in 1640–1; and one may ask whether this was due to his desire to write the *Dabistan* itself. In his text at one place, 1055/ 1645–6 is cited as the current year (*DM*, p. 119). If he had even begun to write only in that year, the project must have shaped itself in his mind much earlier, and his travels, which seemingly detached him from his Parsi family, which probably had now made Gujarat in the Punjab its seat, might really be attributed to his desire to collect material for the book from all possible sources.

There is a passage, to which Rieu has drawn attention,[22] which may give us the light we are seeking. This passage occurs at the beginning of Chapter (*Talim*) II, on Hindus, that immediately follows Chapter I, devoted to the Parsis. It reads:

Since unstable fortune threw this writer away from the Parsis and cast him in the company of the devotees (*samans*) of the idol, and image-worshippers praying to Vishnu (Bishan), it is necessary that, having gathered together the minutiae of the beliefs of this (sect), these should be set out after the [account of the] Parsis. (*DM*, p. 105)

Rieu interprets the passage to mean that 'fortune ... tore him from his Parsi surroundings ... to make him the associate of Hindu votaries.'[23] This is possible; but, perhaps, the author by 'unstable fortune' (*rozgar-i napaydar*) does not have any hostile fate in mind, but only makes a statement of the simple fact that he began with a Parsi environment, but then later—which was, as we have established, in or about 1050/1640–1—he left his Parsi family for long durations, during which he mixed notably with Hindus. The passage does not necessarily mean that such mixing with Hindus and detachment from the Parsi environment for this purpose were against his will.

The solution of the mystery of why the author, indeed, deliberately took to the life of travel and exploration of religious diversities, as he now did, may possibly be sought in the posthumous influence of one man, Azar Kaiwan. The *Dabistan* gives to Azar Kaiwan precedence over even Zoroaster in its description of the religion of the Parsis with which the book begins. The Sipasis, also called Yazdanis, Izidis or Abadis or Azars (these being among alternative names) are described as a monotheistic sect different from Zoroastrians, over whom it is given precedence. To this sect belonged Azar Kaiwan, 'possessed of all sciences' (*zul 'ulum*) and 'the Great Philosopher' (*filsufi azam*). He had come from Iran to settle in Patna, where he died in 1027/1617 at the age of 85 years (*DM*, p. 27).[24] He had numerous disciples, whom our author describes at length. It would become clear from reading his detailed account of Kaiwan and his disciples (pp. 26–44), that the author was affiliated to this sect. It may be recalled that it was in 1033/1623–4, that he was taken as a child from Patna to Agra, so that presumably earlier his family had lived at Patna with the community of Azar Kaiwan's followers. Mobad Hoshyar I, who appears virtually as his guardian during his childhood, was himself a disciple of Azar Kaiwan (pp. 32–3). From the account of the latter's life and teachings given by the *Dabistan* (pp. 26–31), it transpires that he believed in an absolute monotheism, inclining towards pantheism, pursued an ascetic life, and avoided animal-killing and meat eating. A mystic, his opponent was the self (*nafs*); and he declared that asking anyone to adopt one's religion was nothing but an assertion of *nafs*. Though his closest disciples were Parsis, he had Muslim followers too; and his disciples in turn had Muslim, Hindu, Jewish and Christian followers, whom the author knew, or knew of, by name and repute.[25] An affinity was seen particularly with Sufism; and one of Azar Kaiwan's disciples, Kochik Bahram (d. 1048/1638–9) translated the Arabic works of Shihabuddin *Maqtul*, the famous Sufi, into Persian. The author himself sums up the views of Azar Kaiwan and his followers—'the Abadi Mystics' (*darveshan-i Abadiya*) as follows:

When anyone, stranger to their own faith (*kesh*) becomes acquainted with the community of this sect, they do not speak ill of him and commend the path of his religion, and accept whatever he says, omitting nothing by way of respect and courtesy, on account of their own faith. This is because they believe that God can be reached through every religion ... They do not hold it proper to hurt anyone without gain. If someone has some work with them, whether for salvation or for this world, they do all they can to be with him and assist him. They abstain from all practices of intolerance, malice, jealousy and hatred or preference of one community (*millat*) over another, and of one religion (*kesh*) over another. They consider the learned, the mystics, the upright ones and God worshippers of every religion their friends, and they do not call ordinary people bad,[26] nor denounce the worldly ones. They say, of him who does not seek religion, of what use is denouncing the world to him? Such denunciation [they say] is the act of the envious. They do not share their secrets with strangers nor tell others of what someone has told them. (*DM*, p. 42)[27]

After reading this in the context of the known facts of the author's life, there should remain little doubt that, given the basic position of Azar Kaiwan's school or sect that all religions have the capacity to reach God, and the essential truths are few, the author was driven to explore the beliefs of all religions to discover how much of these truths were in fact shared by them.

If this was his objective when 'Fate' separated him from his Parsi environment, it may be assumed that he was by now, at twenty-five years or so in age, himself a religious man of some status. Otherwise, the poetic title 'Mobad' could hardly been claimed by him without an air of presumption. Such status probably explains a curious sentence in the *Dabistan*. This occurs in the author's account of Sikhism. He had met, he says, Guru Hargobind at Kiratpur in 1052/1642–43; and Guru Hargobind 'in his letters was pleased to remember the writer by the title of Nanak, who was the preceptor of this sect' (*DM*, p. 190).[28] Such courtesy could hardly have been extended to the author unless the Sikh Guru had seen in the latter a religious divine who held the same monotheistic principles as the Sikhs did. In fact, our author does point out that the sect of Sipasis or Yazdanis, to which, as we have seen he belonged, had the same outlook of reverence towards the assembled body as the Sikhs had, for 'that sect (of Sipasis too) has the belief that when a large number devote themselves to the doing of a thing, it would certainly get done' (*DM*, p. 192).

There seems little doubt, then, that the author of the *Dabistan* was a priest of the Sipasi/Abadi sect of the Parsis. There is much justice in Rieu's comment that 'his description of Islamism is that of a well-informed outsider, not of a born and bred Muslim'.[29] Though one could argue that this might be because of his anxiety not to identify himself with any particular religion, including Islam, one would then not be able to explain why he should have offered such a 'glowing account' (in Rieu's words) of the Sipasis, or rather, of Azar Kaiwan and his followers.

As against this conclusion about the author's Parsi antecedents, the personal name of Mirza Zulfiqar assigned to him by Azad Bilgrami and later scribes of the book can well be urged. It has been reported that a *diwan* (collection of verses) of 'Mobad' (as poetic title) has been discovered at Patna, and the personal name of the author given there is Zulfiqar Ardastani. From this fact it has been asserted that he migrated to India during the reign of Shah Jahan (1628–58), received instruction in 'the common syllabus taught by Muslim theologians', whereafter 'he turned to the Zoroastrians and Brahmans in succession'.[30] It will be seen, however, in the light of our collection of facts of the author's life in the *Dabistan* itself, that he was in India as an infant, as early as 1619 in the reign of Jahangir, and that from that very time he was in the company of Paris.

If, then, Zulfiqar was really used as a personal name by our author, such use was probably for convenience only in society where Muslims were more acceptable than Parsis. In his account of Azar Kaiwan's followers, he refers to such a practice as a kind of device adopted for appearances (*suri*). Thus, one of Azar Kaiwan's disciples, Farzana Bahram, 'adopted the suri discipleship of Khwaja Jamaluddin Mahmud, one of the pupils of Mulla Jamaluddin Dawani' (*DM*, p. 32). Of four votaries of the Samradi (Parsi) sect, whom the author met in Kashmir in 1048/1638–39, he says that all the four 'also had Muslims names' (p. 60). A follower of the Parsi Akhshi sect, Shaidao, whom the author met in Kashmir in 1040/1630–31, 'was known (publicly) by the name of Shamsuddin' (p. 63). Zulfiqar could then well have been the author's public name without any actual affiliation to Islam.

One may, finally, note that the extensive knowledge of Persian literature, and Islamic practices and beliefs that the *Dabistan* displays, does not militate in any manner against the author being a Parsi. The followers of Azar Kaiwan, whom he describes, were uniformly well versed in Persian and Arabic. They wrote books in Persian: Mobad Hoshyar I, the author's guardian, wrote *Surud-i Mastan* (*DM*, p. 23); Mobad Sarosh, *Jam-i Kaikhusravi* (p. 35);[31] Kochik Bahram rendered the Arabic writings of the Shaikh of *Ishraq*, Shihabuddin *Maqtul* into Persian (p. 37);[32] and Mobad Hoshyar ibn Khurshid wrote *Watira-i Mobadi* (p. 36). Shaidosh on his deathbed went on reciting two couplets of Hafiz.[33]

This background explains why the author, encountering a belief or practice, which to him seems to have a universal value, expresses his recognition of this fact by an apt quotation out of an exceptionally large store of Persian poetry, where we have not only great classical poets, like Sa'di, Rumi ('Maulavi-i Manavi') and Hafiz, but also more recent poets like 'Urfi' and Faizi, and the author himself. To understand the author's religious position, it is necessary to realize that to him not Islam in its theology, but Persian Sufic poetry in its eminent nobility, represents the ultimate truth, the same that Azar Kaiwan and his followers (including the author) also saw in their own version of their ancient faith.

The question whether the author of the *Dabistan* was a Parsi or Muslim can be asked (and answered) in traditional terms: His own text leaves us in no doubt that he was of Parsi upbringing and did not convert to Islam. But, in terms that Azar Kaiwan set forth and the author believed in, the question was, perhaps, irrelevant; Mirza Zulfiqar 'Mobad' was a man of God, a seeker of universal truth. That he is so modest about his own identity is tantalizing for us: what we should surely not do to trace the identity of a man who has left behind so wonderful a book, so multi-layered in its truths, and with so many insights for him who would explore? And yet his indifference to his own name and identity may be understood if we realize that for 'Mobad', the 'self' was of no moment when set beside the great search for the secrets of the spirit in which he had joined. Among its many vices, there were surely some virtues too in a civilization that could produce such a man and such a book nearly three hundred and fifty years ago.

NOTES

1. See D.N. Marshall, *Mughals in India*, Bombay, 1967, I, p. 299, for an incomplete list of the catalogued MSS.

2. Ali Asghar Mustafawi's edn, Teheran, 1361 Solar/1982 is a mere offset reprint of this edition, with a rather light-weight introduction added.

3. Marshall reports earlier editions, Teheran, 1260/1844, and Bombay, 1266/1849–50 and 1277/1860–1.

4. Data about translations derived from C. Rieu, *Catalogue of the Persian MSS in the British Museum*, London, 1879, p. 142a.

5 Ibid., p. 141b.

6. See Jivanji Jamshedji Modi, 'A Parsee High Priest (Dastur Azar Kaiwan, 1529–1614 AC) with his Zoroastrian Disciples in Patna in the 16th and 17th Century AC', *Journal of the KR Cama Oriental Institute* (hereafter *JKRCOI*), XX (1932), p. 7 and n.

7. Under the title *Nanak Panthis*, originally appearing in *Journal of*

Indian History, xix (2). Characteristically, the translator commends the author of the *Dabistan-i Mazahib* for giving 'an impartial account of what he saw and heard of the Sikhs and their Gurus during his contact with them' (p. 3).

8. While rejecting the identification of the author of *Dabistan* with Muhsin Fani, J.J. Modi (*JRCOI*, xx, pp. 8–11) still falls into the error of accepting the date of the death of Muhsin Fani as that of our author.

9. As stated, for example, in the title given to the *Dabistan* in Br. Mus. MS. Add. 7613 (Rieu, *Catalogue of the Persian MSS* ..., I, 143a).

10. Br. Mus. MSS. Add. 16,670 (AD 1792) and Add. 16,671 (AD 1797); Rieu, I, p. 142b.

11. *Ghiyas ul Lughat*, s.v. *mobad*. Muhammad Ghiyasuddin, the author of this very comprehensive dictionary, completed it in 1242/1826–7.

12. Rieu, *Catalogue of the Persian MSS* ..., I, pp. 142a–3a.

13. *Maasir ul Kiram*, Hyderabad (Dn), 1910, I, p. 22.

14. *Dabistan or School of Manners*, tr. D. Shea and A. Troyer, London, 1843, I, pp. xii–xv.

15. Rieu, I, pp. 141a–2a.

16. There is no sanction in the *Dabistan* for Modi's statement that the author was born in Persia and then brought to India (*JRKCOI*, xx, p. 9).

17. For Jahangir's meetings with Jadrup, see *Tuzuk-i Jahangiri*, ed. Saiyid Ahmad, Ghazipur and Aligarh, 1863–4, pp. 175–6, 250–3, 279–81. His description of Jadrup matches that of Chatrupa in the *Dabistan*, pp. 146–7; the *Dabistan* also speaks of the high regard that Jahangir had for Jadrup.

18. Cf. Modi, *JKRCOI*, xx, pp. 40–1.

19. This Shaidab, probably for convenience, also bore the name Shamsuddin.

20. There seems to be no sanction in the *Dabistan* for Modi's suggestion (*JRKCOI*, xx, pp. 9–10) that he visited Navsari, the famous Parsi settlement near Surat, and obtained information about Zoroastrianism from Dastur Birzo Kamdin there.

21. Paikar Pazhoh and Jahan Nur.

22. Rieu, I, p. 142a.

23. Ibid. Rieu is right in contesting the reference to 'the Shores of Persia' in the Shea-Troyer translation, II, p. 2.

24. For a reconstruction of Azar Kaiwan's life, mostly based on the *Dabistan*, see Modi, *JKRCOI*, xx, pp. 25–34.

25. Cf. Modi, *JKRCOI*, xx, pp. 34–51, for information on thirteen Zoroastrian and ten non-Zoroastrian followers of Azar Kaiwan.

26. I take it that *nez* here is a mistranscription for *bad*.

27. Modi, *JKRCOI*, xx, pp. 56–75, draws up a list of the beliefs of Azar Kaiwan and his disciples and traces their antecedents; on pp. 75–85 he compares them with those of earlier Zoroastrian tradition. A very perceptive and sympathetic treatment will be found in H. Corbin, 'Azar Kayvan',

Encyclopaedia Iranica, ɪ, pp. 183–7, where the *Ishraqi* antecedents of the school are strongly brought out.

28. There is no justification in the text for Ganda Singh's rendering: 'Guru Hargobind in his letters to the Chronicler remembered [himself] by the title of Nanak who is the spiritual head of this sect' (*Nanakpanthis*, tr., p. 20).

29. Rieu, ɪ, p. 141b. The editor of the Teheran reprint of *DM*, editor's preface, xvii, justifiably points out that it would have been very difficult for a Muslim to attribute the original foundations of Mecca and Medina to Parsi shrines of the Moon (*mah*) as the author does (pp. 15–16).

30. Nabi Hadi, *Dictionary of Indo-Persian Literature*, New Delhi, 1995, pp. 360–1.

31. This work is extant (pub. Sayyid Abdul Fattah '*urf* Mir Ashraf Ali, Bombay, 1848), but the author gives his own name as Khuda Jui (God-seeker); this may well be his pen-name (cf. Modi, *JKRCOI*, xx, pp. 20–1).

32. He was also the author of *Azhrang-i Mani* (*DM*, p. 36), which may be the *Shahristan*, litho. pub. Bombay, 1851, and described by Modi, *JKRCOI*, xx, pp. 21–3.

33. *Khurram an roz kazin manzil-i wiran bi-rawam*, etc. ('Happy the day I leave this desolate stage of journey'), *DM*, p. 38. The author himself quotes from an elegy he composed for Shaidosh upon his death in 1040/ 1630–1 (p. 39).

20

Muslims' Perceptions of Judaism and Christianity in Medieval India

I

As is well known, Islam arose in Arabia which, alongside the pagan communities, had a large number of tribes and groups which professed Judaism and Christianity. So far as we know, the relations between the Jews and Christians and their Arab neighbours in pre-Islamic times were cordial, or were not at any rate adversely affected by differences of faith. In its self-view Islam represented both a continuation and a supersession of the two earlier Semitic faiths. The Jewish Gospel as well as the New Testament had originally represented divine messages, and so those who followed them were 'People of the Book', to be distinguished from the 'Infidels'. But the Gospel texts, the Quran itself had claimed, had suffered from unauthorized deletions and insertions; and this claim, of course, created a fundamental point of disagreement between the Muslims, on the one hand, and the Jews and Christians on the other. Nonetheless, early Muslims seemed fairly familiar with both the earlier Semitic religions.

Among the learned the familiarity would last longer and be preserved in areas where Jews and Christians were no longer be encountered. Alberuni completed his work *Kitab-al Hind*, *c.* 1035, in Ghaznavide Punjab; yet his knowledge of Jewish and Christian precepts and practices seems considerable. It is possible that some of this knowledge came from the work of al-Iranshahri, a Persian writer in Arabic, which has not survived.[1] Alberuni well knew the Jewish custom of levirate,[2] and shows familiarity with how the Jews represented God:

Similar to this [Hindu Om] is the manner in which the Jews write the name of God, viz. by three Hebrew *Yods*. In the (Torah) the word is written YHVH and pronounced *Adonai*; sometimes they also say *Yah*. The word *Adonai* which they pronounced is not expressed in writing.[3]

This statement shows that Alberuni had access to the text of the

Old Testament, for he refers to both the Jewish and Christian Testaments being in Hebrew and Syriac. Presumably using Arabic translations from Syriac, he shows considerable familiarity with the use of the word 'Eloah' in Hebrew used for God as well as a god, quoting from Gen. vi. 4; Job i. 6; Exod. vii. 1; and Psalms lxxxii.[4] Similarly, he cites 'the Second Book of Kings', about the loss of David's son borne by Uriah's wife and God's promise of another son to him whom he would 'adopt as his own son'.[5] Of the Christian gospel, Alberuni shows equal if not greater grasp. He argues that, unlike Arabic, the language of the New Testament has a looser meaning attached to the words 'father' and 'son'. 'By *the son* [of God] they (the Christians) understand most especially Jesus, but apply it also to others besides him'. He tellingly quotes the prayer, 'O our father which art in Heaven' (Matt. vi, 9); and Jesus's promise that he is going to 'his father and to their father' (John xx, 17).[6] Alberuni considers the Trinity to be not inconsistent with monotheism, for he says that the Christians 'distinguish' between the Three Persons (the Trinity) and give them separate names, Father, Son and Holy Ghost, but unite them into one substance.[7] Elsewhere he shows familiarity with the ranks of the Church, speaking of the bishops, metropolitans, *catholici* and patriarchs, and of the lower clergy, namely the presbyter and deacon.[8] Presumably, he knew more of the Eastern than of the Roman Church, for he never mentions the Pope.

Alberuni admired the Christian doctrine of non-violence as enshrined in the New Testament: 'to offer to him who has beaten your cheek the other cheek, also to bless your enemy and pray for him. Upon my life, this is a noble philosophy.' But in practice it had been otherwise: 'ever since Constantine the Victorious became a Christian both sword and whip have ever been employed, for without them it would be impossible to rule.'[9] Alberuni's admiration for Christ's message shows also in a passage in his Preface:

The Messiah expresses himself in the Gospel to this effect: 'Do not mind the fury of kings in speaking the truth before them. They only possess your body, but they have no power over your soul' (Cf. Matt. x, 18, 19, 28; Luke, xii, 4). In these words the Messiah orders us to exercise moral courage.[10]

It seems from these passages that, besides reliance on the translations of the Gospel and al-Iranshahri, Alberuni had some contacts with the Jewish and Christian communities in Central Asia, although he nowhere directly refers to them. But soon after him, at least in northern India, the Jews and Christians alike seem to have become distant entities, only to be heard of in anecdotes or to be mentioned in hypothetical or rhetorical contexts, though the references themselves are not unfriendly.

On 9 November 1317, the Sufi saint Shaikh Nizamuddin, while declining to ask a Hindu to convert to Islam, related this anecdote about Khwaja Bayazid Bustami, the great Sufi saint:

A Jew had a house near that of Khwaja Bayazid Bustami. When Khwaja Bayazid died, people asked the Jew, 'why do you not become a Muslim?' The Jew replied: 'What kind of Muslim should I be? If Islam is what Bayazid followed, I am not equal to following it; if it is what you follow, then I am repelled by such Islam!'[11]

When Nizamuddin himself died, it was claimed in verse that 'Muslims, Hindus, Christians ('Tarsa') and Magians crowned their heads with the dust of the door of his tomb.'[12] This is, surely, rhetoric, in so far as the Christians and the Magi are concerned. There is no evidence that there was any community of Christians settled at Delhi in the fourteenth century.

II

The living relationship with Christianity (if not immediately with Judaism as well) was re-established with the arrival in strength of the Portuguese following Vasco da Gama's voyage terminating at Calicut in 1498. Not surprisingly, it was now the Catholic version of Christianity which Muslims in India began mainly to encounter. On 21 June 1578 there arrived at Akbar's court a Portuguese (*firangi*), who was a merchant in Bengal, Prtb tar (?) by name, accompanied by his wife Fashurna (?), and he introduced to Akbar the practice of monogamy that the Christian laity had to follow — an imposition, he said, of the celibate clergy.[13] But it was with the arrival of the first Jesuit mission in 1580 that there was a much livelier appreciation of Christianity. Unfortunately, Akbar's adviser and minister Abul Fazl, who met the mission, has not left his description of Christianity or even an account of his meeting with the Jesuits in his writings,[14] the gap being filled by 'Abdul Qadir Badauni, the historian, a critic of both Akbar and Abul Fazl. Placing the Jesuit arrival a year before the actual one, he sets forth the picture of Christianity that Akbar's court now obtained.

There came experienced theologians from Europe (*Afranja*), whom they call 'Padre' (*Padhari*). Their absolute legislator (*Mujtahid-i Kamil*), who can alter all decrees in view of circumstances of the time, and kings too cannot defy his authority, is called the 'Pope' (*Papa*). They brought the Bible (*injil*) and gave arguments in favour of the Trinity, and proving the truth of Christianity (*nasraniyat*), began to spread the Christian faith (*millat-i Isawi*). His Majesty instructed Prince Murad to take some lessons from the Bible, and Shaikh Abul Fazl was appointed to translate it. In place of the invocation 'In the name of God', this sentence occurred (in the Gospel): 'O whose name is Jesus Christ (*Zhazhu Kristu*)', i.e. 'O whose name is Benevolent and Bountiful'. ... These accursed people brought in a description of *Dajjal* (Anti-Christ) and applied his attributes to our Prophet, peace be on him, the very opposite of all *Dajjals*.[15]

It may be observed in passing that there must have been much interest at this time at Akbar's court in the Pope's authority to 'alter all decrees' of religion in his capacity as *Mujtahid-i Kamil*, the legal 'innovator' with absolute authority, because a more limited role as legislator in Islamic matters had been sought for Akbar himself through the theologians' declaration (mahzar) of 1579;[16] and Abul Fazl had argued that, had the great jurist Abu Hanifa been alive now, he would have authored a different system of law.[17] In any case, the first Jesuit mission ignited some interest at the court in the Bible. It was obvious that by now there were no Arabic or Persian versions of the Gospel available, as they apparently were to Alberuni. In a letter dated 14 April 1582, carried by his envoy Sayyid Muzaffar Khan to Goa, Akbar wrote (Abul Fazl's draft) to 'the scholars of Europe' (*danayan-i firang*), the emperor not only asked for a scholar to be sent to him to explain the tenets of Christianity, but also went on to add:

It has reached our august ear that divine books like the Torah, the Gospel (*Injil*) and the Psalms (*Zabur*) have been rendered into the Arabic and Persian languages; if these books, so translated or not, from which general benefit would follow, are available in that country, these may be sent to us.[18]

Unfortunately, our sources do not indicate any tangible consequences of this curiosity regarding Christianity during the time of Akbar and Jahangir. References to Christian practices or beliefs remain casual or incidental. In his book on ethics, Badauni mentions Christian books on ethics, but gives no title;[19] elsewhere, he recalls from his personal knowledge that Christians and Jews like the Hindus, not only regard music as permissible, but consider it a part of worship.[20]

This is a little more specific evidence of actual observation of Christian (and Jewish?) practices, but it hardly denotes penetration.

III

The lack of interest in Christian theology at the Mughal court, if one goes by what came to be written in Persian, rather than by Mughal painting, which in its later phase has distinct traces of Christian influence both in its themes and in its symbolisms,[21] is surprising. This indifference was not shared by a man, however, who appears to have devoted his life to an unbiased collection of data about diverse religions. For reasons not known, he conceals his name from us in his book, the *Dabistan-i Mazahib* ('School of Religions').[22] But Azad Bilgrami gives his name as Mirza Zulfiqar with the pen name Mobad;[23] and the latter, indeed, appears in the *Dabistan*. His autobiographical details in the book are consistent with his having some Parsi connections.[24] The author refers to 1645–6 as the current year at one place;[25] later dates occur in the text, the last traceable date being 1653,[26] when he was in the Golkunda kingdom, though most of his life was spent in various parts within the Mughal Empire.

In the *Dabistan-i Mazahib* there is a full chapter on Judaism.[27] The author says he had been unable to meet any follower of that religion; but in 1647 he came to Haidarabad, capital of the Golkunda kingdom, where he met the famous Muhammad Sa'id 'Sarmad'.[28] Presumably, from what Sarmad told him, he writes that Sarmad belonged to

a family of the Jewish learned, of the class whom they call Rabbis (*arbanniyun*); after obtaining knowledge of the beliefs of the Rabbis and reading the Torah, he became a Muslim, and studied the sciences while attending upon some of the Iranian scholars.

Coming to India, he turned a mystic and attached to himself a young Hindu boy of Thatta, Abhay Chand, to whom he taught the Torah, the Psalms and other texts.[29] It was from Sarmad and Abhay Chand that the author's information about Judaism came.

The authenticity of this information can fortunately be checked by a means that Abhay Chand has provided for us through the *Dabistan*. At the request of the author he translated 'a small portion of the Torah' from the original Hebrew into Persian, 'Mobad' had this translation closely checked by Sarmad, and then put this 'story of Adam' in his book verbatim.[30] The translation runs from the beginning of Genesis to

Genesis vi. 8. The accuracy and completeness of the translation is admirable, every sentence and clause of the Genesis i-vi.8, being present, the placing of words in the Persian text making it obvious that a literal translation of the Hebrew was being attempted: thus verbs mostly precede the subjects, for example *guft khuda*, instead of *khuda guft*.

Comparing it with the revised version, one finds the Abhay Chand translation more convincing at many points. Thus, for example, where Abhay Chand translates: 'and God's wind used to blow over the face of the water', the R.V. Gen. i.2 has: 'and the spirit of God moved upon the face of the water'. Or again upon Cain's appeal to God, 'And God said unto Cain (Qabil), "But whoever killeth Cain shall have chastisement visited upon him upto seven generations"' (Abhay Chand), the corresponding words in R.V. Gen. iv. 15 are: 'And the Lord said unto him: "therefore whosoever slayeth Cain, vengeance shall be taken from him sevenfold".' 'Wind' for 'Spirit', and 'seven generations' for 'sevenfold".' appear clearly to be better choices. Abhay Chand, a poet in Persian himself,[31] naturally uses the Arabicized forms of biblical names, just as the R.V. uses the English forms. But all the names of Adam's descendants with the precise ages assigned to them, are exactly given without any slip whatsoever.

We should therefore be left in no doubt that Sarmad and Abhay Chand knew Hebrew, had the Hebrew Gospel (Old Testament) with them and were closely acquainted with its contents. Sarmad was, therefore, being truthful when he claimed a Rabbinic past.

The Jewish creed, according to Sarmad, was as follows:

1. God has a physical existence, and resembles man, who is created in His image; and sometimes He diffuses like rays [throughout the creation].

2. In the Torah and Psalms it is stated that the Soul has an invisible (lit. light, *latif*) body, existing in the human frame, the body of the senses.

3. The reward and punishment of the Last Day shall be in this creation. Suppose a person lives for 120 years: this constitutes one 'day'. Upon his death it becomes 'night'. Then all the elements of his body scatter; after some 12 years pass, they assemble again to put life into the same person (Cf. Dan. xii. 2). Another 'day' begins — and so the cycle goes on.

4. All elements that exist are found in the human body.

5. The Jews deny the prophethood of Christ and say he was a liar. The arguments that Christians bring forth based on

statements in the Torah are futile, since the statements they quote were made by Isaiah, (*Ishiya*) for himself, not Christ [cf. Isaiah ix. See also 10 below].

6. Abraham was not a Prophet but *Wali*, the Friend of God [cf. 2 Chron. xx. 7; Rom. iv. 11], which is a higher position than that of a Prophet.

7. In the Torah there is no mention [contrary to the Quran] of the Pharaoh claiming to be God. He was cruel and oppressed the Israelites, and disregarded Moses's admonitions; it was for this that he was chastised [Cf. Ex. xiv].

8. Aaron (Harun) was not a partner in the Prophethood of Moses, but was his *khalifa* (spokesman or successor) [cf. Ex. iv. 14–16; Num. xii, xvii, xviii, xx; Dieut. x. 6].

9. David sent Uriah to his death, because he was desirous of his wife, from whom he begat Solomon [2 Sam. xi, xii; 1 Chron. iii. 5. There is silence in the Quran on this matter].

10. Christ was not a Prophet. The words 'They broke my hands, and legs, and counted my bones' [cf. Psalms xxxv, 15, 16 and c], which Christians cite as referring to Christ, were spoken by David for himself.

11. In the Torah it is said that if the Israelites commit evil deeds, inevitably Muhammad would come. Sarmad said that although the name of the Prophet is found in the Torah, it is in a context which suggests another meaning. Even if it is taken as the name of the Prophet, it is a warning to Bani Israel not to join his faith (cf. Ezek, xxxviii). 'On this he spoke with much insistence.'

12. No outsider can enter the religion of the Jews. The circumcision prescribed by the law of their Prophet applies to them alone.

13. A Prophet is to be present and alive at all times to put into effect the law of the Torah.[32]

It is obvious that points 5–11 belong to one class, where Sarmad points out Jewish objections to Christian and Muslim interpretations of certain passages of the Old Testament or to the Muslim version of the biblical tradition. He obviously had access to the Hebrew scriptures, even though as in point 10, he may not have been literally quoting from the Bible. But the other points in which Sarmad represents Jewish

Rabbinic beliefs require a commentary.

On the perception of God, one may not fault Sarmad for inaccuracy. If 'God created man in his own image; in the image of God created He him' (Gen. i. 27; Abhay Chand has also translated this portion), then an anthropomorphic conception of God must follow. This has to be reconciled with the universal presence of God and His absolute power; and so the formulation of Jewish faith in point No. 1 seems unexceptionable. So also the concept of the Soul (point 2).

But point (3) is totally against the Rabbanic theology of the Day of Judgement. The soul remains suspended after death, until the dead are aroused on the Day of Judgement. Dan. xii. 2 describes the Day of Judgement rather than any reawakening by a physical assemblage of elements of the previous body in this life. Sarmad's representation of Judaism seems to encompass the soul's temporary suspension ('sleep') after death, but not the concept of the Day of Judgement — a basic idea that has been so strongly inherited by Christianity and Islam from Judaism. In fact, Sarmad seems to attribute to Judaism something very akin to the *Nuqtavi* view of coming together of the scattered elements of the dead physical frames in new bodies with the same or even merged souls.[33] One can, therefore, suggest that either the Jews in Iran had developed a heretical doctrine paralleling that of the *Nuqtavis*, or that Sarmad being personally impressed by the latter, was reading into the Jewish creed something which was not there.

It is significant that Sarmad knew that Judaism was not a proselytizing religion and had no room for outsiders (point 12). As for the necessity of the Prophets (point 13), it must be assumed that Sarmad had in mind the successive generations of biblical Prophets and the indispensability of their missions at that time; it is difficult to imagine him saying that the Jews had a Prophet living currently among them as well.

IV

The *Dabistan-i Mazahib* has a chapter on Christianity[34] immediately following the one on Judaism. The account is far more self-confident than the previous one. The author tells us that he met some of the Christian learned; and that his information was especially derived from 'a French *Padre* (*Padri-i fransai*)), whom the people from Portugal and Goa, who are in India and the Port of Surat, hold in high regard and whom the author met at the Port of Surat in 1057/1647'. The chapter is divided into three portions: (1) Christ; (2) beliefs of Christians; and (3) practices of Christians.

It becomes immediately apparent that the *Dabistan*'s account is entirely and genuinely derived from a detailed and accurate Roman Catholic transmission and is nowhere in the slightest influenced by the traditional Muslim beliefs about Christians or by the Quranic narrative as against the biblical one. The account of Christ begins by giving the date of his birth in terms of the usual Christian calculations from the Bible (31,909 years from Creation; 2,957 from Noah's flood; 752 years from the foundation of Rome; and 42 years from the accession of [Augustus'] Caesar, which suit the traditional date of the founding of Rome (753 BC) and the actual date of Augustus' seizure of power after the death of Julius Caesar (44 BC). It goes on to say that the virgin birth of Christ was predicted by Isaiah, the father of David, in these words: 'From Jesse's seed a branch springs forth; a flower blooms forth in that branch, within which [flower] the spirit of God settles. A virgin eats the fruit and bears a son.'[35] Perhaps, this is a reference to Isaiah XI.1–2, though the reference to the virgin does not occur there.[36] It goes on to describe the crucifixion of Christ by consent of Pontius Pilate ('Filatas') upon the insistence of the Jews, though Pilate himself washed his hands off the deed. But the Jews took the responsibility, which burden they still bear[37] — the standard basis of Christian anti-Semitism. The author goes on to tell us that three pictures were made of the blood-stained Jesus on the cross, one kept at the city of Shahin (?) in Portugal, displayed twice every year; one at Milan in Italy; and another at Rome.[38] This information again suggests close familiarity with Catholic pilgrim-places in Europe, on the part of the author's informant.

Coming to Christian beliefs, the author puts the first one as belief in Christ being *filius* ('filyus', carefully spelt letter-by-letter with vowels written out), that is the Son of God. He then classifies the basic Christian beliefs into those that relate to the Divinity of Christ, and those that relate to the person of Christ. He carefully spells out the word *Deus* (Diyos) for God, and sets out the belief in him as Creator, the Giver of Paradise, the Source of Peace, the Father of Christ. There is also the specific belief in the Holy Spirit (*Ruh-i Pak*, the pure Spirit), which, with God and Christ, completes the Trinity. The second set of beliefs relates to Christ being the Son of God coming from the womb of Virgin Mary ('Mariam') through the Holy Spirit (*ruhu'l quds*); to Christ mounting on the cross for the salvation of humanity, dying and being buried; to Christ's coming being foretold by the earlier Prophets; to his resurrection and ascension on the third day of his crucifixion; and to his appearance on the Day of Judgement to judge 'the living and the dead'. The Christians believe that the Trinity really constitutes One; and the Son of God came to die for the salvation of man. This statement with numbered beliefs[39] is obviously based on the Nicene Creed, as finally framed (the Nicaeno Constantinopolitan Creed, 381), with some necessary elaborations and explanations.[40]

The statement of the central creed is followed by the description of the four places where the dead souls go to: Hell, Purgatory ('Parkatori'/'Pargatori'); 'Leno', for those who die young; and Paradise. The Christian belief that on the Day on Judgement souls will unite with their bodies is also noted.[41]

The third portion deals with the morals, rituals and practices of the Christians. It mentions the Sunday sermons and the mass as well as the confessions (*kanfiya*) which must be offered once a year. It mentions the sacraments ('sakarmaint'), including payment of tithe, confirmation ('konfarmashayo'), eucharist ('senokrista'), penitence ('panitanshia'), extreme unction ('astrima onshia'), marriage ('matrimonia'), etc.[42]

The Pope is also mentioned: 'The successor of Christ they call Pope ('Pap'); and it is settled that he does not lead anyone to error, since Lord Christ in the Holy Bible has given him some pledges'.[43] After further details of Christian beliefs and practices, all on the basis of Catholic teaching, the author ends by saying that 'the Bible (New Testament) in the language of Christ has been rendered into many languages such as Hebrew, Greek, Latin — which is the language of the learned of Europe — and Syriac; and all of these they regard as the Word of God.'[44]

As already noted, Christianity is portrayed here in its Catholic garb only, and no hint is offered of the Reformation which had torn Christianity for well over a century and a quarter. Not only are the propositions of Protestantism (varied as they were) ignored, but the very existence of Protestantism side-stepped. Clearly, Mobad's French Padre either did not regard Protestants as Christians or did not wish to confuse matters by referring to their heresies. Apparently too, Mobad did not meet any Dutch or English merchant or clergyman sufficiently interested in transmitting his beliefs to him.

In his account of both Judaism and Christianity, Mobad's clinical neutrality is striking. Not for him the usual Muslim declamations of disapproval when one is obliged to quote or describe something against the traditions or creed of Islam. This attitude he maintains throughout his book, especially while reproducing arguments of votaries of one religion against those of another, as in the long section, 'Account of Debate between Religions'.[45] Here, for instance, he represents the Christian winning in the debate with the Muslim, over the authenticity of the Bible. If the Bible has undergone alterations, as the Muslims allege, then the latter should be able to produce the true text of the Bible, just as the Christians have the true text of the Old Testament ('Torah') which they share with the Jews, besides having their own *Injil*, or New Testament. The Christian similarly succeeded in showing that Prophet Muhammad's miracle of breaking the moon in twain could not have taken place. But the Jews brought arguments to prove that the virginity of Mary was disputable, and that the crucifixion of Christ was not predicted in the Psalms of David.[46] We have here, therefore, impartiality of a very high order, for which there can surely be found few parallels in the Islamic and Christian worlds of the seventeenth century.

V

So far as we can find, the *Dabistan-i Mazahib* (1553) had no successor; and surprisingly little intellectual curiosity is diplayed in the Indo-Muslim literature during the succeeding hundred years in the religion of the Europeans. Christianity was tolerated but not studied. It was almost the same story as with European technological appliances; they were used, but not, but for rare exceptions, reproduced. There was apparently no perception that Christianity was a challenging religion, so that Muslims should have need for studying it in order to controvert it. In other words, they lacked the motive which led so many Christian missionaries to study Islam and Hinduism. The indifference exhibited towards Christianity was not then a product of enmity; it was a product of a belief in coexistence, taking the Quranic verse, 'To you your religion, to me mine' in the most literal sense. It is interesting that Bernier (1667) attributes such a notion to the Brahmans as well: 'I found it impossible to convince them that the Christian faith was designed for the whole earth.'[47] With this comfortable vision, it was possible to look into one's own faith alone, and not polemicize with others. It is, then, a disturbing thought that tolerance could also generate inertia, which, on the other hand, was such a stranger to the actively proselytizing, intolerant True Apostolic Church of Rome.

NOTES

1. *Alberuni's India*, tr. E.C. Sachau, London, 1910, I, pp. 6–7.
2. Ibid., p. 109.
3. Ibid., p. 173–4.
4. Ibid., pp. 36–8.
5. Ibid., p. 38.
6. Ibid.
7. Ibid., p. 94.
8. Ibid., II, p. 15.
9. Ibid., p. 161.
10. Ibid., pp. 4–5.
11. Amir Hasan Sijzi, *Fawa'idu'l Fawad*, ed. M. Latif Malik, Lahore, 1966, p.
12. Mir Khurd, *Siyarul Auliya*, ed. Chiranji Lal, Delhi, 1985, p. 155. The work was completed after 1387, but most of the text was written much earlier.
13. *Akbarnama*, Bib. Ind. ed., III, p. 243 to be read with the passage in the earlier version of the work, B. L. MS. Add. 27, 247, f. 294b.
14. Abul Fazl does, however, refer under the year 1579–80 to the agitation caused by the Jesuit mission: 'at this time, the Christian scholars (*filsufan-i Nisara*) submitted strong arguments against the worldly learned of Muslim law at the imperial court; and learned controversy ensued' (*Akbarnama*, III, p. 272).
15. Abdul Qadir Badauni, *Muntakhab-ut Tawarikh*, Bib. Ind. II, p. 260.
16. For its text, see Nizamuddin Ahmad, *Tabaqat-i Akbari*, Bib. Ind., II, pp. 344–6; Badauni, II, pp. 271–2. See also M. Athar Ali, 'Towards an Interpretation of the Mughal Empire', *JRAS*, I, London, 1978 [Chapter 6].
17. Badauni, III, p. 79.
18. *Insha'i Abul Fazl*, Nawal Kishore, 1280/1864, pp. 37–9.
19. *Nijat'ur Rashid*, ed. S. Moinul Haq, Lahore, 1972, pp. 21–2.
20. Ibid., pp. 210–11.
21. Percy Brown, *Indian Painting under the Mughals, A.D. 1550 to A.D. 1750*, 1924, pp. 163–79; Ashok Kumar Das, *Mughal Painting During Jahangir's Time*, Calcutta, 1978, pp. 229–50.
22. I have used the edition ed./pub. by Ibrahim bin Nur Muhammad, Bombay, 1292/1875.
23. *Ma'asirul Kiram*, I, Hyderabad Dn, 1910, p. 22.
24. See esp. *Dabistan–i Mazahib*, p. 147. [See Chapter 19]
25. Ibid., p. 119.

26. Ibid., p. 153.

27. Ibid., pp. 194–202.

28. Ibid., p. 191.

29. Ibid., pp. 194–5.

30. The text runs from p. 196 to 202, constituting sec. 2 of the chapter on the Jews.

31. Ibid., p. 195.

32. Ibid., pp. 195–6.

33. A good exposition of the *Nuqtawi* theory is given in the *Dabistan-i Mazahib* itself, pp. 343–7.

34. *Dabistan-i Mazahib*, pp. 202–8.

35. Ibid., p. 202. Isha is the form given to Jesse's name. Ishas, adds the *Dabistan*, was the father of David.

36. 'And there shall come forth a shoot out of the stock of Jesse, and a branch out of his roots shall bear fruit; and the spirit of the Lord shall rest upon him', etc. (revised version).

37. *Dabistan-i Mazahib*, pp. 202–3.

38. Ibid., p. 203.

39. Ibid., pp. 203–4.

40. See the translation of the creed in Henry Bettenson, *Documents of the Christian Church*, London, 1954, pp. 36–7.

41. *Dabistan-i Mazahib*, p. 204.

42. Ibid., pp. 205–6.

43. Ibid., p. 206.

44. Ibid., p. 208.

45. Ibid., pp. 254–68.

46. Ibid., p. 258.

47. François Bernier, *Travels in the Mogul Empire*, tr. A. Constable, 2nd edn, rev. V.A. Smith, London, 1916, p. 328.

THE POLITICS OF EMPIRE

The Religious Issue in the
War of Succession, 1658–9

The war of succession among Shah Jahan's sons, which shook the Mughal Empire when it was at its height, by its extremely dramatic interest, called forth a spate of accounts which by their variety of detail, described from all points of view and with all degrees of credibility, almost overwhelm the modern student. Sir Jadunath Sarkar provided for the first time a coherent description of the war of succession, by picking out the most reliable accounts and rejecting those based on hearsay or later tradition. Great as the value of the Sir Jadunath's work was, his account suffered from an emphasis on pure description, with little attempt at analysis. Yet, the war of succession is an event which perhaps more than any other, stands in need of scientific analysis.

The war of succession has been considered a decisive turning point by historians who choose to view the whole history of medieval India as largely a struggle between two communities. Shibli put the weight of his great authority in favour of this interpretation: The Hindus, benefiting from the policy of tolerance of Akbar, were getting out of hand and even persecuting the Muslims. Dara Shukoh was a traitor within the Islamic political community who sought to open the gates fully to the Hindus. Aurangzeb, therefore, rallied the Muslims together and fought essentially for the faith, not for the throne.[1]

Others who did not share the same partisan feeling for Aurangzeb, mainly looking at his later policy, and Dara's intellectual eclecticism, hastened to accept this interpretation and declared that the war was a struggle between two opposite policies, those of religious tolerance and Muslim orthodoxy.[2]

Recent work on the subject has tended to assume this interpretation with only minor qualifications. On the one hand, R.P. Tripathi admits it only to the extent that religion served as a war cry to rally Aurangzeb's supporters.

It was also deemed necessary to find out an effective slogan for the war and the cry that was raised was the defence of the law of Islam from the heresies of Dara whether Shah Jahan was alive or dead. Should the emperor be still

alive, they would free him from the thraldom and tyranny of that idolator!
They arrogated to themselves the honour of being the defenders of Islam.[3]

On the other hand, the supporters of the old interpretation flourish
in strength, and it has been considerably enlarged and embellished with
facts and theories.[4] Proclaimed by so many writers of textbooks[5], that
interpretation has already become a set dogma which, it would seem,
nothing can shake.

Yet, those who made such statements do not seem to have troubled
to ask themselves whether Aurangzeb in fact ever raised the slogan of
'Islam in Danger' in order to gain the throne. This question, it must be
remembered, is quite different from whether Aurangzeb later on tried
to build an Islamic state or persecuted Hinduism. What we wish to
enquire here is whether a new religious policy was the chief, or at least
the declared, object for which the war of succession was fought.

There is a very interesting document which has come to light from
the Udaipur records. This is a nishan, or princely order, which
Aurangzeb sent to Rana Raj Singh of Mewar. This bore the impression
of his palm and it is obvious that Aurangzeb attached very great
importance to its contents. Assuring the Rana of his sympathy and
pledging himself to restore the parganas of Mandalgarh, etc. which
Shah Jahan had detached from his territory, Aurangzeb makes the
following declaration:

That loyal one (i.e. the Rana) has become the recipient of thousands of
royal favours. Because the persons of the great kings are shadows of God,
the attention of this elevated class (of Kings) who are the pillars of the
great (i.e. God's) court, is devoted to this, that men belonging to various
communities and different religions should live in the vale of peace and
pass their days in prosperity, and no one should interfere with the affairs
of another. Any one of this sky-glorious group (i.e. the kings) who resorted
to intolerance, became the cause of dispute and conflict and of harm to the
people at large, who are indeed a trust received from God. In reality, he
(such a king) thereby endeavoured to devastate the prosperous creations
of God and destroy the foundations of God's fabric, which is a habit
deserving to be rejected and cast off. God willing, when the Truth comes
into its own and the wishes of the sincerely loyal ones are fulfilled (i.e.
when Aurangzeb gains the throne), the benefits of the revered practices
and established regulations of my great ancestors, who are so esteemed
by the worshipful ones, will cast lustre on the four-cornered, inhabited
world.[6]

What is this but a pledge that the contender for the throne had no intention to change the religious policy of his predecessors? Would a man who was raising a religious war cry at the time, have condemned in such ringing tones any attempt at intolerance or religious discrimination? Whether Aurangzeb was sincere in making this declaration is beside the point. What is significant is that rather than stress the religious issue, he was anxious to avoid it by declaring himself on the side of the established imperial policy.

It is interesting to note in this connection that Aurangzeb seems to have underplayed the charge of heresy against Dara Shukoh, before the battle of Samugarh placed victory decisively in his hands.

It is true that in the preamble to his agreement (*ahadnama*) with Murad Bakhsh, Dara Shukoh is denounced as the 'Prince of Heretics' (*ra'is al-mulahida*).[7] It is also stated by a historian that prior to his marching out from Burhanpur, Aurangzeb sought the blessing of Shaikh Abdul Latif of Burhanpur on the ground that he was going to fight a heretic.[8] These were, however, formal declarations. Even a partisan of Aurangzeb like Aqil Khan Razi did not take them seriously: he omits the preamble to the ahadnama and nowhere through his accounts refers to Dara's heresy as a cause of the war. How serious Aurangzeb himself was in this allegation is revealed by his own reply to a letter he received from princess Jahan Ara after the battle of Dharmat. This reply contains his charge sheet against his elder brother. The whole consists merely of accusations that Dara had throughout tried to thwart or even kill Aurangzeb. The only possible reference — that is, possible if read alone — to Dara's religious views is in the statement that 'his actions are always contrary to (the principles) of the Empire, faith and religion and injurious to the interests of the country and the people.' Sandwiched between the 'Empire' and 'country and people' *faith* and religion can only have a formal significance, for a man who violated the interests of the Empire was supposed ipso facto to have violated the principles of his faith. That this is really so is shown by the fact that Aurangzeb proceeds to illustrate his statement only by allegations of a political nature, chiefly that, by bringing about the withdrawal of Mughal contingents from the Bijapur campaign in 1657, Dara had harmed the larger interests of the Empire and exposed Aurangzeb and his troops to grave danger.[9]

Manucci purports to give us a letter from Aurangzeb to Murad calling upon him to join in a campaign against Dara, 'the infidel and idolator' as well as against Shuja 'a heretic'.[10] But this is obviously a fruit of his imagination for Aurangzeb and Murad were then in alliance with Shuja, and one of the complaints against Shah Jahan and Dara that Aurangzeb was then raising was that they had sent 'a grandson of Parwez' (Sulaiman Shukoh) to destroy Shuja, his elder brother.[11]

It was only after Samugarh, when special reason had to be given to abandon the aim stated till then, namely the replacement of Dara in the counsels of Shah Jahan, that Dara's heresy was proclaimed to be his chief and unpardonable crime. It was first brought up in a private interview with Jahan Ara Begam.[12] It is also noteworthy that the official history of the first decade of Aurangzeb's reign, the *Alamgir Nama* of Muhammad Kazim gives its detailed account of Dara's heresy not to explain Aurangzeb's taking up arms against him, but to justify his execution.[13]

There is also no proof in either the actions of any contenders or in the behaviour of any section of the nobility, that the war of succession was regarded as a war between two faiths. Proofs that have till now been offered can by no means command the confidence of any sober student of history. I.K. Ghori says, for example, that

It was under this impression that Aurangzeb appealed to the religious sense of the imperial commanders that they should support him in the struggle ahead against the heretic Dara. As the rumour of Shah Jahan's death still needed confirmation, large scale desertions to Aurangzeb did not take place, but even then twenty Muslim commanders of the imperial army decided to disobey the summons and joined hands with him.[14]

In support of this statement Ghori has cited Manucci and Sadiq Khan. The statement is made by neither of them, but by Abul Fazl Mamuri, and he too speaks only of twenty commanders and not of twenty Muslim commanders.[15] The actual facts in this case are these: On falling ill, Shah Jahan issued, allegedly on the advice of Dara Shukoh, a number of farmans to the imperial officers serving in the Deccan to start for the court at once. Mahabat Khan and Satar Sal Hada at once left for the court along with their contingents.[16] But Najabat Khan and Mir Jumla were sympathetic to Aurangzeb and decided not to leave the Deccan.[17] Shah Nawaz Khan Safvi, a leading noble of Shah Jahan, was also in the Deccan when Aurangzeb was making preparations for the war of succession. He refused to side with Aurangzeb and so was treacherously arrested.[18]

Thus, there is no question of Muslim officers unanimously aligning themselves with Aurangzeb. On the contrary, a plausible case can be made out that Aurangzeb succeeded in obtaining support from a very large number of Rajputs.[19] Aurangzeb's nishans to Rana Raj Singh of

Mewar leave us in no doubt that the head of the most illustrious house in Rajasthan was in sympathy with Aurangzeb. A bargain had been struck whereby in return for the Rana's support, Aurangzeb was to restore to him the parganas lost by him in 1654. This pledge Aurangzeb hastened to fulfil as soon as he occupied the throne.[20] The correspondence of Mirza Raja Jai Singh reveals him as a secret partisan of Aurangzeb who sabotaged the whole military effort of Dara Shukoh. There is no need to enlarge upon this here because Qanungo has established it beyond any reasonable doubt.[21] It only remains for us to quote the rebel Akbar's taunt made in a letter to his father in 1681:

Perhaps, it has not been brought to your (Aurangzeb's) notice that Dara Shukoh was in reality prejudiced against, and hostile to, this race (the Rajputs). He saw the results of this. If he had made friends with them from the first, he would not have fared as he did. ...[22]

As for the Shias, it is only Bernier and Manucci[23] who make out Shuja to have been a special favourite with them. Since Manucci had read Bernier, the latter is probably the sole authority for the statement. That this should be considered sufficient evidence for postulating a Shi'ite candidate for the throne is surprising — more so, when we find a historian of R.P. Tripathi's stature doing so.[24] Iranian nobles like Mir Jumla and Shaista Khan were on the side of Aurangzeb and Shah Nawaz Khan Safvi on that of Dara. Indeed, Murad Bakhsh himself was popularly suspected of having Shi'ite leanings.[25] Where then are the Shias who are supposed to have sided with Shuja?

The final test for all this theorization is whether the nobles were actually divided in their loyalties to the contending princes on communal, racial or any other lines. No such study of the individual nobles has been so far attempted, although there is sufficient contemporary material to make an adequate enumeration and classification possible. Mere reliance on eighteenth-century works like the *Ma'asir-ul Umara*, or *Tazkirat-ul Umara* will give a wholly misleading picture, because they cover only the barest fraction of the officers involved. I have made lists of the supporters of Aurangzeb, Dara and Murad before the battle of Samugarh, as also those of Shuja, from all the available sources which are accessible to us. These are the *Alamgir Nama* by Muhammad Kazim; *Alamgir Nama* by Hatim Khan; *Ma'asir-i Alamgiri* by Saqi Mustaad Khan; *Tarikh-i Aurangzeb* by Abul Fazl Mamuri; *Futuhat-i Alamgiri* by Isar Das Nagar; *Waqi'at- i Alamgiri* by Aqil Khan Razi; *Adab-i Alamgiri*; *Amal-i Salih* by Salih Kambu; *Tuhfa-Shah Jahani* by Sidhari Lal; *Mirat-i Jahan-Numa* and *Mirat-ul Alam* by Bakhtawar Khan;

Khulasat-ut Tawarikh by Sujan Rai Bhandari; *Tarikh-i Shah Jahani* by Sadiq Khan; *Nuskha-i Dilkusha* by Bhimsen; *Storia Do Mogor* by Manucci; *Travels in the Mughal Empire* by Bernier; the *Ma'asir-ul Umara* by Shah Nawaz Khan and *Tazkirat-ul Umara* by Kewal Rai.

On the basis of this study, the following facts emerge:

There were 87 nobles holding the ranks of 1000 *zat* and above who are known to have supported Dara Shukoh in the war of succession; out of these 23 were Iranis, 16 Turanis, 1 Afghan, 23 other Muslims, 22 Rajputs and 2 Marathas.

Out of 124 nobles holding the ranks of 1000 and above who supported Aurangzeb, 27 were Iranis, 20 Turanis, 23 other Muslims, 9 Rajputs, 10 Marathas and 2 other Hindus.

Shah Shuja is known to have been supported by ten nobles of 1000 and above, out of whom 1 was Irani, 3 Turanis, 1 Afghan and 5 other Muslims.

There were 11 mansabdars of 1000 and above who supported Murad Bakhsh; out of these there was 1 Irani, 1 Afghan, 7 other Muslims and 2 Rajputs.

These figures show more conclusively than anything else that all religious and racial sections in the nobility were divided in their loyalties. This is quite clear in the case of both Dara and Aurangzeb who had among their supporters members of all important sections. Twenty-three Hindu nobles (11 Rajputs, 10 Marathas and 2 other Hindus) supported Aurangzeb and Murad, as against 24 Hindu nobles (22 Rajputs and 2 Marathas) backing Dara Shukoh. These figures do not show any alignment of nobles on merely religious lines. Indeed, if Aurangzeb had made any statement or committed any action hostile to any community, this would have been disastrous for his cause, because amidst a generally apathetic nobility, a big section solidly opposing him could have made all the difference.

The absence of any anti-Hindu or anti-Rajput bias in Aurangzeb's effort to gain the throne may surprise those who concentrate only on Aurangzeb's later religious policy, with its temple destruction and *jizya* and his war with Marwar and Mewar in 1680. But a careful student of his reign might look more closely at what immediately followed on the war of succession. Never since the recall of Man Singh from Bengal in 1606 by Jahanagir had an important governor-ship been conferred on a Rajput. Aurangzeb made Jai Singh the nominal, as well as the actual viceroy of the Deccan, perhaps the most important post in the whole Empire, and Jaswant Singh was twice appointed governor of Gujarat. Never since the death of Akbar had there been a Hindu diwan (finance minister) of the Empire. Now Aurangzeb appointed Raja Raghunath to this post. The well-known Benaras farman[26] is a testimony to his attempt to follow his pledge given in the nishan to Rana Raj Singh, which was to ensure that no one interfered in the religion of another.

It is beyond the scope of this article to examine why and how Aurangzeb's policy changed in later days. Nevertheless, one reason usually advanced for this, namely that it began with the war of succession in reaction to the increasing Rajput or Hindu penetration of the imperial services under Shah Jahan, can no longer be held, since in fact there was no movement against it. And even if there was one, Aurangzeb had nothing to do with it in 1658–9.

NOTES

1. Maulana Shibli, *Aurangzeb Alamgir per ek nazar*, Aligarh, 1922, In English he has been followed by Faruki, *Aurangzeb and His Times* (see esp., pp. 28–9, 47–8) and by I.H. Qureshi in *A History of Freedom Movement* (*being the History of Muslim Struggle of Hind-Pakistan*), Karachi, vol. I, p. 23.

2. Cf. S. Lane-Poole, *Aurangzeb*, p. 42: 'Dara might have been a lesser Akbar' and cf. S.R. Sharma, who declares, 'when Aurangzeb became the King of India Muslim theology triumphed in him' (*Religious Policy of the Mughal Emperors*, p. 118).

3. *Rise and Fall of the Mughal Empire*, p. 482.

4. An example of such effort is to be found in Iftikhar Khan Ghori's attempt to substantiate what was only suggested hitherto by various scholars, that the war of succession was a war not only between Hinduism and Islam, but also between Shi'ism and Sunnism. *Journal of the Pakistan Historical Society*, III, part II, pp. 97–119.

5. See, for example, the two text books so widely used: A.L. Srivastava, *Mughal Empire*, pp. 320, 323, 334, 339; and S.R. Sharma, *Mughal Empire in India*, vol. II, p. 503.

6. Shyamaldas, *Vir Vinod*, II, pp. 419–20, note. This great history of Mewar reproduces in this note the whole text of the *nishan*; it is followed by other *nishans* as well.

7. *Adab-i-Alamgiri*, f. 84a–85a; printed in Najib Nadvi, *Ruq'a vt-i Alamgir*, pp. 264–5. Kamwar; *Tazkira-i Salatin-i Chaghtai*, MS f. 211b–212b.

8. Mamuri, *Tarikh-i Aurangzeb*, f. 86b; Khafi Khan, II, p. 11.

9. The whole letter is reproduced in *Waqi'at-i Alamgiri*, ed. Zafar Hasan,

Aligarh, 1946, pp. 50–2.

10. Manucci, I, pp. 247–8.

11. *Waqi'at-i Alamgiri*, p. 50. It was actually Murad who had accused Dara of heresy (*Ruqu'at-i Alamgir*, p. 372).

12. *Futuhat-i Alamgiri*, f. 27a. It is to be noted, however, that the earlier and more reliable *Waqi'at-i Alamgiri* in its accounts of the same interview does not put any such statement in the mouth of Aurangzeb.

13. *Alamgirnama*, p. 432.

14. *Journal of the Pakistan Historical Society*, VIII, part II, p. 100.

15. *Tarikh-i Aurangzeb*, f. 96a–b.

16. *Waqi'at-i Alamgiri*, pp. 23, 26; Hatim Khan, *Alamgirnama*, f. 86; *Amal-i Salih*, III, p. 282; *Tuhfi Shah Jahani*, f. 28; Manucci, I, p. 251.

17. Hatim Khan, *Alamgirnama*, f. 9a. Cf. *Waqi'at-i Alamgiri*, pp. 27–8. Mir Jumla was arrested with his own consent and his entire contingent, treasure and property were appropriated by Aurangzeb (Khafi Khan, II, p. 9; *Tuhfa-i Shah Jahani*, f. 29a; Manucci, I, p. 250).

18. *Adab*, f. 245; *Mirat-ul Alam*, ff. 107a, 90b; *Amal-i Salih*, III, pp. 282–3; Hatim Khan, *Alamgirnama*, ff. 12a, 15b; *Waqi'at-i-Alamgiri*, p. 31; *Khulasat-ut Tawarikh*, p. 493; Khafi Khan, II, p. 12.

19. This statement questions one of the most cherished assumptions of the communal interpretation: When the conflict for the throne started, Dara Shukoh was supported by the Rajputs and others who viewed the rise of orthodoxy with distaste (*A History of the Freedom Movement of Pakistan, 1707–1947*, vol.I, p. 23) "he (Dara) ... was friendly to Hindus and popular with the Rajput aristocracy ... while Aurangzeb was a staunch Sunni and bitterly hostile to non-Muslims" (A.L. Srivastava, *Mughal Empire*, p. 320).

20. *Vir Vinod*, II, p. 426–7.

21. *Dara Shukoh*, pp. 167–78.

22. Royal Asiatic Society, London, MS 173. I owe this reference to my friend and colleague, Irfan Habib.

23. Bernier, *Travels*, p. 8; Manucci, *Storia Do Mogor*, I, p. 228.

24. *Rise and Fall of the Mughal Empire*, p. 479.

25. Hatim Khan, *Alamgirnama*, MS Br. Add. 26, 233, ff. 7b–8a.

26. *Journal of Asiatic Society of Bengal*, 1911, p. 689. There are two grants to Jain religious devotees from this early period which have been published (*Journal of the Pakistan Historical Society*, 1957, V, part IV, pp. 252–4).

22

Causes of the Rathor
Rebellion of 1679

Aurangzeb's policy towards the Rajputs, especially his handling of
the question of succession to the *gaddi* of Marwar after the death of
Jaswant Singh (1678), is clouded by considerable controversy. The
discrepancies in chronicles about events of the Rathor Rebellion of
1679 have long been the despair of historians and we find important
factual gaps in the account given in the monumental *History of
Aurangzeb* by Sir Jadunath Sarkar. Fortunately, however, we now
have the monthly dispatches of the official news-writer of Ajmer,[1]
covering precisely this period (1678–80). Written with the object of
providing accurate information to the court, covering the entire
province of Ajmer, which included all the chief Rajput states, it gives
us detailed reports of events, negotiations and other transactions taking
place at the time. This enables us to have a pretty clear picture of
what actually took place during these critical years, the nature of the
policy of Aurangzeb, and the viewpoints of the several sections of the
Rajputs. On the basis of this, we are now able to trace in detail, with
considerable confidence in the reliability of our information (for the
news-writer was not writing for public consumption, but for the
knowledge of the emperor himself), the succession of events
following the death of Jaswant Singh and leading to the rebellion of
1679–80.

When Jaswant Singh died in December 1678, he left no son. At his
death he was also heavily in debt to the imperial treasury.[2] Iftikhar
Khan, the governor of Ajmer reported in Ziqad, AH 1089 (January
1679) that the late raja and his forefathers had hoarded a large amount
of cash and treasure in the fort of Siwana.[3] So a search was made for
the hidden treasure in order to satisfy government claims, but it yielded
nothing.[4] Then an order was issued in Zilhij (February 1679) that the
entire property belonging to the raja should be escheated.[5] Earlier,
Kesri Singh Mutasaddi along with Raghunath Singh and other Rajputs
had prepared a list of the entire property belonging to the late raja and
presented it before Iftikhar Khan (Ziqad, January 1679).[6] Pending his

decision about the succession, Aurangzeb declared in the same month that the whole of Marwar, including the capital, with the exception of only two parganas, was to be resumed to the khalisa, and royal officials were deputed to take charge. This aroused the indignation of the Rathors, who declared that if Jodhpur, the seat of their clan and the place where the mourning of the dead king was taking place, was taken into the khalisa, the prestige of the Rathors would be adversely affected. They came to Iftikhar Khan and represented as follows: 'During the rule of the Mughal dynasty, no *bumi* or *zamindar* has been turned out of his native place (watan) even on the commission of any specific fault. The Rathors, who have always been loyal and faithful, ask simply that they be not subjected to exile.' They were prepared to give over the whole of Marwar, but not the ill-fortified town of Jodhpur.[7] Iftikhar Khan suggested to the Rajputs (February 1679) that they should accompany him to the court so that their demands might be fulfilled. The Rajputs refused. Iftikhar Khan defended the imperial resumption of Jodhpur to the khalisa on the ground that according to the rules, watan could not be conferred upon either a woman or a servant.[8] Aurangzeb in the meanwhile had issued another order designed to placate the deceased raja's officers. All of them were to be confirmed in the pattas or assignments granted to them by Jaswant Singh, these being now formally considered their jagirs so that against these they would receive corresponding mansabs from the imperial court.[9] Jaswant's Singh's officers declined this offer, possibly (for this is not stated) because they thought it would lead to the permanent disruption of the Marwar kingdom. When pressed by Iftikhar Khan, they declared that though they knew they could not resist the imperial army, they had decided to die rather than submit.[10]

The situation was further complicated when, to the relief of Jaswant Singh's officers, the news arrived in March or April that the two wives of Jaswant Singh had given birth to two sons. This meant that they had now a candidate, in the person of Ajit Singh, one of the posthumous sons, whom they could present for the Marwar throne.

The Emperor too seems to have accepted the genuineness of the two sons (one of whom died shortly after birth) without question. Thus we read in the Ajmer news-letters that the fort of Pokhran had been conferred on Rawal Amar Singh, but after the birth of Jaswant Singh's posthumous sons, the Rawal was informed (Rabi I = May 1679) that the grant was being revoked, as sons had been born to Jaswant Singh, and the Emperor was favourably disposed towards them.[11]

But soon after, Aurangzeb conferred the *tika* on Indar Singh on the payment of thirty-six lakh rupees as succession fee.[12] The appointment of Indar Singh as Raja of Jodhpur came as a great surprise to the Rathors. Till now, Aurangzeb had not taken any decision about the succession to the Marwar throne. It is significant that before the birth of the two posthumous sons of Jaswant Singh, his officers could not suggest any name for the incumbent of the gaddi, which meant, as Iftikhar Khan pointed out, that they were arguing for the retention of Marwar in the hands of the 'women and servants' of the late raja, a position hardly acceptable in the circumstances of the time. As for Indar Singh (grandson of Amar Singh, elder brother of Jaswant Singh), he belonged to a line hostile to Jaswant Singh and his followers, and his attempt to secure succession to the Jodhpur gaddi had been opposed by most of the Rathor leaders.[13]

There was another claimant still in the person of Anup Singh, son of Rao Karan, who had the rank of 2500/2000.[14] He had offered forty-five lakh rupees as succession fee.[15] Anup Singh was a blood relation of Jaswant Singh, but since his relationship to the principal royal line was remote, his claims were not entertained.[16]

When Rani Hadi, the chief queen of Jaswant Singh and other Rajput leaders heard (Jamada I = June 1679) that the tika had been conferred on Indar Singh, they sharply protested against it and said it would have been better if the previous order for including Jodhpur into the khalisa had been maintained rather than that Jodhpur be handed over to Indar Singh.[17]

Already in Rabi I (April 1679), before Indar Singh had received the tika, Tahir Khan, *qila'adar* of Jodhpur, had suggested to the Rathors that they could please the emperor by demolishing all the temples within the state and constructing mosques in their place. The Rajputs, when they heard this, were very indignant. But when the message was carried to Rani Hadi, Jaswant's chief queen, who was inside the fort as the titular leader of the Rathors, she declared that he (Tahir Khan) could do as he pleased for the good of the Rathors: 'If Jodhpur was conferred on the sons of the late Raja, the Rajputs undertook to demolish all the temples in the state of Marwar.'[18]

That the Rathors' reaction to Aurangzeb's decision stemmed solely from a sense of indignation at the appointment of Indar Singh and not from any resentment over the larger issues involved in Aurangzeb's policy—specially his discriminatory measures against the Hindus—

becomes clear from the way the Rathors pressed the case for Ajit. We have just seen that they declared that they preferred the khalisa or imperial administration to Indar Singh.

They now proclaimed that if only the tika was given to Ajit Sigh, they would be more loyal than the king in carrying out Aurangzeb's pet projects, the collection of the jizya and the destruction of temples within Marwar. It may be noted that there is no suggestion anywhere that Indar Singh had given such a pledge to secure the tika.

Two months later (Jamada I = June 1679), when Indar Singh had been appointed raja, two spokesmen of the Rathors, Ram Bhati and Sonak Rathor, went to Qazi Hamid of Jodhpur and represented as follows:

The *zamindari* of the country of Marwar was the property of Raja Jaswant Singh and after his death by the law of inheritance the *zamindari* of the country devolves on his sons. In the presence of the sons of the late Jaswant Singh, Indar Singh had no right to succeed. If the *watan* and the *zamindari* was conferred on the sons of the deceased Raja, the Rajputs undertook to demolish all the temples of Jodhpur and construct mosques instead. The Rajputs were also prepared to promulgate the law of the *shari'at* and to carry out the orders of the Emperor to whatever effect. We want to know the law of the *shari'at* in this case. The Qazi gave them no answer and forwarded the case to Qazi Shaikhul-Islam (Chief Qazi at the Court).[19]

Tahir Khan also reported in the same month to the emperor that the Rajputs were prepared to demolish all the temples within the Jodhpur state, to promulgate Islam and to offer a bigger peshkash than that offered by Indar Singh, if the latter's appointment as the Raja of Jodhpur was cancelled.[20] The imperial *waqai'navis* in Jamada I (June 1679) reported flatly that 'the root cause of the Rajput rebellion is Indar Singh, because he is intensely unpopular in Marwar and no one likes him. The Rajputs would be agreeable and pleased if Jodhpur is included in the khalisa permanently.'[21]

The next month Ram Bhati and Sonak Rathor again pleaded with Tahir Khan:

We are prepared to obey the laws of the *shariat* and the imperial laws. Why then is Jodhpur not included in the *khalisa*? The entire Rajput community is agreeable to it. If Jodhpur is taken into *khalisa* there can be no rebellion. The root cause of the entire rebellion is Indar Singh because he is intensely unpopular in Marwar and no one likes him and none wants him.[22]

When the Rajputs failed to get the appointment of Indar Singh cancelled, they asked Tahir Khan in Jamada II (July 1679) to leave Jodhpur because they had decided to oppose Indar Singh and offer him battle.[23] Chauhar Mal, the *mutasaddi* of Indar Singh, could not enter Jodhpur owing to the opposition of the Rajputs.[24]

This was a prelude to the rebellion. The flight of Ajit from the court, arranged by Durga Das, followed. Aurangzeb's acceptance of a false Ajit as the true one, and his firm refusal to recognize the genuineness of the real Ajit barred the way to any compromise. The news-reporter of Ajmer reported a conversation between Sujan Singh Rathor and Padshah Quli Khan, in which, the former protesting his loyalty to the emperor asserted the genuineness of the real Ajit and said that Durga Das, Sonak and other Rathors were fighting only for the sake of Ajit and they would not otherwise have been able to resist Raja Indar Singh.[25] When this report was presented to Aurangzeb, he gravely censured the news-reporter for giving credence to such statements.[26]

The *Waqai'Ajmer* thus presents us with a mass of new information which enables us to reinterpret the events leading to the Rajput War. It seems to me that the basic assumptions postulated by Sir Jadunath Sarkar to explain the causes of the war cannot be easily accepted in the light of this information. Sarkar assumes, in the first place, that though Jaswant Singh had no son, Aurangzeb could have immediately appointed Indar Singh, 'a loyal grandee', and his failure to do so suggests that he wanted to destroy the Marwar Kingdom.[27] But we have seen that if Indar Singh was not appointed for five months, it was solely because he was not acceptable to the Rathors, who throughout expressed their hostility to him in no uncertain terms.

The second assumption put forward by Sarkar is that Aurangzeb wanted to make Jaswant's state 'a quiescent dependency' or 'a regular province of the Empire, for Hindu resistance to the policy of religious persecution must be deprived of a possible efficient head'.[28] But again, we see that if this was Aurangzeb's real objective, this could have been secured best by accepting Ajit. His partisans were ready to destroy temples and enforce the shari'at—things for which Indar Singh never gave his consent. Moreover, Ajit was a baby at the time, and even if Aurangzeb had seen (mistakenly) the marks of future greatness in this baby, it was obvious that simply because of his age Ajit could not, at least for a decade and a half, have become the 'efficient head' of any Hindu resistance.

The only plausible support for Sarkar's argument lies in the delay

of five months which Aurangzeb allowed before appointing Indar
Singh. There is, however, a possible explanation which arises from
the *Waqai'Ajmer*. The Rathors were opposed to Indar Singh, and
their opposition was fortified by the news that two queens of Jaswant
were pregnant and might well bear sons. But how could it be known
for certain that these would be sons? Aurangzeb might have thought
that in case the children turned out to be daughters—for which there
was, after all, even chance—the whole issue would be simplified,
since the Rathors would no longer have any candidate to pit against
Indar Singh. In case they turned out to be boys, Aurangzeb's task
would be no less difficult whether he appointed Indar Singh before or
after their birth.

It has also not been appreciated that Aurangzeb might have
preferred Indar Singh to Ajit for quite the opposite reason to what
Sarkar has suggested. There is no reason to believe that Indar Singh
was incompetent. In 1678 he was already holding the rank of 1000/
1000 (700x2–3h) and had served with some distinction in the
Deccan.[29] It could be urged that Aurangzeb wanted an able officer,
not a baby, to head the Marwar state so that peace and order might be
maintained in that strategic state (it lay astride the main Agra–
Ahmadabad route) and it might continue to supply military contingents
to the Mughal armies. It is also to be remembered that Aurangzeb
was not stepping beyond custom and precedent in overlooking Ajit's
claim and selecting Indar Singh. Jahangir had asserted this imperial
prerogative in no uncertain terms sixty-five years earlier in the case
of Bikaner.[30] Similarly, he had rejected the claims of Man Singh's
grandson, Maha Singh, to the Amber throne, despite the fact that
Rajput custom had prescribed his succession.[31]

In appraising Aurangzeb's policy towards Marwar, we should
perhaps guard against the assumption made, without much historical
basis, that it was a part of his alleged anti-Rajput policy. Aurangzeb's
first twenty years showed little signs of hostility towards the Rajputs.
In his first two regnal years, zat ranks amounting to 12,600 making
up 14.16 per cent of the total additions, and sawar ranks amounting
to 11,900 making up 22.04 per cent, were bestowed upon Rajput
officers.[32] This should be considered in the light of the fact that in
Shah Jahan's thirtieth regnal year, Rajputs holding zat ranks of 1000
and above held 18.9 per cent of the total zat and 24 per cent of the
sawar mansabs.[33]

This shows only a very marginal, in fact, insignificant change in
the position of the Rajputs among mansabdars. Indeed, whereas there

was no Rajput officer throughout the reign of Shah Jahan holding the rank of 7000, Jai Singh and Jaswant Singh—the latter, despite his role at the battle of Dharmat and Khajwah—were promoted by Aurangzeb to 7000/7000 each.[34] The representation of the Rajput mansabdars holding the rank of 1,000 and above during the first twenty years of Aurangzeb's reign (1658–78) was 14 per cent.[35] This is not at par with the proportion of 18 per cent Rajput mansabdars of the rank of 1000 and above during Shah Jahan's reign,[36] and this may be held to mark a decline. It should be remembered, however, that this was a decline generally shared by all the non-Deccani elements.

The rebellion of the Rathors and Sisodias was not really a 'Rajput rebellion', if by that is meant that the majority of the Rajputs were involved in it. The Kachwahas, the Haras, the Bhatis, the Rathors of Bikaner, all remained loyal to the Mughals.

Yet, while most of the Rajputs had not so far been alienated by Aurangzeb's policy as to rebel against him, the Rajput rebels too were not completely friendless within the rest of the Mughal nobility. The very fact that Prince Akbar should have staked his fortune and placed himself at the head of the rebels shows that he expected some support from within the nobility. Tahawwur Khan, his main supporter, enjoyed no mean status. In actual fact, Bahadur Khan Kokaltash, the leading noble of Aurangzeb at the time, was said to have advised Aurangzeb that he should recognize Ajit Singh.[37]

On the whole, though one must not be dogmatic, it seems that the origin of the rebellion of 1679 lay in the clan rivalries and disputes among the Rajputs themselves. As long as the imperial power was strong it could overrule the claims of one clan or party against another without danger of rebellion. Jahangir had done it in the case of the Kachwahas without provoking any armed opposition. Under Aurangzeb, however, such an assertion of imperial authority was not quietly accepted, perhaps because the Rathors felt that they could defy imperial government with some chance of survival, if not success. For such an attitude on their part, Aurangzeb's involvement in the north–west and in the Deccan, and the series of internal rebellions starting with the Jats, all were perhaps responsible.

NOTES

1. The original copy of the *Waqai'Ajmer* is in the Asifiyah Library,

Hyderabad. I have used a transcript from the original in the Research Library, Dept. of History, AMU, Aligarh.

2. Ali Muhammad Khan, *Mirat-i-Ahmadi*, I, ed. Nawab Ali, Baroda 1927–8, 1930, I, p. 277.

3. *Waqai'Ajmer*, p. 74.

4. *Ma'asir-i-Alamgiri*, p. 172.

5. *Waqai Ajmer*, pp. 84, 92.

6. Ibid., p. 81.

7. Ibid., pp. 80–3.

8. Ibid., pp. 117–18.

9. Ibid., p. 114.

10. Ibid., p. 116.

11. Ibid., p. 194.

12. *Ma'asir-i-Alamgiri*, pp. 175–6; *Dilkusha*, f. 76a; *Ma'asir-ul-Umara*, II, p. 236.

13. The Rathors represented to Iftikhar Khan that Abdur Rahim should be sent to Jodhpur as *kotwal* and an experienced *karori* should be appointed at Jodhpur and the tika should not be conferred on Indar Singh till it was found whether a son was born to the late Raja Jaswant Singh. (*Waqai Ajmer*, p. 141).

14. Hadi Kamwar Khan, *Jazkiratu-s Salatin-i Chaghala,* M.A. Library, MS Lytton 40/2 (hereafter referred to as Kamwar), f.277b

15. *Waqai' Ajmer*, p. 107.

16. For the detailed biography of Anup Singh, see *Vir Vinod*, II, pp. 498–500; *Ma'asir-ul-Umara*, II, pp. 289–91.

17. *Waqai'Ajmer*, p. 241.

18. Ibid., p. 167.

19. Ibid., pp. 245–6.

20. Ibid., p. 244.

21. Ibid., p. 270.

22. Ibid., pp. 277–8.

23. Ibid., p. 288.

24. Ibid., p. 280.

25. Ibid., p. 633.

26. Ibid., p. 645.

27. *History of Aurangzib*, vol. III, p. 369.

28. Ibid., p. 368.

29. *Selected Documents of Aurangzeb's Reign*, p. 121; *Ma'asir-ul-Umara*, II, p. 236; After his appointment as Raja of Jodhpur, Indar Singh was promoted to the rank of 3000/2000.

30. *Tuzuk*, p. 106.

31. Ibid., p. 130.

32. See M. Athar Ali, *The Mughal Nobility under Aurangzeb*, p. 24.

33. This is based on Waris's list of mansabdars.

34. For further elucidation of this point, see my article, 'The Religious Issue in the War of Succession 1658–59' this volume, pp. 238–45.

35. See my book, *The Mughal Nobility Under Aurangzeb*, p. 35.

36. Ibid., p. 24.

37. *Futuhat-i-Alamgiri*, f. 75a–b; *Ma'asir-i-Alamgiri*, p. 168. Tahir Khan was deprived of his *mansab* because he did not try to stop Ajit Singh from entering Jodhpur (Kamwar, f. 266a).

23

Provincial Governors Under Aurangzeb
An Analysis

The post of the governor of a province in the Mughal Empire was a very important one. The Empire was divided into a number of subas, or provinces, each of which had as the head of its administration an officer known variously as *nazim, sahib-i suba, subedar, faujdar-i suba*, etc. Like the two principal ministers at the centre, the diwan and the *mir bakhshi*, the provincial governors were generally appointed from amongst officers holding the highest ranks or mansabs. It can be said that they formed, at any time, the hard core of the ruling bureaucracy.

The jurisdiction and powers of the governors have been discussed often enough[1], but, so far as the present writer is aware, no attempt has been made to examine the nature and tenures of appointments and the kinds of persons appointed as governors from a study of the actual appointments in all the provinces. The present chapter is based on an investigation of such appointments during the entire reign of Aurangzeb (1658–1707). The period is a long one, and may be considered sufficiently long to enable us to draw inferences from our record with some confidence.

As is well known, only the first ten years of Aurangzeb's reign are covered by the detailed official chronicle, the *Alamgir Nama*. For the remaining period of nearly four decades, we have to obtain our information from sources which are by no means as easily accessible or, alternatively, as reliable. I have compiled my own list principally from the akhbarat, supplementing them from the numerous chronicles, memoirs and epistolary collections, largely in manuscript. At the risk of taking up too much space, I have given detailed references to substantiate my list.

The main table which seeks to give for each province a list of its governors, with the full duration of their terms of office in terms of the regnal years of Aurangzeb, is not, by the nature of our sources, complete and without blanks. But it can be claimed that the information is virtually complete for all the major provinces. It is also possible that in the case of some of the Deccan provinces, where there is a blank, it is to be explained by the fact that no governor was appointed, the province being regarded as part of the superior viceroyalty of the Deccan. Even so, the limits to which our information extends can be judged from the fact that out of 1059 possible entries in our table, we are in fact able to record 853.[2]

In preparing the tables, certain assumptions have been found necessary. For example, a distinction has been made between deputies of princes, who acted as governors on behalf of the princes, who were formally appointed, and deputies of ordinary governors. The names of the former have been recorded, while the latter have been ignored. In analysing the main table again, the princes who governed through deputies are not treated as governors at all (generally such princes governed another province directly in person), while the deputies have been regarded at par with ordinary governors: it being not possible to consider one province having at any time two governors.

As stated already, our record shows 853 years during which provincial governors are known to have held office. The number of appointments known is 337 and the number of persons serving as governors is 137. In other words, on an average, each single term of a governor lasted only a little more than two and a half years, while on an average again each governor was appointed to about two terms and to a total of about 6 years and 2 months.

Naturally, in actual fact the range of variations was very great. There is record of single terms of office as governors extending to 23, 17, 14, and 12 years.[3] At the same time, single persons serving as governors in different provinces, held office for totals of 41, 30, and 25 years.[4] On the other hand, officers were appointed and dismissed or transferred within the same year.[5]

But, on the whole, we can say from the analysis of the table that the Mughal court did not approve of long terms for governors, and generally transferred or recalled them after two or three years. Moreover, it was still rare for high officers to make careers as governors only: the men once appointed as governors could generally expect to serve only for one other term. In other words, governorship was by no means the office which the highest nobles necessarily enjoyed or which they might treat as the basis or instrument of their power. These facts are significant for any consideration of the ways in which the Mughal emperors maintained the authority of the central government.

It is also possible to analyse the duration of the terms of governors, according to provinces. Table 1 gives the duration of each term province-wise. It does not seem that any particular policy regarding a

TABLE 1

Duration of Terms of Governors

Province	Number of Years for which Appointment are Known	Number of Actual Appointments as Governor	Average tenure of Governors
Bengal	51	8	6 years 4½ months
Orissa	46	16	2 years 10½ months
Bihar	51	14	3 years 7½ months
Ilahabad	48	18	2 years 7½ months
Awadh	37	24	1 year 6½ months
Agra	46	28	1 year 7½ months
Delhi	43	10	4 years 3½ months
Lahore	49	22	2 years 2½ months
Kashmir	51	15	3 years 4½ months
Kabul	51	10	5 years 1 month
Multan	40	17	2 years 4 months
Sind	51	15	3 years 4½ months
Ajmer	38	20	1 year 10½ months
Gujarat	51	11	4 years 7½ months
Malwa	46	17	2 years 8 months
Deccan	40	19	2 years 1 month

province was behind the longer or shorter terms there. It may be said, in general, that the provinces where conditions were more stable, like Bengal, Gujarat, Kabul, Delhi, or Kashmir were allowed to have governors serving for terms longer than elsewhere.

The analysis of the social and personal antecedents of the individual governors yields certain interesting results. In the first place, we find that out of 137 governors, seven were princes, and of the remaining

130, 97 were *khanazads*, that is their fathers or senior relations had previously been in service. This gives a ratio of 74.6 per cent. It seems that there was a special preference for khanazads in appointments as governors, since their ratio in the general ranks of the nobles was not so high. Out of 141 mansabdars holding 3000 zat and above during the first part of Aurangzeb's reign, 1658–78, 86 or 61 per cent were khanazads and among the 486 nobles of 1000 zat or above, in the same period, only 213 or about 44 per cent are known to have been khanazads. During the remainder of Aurangzeb's reign, of 212 nobles of 3000 and above, only 94 or 44.3 per cent were khanazads; and of 575 nobles of 1000 and above only 272 or 47 per cent.[6] In both the highest ranks and the middle, therefore, the ratio of the khanazads was about half; but among governors it was three-fourths.[7] The only explanation for this seems to be that the office of governor was deemed to be of considerable trust and was only conferred on those nobles who had been in service for, so to speak, more than a generation.

Another aspect to be considered is the racial and religious composition of the class of governors. Table 2 gives this composition; and for comparative purposes, the figures of corresponding categories among the nobles of 1000 zat and above are also given. A glance at

TABLE 2

Racial and Religious Composition of Governors

	Iranis	Turanis	Afghans	Indian Muslims	Other Muslims	Rajputs and Hindus	Total
Governors other than Princes	63	29	6	19	9	4	130
%	26.3	22.3	4.6	14.6	6.9	3.0	
Mansabdars of 3000 *zat* and above, 1658–78	55	25	12	14	7	28	141
%	39.0	17.7	8.5	9.9	4.3	19.8	
Mansabdars of 3000 *zat* and above, 1679–1707	54	28	14	28	26	62	212
%	25.5	13.4	6.6	13.4	12.3	19.2	

this table would show that the predominance of the Iranis in the higher ranks of the nobility is emphasized still further among the governors.

The proportion of Turanis and Indian Muslims corresponds, but the Rajputs, other Hindus, Afghans and Deccanis generally were not appointed governors in numbers commensurate with their numerical strength in the higher nobility. This may have been due to the court's hesitation in appointing men who might have zamindari or local interests.

An attempt has been made to discover if any change occurred in the composition of the governors by tabulating the composition year by year. Table 3 brings out the fact, already well known, that during the last years of Aurangzeb's reign, a very large number of provinces were given over to princes. Their number, even when the cases where they governed through deputies are excluded from consideration, was very large. Of the twenty-three persons known to have held office as provincial governors in the forty-seventh regnal year, as many as seven were princes.

The fortunes of the Iranis, despite the anti-Shiite tendencies sometimes ascribed to Aurangzeb, show a remarkable degree of constancy. It was only during the last five years that they seem to lose ground, but this is, perhaps, because of the appointment of princes. The Turanis almost disappear in the middle years of the reign, but recover during the last years. This is probably owing to the rising strength of the Turani group headed by Ghaziuddin Khan Firoz Jang.[8]

Before concluding this paper, it may be pointed out that the information contained in the main table about the governors of each province can also be of interest to students of local or regional history, for whom it may not be possible to explore the entire range of the source material. To this extent besides its analytical value, the record of governors may have value simply as a repository of information. It may also be considered whether a similar enquiry should be attempted for the reigns of the other Mughal emperors, so that we should then form a comparative view and be in a position to assess more precisely the play of various tendencies over a still longer period of time. It is hoped that the present paper will have shown that such an enterprise, though requiring much labour, may not entirely be a fruitless exercise.

TABLE 3

Racial and Religious Composition of Governors in Each Year

(1) R.Y.	(2) Number of Governors known to be holding post during the year (including deputies of princes)	(3) Princes (not governing through deputies)	(4) Iranis	(5) Turanis	(6) Afghans	(7) Other Indian Muslims	(8) Deccanis (of Indian origin but not including Marathas)	(9) Rajputs and other Hindus	(10) Race not known	(11) Remarks
1.	17	1	10	3	—	2	—	—	1	
2.	22	1	10	5	—	4	—	1	1	One Irani was of Deccani origin
3.	17	—	9	4	—	1	—	1	2	One Irani was of Deccani origin
4.	19	—	11	3	1	1	—	1	2	One Irani was of Deccani origin

(1)	(2)	(3)	(4)	(5)	(6)	(7)	(8)	(9)	(10)	(11)
5.	16	—	11	3	—	1	—	—	1	One Irani was of Deccani origin
6.	21	1	12	6	—	1	—	—	1	
7.	20	1	12	5	—	1	—	—	1	
8.	18	1	11	3	—	1	—	1	1	
9.	21	—	13	4	1	1	—	—	1	
10.	24	1	14	6	—	2	—	1	1	
11.	17	1	10	3	—	1	—	—	2	
12.	19	1	12	2	—	3	—	—	1	
13.	22	1	14	3	—	3	—	—	1	
14.	21	1	12	3	—	4	—	1	—	
15.	20	—	11	5	—	3	—	1	—	
16.	13	—	9	3	—	1	—	—	1	
17.	15	—	11	2	—	1	—	—	1	
18.	19	—	13	2	1	2	—	—	1	
19.	20	2	12	3	—	2	—	—	1	
20.	20	3	11	3	1	1	—	—	1	
21.	17	4	9	2	—	1	—	—	1	
22.	19	2	12	2	—	2	—	—	1	One Indian Muslim was of Deccani origin
23.	16	1	12	2	—	1	—	—	—	

(1)	(2)	(3)	(4)	(5)	(6)	(7)	(8)	(9)	(10)	(11)
24.	16	—	13	1	—	1	—	—	1	
25.	16	—	12	1	—	3	—	—	—	
26.	14	—	13	—	—	1	—	—	—	
27.	14	—	12	2	—	—	—	—	—	
28.	16	—	13	3	—	—	—	—	—	
29.	17	—	12	2	—	2	—	1	—	
30.	18	—	15	1	—	1	—	1	—	One Irani was also a Deccani
31.	19	1	14	1	—	3	—	—	—	One Irani was of Deccani origin
32.	15	—	11	1	—	3	—	—	—	
33.	14	1	12	1	—	—	—	—	—	
34.	11	—	11	—	—	1	—	—	—	
35.	12	—	11	1	—	1	—	—	—	
36.	17	—	14	1	—	2	—	—	—	
37.	23	—	18	2	—	2	1	—	—	One Irani was of Deccani origin
38.	24	—	19	1	—	3	1	—	—	
39.	23	1	16	1	—	3	1	—	1	One Irani was of Deccani origin

(1)	(2)	(3)	(4)	(5)	(6)	(7)	(8)	(9)	(10)	(11)
40.	22	1	15	2	—	3	—	—	1	One Irani was of Deccani origin
41.	18	3	10	1	—	3	—	—	1	One Irani was of Deccani origin
42.	23	4	11	1	1	4	1	—	1	One Irani was of Deccani origin
43.	25	4	13	2	1	4	1	—	—	One Irani was of Deccani origin
44.	25	1	15	3	—	4	1	—	1	One Irani was of Deccani origin
45.	27	2	15	4	—	5	1	—	—	One Irani was of Deccani origin
46.	24	4	12	4	—	4	—	—	—	One Irani was of Deccani origin

(1)	(2)	(3)	(4)	(5)	(6)	(7)	(8)	(9)	(10)	(11)
47.	23	7	8	4	—	2	—	1		One Irani was of Deccani origin
48.	21	5	7	3	3	2	—	1	1	Two Afghans were also Deccanis
49.	20	6	7	4	—	1	—	1	1	
50.	18	3	7	5	—	1	1	—		
51.	17	3	6	5	—	1	1	—		

271

TABLE 4

Provincial Governors Under Aurangzeb

For convenience in reproduction, the table has been divided into five
parts, as follows: (a) Bengal, Orissa, Bihar, Ilahabad and Awadh; (b)
Agra, Delhi, Lahore, Kashmir and Kabul; (c) Multan, Sind, Ajmer,
Gujarat and Malwa; (d) Deccan, Bedar, Khandesh, Berar and
Aurangabad; and (e) Bijapur and Golkunda.

The abbreviations used to indicate the racial origin are:

P	Prince
I	Irani
T	Turani
R	Rajput
Af	Afghan
Ind.	Other Indian Muslim
Dec	Deccani
I-Dec	Irani Deccani
H	Hindu
(d)	Stands for 'died in office'

Table 4 (a)

R.Y.	Bengal	Orissa	Bihar	Ilahabad	Awadh
1.			Daud Khan Qureshi (Ind.)	Khan-i-Dauran, Nasiri Khan (T)	Iradat Khan (I)
2.	Mir Jumla (I-Dec)	Khan-i-Dauran, Nasiri Khan (T)	,,	,,	Fedai Khan, Azam Khan (I)
3.	,,	,,	,,	Bahadur Khan (I)	Murad Khan
4.	,,	,,	,,	,,	,,
5.	,, (d)		,,	,,	,,
6.	Shaista Khan (I)		Yadgar Beg, Lashkar Khan	,,	,,
7.	,,		,,	,,	,,
8.	,,	,,	,,	,,	Saf Shikan Khan, Muhammad Tahir (I)
9.	,,	,,	,,	,,	,,
10.	,,	,, (d) Tarbiyat Khan Birlas (T)	,,	Alahwardi Khan (I)	,,
11.	,,	,,	Ibrahim Khan (I)	,,	Fedai Khan, Azam Khan Koka
12.	,,	Safi Khan (I)	,,	,, (d) Amir Khan, Mir Miran (I)	,,
13.	Shaista Khan (I)	Saf Shikan Khan, Muhammad Tahir (I)	Ibrahim Khan (I)	Amir Khan, Mir Miran (I)	Fedai Khan, Azam Khan (I) (T) Tarbiyat Khan Birlas

273

R.Y.	Bengal	Orissa	Bihar	Ilahabad	Awadh
14.	,,	,,	,,	Daud Khan (Ind.)	,,
15.	,,			,,	
16.	,,	,,	,,	Hasan Ali Khan Bahadur (I)	
17.	,,	Rashid Khan, Ilhamullah (Ind.)	Amir Khan, Mir Miran (I)	,,	Mir Ahmad, Saadat Khan (I)
18.	,,		Tarbiyat Khan Birlas (T)	,, ,,	Namadar Khan (I)
19.	,,	Shaista Khan (I)	,,	Himmat Khan, Mir Isa (T)	Tarbiyat Khan Birlas (T)
20.	Fedai Khan, Azam Khan Koka (I)	Prince Azam (Nurullah Khan) (Dy)	,, Prince Azam	,,	Namadar Khan (I)
21.	Prince Azam		Saif Khan Saifuddin Mahmud (T)	,,	Tahawwur Khan (I)
22.		Shaista Khan (I)	,,	,,	Abu Muhammad Khan Bijapuri (Ind–Dec)
23.	Shaista Khan (I)	,,	,,		
24.	,,	,,	,, Safi Khan (I)		
25.	,,	,,	,,		
26.	,,	,,	,,		

R.Y.	Bengal	Orissa	Bihar	Ilahabad	Awadh
27.	,,	,,	,, (I)	Saif Khan, Saifuddin (T)	
28.	,,	,,	,,	,, (d) Muhtasham Khan, Mir Ibrahim (I)	
29.	,,	,,	,,	Himmat Khan, Muhammad Hasan (I)	
30.	,,	,,	,,	,,	
31.	,,	,,	,,	,,	
32.	Ibrahim Khan (I)	Abu Nasar Khan (I)	,,	Bahadur Khan Koka (I)	Kamar Khan (I) Himmar Khan, Muhammad Hasan (I)
33.	,,	,,	,,	,,	
34.	,,	,,	,,	Himmat Khan, Muhammad Hasan (I)	
35.	,,	,,	,,	,,	
36.	,,	,,	,,	,,	
37.	,,	Kamgar Khan (I)	Mukhtar Khan, Qamruddin (I)	Buzurg Umaid Khan (I) ,, (d) Sipahadar Khan, Nasiri Khan (I)	Khuda Band Khan (I)
38.	,,	,,	Fidai Khan (I)	,,	Askar Khan Hyderabadi (I-Dec)

R.Y.	Bengal	Orissa	Bihar	Ilahabad	Awadh
39.	Ibrahim Khan (I)	Akram Khan	,,	Sipahdar Khan, Nasiri Khan (I)	Askar Khan Hyderabadi (I-Dec)
40.	Prince Azim-uz-Shan	,,	,,		
41.		,,	,,	Ibrahim Khan (I)	Asadullah, Ikram Khan (Ind.)
42.	,,	,,	,,	,,	Zabardast Khan, Mohd. Khalil (I)
43.	,,	Zabardast Khan, Muhd. Khalil (I)	,,	Sipahadar Khan, Nasiri Khan (I)	Shamsher Khan Qureshi (Ind.)
44.	,,	Ghazanfar Khan (d) (T) Askar Khan Hyderabadi (I-Dec)	,,	,,	Zabaardast Khan, Muhd. Khalil (I)
45.	,,	,,		,,	Muhaammad Murad Khan (T)
46.	,,	,,	Shamsher Khan Qureshi (Ind.)	Fedai Khan, Salih Khan (I)	
47.	,,	Kamgar Khan (I)	Prince Azim-us-Shan	Sipahadar Khan, Nasiri Khan (I)	Shamsher Khan Qureshi (Ind.)
48.	,,	Murshid Quli Khan (Ind.)	,,	,,	,,
49.	Farrukh Siyar (Dy)	,,	,,	,,	Mirza Khan Alam (T) Abu Nasar Khar (I)
50.	,,	,,	,,	,,	,,
51.	,,	,,	Sarbuland Khan (T) (Dy.)	,,	,,

Table 4 (b)

R.Y.	Agra	Delhi	Lahore	Kashmir	Kabul
1.	Shaista Khan (I)	Siyadat Khan(d) (I)	Khalilullah Khan (I)	Itemad Khan, Ashraf Khan (I)	Mahabat Khan (I)
2.	Mukhlis Khan (Ind.) Saif Khan (T)	Danishmand Khan (I)	,,	,,	,,
3.	Wazir Khan (I)		,,	Ibrahim Khan (I)	,,
4.	,,		,, (d)	,,	Amir Khan (I)
5.	,,	Hoshdar Khan (I)		Islam Khan (T)	,,
6.	Islam Khan (T) Hoshdar Khan (I)	,,	Ibrahimn Khan (I)	,,	,, ,,
7.	,,	Safi Khan (I)	,,	Saif Khan (T)	,,
8.	,,	,,	,,	,,	,,
9.	,,	,,	,,	Mubariz Khan (T)	,,
10.	,,	,,	Mohammad Amin Khan (I)	,,	,,
11.	,,	Danishmand Khan (I)	,,	,,	Mahabat Khan (I)
12.	,,	Danishmand Khan (I)	,,,	,,	,,
13.	,,	,, (d)	Saif Khan (T)	,,	,,

277

R.Y.	Agra	Delhi	Lahore	Kashmir	Kabul
		Namdar Khan (I)	Fidai Khan, Azam Khan (I)		Muhammad Amin Khan (I)
14.	Namdar Khan (I)		,,	Iftikhar Khan, Mir Sultan Husain (I)	,,
15	Sar Buland Khan (T) Himmat Khan Mir Isa (T)		Fidai Khan, Azam Khan (I)	Iftikhar Khan, Mir Sultan Husain (I)	Mahabat Khan (I)
16.	,,	Safi Khan (I)	,,	,,	
17.	Mutamad Khan, Khwaja Nur		,,		Fidai Khan, Azam Khan (I)
18.	,,	,,	Amanat Khan, Mirak Muinuddin Ahmad (I)	,,	,,
19.		,,	,,	Qiwam Uddin Khan (I)	,,
20.	Hasan Ali Khan Bahadur (I)	,,	,,	,,	,,
21.	Shaista Khan (I)	,,	Qiwam Uuddin Khan (I)	Ibrahim Khan (I)	Amir Khan, Mir Miran (I)
22.	Safi Khan (I)	,,	,,	,,	,,

R.Y.	Agra	Delhi	Lahore	Kashmir	Kabul
23.	,,		Prince Azam (Lutfullah Khan (Dy.) (Ind.)	,,	,,
24.	Ibadullah Khan	Aqil Khan (I)	,,		,,
25.	Syed Munawwar, Lashkar Khan (Ind.)	,,	,,	,,	,,
26.	Muhtasham Khan, Mir Ibrahim (I)	,,	Mukarram Khan, Mir Ishaq (I)	,,	,,
27.	Safi Khan (I)	,,	,,	,,	
28.	Mukarram Khan (I)	Aqil Khan (I)	Mukarram Khan, Mir Ishaq (I)	Ibrahim Khan (I)	Amir Khan, Mir Miran (I)
29.	Sipahdar Khan, Nasiri Khan (I)	,,	,,	Hafizullah Khan (Ind.)	,,
30.		,,	Sipahdar Khan, Nasiri Khan (I)		,,
31.	,,	,,	Muhammad Ibrahim, Mahabat Khan Hyderabadi (I-Dec) ,, (d)	,,	,,
32.		,,	Prince Azam	,,	,,
33.		,,		Muzaffar Khan, Muhammad Baqa (I)	,,

R.Y.	Agra	Delhi	Lahore	Kashmir	Kabul
34.		,,	Bahadur Khan (I)		,,
35.		,,	,,	,,	,,
36.	Itiqad Khan (I)	,,	,,	Abu Nasar Khan (I)	,,
37.	Shaista Khan (I)	,,	Mukarram Khan, Mir Ishaq (I)	,,	,,
38.	Fedai Khan, Salih Khan (I) Mukhtar Khan (I)	,,	,,	,,	
39.	,, Prince Muazzam	,,	,,	,,	,,
40.	Itiqad Khan (I)	,, (d) Mohd. Yar Khan (I)	,,	,,	,,
41.	Mukhtar Khan (I) Itiqad Khan (I)	,,	Abu Nasar Khan (I)	Fazil Khan Burhanuddin (I)	,,
42.	Itiqad Khan (I)	Mohd. Yar Khan (I)		Fazil Khan Burhanuddin (I)	Aqil Khan (d) (I) Prince Muazzaam
43.	,,	,,	Ibrahim Khan (I) Prince Muazzam	,,	,,
44.	,,	,,	,, Fazil Khan (I) (Dy)	,,	Nasir Khan (Dy)

R.Y.	Agra	Delhi	Lahore	Kashmir	Kabul
45.	,,	,,	Saf Shikan Khan, Mohd. Shuja (I) (Dy.)	,, (d) Ibrahim Khan (I)	,, Sher Zaman (Dy.) (Ind.)
46.	,, (d) Mukhtar Khan Qamruddin (I)	,,	Zabardast Khan Muhd. Khalil (I) (Dy.)	,,	,,
47.	,,	,,		,,	,,
48.	,,	,,	Zabardast Khan, Muhd. Khalil (I)	,,	,,
49.	,,	,,	Prince Muazzam Munim Khan (T) (Dy.)	,,	,,
50.	,,	,, ,,		Nawazish Khan, Mukhtar Beg (T)	,, ,,
51.	,,	,,	,,	,,	,, ,,

281

Table 4 (c)

R.Y.	Multan	Sind	Ajmer	Gujarat	Malwa
1.	Lashkar Khan, Yadgar Beg	Qabad Khan (T)	Tarbiyat Khan Birlas (T)	Shah Nawaz Khan Safvi (I)	Jafar Khan (I)
2.	,,	,,	,,	Jaswant Singh (R)	,,
3.	Tarbiyat Khan Birlas (T)	Lashkar Khan, Yadgar Beg	Marhamat Khan	,,	,,
4.	,,	,,	,,	Qutbuddin Khan (Af)	,,
5.	,,	,,		Mahabat Khan (I)	,,
6.	,,	,,		,,	,,
7.	,,	Qabad Khan (T) Ghazanfar Khan (I)		,,	Najabat Khan (T) ,,(d) Wazir Khan, Muhd. Tahhir (I)
8.	,,	,,		,,	,,
9.	Saif Khan (T)	,,	,,		,,
10.	,,	,, (d) Syed Izzat Khan (Ind.)	Abid Khan (T)	Bahadur Khan Koka(I)	,,
11.	Tahir Khan (T) Lashkar Khan, Yadgar Beg	,,	,,	,,	,,
12.	,,	,,	Izzat Khan (Ind.)	,,	,,
13.	Mubariz Khan (T)	,,	,,	,,	,,
14.	Abid Khan (T)	,,	,,	Jaswant Singh (R)	,,

R.Y.	Multan	Sind	Ajmer	Gujarat	Malwa
15.	Abid Khasn (T)	Syed Izzat Khan (Ind.)	Izzat Khan (Ind.)		Wazir Khan (d) (I) Amir Khan, Mir Miran (I)
16.	,,	,,		Muhd. Amin Khan (I)	Islam Khan Rumi (T)
17.	,,	,,		,,	,,
18.	Dilir Khan (Af.)	,,	Darab Khan (I) Amanat Khan, Syed Ahmad Khan Khattab	,,	,,
19.	Prince Azam	,,		,,	,, (d) Prince Akbar
20.		,,	,,	,,	,,
21.	Prince Akbar		Syed Hamid Khan (T) Iftikhar Khan (I)	,,	,,
22.	,, Izza Khan (Ind.) (Dy.)	Khanazad Khan (I)	Badshah Quli Khan, Tahawwur Khan (I)	,,	Mukhtar Khan, Mir Shamsuddin (I)
23.	,,	,,	Inayat Khan (I)		,,
24.		,,	,,	,, (d)	,,
25.		,,	,, (d)	Mukhtar Khan Mir Shamsuddin (I)	Muftakhar Khan, Khan-i-Zaman (I)
26.		,, Sardar Khan, Dildost (T)		,,	,,
27.		,,		,,	,, (d)
28.				,, (d)	Mughal Khan, Arab Shaikh (d) (T)
29.		Sardar Khan, Dildost (T)		I Shuja'at Khan (I)	Prince Azam Rai Rayan Muluk Chaand (dy.) (H)

R.Y.	Multan	Sind	Ajmer	Gujarat	Malwa
30.		,,		,,	Muluk Chand (Dy) (H) (d) Mir Khan Behmani (Ind.)
31.	Makarnat Khan, Muhd. Mansur (I)	Murid Khan, Muhd, Masib (T)	Shuja'at Khan (I)	,,	
32.	,,	Zabarrdast Khan, Qadirdad Khan (T) (d)	Safi Khan (I)	,,	
33.	,,	Abu Nasar Khan (I)	,,	,,	
34.		,,	,,	,,	
35.		Hafizullah Khan (Ind.)	,,	,,	
36.		,,	,,	,,	
37.	Alah Yar Khan (T)	,,	,, (d)	,,	Bahadur Khan Koka (I)
38.	Mukarram Khan, Mir Ishaq (I)	,,	Mujahid Khan, Syed Hamid (T)	,,	Mirza Askar, Wazir Khan (I)
39.	,,	,,	Tarbiyat Khan, Mir Khalil (I) Mujahid Khan, Syed Hamid (T)	,,	Mukhtar Khan, Qamruddin (I)
40.	Alah Yar Khan (T) Prince Muizuddin	,,	Abdullah Khan Barha (Ind.)	,,	
41.	Prince Muizuddin	Hafizullah Khan (Ind.)	Abdullah Khan Barha (Ind.)	Shuja'at Khan (I)	Mukhtar Khan Qamruddin (I)

R.Y.	Multan	Sind	Ajmer	Gujarat	Malwa
42.	,,	,,	,,	,,	,,
43.	,,	,,	,,	,,	,,
44.	Mohd. Rafi (I) (Dy.)	,,	,,	,,	,,
45.		,, (d) Khanazad Khan, Sa'id Khan (T)	,,	,, (d)	Abu Nasar Khan, Shaista Khan II (I)
46.	,,	,,	,, (d) Hasan Ali Khan Barha (Ind.)	Prince Azam	,,
47.	,,	,, Prince Muizuddin, Amin Uddin Khan (Dy.)	Prince Azam	,,	Prince Bidar Bakht Jai Singh Sawai (R) (Dy.)
48.	,,	,, Yusuf Khan Tarin (Af.) (Dy)	,,	,,	,,
49.	,, ,,	,, Ahmad Yar Khan (Dy.)	Sar Andaz Khan Panni (Af.) (Dy.) Zabardast Khan, Muhd. Khalil(I)	,,	Jai Singh Sawai (R) (Dy.) Khan-i-Alam Hyderabadi (Ind.-Dec)
50.	,,	,, Ahmad Yar Khan (Dy.)		Ibrahim Khan (I)	,,
51.	,,	,, Ahmad Yar Khan (Dy.)		,,	,,

Table 4 (d)

R.Y.	Deccan	Bedar	Khandesh	Berar	Aurangabad
1.	Prince Muazzam		Wazir Khan (I), Mir Jumla (I)	Syed Salabat Khan, Ikhtisas Khan (Ind.)	
2.	,,			Shah Beg Khan (T), ,,	
3.	Shaista Khan (I)	Khan-i-Zaman, Mir Khalil (I)			
4.	,,				
5.	,,	,,			
6.	Prince Muazzam	,,			
7.	,,	,,	Wazir Khan(I), Daud Khan Qureshi (Ind.)		
8.	Mirza Raja Jai Singh (R)		,,		Khan-i-Zaman, Mir Khalil (I)
9.	Dilir Khan (Af.)	Khan-i-Zaman, Mir Khalil (I)	,,	Irij Khan (I)	,,
10.	Prince Muazzam		,,	Daud Khan Qureshi (Ind.)	
11.	,,		Mukhtar Khan, Mir Shamsuddin (I)		
12.	,,		Daud Khan Qureshi (Ind.)		

286

R.Y.	Deccan	Bedar	Khandesh	Berar	Aurangabad
13.	,,	Mukhtar Khan	,,		
14.	,,	Mir Shamsuddin (I)	Hoshdar Khan (I)		
15.	Bahadur Khan Koka (I) Bahadur Khan Koka (I)	Mukhtar Khan (I) Qalandar Khan (T)	Hoshdar Khan (d) (I) Mukhtar Khan, Mir Shamsuddin (I)		
16.	,,		,,		
17.	,,		,,		
18.	,,		,,	Khan-i-Zaman, Mir Khalil (I)	
19.	,,	Khan-i-Zaman, Mir Khalil (I)	,,		
20.	Dilir Khan (Af.)		,,		
21.	Prince Shah Alam				
22.	,,				
23.	Bahadur Khan Koka (I)		Bahadur Khan Koka (I)		
24.	,,		Irij Khan (I) Khan-i-Zaman, Mir Khalil (I)		
25.	,,		Mighal Khan (T) Lashkar Khan, Syed Munawwar Khan (Ind.)		

287

R.Y.	Deccan	Bedar	Khandesh	Berar	Aurangabad
26.	,,	Mir Shamsuddin Mukhtar Khan Sabzwari (I)	,,		
27.	Safi Khan (I)				
28.	Amanat Khan, Mirak Moinuddin (I) (d)		Khan-i-Zaman, Mir Khalil (I)	Irij Khan (I)	
29.	Haji Shafi Sabzwari (I)	Qulich Khan (T)	Prince Azam Mir Khan (Ind.) (Dy.)	Irij Khan (d) (I) Hasan Ali Khan Bahadur (I)	
30.	,,			,, (d) Muhd. Ibrahim, Mahabat Khan (I-Dec.)	
31.	,,			Prince Kam Bakhsh	
32.					
33.					
34.					
35.					
36.		Abdullah Khan (Ind.) Lashkar Khan, Munawwar Khan (Ind.)	Inayat Khan II (I) Marahmat Khan,	Nawazish Khan Rumi (T)	
37.		Abdullah Khan (Ind.)	Dindar Khan (I)	,, Ali Mardan Khan (Dec.)	
38.	Diyanat Khan, Mir Abdul Qadir (I)		,,	,,	
39.	,,	Khanazad Khan, Ruh Ullah Khan (I)	Inayat Khan II (I)	,,	

288

R.Y.	Deccan	Bedar	Khandesh	Berar	Aurangabad
40.		,,	,,		
41.	Hasan Ali Khan Barha (Ind.)		Najabat Khan Bahrawar Khan (T)	Prince Kam Bakhsh	
42.		Ali Mardan Khan (Dec)	Najabat Khan, Bahrawar Khan (T) Mutaqad Khan, Mohd. Quli (T)	Prince Kam Bakhsh Askar Khan (I-Dec)	
43.	Najabat Khan, Bahrawar Khan (T)	,,		,,	
44.	,,	Khuda Band Khan (I)	Sadruddin Mohd. Khand(I)	Khuda Band Khan (I) Ali Mardan Khan (Dec)	
45.	Lutfullah Khan (Ind.)	,,	Najabat Khan, Bahrawar Khan (T)		
46.	Prince Bedar Bakht	,,	,,	Firoz Jung (T)	
47.	,,	,,	Prince Bedar Bakht	,,	
'48.	,,		,, Mir Ahmad Khan (T) (Dy)	,, ,,	
49.	Prince Azam		Prince Azam	,, ,,	
50.			Najabat Khan, Bahrawar Khan (T)		
51.			Chin Qulich Khan (T)	,,	

Table 4 (e)

R.Y.	Bijapur	Golkunda	R.Y.	Bijapur	Golkunda
1.	Mir Muhd. Hasan Ruhullah Khan II (I)		12.		
2.	Abdullah Khan Barha (Ind.)		13.	Mamur Khan (Af.)	Jan Sipar Khan (I)
3.	,, Lashkar Khan, Munawwar Khan Barha (Ind.)		14.	Lutfullah Khan (Ind.)	,,
4.			15.	,,	,,
5.			16.	,, Chin Qulich Khan (T)	,, (d) Prince Kam Bakash Rustam Dil Khan (I) (Dy.)
6.			17.		
7.		Jan Sipar Khan (I)	18.	,,	Syed Muzaffar Khan (Ind.)
8.		,, Jan Nisar Khan, Abul Makarim (I)	19.	,,	Prince Kam Baksh Daud Khan Panni (Dy.) (Af.)
9.	Lashkar Khan, Munawwar Khan (Ind.)	,,	20.	,,	,,
10.	,,		21.		
11.	,,	Rustam Dil Khan (I)	22.	Prince Kam Baksh	Rustam Dil Khan (I) (Dy.)

REFERENCES TO TABLE 4

Authorities are give for each term of governorship, indicated by the years it covered.

BENGAL

Years		
	2–5	*Alamgir Nama*, 462, 484, 492, 592, 676, 741, 761, 778; *Ma'asir-i Alamgiri*, 32, 45; *Ma'asir-ul-Umara*, III, 530–55.
	6–19	*Alamgir Nama*, 848, 855, 882, 919, 941, 958, 1057; *Ma'asir-i-Alamgiri*, 45, 159; *Ma'asir-ul-Umara*, II, 690–707.
	20	*Ma'asir-i-Alamgiri*, 159, 168; *Ma'asir-ul-Umara*, I, 247–53.
	21–2	*Ma'asir-i-Alamgiri*, 161, 168, 171, 180, 181; *Akhbarat*, 21 R.Y.
	23–31	*Ma'asir-i-Alamgiri*, 181; *Ma'asir-ul-Umara*, II, 690–707; *Riyazus Salatin*, 222–3.
	32–40	*Ma'asir-i-Alamgiri*, 236, 387, 497; *Tazkara-i-Salatin-i-Chaghta*, 299b; *Akhbarat*, 36 R.Y., 38 R.Y., 39 R.Y., 40 R.Y.; *Ma'asir-ul-Umara*, I, 295–301.
	41–51	*Ma'asir-i-Alamgiri*, 387, 432, 470; *Akhbarat*, 47 R.Y.

ORISSA

Years		
	2–10	*Alamgir Nama*, 474, 1050, 1067; *Ma'asir-ul-Umara*, I, 872–85; *Ma'asir-i-Alamgiri*, 62, 90; *Akhbarat*, 10 R.Y.
	11	*Akhbarat*, 11 R.Y.; *Ma'asir-ul-Umara*, I, 493–8.
	12	*Ma'asir-i-Alamgiri*, 90; *Akhbarat*, 11 R.Y; *Ma'asir-ul-Umara*, II, 740–2.
	13–14	*Akhbarat*, 14 R.Y.; *Ma'asir-ul-Umara*, II, 738–40.
	18–19	*Ma'asir-i-Alamgiri*, 150; *Ma'asir-ul-Umara*, II, 303–5.
	21	*Ma'asir-i-Alamgiri*, , 161; *Akhbarat*, 21 R.Y.
	22–30	*Ma'asir-ul-Umara*, II, 690–707.
	31–6	P. Acharya, *Two Forgotten Mughal Subedars of Orissa*, PIHC, 1950, pp. 219–21; *Tazkara-i-*

Salatin-i-Chaghta, 294b; Arkan-i-Ma'asir-i-Taimuriya, 124a.

37–8   *Akhbarat*, 37 R.Y., 38 R.Y.

39–42   P. Acharya, *Two Forgotten Mughal Subedars of Orissa, PIHC,* 1950, pp. 219–21.

43   *Akhbarat*, 43 R.Y.

44–6   *Akhbarat*, 44 R.Y., 46 R.Y.; *Dilkusha*, 95a.

47–51   *Ma'asir-i-Alamgiri*, 482–83; *Akhbarat*, 47 R.Y., 48 R.Y.; *Ma'asir-ul-Umara*, III, 751–5.

BIHAR

Years   1–7   *Alamgir Nama*, 286, 419, 513, 589, 648, 755, 866, 877; *Ma'asir-i-Alamgiri*, 37.

            8–10   *Alamgir Nama*, 877, 972; *Ma'asir-ul-Umara*, III, 168, 171.

            11–16   *Ma'asir-i-Alamgiri*, 71, 150; *Ma'asir-ul-Umara*, I, 295, 301.

            17–18   *Ma'asir-i-Alamgiri*, 148; *Ma'asir-ul-Umara*, I, 277–8.

            19–20   *Ma'asir-i-Alamgiri*, 148, 157; *Akhbarat*, 20 R.Y.

            21–3   *Ma'asir–i-Alamgiri*, 169, *Tazkira-i-Salatin-i-Chaghta*, 265a; *Ma'asir-ul-Umara*, II, 479–85.

            24–6   *Ma'asir-i-Alamgiri*, 226; R.R. Diwakar, *Bihar Through the Ages*, 498; Bhim Sen, *Nuskha-i-Dilkusha*, 80b.

            27–36   *Ma'asir-i-Alamgiri*, 348; *Ma'asir-ul-Umara*, I, 453–4; *Arkan-i-Ma'asir-i-Taimuriya*, 127a; *Bihar Through the Ages*, 498–9.

            37   *Ma'asir-i-Alamgiri*, 369–70.

            38–45   *Akhbarat*, 38 R.Y., 39 R.Y., 40 R.Y., 43 R.Y., 44 R.Y., 45 R.Y.; *Ma'asir-i-Alamgiri*, 369, 433.

            46   *Akhbarat*, 46 R.Y., 47 R.Y.

            47–51   *Akhbarat*, 47 R.Y.; *Ma'asir-i-Alamgiri*, 470; *Bihar Through the Ages*, 499.

ILAHABAD

Years   1–2   *Alamgir Nama*, 349, 465, 486.

            3–9   *Alamgir Nama*, 465, 486, 564, 858, 860, 979, 986, 1056; *Ma'asir-i-Alamgiri*, 58.

10–11   *Alamgir Nama*, 1056; *Ma'asir-i-Alamgiri*, 82; *Akhbarat*, 10 R.Y.

12–15   *Akhbarat*, 14 R.Y.; *Ma'asir-i-Alamgiri*, 82, 110; *Ma'asir-ul-Umara*, II, 32–7.

16–18   *Akhbarat*, 19 R.Y.; *Ma'asir-i-Alamgiri*, 150, 153; *Ma'asir-ul-Umara*, I, 593–9.

19–23   *Akhbarat*, 19 R.Y.; *Ma'asir-i-Alamgiri*, 150, 153, 181, 187; *Ma'asir-ul-Umara*, III, 946–9; *Akhbarat*, 23 R.Y.

27–8   *Akhbarat*, 28 R.Y.; *Ma'asir-i-Alamgiri*, 246–7.

29–32   *Akhbarat*, 30 R.Y.; *Ma'asir-i-Alamgiri*, 282; *Ma'asir-ul-Umara*, III, 449–51.

33   *Ma'asir–i-Alamgiri*, 335.

34–6   *Akhbarat*, 34 R.Y.; 36 R.Y.; *Ma'asir-i-Alamgiri*, 338, 348, 365.

37–40   *Akhbarat*, 37 R.Y., 38 R.Y.; *Ma'asir-i-Alamgiri*, 365, 387; *Ma'asir-ul-Umara*, III, 949–51.

41–3   *Akhbarat*, 43 R.Y.; *Ma'asir-i-Alamgiri*, 387.

44–5   *Akhbarat*, 44 R.Y.; *Ma'asir-ul-Umara*, III, 949–51.

46   *Akhbarat*, 46 R.Y.

47–51   *Ma'asir-i-Alamgiri*, 481, 496; *Akhbarat*, 47 R.Y., 48 R.Y.; *Tazkara-i-Salatin-i-Chaghta*, 286b; *Ma'asir-ul-Umara*, III, 949–51.

AWADH

Years   1   *Alamgir Nama*, 127, 202.

            2   *Ma'asir-ul-Umara*, I, 248.

            3–8   *Alamgir Nama*, 927; *Ma'asir-ul-Umara*, III, 583–6

            9–10   *Akhbarat*, 19 Rajab, 9 R.Y.; *Ma'asir-ul-Umara*, II, 739.

            11–12   *Ma'asir-i-Alamgiri*, 104; *Ma'asir-ul-Umara*, I, 250.

            13–14   *Akhbarat*, 13 R.Y.; *Ma'asir-i-Alamgiri*, 104; *Ma'asir-ul-Umara*, I, 297.

            17   *Ma'asir-i-Alamgiri*, 143; *Akhbarat*, 18 R.Y.

            18–20   *Akhbarat*, 18 R.Y., 19 R.Y., 2 R.Y.; *Ma'asir-i-Alamgiri*, 143.

21   *Ma'asir-i-Alamgiri*, 171.

22   *Ma'asir-i-Alamgiri*, 171.

32   *Tazkara-i-Salatin-i-Chaghta*, 289a; *Akhbarat*, 32 R.Y.

33   *Ma'asir-i-Alamgiri*, 335; *Ma'asir-ul-Umara*, III, 950.

37   *Akhbarat*, 37 R.Y.

38–40   *Akhbarat*, 38 R.Y., 40 R.Y.; *Ma'asir-i-Alamgiri*, 369.

41–2   *Ma'asir-i-Alamgiri*, 397; *Akhbarat*, 42 R.Y.

43–6   *Akhbarat*, 43 R.Y.; 44 R.Y., 45 R.Y., 46 R.Y., 47 R.Y.

47–8   *Akhbarat*, 47 R.Y.; *Ma'asir-i-Alamgiri*, 470.

49   *Ma'asir-i-Alamgiri*, 516.

50–1   *Ma'asir-i-Alamgiri*, 516.

AGRA

Years   1   *Alamgir Nama*, 226, 229.

2   *Alamgir Nama*, 294, 433.

3–5   *Alamgir Nama*, 481, 564, 741, 759, 819.

6–13   *Akhbarat*, 9 R.Y., 12 R.Y., 13 R.Y.; *Alamgir Nama*, 823, 839, 842, 871, 873, 883, 933, 978; *Ma'asir-i-Alamgiri*, 50, 93.

14   *Ma'asir-i-Alamgiri*, 112; *Akhbarat*, 15 R.Y.

15–16   *Akhbarat*, 15 R.Y.; *Ma'asir-i-Alamgiri*, 118, 120.

17–18   *Akhbarat*, 17 R.Y.; *Ma'asir-i-Alamgiri*, 132.

20   *Akhbarat*, 20 R.Y.; *Ma'asir-i-Alamgiri*, 158.

21–2   *Akhbarat*, 21 R.Y., 22 R.Y.; *Ma'asir-i-Alamgiri*,

23   *Akhbarat*, 22 R.Y.; *Ma'asir-i-Alamgiri*; 180; *Ma'asir-ul-Umara*, II, 740–2.

24   *Akhbarat*, 24 *Rajab*, 24 R.Y.

25   *Akhbarat*, 25 R.Y.; *Ma'asir-ul-Umara*, II, 467.

27   *Ma'asir-i-Alamgiri*, 246.

28–9   *Ma'asir-i-Alamgiri*, 246.

30–1   *Akhbarat*, 30 R.Y.

36–7   *Akhbarat*, 36 R.Y., 37 R.Y.; *Ma'asir-i-Alamgiri*, 351, 368.

38	*Akhbarat*, 38 R.Y.; *Ma'asir-i-Alamgiri*, 368–70.
39	*Ma'asir-i-Alamgiri*, 372; *Akhbarat*, 39 R.Y.
40	*Akhbarat*, 40 R.Y.; *Ma'asir-i-Alamgiri*, 392.
41–5	*Akhbarat*, 43 R.Y., 44 R.Y., 45 R.Y.; *Ma'asir-i-Alamgiri*, 392.
46–51	*Akhbarat*, 46 R.Y.; *Ma'asir-i-Alamgiri*, 460, 498; *Ma'asir-ul-Umara*, III, 655–60.

DELHI

Years

1	*Alamgir Nama*, 129, 146, 161.
2	*Alamgir Nama*, 415, 464.
5	*Alamgir Nama*, 839.
6–7	*Alamgir Nama*, 839; *Ma'asir-ul-Umara*, II, 740–2.
8–10	*Alamgir Nama*, 937, 961, 979; *Akhbarat*, 9 R.Y.; *Ma'asir-ul-Umara*, II, 30–2.
12–13	*Ma'asir-i-Alamgiri*, 105; *Ma'asir-ul-Umara*, II, 30–2.
17–21	*Akhbarat*, 17 R.Y., 18 R.Y.,; *Ma'asir-i-Alamgiri*, 132, 147; *Ma'asir-ul-Umara*, II, 740–2
24–40	*Ma'asir-i-Alamgiri*, 195, 383; *Akhbarat*, 37 R.Y., 38 R.Y., 39 R.Y.; *Ma'asir-ul-Umara*, II, 821–3
41–51	*Akhbarat*, 43 R.Y., 44 R.Y., 45 R.Y., 46 R.Y., 47 R.Y., 48 R.Y.; *Ma'asir-i-Alamgiri*, 384, 462; *Ma'asir-ul-Umara*, III, 708–9.

LAHORE

Years

1–4	*Alamgir Nama*, 215, 229, 341, 419, 473, 574, 608, 615, 631, 661.
5–10	*Alamgir Nama*, 776, 818, 840, 846, 855, 1058, 1065, 1067; *Ma'asir-i-Alamgiri*, 62–4.
11–13	*Akhbarat*, 13 R.Y.; *Alamgir Nama*, 1067.
14–17	*Akhbarat*, 15 R.Y.; *Ma'asir-ul-Umara*, I, 247–52.
18–20	*Ma'asir-i-Alamgiri*, 150; *Ma'asir-ul-Umara*, I, 258–68.
21–3	*Ma'asir-i-Alamgiri*, 166, 169, 188.
24–5	*Akhbarat*, 25 R.Y.; *Ma'asir-i-Alamgiri*, 188.

26–30   *Ma'asir-i-Alamgiri*, 283; *Ma'asir-ul-Umara*, III, 697.

31   *Ma'asir-i-Alamgiri*, 283.

32   *Ma'asir-ul-Umara*, III, 632.

33   *Ma'asir-i-Alamgiri*, 338.

34–6   *Akhbarat*, 34 R.Y., 36 R.Y.; *Ma'asir-i-Alamgiri*, 338.

37–40   *Akhbarat*, 38 R.Y., 39 R.Y., 4 R.Y.; *Ma'asir-i-Alamgiri*, 360, 386.

41   *Ma'asir-i-Alamgiri*, 386.

43–6   *Akhbarat*, 43 R.Y., 44 R.Y., 45 R.Y., 46 R.Y.; *Ma'asir-i-Alamgiri*, 423.

48   *Ma'asir-i-Alamgiri*, 496.

49–51   *Ma'asir-i-Alamgiri*, 496, 497, 519.

KASHMIR

Full information on the Mughal governors of Kashmir is given in *Tarikh-i-Kashmir* by Narayan Kaul folios unmarked (Aligarh: Subhanullah Collection No. 954/13). References given below are to authorities other than the *Tarikh-i Kashmir*, wherever they supplement or corroborate its information.

Years

1–2   *Alamgir Nama*, 196, 210, 302, 564.

3   *Alamgir Nama*, 564, 634; *Ma'asir-i-Alamgiri*, 38.

4–5   *Alamgir Nama*, 634, 823, 832.

6–8   *Alamgir Nama*, 832, 838, 843, 877, 921, 957; *Ma'asir-i-Alamgiri*, 52.

9–11   *Akhbarat*, 10 R.Y.; *Alamgir Nama*, 957, 1064; *Ma'asir-i-Alamgiri*, 63, 83.

12–13   *Akhbarat*, 12 R.Y., 13 R.Y., *Ma'asir-i-Alamgiri*, 83, 112.

14–18   *Ma'asir-i-Alamgiri*, 112, 125; *Ma'asir-ul-Umara*, I, 254.

19–20   *Ma'asir-i-Alamgiri*, 151, 163, 165.

21–8   *Ma'asir-i-Alamgiri*, 163, 236; *Ma'asir-ul-Umara*, I, 298.

29–32   *Tarikh-i Azmi*, f. 163b.

33–5   *Tazkara-i-Salatin-i-Chaghta*, 273a.

36–40   *Akhbarat*, 36 R.Y.; *Ma'asir-i-Alamgiri*, 386; *Ma'asir-ul-Umara*, I, 292.

41–45   *Akhbarat*, 43 R.Y., 44 R.Y., 45 R.Y.; *Ma'asir-i-Alamgiri*, 386, 424, 432.

46–49   *Akhbarat*, 45 R.Y., 48 R.Y.; *Ma'asir-i-Alamgiri*, 497, 512.

50–51   *Ma'asir-i-Alamgiri*, 497; *Ma'asir-ul-Umara*, I, 246–7.

KABUL

Years

1–3   *Alamgir Nama*, 129, 194, 219, 229, 302, 341, 397, 419, 442, 454, 485, 564, 624, 634, 661; *Ma'asir-i-Alamgiri*, 38.

4–10   *Alamgir Nama*, 661, 741, 761, 842, 847, 937, 972, 1042, 1044; *Ma'asir-i-Alamgiri*, 38, 57, 61.

11–12   *Ma'asir-i-Alamgiri*, 71, 84, 104.

13–14   *Ma'asir-i-Alamgiri*, 104; *Ma'asir-ul-Umara*, III, 616.

15–16   *Ma'asir-i-Alamgiri*, 136; *Ma'asir-ul-Umara*, III, 593.

17–19   *Ma'asir-i-Alamgiri*, 136, 157.

20–42   *Ma'asir-i-Alamgiri*, 157, 170, 270, 394; *Akhbarat*, 39 R.Y., 40 R.Y.

43–51   *Ma'asir-i-Alamgiri*, 394–95, 482, 497; *Akhbarat*, 45 R.Y.

MULTAN

Years

1–2   *Alamgir Nama*, 210, 214, 217, 428, 485.

3–8   *Alamgir Nama*, 485, 589, 608, 614, 845, 966; *Ma'asir-i-Alamgiri*, 35.

9–10   *Akhbarat*, 10 R.Y.; *Alamgir Nama*, 1049.

11–13   *Ma'asir-i-Alamgiri*, 74, 104, 105; *Akhbarat*, 13 R.Y.

14–17   *Akhbarat*, 18 R.Y.; *Ma'asir-i-Alamgiri*, 110, 140.

18   *Ma'asir-i-Alamgiri*, 140, *Akhbarat*, 18 R.Y.

19–20   *Akhbarat*, 19 R.Y., 20 R.Y.; *Ma'asir-i-Alamgiri*, 149, 157.

21–22   *Akhbarat*, 21 R.Y., 22 R.Y.; *Ma'asir-i-Alamgiri*, 166, 173.

31–3   Isar Das, *Futuhat-i-Alamgiri*, 133b; *Akhbarat*, 32
         R.Y.

37   *Akhbarat*, 37 R.Y.

38–9   *Akhbarat*, 38 R.Y.; *Ma'asir-ul-Umara*, III, 697.

40–51   *Akhbarat*, 40 R.Y.; 43 R.Y., 44 R.Y., 45 R.Y., 47
         R.Y., 48 R.Y.; *Ma'asir-i-Alamgiri*, 432, 470, 497.

SIND

Full information on the Governors of Sind and their periods of office is
given in the *Tuhfatul Kiram*, III, 96–99, the entire reign of Aurangzeb being
covered. Its information is confirmed in each case where other evidence is
available. References given below are to authorities other than the *Tuhfatul
Kiram*.

Years   1–2   *Alamgir Nama*, 217, 282, 290, 485, 623.

             3–6   *Alamgir Nama*, 485, 877.

             7–9   *Alamgir Nama*, 864, 1048.

             10–21   *Alamgir Nama*, 1048; *Ma'asir-i-Alamgiri*, 173.

             22–6   *Akhbarat*, 22 R.Y.

             27–30   *Tazkara-i-Salatin-i-Chaghta*, 268b.

             35–45   *Akhbarat*, 38 R.Y., 43 R.Y., 44 R.Y., 45 R.Y.;
                     Ma'asir-i-Alamgiri, 407, 432, 440.

             46   *Ma'asir-i-Alamgiri*, 440.

             47–51   *Akhbarat*, 47 R.Y.; 48 R.Y.; *Ma'asir-i-Alamgiri*,
                     470, 497.

AJMER

Years   1–3   *Alamgir Nama*, 119, 311, 336, 568, 593.

             4   *Alamgir Nama*, 593.

             10–11   *Alamgir Nama*, 1056; *Ma'asir-ul-Umara*, III, 121.

             12–15   *Akhbarat*, 12 R.Y., 15 R.Y.

             19–20   *Akhbarat*, 19 R.Y., 20 R.Y., *Ma'asir-i-Alamgiri*,
                     150–151, 158, 165; *Tazkara-i-Salatin-i-Chaghta*,
                     262b.

             21–2   *Waqai Ajmer*, 116–118; *Akhbarat*, 22 R.Y.; *Ma'asir-
                     i-Alamgiri*, 165, 173.

             23   *Waqai Ajmer*, 633; *Ma'asir-i-Alamgiri*, 173, 179.

             24–6   *Ma'asir-i-Alamgiri*, 206, 213, 223.

31–7   *Akhbarat*, 32 R.Y., 36 R.Y., 37 R.Y.

38   *Akhbarat*, 38 R.Y.

29   *Akhbarat*, 39 R.Y.

40–6   *Akhbarat*, 40 R.Y., 42 R.Y., 43 R.Y., 44 R.Y., 45 R.Y., 46 R.Y.

47–8   *Ma'asir–i-Alamgiri*, 473, 497; *Akhbarat*, 46 R.Y., 47 R.Y., 48 R.Y.

49–50   *Ma'asir-i-Alamgiri*, 497; *Ma'asir-ul-Umara*, I, 300.

GUJARAT

Years   1   *Alamgir Nama*, 21, 296; *Mir'at-i-Ahmadi*, I, 241.

          2–4   *Alamgir Nama*, 332, 346, 404, 485, 568, 592, 636, 647, 754; *Mir'at-i-Ahmadi*, I, 244, 253.

          5–9   *Alamgir Nama*, 754, 737, 755, 1056; *Ma'asir-i-Alamgiri*, 41; *Mir'at-i-Ahmadi*, I, 253–66.

          10–13 *Alamgir Nama*, 1056; *Dilkusha*, 41a; *Mir'at-i-Ahmadi*, I, 267–76.

          14–15 *Mir'at-i-Ahmadi*, I, 276, 288; *Ma'asir-i-Alamgiri*, 121, 182, 189, 198, 216, 219.

          16–24 *Mir'at-i-Ahmadi*, I, 289–303.

          25–8 *Ma'asir-i-Alamgiri*, 219–20, 247; *Akhbarat*, 25 R.Y.; *Mir'at-i-Ahmadi*, I, 303–10.

          29–45 *Mir'at-i-Ahmadi*, I, 311–45; *Ma'asir-i-Alamgiri*, 383, 395, 441.

          46–9 *Ma'asir-i-Alamgiri*, 397, 442, 473, 512; *Mir'at-i-Ahmadi*, I, 346–56.

          50–1 *Mir'at-i-Ahmadi*, I, 369; *Ma'asir-i-Alamgiri*, 497, 512.

MALWA

Years   1–6   *Alamgir Nama*, 162, 229, 419, 434, 485, 590, 634, 741, 761, 837, 842, 855, 873; *Ma'asir-i-Alamgiri*, 47, 48.

          7–14 *Alamgir Nama*, 873, 880, 1036; *Ma'asir-i-Alamgiri*, 120; *Akhbarat*, 13 R.Y., 15 R.Y.

          15–19 *Akhbarat*, 15 R.Y., 19 R.Y.; *Ma'asir-i-Alamgiri*, 120, 151.

          20–1 *Akhbarat*, 19 R.Y., 20 R.Y.; *Ma'asir-i-Alamgiri*, 152.

22–4   *Akhbarat*, 22 R.Y., 25 R.Y.; *Ma'asir-i-Alamgiri*,
        174, 220.

25–7   *Akhbarat*, 25 R.Y.; *Ma'asir-i-Alamgiri*, 220, 246.

28   *Ma'asir-i-Alamgiri*, 246, 261; *Akhbarat*, 28 R.Y.

29–30   *Ma'asir-i-Alamgiri*, 273.

31   *Tazkira-i-Salatin-i-Chaghta*, 289b; *Selected
        Documents of Aurangzeb's reign*, 173.

37–8   Lindesiana, *Diplomatic Correspondence of
        Aurangzeb*, folios unmarked; *Mir'at-i-Aftab Numa*,
        594; *Ma'asir-ul-Umara*, 1,810–11.

39–44   *Akhbarat*, 39 R.Y., 40 R.Y., 42 R.Y., 43 R.Y., 44
        R.Y.,; *Ma'asir-i-Alamgiri*, 442; *Ma'asir-ul-Umara*,
        III, 655–60.

45–6   *Akhbarat*, 45 R.Y., 46 R.Y.,; *Ma'asir-i-Alamgiri*,
        441–2; *Ma'asir-ul-Umara*, I, 292–3.

47–9   Inayatullah, *Ahkam-i-Alamgiri*, 62b; *Ma'asir-i-
        Alamgiri*, 498; *Akhbarat*, 48 R.Y.

50–1   *Ma'asir-i-Alamgiri*, 512.

DECCAN

Years   1–2   *Alamgir Nama*, 219, 338, 416.

        3–5   *Alamgir Nama*, 416, 446, 462, 485, 564, 578, 592,
                627, 634, 741, 761; *Ma'asir-i-Alamgiri*, 32.

        6–7   *Alamgir Nama*, 819, 854, 869, 874, 879; *Ma'asir-
                i-Alamgiri*, 45.

        8–9   *Alamgir Nama*, 903, 904, 907, 913, 919, 924, 970,
                971, 988, 1009, 1020, 1022, 1036; *Ma'asir-i-
                Alamgiri*, 52, 71.

        10–14   *Alamgir Nama*, 1029, 1037; *Ma'asir-i-Alamgiri*, 60.

        15–19   *Ma'asir-i-Alamgiri*, 124, 161, 169.

        20   *Ma'asir-i-Alamgiri*, 161.

        21–2   *Ma'asir-i-Alamgiri*, 169.

        23–6   *Ma'asir-i-Alamgiri*, 189, 205.

        27   *Akhbarat*, 27 R.Y.; *Ma'asir-i-Alamgiri*, 243.

        28   *Akhbarat*, 28 R.Y.

        29–31   *Akhbarat*, 28 R.Y., 30 R.Y.

        38   *Akhbarat*, 38 R.Y.

        42   *Akhbarat*, 42 R.Y.

43–5   *Akhbarat*, 43 R.Y., 44 R.Y., 45 R.Y.; *Ma'asir-i-Alamgiri*, 441.

46–8   *Ma'asir-i-Alamgiri*, 461, 470, 483; *Akhbarat*, 46 R.Y.

49   *Ma'asir-i-Alamgiri*, 496.

BEDAR (Zafarabad)

Years   4–7   *Alamgir Nama*, 624; *Ma'asir-ul-Umara*, I, 788.

14   *Akhbarat*, 14 R.Y.; *Ma'asir-ul-Umara*, III, 622.

15   *Akhbarat*, 15 R.Y.

20   *Akhbarat*, 20 R.Y.; *Ma'asir-i-Alamgiri*, 158.

29   *Akhbarat*, 29 R.Y.; *Ma'asir-i-Alamgiri*, 263.

36   *Akhbarat*, 36 R.Y.

37   *Akhbarat*, 37 R.Y.

38   *Akhbarat*, 38 R.Y.

39–40   *Akhbarat*, 39 R.Y., 40 R.Y.; *Ma'asir-i-Alamgiri*, 384, 385.

42–3   *Akhbarat*, 42 R.Y., 43 R.Y.

44–7   *Akhbarat*, 44 R.Y., 45 R.Y., 46 R.Y.; *Ma'asir-i-Alamgiri*, 432.

KHANDESH (BURHANPUR)

Years   1–2   *Alamgir Nama*, 129, 196, 219, 233, 439, 440.

7–8   *Alamgir Nama*, 873, 972; *Ma'asir-i-Alamgiri*, 49.

9–10   *Alamgir Nama*, 972, 1027.

11–13   *Dilkusha*, 40b; *Akhbarat*, 14 R.Y.; *Ma'asir-i-Alamgiri*, 110; *Ma'asir-ul-Umara*, II, 32–7.

14   *Akhbarat*, 14 R.Y.; *Ma'asir-i-Alamgiri*, 110.

15–20   *Akhbarat*, 15 R.Y.; *Ma'asir-i-Alamgiri*, 144; *Ma'asir-ul-Umara*, III, 620–3.

23   *Ma'asir-i-Alamgiri*, 206.

24   *Ma'asir-i-Alamgiri*, 206, 209, 217, 220; *Akhbarat*, 24 R.Y.

25–6   *Akhbarat*, 25 R.Y.; *Ma'asir-i-Alamgiri*, 220.

28   *Akhbarat*, 28 R.Y.

29   *Ma'asir-i-Alamgiri*, 262.

36   *Akhbarat*, 36 R.Y.

37–8	*Akhbarat*, 37 R.Y., 38 R.Y.	
39	*Akhbarat*, 39 R.Y.	
40–2	*Akhbarat*, 40 R.Y., 41 R.Y.	
43	*Akhbarat*, 43 R.Y., *Ma'asir-i-Alamgiri*, 387, 433.	
44	*Akhbarat*, 44 R.Y.; *Ma'asir-i-Alamgiri*, 433.	
45–6	*Akhbarat*, 45 R.Y., 46 R.Y.; *Ma'asir-i-Alamgiri*, 470.	
47–8	*Akhbarat*, 47 R.Y., 48 R.Y.; *Ma'asir-i-Alamgiri*, 470, 480.	
49	*Ma'asir-i-Alamgiri*, 496.	
50	*Ma'asir-i-Alamgiri*, 512.	
51	*Dilkusha*, 161b.	

BERAR

Years		
1–2	*Alamgir Nama*, 191.	
3	*Alamgir Nama*, 476.	
9	*Alamgir Nama*, 1023.	
10	*Alamgir Nama*, 1032.	
18	*Akhbarat*, 18 R.Y.; *Ma'asir-i-Alamgiri*, 144.	
28	*Ma'asir-i-Alamgiri*, 262.	
29–30	*Akhbarat*, 30 R.Y.; *Ma'asir-i-Alamgiri*, 278, 281.	
31	*Ma'asir-i-Alamgiri*, 302.	
36	*Akhbarat*, 36 R.Y.	
37–9	*Akhbarat*, 37 R.Y., 38 R.Y., 39 R.Y.	
41	*Ma'asir-i-Alamgiri*, 390, 396.	
42–3	*Akhbarat*, 42 R.Y., 43 R.Y.; *Ma'asir-i-Alamgiri*, 396.	
44–5	*Akhbarat*, 44 R.Y., 45 R.Y.; *Ma'asir-i-Alamgiri*, 432.	
46–51	*Akhbarat*, 46 R.Y., 47 R.Y.; *Ma'asir-i-Alamgiri*, 461, 470, 480 483, 493.	

AURANGABAD

Years		
8–9	*Alamgir Nama*, 972.	

BIJAPUR (DAR-UL-ZAFAR)

Years		
	30	*Ma'asir-i-Alamgiri,* 282, 299.
	31	*Ma'asir-i-Alamgiri,* 327.
	32	*Akhbarat,* 32 R.Y.; *Ma'asir-i-Alamgiri,* 329.
	38–40	*Akhbarat,* 38 R.Y., 39 R.Y., 40 R.Y.
	42–3	*Akhbarat,* 42 R.Y., 43 R.Y.; *Ma'asir-i-Alamgiri,* 412.
	44	*Akhbarat,* 44 R.Y., 45 R.Y.
	45–60	*Akhbarat,* 46 R.Y., 47 R.Y., 48 R.Y., 49 R.Y.; *Ma'asir-i-Alamgiri,* 441, 471, 474, 480, 494, 496, 498, 518; *Dilkusha,* 157b.
	51	*Dilkusha,* 158a; *Ma'asir-i-Alamgiri,* 520.

GOLKUNDA

	36–7	*Akhbarat,* 36 R.Y., 37 R.Y.
	38–9	*Akhbarat,* 38 R.Y., 39 R.Y.
	40	*Akhbarat,* 40 R.Y.
	42–5	*Ma'asir-i-Alamgiri,* 439; *Akhbarat,* 42 R.Y., 43 R.Y., 45 R.Y.
	47	*Akhbarat,* 47 R.Y.
	48–9	*Ma'asir-i-Alamgiri,* 483, 494, 496, 497.

NOTES

1. For the best study of the subject, see P. Saran, *Provincial Government of the Mughals,* (1526–1658), Allahabad, 1941.

2. The reign lasted fifty-one years; so each province carries 51 entries, except for Bijapur and Golkunda, which being annexed later in the reign, carry 20 and 19 entries respectively.

3. Amir Khan served in Kabul for 23 years; Aqil Khan in Delhi for 17 years; also Shujaat Khan in Gujarat for 17 years. Shaista Khan served in Bengal for 14 years in a single term. Izzat Khan served in Sind for a continuous term of 12 years.

4. Ibrahim Khan s/o Ali Mardan Khan served as governor for 41 years in different provinces. Shaista Khan served for 30 years and Bahadur Khan Koka for 25 years.

5. Muhammad Ibrahim Khan Qureshi was appointed in Bihar in the 46th r.y. but was removed in the same year. Muhtashim Khan was appointed in Ilahabad in the 23rd R.Y., and removed the same year. Dilir Khan was appointed in Multan in the 18th R.Y. and dismissed in the same year. Khudaband Khan was appointed to Awadh and dismissed in the 32nd R.Y. Such instances may be multiplied.

6. See my book, *The Mughal Nobility under Aurangzeb*, pp. 12, 36.

7. This cannot be owing to any subjective reasons, such as any closer enquiry into the antecedents of governors. I have used the same list of nobles, given at the end of my book, to establish the antecedents of governors.

8. For this faction, see S. Chandra, *Parties and Politics at the Mughal Court*, 1707–40, Aligarh, 1959, p. 9.

THE EMPIRE AND CONTEMPORARY
POWERS

24

'International Law' or Conventions Governing Conduct of Relations between Asian States, Sixteenth and Seventeenth Centuries

Modern international law has developed out of the conventions governing the conduct of relations between European states. However, as states also existed outside Europe, and they had to evolve traditions and norms in conducting relations with one another, in dealing with one another's subjects, and so on, systems of primitive 'International Law', both 'public' and 'private', existed outside of Europe as well. Taking only the medieval and early modern periods and omitting the Americas, one could broadly say that two such major systems, outside of Christendom, can be identified. The first embraced the Islamic states of Asia (including India) and North Africa; and the second revolved around the Celestial Empire. The spheres of these systems intersected: notably, the Islamic with the Christian or European in the Mediterranean (seen especially in the relations of the Ottoman Empire with European powers). But, in spite of uniformities in the intersecting systems such as found in the sixteenth-century Mediterranean by Braudel, the systems by and large remained isolated, with mutual contacts as mere episodes or, at best, secondary aspects only.

My purpose is to study the first of these two systems, with special focus on the Indian Mughal Empire in the sixteenth and seventeenth centuries.

A word may be put in about the theory or tradition which the Mughal Empire had inherited. As is well known, formal Islamic jurisprudence remains enmeshed in the fiction of the caliph or imam, a single law-enforcing authority in the entire Muslim community, and does not have any provisions for a situation in which not one caliph, but various sultans, are in independent, sovereign control of different parts of the *Daru-l Islam*, the Islamic world. As such, relations between sovereign states, contracts between subjects of various states, law of the high seas, etc., are not known to Islamic law. However, in all these spheres conventions and practices developed in time under various influences, among which mercantile custom had also perhaps its due place. These conventions are often incidentally referred to by historians, when they condemn particular actions, such as affront to envoys, or use of epithets or complimentary adjectives in communications, or ill-treatment of subjects of another ruler. These also figure in litigation, and such documents of jurists, as fatwas, or interpretations of the law. Though the formal body of Islamic law might exclude International law, jurists sitting in judgment in actual disputes had to grapple with cases involving contracts between subjects of different states, crimes on high seas, disposal of shipwrecks, and so on. One of the important aspects of interstate relations was the protection of other sovereigns' subjects in one's state and of one's own subjects on high seas and in other states.

In the Mughal Empire, the Emperor's own subjects were entitled to compensation if they were subjected to robbery within the towns and on the roads in daylight. This obligation is imposed on the kotwal, head of town police, and, outside the towns, on the Revenue Collector, in Abul Fazl's record of the official regulations of the Mughal Empire, the *A'in-i Akbari*, c. 1595.[1] The official regulations of the reign of Shah Jahan (1628–58) similarly insisted that 'if anywhere anything is lost, the officers having revenue jurisdiction there are obliged to pay compensation as well as a fine for their negligence.'[2] Niccolao Manucci (c. 1700) recognized the prevalence of this regulation, observing that 'the *faujdars* have to supervise the roads, and should any merchant or traveller be robbed in daylight, they are obliged to pay compensation.'[3]

Now, in extending this entitlement, the Mughal administration made no distinction between its own subjects and those of other sovereigns. This becomes clear from the claims it entertained from the English East India Company's servants, even though there were no specific formal provisions for such claims in any special mandates or farmans obtained by the Company. In 1619, in spite of the fact that the obligation for paying compensation fell upon a member of 'the cheefe nobilitie' within whose jurisdiction (near Surat) a robbery of the Company's caravan occurred, the local qazi, being the 'notarye publicke', issued a certificate of the loss sustained.[4] In 1650, when a robbery occurred near Agra, the emperor ordered that either the goods should be recovered, or compensation be provided by 'the Governor of the district', on the basis of the report of the official 'news-writers' ('vaka novies' = waqi'a-navis), even before the petition on the Company's behalf was submitted.[5]

With this principle firmly held applicable to all, subjects or non-subjects, in respect of its own territories, it was natural that the Mughal emperor would hold that a similar protection had to be extended to his own subjects on sea by others, who exercised or could be expected to exercise control over those who perpetrated thefts or piracy overseas. When the English East India Company's vessels seized cargo of Indian merchants plying on the Red Sea trade in 1623, the Mughal authorities demanded restitution, and, upon the Company's failure to do so or to pay compensation, put the English factors at Surat in prison for seven months the next year. Ultimately, full restitution was made by the Company.[6] For the future they were obliged to agree that 'if any other Christian shall offend any man belonging to the Kings port, the English are not to be questioned for it; but if any English man doe commit any offence they are answerable for it.'[7]

At the same time, the Mughal authorities made it clear that their claim of protection on high seas extended only to the subjects of the Mughal emperor. When the Turkish merchants similarly plundered by the English on the high seas, came to Lahore (the then seat of the Court), 'throwing their shashes under their feet and trampelling upon them', in front of the high officers of the court, they were told by Khwaja Abul Hasan, the diwan (finance minister), that 'they wear none of this King's people: he had nothing to do with them.' The argument was that 'both parties (the English and the Turks) being strangers and the act done out of his territories', the Mughal emperor had nothing to do with the Turkish merchants' claims of 85,000 rials-of-eight against the English, though the Turks had been undoubtedly engaged in the Indian trade, and were travelling on an Indian ship, when robbed.[8]

The Mughal authorities reserved the right to stop traffic of their own subjects with a foreign country. In 1640, Emperor Shah Jahan interdicted trade with Iran; the original farman has not survived, but the farman lifting the ban on 16 August 1641 is extant. It shows that the original order prohibited all export of Indian products to Iran by 'merchants'; the rescinding order permitted such exports as well as import of horses and other cargo.[1] While the farman does not specify that the prohibition applied only to the subjects of the Mughals trading with Iran, the report of the Isfahan factors to the Company referred to 'the king of India's inhibition to *his* merchants from trading into Persia.'[9] After the loss of Qandahar to the Persians in 1648, Emperor Shah Jahan again imposed 'restraint to his merchants from trading thither (in Persia).'[10] This ban apparently did not again apply to others, so that the English commerce with Gambroon, carried on from Surat, flourished. Inherent in these orders was, then, the assumption that while the subjects of the two hostile states could be made the object of traffic-interdiction by one of them, 'third parties' could not be expected to be brought under the ban. Such a position would be in absolute accordance with international law, as now propounded, where a sovereign state's right to trade or not trade with another state is absolute, but it has no right to impose its own ban upon neutrals or third parties.

Even more interesting is the absolute absence of any concept of 'extra-territoriality'. Neither at Gambroon in Persia, nor in the Red Sea ports, where *banya* merchants from Gujarat were so numerous, was there any attempt to create 'autonomous' communities, whether under the patronage of the Mughal emperor, or independently of him.[11] There is similarly no indication that in South-East Asia Indian merchants formed any self-governing communities. In the 1640s, a document was submitted to the Surat authorities on behalf of a woman, Fatima, who claimed that when her father, a merchant of Surat died at Achhi (Achin), his slave fictitiously declared himself to have married his master's widow. The widow having protested, the king (*padshah*) of Achin imprisoned the slave, and would have imposed severe punishment on him, if 'the merchants' had not 'pressed and persuaded' the widow to withdraw her complaint, whereafter 'on the petition of the merchants', the King released the slave.[12] The event presumably took place in the 1620s or 1630s. It is clear from this that the entire judicial and penal process was in the hands of the king of Achin. The 'merchants', presumably those from Surat or India, had a locus standi, but only as interested parties. The assumption throughout is that the offence should have been adjudicated where it occurred and by the sovereign authority of that place.

This principle the Mughal authorities applied to their own territory. Foreigners could claim no extra-territoriality, and must be bound by the same laws as applied to the subjects of the Mughal emperor. The English at Ahmadabad learnt early (1622) that they could not claim their cloth back from one of their washermen, when he lost it through a theft committed in his house, since the law was that 'whatsoever in this country is taken by thieves perforce is to be borne by the owner, in whose custody soever.'[13] They learnt (1619, Burhanpur) also that, if they claimed disciplinary control over their factors, the latter's private debts had to be met by them—'the law of this country compelling all principals to make good there respondents acts.'[14] This law gave no end of trouble to the English East India Company, which sought to be absolved of the responsibility of its factors' 'private debts', a position which the Mughal authorities consistently rejected. In one of such later disputes in the 1660s where the English Company in Bengal was compelled to meet the claims against a factor recalled by it, it had further to agree to follow 'the different custom of this country from all others', namely 'if a merchant cannot recover in what is due on such bills (of exchange) (from the drawee), that he shall return them to the person of whom he bought them and receive his money again without interest.'[15]

The Mughal authorities would not, similarly, permit foreign subjects to adopt trappings not permitted to their own. On 20 September 1645 the imperial minister, Sa'dullah Khan, issued a *hasbu-l hukm* expressing alarm at the fact that at Surat the English and the Dutch were allowed to land 200 to 300 armed sailors near the port and their presidents ('kaptan') went about with 200–300 Indian armed retainers in Surat. The landing of only 20–30 armed sailors at any one time was to be permitted; and no armed men were to attend the presidents.[16]

The Mughal emperor, therefore, neither sought nor conceded 'extra-territoriality', his position being similar in this respect to the Qing Empire of China, which was forced to accept this doctrine, along with opium, at the point of the imperialist bayonet in the nineteenth century.[17] In India the full-scale conquest so early superseded the 'extra-territoriality' phase that it hardly finds mention in textbook accounts of the eighteenth century. It must, however, still be asserted that in India too it was a western imposition and had no indigenous origins.

The Mughal sovereign and his counsellors were conscious that their empire was a component of a world-wide system of states. It is true that among these states, they held those situated in the Indian sub-continent, whether in the southern peninsula or in the Himalayas to be subordinate states in various degrees of vassalage. They were not prepared to concede royal titles to any such sovereign. *Raja*, which the Mughal emperors conferred upon their own nobility was not deemed a royal title. The ruler of a large kingdom like Bijapur, the Adil Shah was only Adil Khan in the eyes of the Mughal chancery, and the Qutb Shah of Golkunda was Qutbul Mulk to the Mughals. Regular or occasional exaction of tribute from these rulers was another hallmark of the relationship.

But outside of India, the Mughal emperors, in spite of assuming such titles as *Gaiti Khadiv*, 'Earth's Lord', or *Khalifatu'z Zaman*, 'Caliph of the Age', laid no claim to absolute supremacy over other states. They dealt as equals with the Safavids of Persia (Shah Abbas I was a 'brother' to Jahangir), the Uzbek Khans and the Ottomans (the Sultan of Rum). The statement of Thomas Roe that the Mughal emperor 'this overgrowne eliphant (would not) descend to article or bynde him selfe reciprocally to any prince upon terms of equalety', was more a product of his sense of frustration at the Mughal court's concern for the interests of the Empire's own merchants while treating of his demands, than an accurate statement of the Mughal emperor's attitude.[18]

The realistic attitude of the Mughal emperors was shown in the sensible view they took over the question of salutation expected from envoys of foreign sovereigns. For reasons difficult to understand today, Europeans of the colonial era tended to see in the Chinese kowtow or the Indian form of genuflexion (*sijda*) or deep bow (*taslim, salam*: 'placing the hand thrice upon the head, and as often dropping it down to the ground'), acts of unacceptable humiliation,[19] while they did not attach any stigma of humility to the European ritual of kneeling. Generally, at the Mughal court, Asian envoys performed the mode of salutation current at this court, as Bernier witnessed the Uzbek envoys doing before Aurangzeb, or they observed the form of salutation current at their own courts, as the Persian envoy was seen doing (1661).[20] When the English Ambassador, Sir Thomas Roe, appeared before Jahangir in 1616, he was 'freely granted leave ... to use the customs of my country': Entering the durbar, he made three successive 'reverences' in the European manner.[21] When the Dutch envoy performed salam in the Indian fashion before Aurangzeb, the latter himself desired from him 'a salute *à la Frank'*.[22]

The conventions of protection and immunities granted to envoys, now codified in international law and practice, were also observed, being the product of long-developed traditions of inter-state intercourse in Asia. When Sir Thomas Roe arrived at Surat in 1615, his difficulties with local officials who were not clear about his status were resolved once a farman arrived from the court which, according to Roe, 'contayned a command to all governors of provinces or towns to attend me with sufficient guard and not to meddle with anything that was mine.'[23] Similarly, although tobacco-smoking was strictly prohibited in Iran, Jahangir's ambassador Khan Alam was expressly allowed by Shah Abbas I to smoke in public, much to the discomfort of those present.[24]

There were two aspects of interstate intercourse in which Mughal or perhaps Asian practice was different from the European. There were, first, no permanent representations of one sovereign at the seat of another in the form of embassies or consulates. An embassy was in the nature of a temporary mission, often with specific purposes; and the value of the range of gifts sent with it was an index of the importance that was attached to it by the sovereign who sent it.[25]

Second, the idea of a 'treaty' in the sense of a contractual agreement signed by the plenipotentiaries of two sovereigns, was largely alien to the diplomatic practices in Islamic Asia and India. Such interstate agreements took the form of exchange of letters, or an offer contained in the letter from one sovereign accepted by the other, as, for example, Abdullah Khan Uzbek's offer in a letter of treating the Hindukush as the boundary, accepted by Akbar through his reply (1596).[26] The only 'treaty' known from Mughal history seems to be that of Shalimar (1740), when the victor, Nadir Shah dictated terms to the Mughal emperor in the latter's capital.[27] This was hardly a 'treaty' in any proper sense, since the Mughal emperor was at the time not a free agent.

It is, therefore not surprising that the Mughal court gave very little consideration to the idea of a 'solemn treaty' between Jahangir and James I proposed by Roe on the English subjects' rights and privileges in India.[28] It was not that the Mughal authorities saw the king of England as too insignificant to be treated at par with the Mughal emperor. The entire notion of a treaty itself was foreign to them. What they were willing to do was to issue imperial rescripts to cover points that they could agree to; it was for the other party to record and make arrangements to fulfil its side of the bargain.

Clearly, the Asian version of 'international law' deserves more attention, if we are to understand much of the diplomatic, political and commercial history of the period. Unluckily, interesting as the subject is, little attention has been paid to it, at least among the historians of India. The present paper may be seen as an initial step in any enquiry which can grow almost infinitely in scope, so rich is the evidence.

NOTES

1. *A'in-i Akbari*, ed. H. Blochmann, Calcutta, 1867–77, I, p. 284.

2. Rai Chandrabhan Brahman, *Char Chaman-i Barhaman*, c. 1656, B. L. Add. 18,863, f. 25a–b.

3. *Storia do Mogor*, tr. W. Irvine, Indian Texts Series, Government of India, London, 1907–8, II, p. 451. For a similar duty devolving on the kotwal, see ibid., II, p. 421.

4. *English Factories in India, 1618–21*, ed. W. Foster, pp. 81, 89.

5. *English Factories in India, 1646–50*, ed. pp. 300–1, 302.

6. *English Factories in India, 1624–9*, pp. vi, 59 ('The losses may appear great, but they practically amount merely to a restitution of the money forced from the natives in 1623').

7. Ibid., p. 28.

8. Nat. Paris, Blochet; Suppl. Pers. 482, f. 44a–b.

9. *English Factories, 1637–41*, p. 242 (italics ours).

10. Surat letter to Company, 20 March 1650 (*English Factories, 1646–50*, pp. 307–8).

11. In Persia, the major descriptions of these merchants are by numerous European travellers like Pietro della Valle, Chardin and Tavernier and in the English factory records. A competent modern account of them is yet to be written, that in Riazul Islam, *Indo-Persian Relations*, Teheran, 1970, pp. 171–3, being much too brief. For Gujarati merchants in the Red Sea, there is a definitive study by Ashin Das Gupta, 'Gujarati Merchants and the Red Sea Trade, 1700–1725', *Age of Partnership*, ed. B.B. Kling and M.N. Pearson, Honolulu, 1979, pp. 132–8.

12. Bib. Nationale, Paris: Blochet Sup. Pers. 482, f. 226a–227a.

13. *English Factories, 1622–23*, pp. 40–41.

14. *English Factories, 1618–21*, p. 89.

15. *English Factories, 1668–69*, p. 177.

16. Bib. Nationale, Paris: Blochet Sup. Pers. 482, f. 133a–b.

17. There is a very good critique of the western view that 'extra-territoriality' was an acceptable institution in the Celestial Empire and Asian states generally: Yu Shengwa, 'Vestiges of Colonialist Ideology: An Obstacle to the Study of the History of Sino-Western Relations', *IHR*, ed. V. Jha, xvi (1–2), pp. 223–44, reprinted from *Social Sciences in China*, no. 4, Beijing, 1991.

18. From a letter of 21 August 1617 to the English Ambassador at Constantinople, quoted by W. Foster, *The Embassy of Sir Thomas Roe to India*, London, 1926, p. xliii.

19. See François Bernier, *Travels in the Mogul Empire, AD 1656–1668*, tr. A. Constable, revised by V.A. Smith, London, 1916, pp. 117 (where the ceremony is described) and 119 (where it is said that it 'savours of servility').

20. Ibid., pp. 117, 119, 147–8. Manucci's account of the Persian ambassador being forced to bow is quite fanciful (*Storia do Mogor*, II, p. 50; cf. Riazul Islam, *Indo-Persian Relations*, p. 126 n.)

21. *Embassy of Sir Thomas Roe*, p. 87. See also p. 214, where Jahangir told his officers not to insist that Roe should perform 'size-da' (*sijda*).

22. Bernier, *Travels in the Mogul Empire*, p. 127.

23. *Embassy of Sir Thomas Roe*, p. 65.

24. Jahangir, *Tuzuk-i Jahangiri*, ed. Saiyid Ahmad, Ghazipur and Aligarh, 1863–4, p. 183; Riazul Islam, *Indo-Persian Relations*, p. 75 and n.

25. On the gifts brought by Persian embassies to Jahangir and Aurangzeb, see *Embassy of Sir Thomas Roe*, pp. 262-3; Bernier, *Travels in*

the *Mogul Empire*, pp. 147–8. For the gifts carried by Khan Azam's embassy to Persia, see Riazul Islam, *Indo-Persian Relations*, pp. 74, 233.

26. Abul Fazl, *Akbarnama*, Bib. Ind., Calcutta, 1873–87, III, p. 705.

27. Zahiruddin Malik, *The Reign of Muhammad Shah*, Bombay, 1977, p. 181; Riazul Islam, *Indo-Persian Relations*, pp. 150–2.

28. Editor's introduction to *Embassy of Sir Thomas Roe*, pp. xxxiii, ff.

25

Jahangir and the Uzbeks

The north-western frontier of the Indian empire has ranged over a vast region from beyond the Oxus to as far as the Beas. Under the Delhi Sultans, it generally lay across one part or another of the Punjab. Under Sher Shah the Salt Range in north-western Punjab seems to have formed the border with his newly built fortress of Rohtas, as the key-point in the defence line. Akbar appears to have extended the effective frontier up to the Indus with his great fort of Attock guarding the main ferry across the Indus.[1]

Given the conditions of medieval warfare, none of the frontiers maintained by medieval rulers could be described as satisfactory. The Punjab rivers were all fordable except during the season of inundations. The Indus too was difficult to defend during the winter and early summer with its long course and broad channels in the plains. The Salt Range is really formed of low hills that could be penetrated at any number of points. To the west of the Indus, the Sulaiman Range, which the British made their frontier, was not a possible frontier for any previous Indian government. For one, it is pierced by numerous passess open throughout the year; for another, it was inhabited by Afghan tribes who made regular garrisoning of all the passes by any outside army impossible. A truly 'scientific frontier' in medieval conditions could be secured only if an Indian government held the Hindukush mountains with Kabul and Qandahar as the two great fortresses in the rear commanding the only two possible routes from the north-west into India. It was one of Akbar's great achievements that he ultimately set his frontier at the Hindukush, shifting it from the Indus. It is no accident that the military significance of the Hindukush was well recognized by writers of the Mughal period.[2]

Akbar's empire had in the earlier part of his reign the Indus and not the Hindukush as its frontier. The Hindukush then separated the splinter Uzbek kingdom of Balkh and the Timurid kingdom of Badakhshan on the one hand, and Akbar's brother, Mirza Hakim's principality of Kabul, on the other. But these kingdoms were swept away under the mounting pressure of the Uzbek and Mughal empires just one and half decade befores the end of the century.

In 1585 Abdullah Khan Uzbek attacked Badakhshan and conquered it. The following year (1586) Balkh was annexed by him.[3] On the other hand, in 1585 Mirza Hakim died and Kabul was henceforth governed directly by Akbar.[4] For the moment Akbar seemed to have even thought of challenging the Uzbek occupation of Balkh and Badakhshan.

But, whatever their proclaimed or secret ambitions, neither of the two rulers dared in practice to contest the other's annexations, and thus more by accident than design, had to acknowledge the Hindukush as their boundary. This recognition was made explicitly by Akbar when he wrote to Abdullah Khan Uzbek that Hindu-Koh (Hindukush) be fixed as the frontier of the two empires; and it seems that Abdullah Khan too agreed to this.[5]

II

In 1598 Abdullah Khan Uzbek died and was succeeded by his son Abdul Mumin who was killed after a short reign of six months.[6] Civil war then broke out in Trans-Oxiana. Shah Abbas, who was waiting for such an opportunity, occupied Khurasan. The nobles of Bukhara in frustration offered the throne of Trans-Oxiana to Jan Mohammad so that law and order could be restored and the safety of the kingdom ensured. Jan Mohammad refused the offer and his son Din Mohammad ascended the throne of Trans-Oxiana, who, within a few days of his accession, died fighting against Shah Abbas in the vicinity of Herat.[7] After the death of Din Mohammad, his brother Baqi Mohammad ascended the throne and inflicted a crushing defeat on the Shah of Persia.[8] Baqi Mohammad Khan was succeeded by his brother, Wali Mohammad Khan.[9] After the accession of Wali Mohammad Khan, the nobles and the Uzbek leaders cooperated with him as a result of which stability in the Uzbek kingdom was restored. Wali Mohammad Khan treated his nephews with the utmost affection and consideration. He bestowed the province of Samarqand on Imam Quli Khan and the provinces of Balkh, Andkhud, Sherghan, etc. on Nazr Mohammad Khan. Wali Mohammad Khan also placed two of his reliable officers as *ataliq*s ('guardians'with each of his cousins. For a long time Imam Quli Khan and Nazr Mohammad Khan obeyed their uncle Wali Mohammad Khan. Subsequently, Imam Quli Khan killed his ataliq and rebelled. Wali Mohammad Khan was hurt at the behaviour of his nephew and proceeded towards Samarqand to suppress the revolt. Imam Quli Khan fled to Balkh and joined his brother Nazr Mohammad

Khan who also killed his ataliq and rebelled. Both brothers made a joint
front against Wali Mohammad Khan and wanted to expel him from
Trans-Oxiana.[10] As a result of this combination the position of Wali
Mohammad Khan became critical and he fled to Persia. But news of
support from some of the Uzbek chiefs tempted him to return to his
kingdom, and oppose Imam Quli in a battle near Samarqand. Victory
however went to Imam Quli, and Wali Mohammad Khan was captured
and then beheaded at his orders.[11]

In 1611 Imam Quli Khan was proclaimed as the king ('Khan')of
Bukhara and he assigned Balkh and Badakhshan to his younger brother,
Nazr Mohammad Khan.[12] Nazr Mohammad united these two territories
which in the course of time became virtually a separate kingdom.
Henceforth, the Mughals had to deal primarily with this kingdom,
though it continued formally to be a part of the Uzbek Empire.

III

The disturbed condition of the Uzbek Empire at the time of Jahangir's
accession in 1605 appears to have led him to dream of reconquering
his 'ancestral lands'—a project which, he says, was very dear to his
father, Akbar's heart.[13]

It seems that in anticipation of such an opportunity Jahangir adopted
an attitude of coolness towards the Uzbeks, while from the very
beginning of his reign he cultivated relations of friendship with the
Safavid Empire, the traditional enemy of the Uzbeks. Thus, in the
first one and a half decadeof the reign there was virtually no contact
between the Mughal and the Uzbek courts, let alone a formal exchange
of envoys between the two rulers. In fact, at one time Imam Quli
appears to have received reports that Jahangir was contemplating an
expedition to Badakhshan (possibly to synchronize with some Persian
action against the Uzbeks).[14]

However, two factors, both following from the increased power
of Shah Abbas of Persia, led to a thawing of this diplomatic 'freeze'.
From 1614 to 1617 the Uzbeks had been attacking and plundering
parts of the Persian possessions of Khurasan; and both Imam Quli
and Nazr Mohammad cooperated in these aggressive operations. But
an Uzbek reverse near Merv in 1617 was followed by the march of a
very large Persian army to the border of Trans-Oxiana. The Uzbeks
were cowed by this show of force and were compelled to seek peace
with the Shah.[15] From now on, in view of the Persian threat to their
dominions, it must have appeared to them expedient to enter into

better relations with Jahangir, and to secure their rear from the other side. On the other hand, despite many exchanges of envoys, presents and letters between Mughal and Persian emperors, Shah Abbas had never explicitly abandoned his claim on Qandahar, the bone of contention between the Safavids and the Mughals. In 1620–1, his envoy Zanbil Beg actually raised the matter of Qandahar with Jahangir, and this must have made the Mughal emperor uneasy about Persian intentions. A natural antidote to the Persian menace was an alliance with the Uzbeks; and so in Jahangir's eyes, too, good relations with the Uzbeks became good policy.

The first step in this direction was taken in 1621 when the mother of Imam Quli sent to Nur Jahan a formal letter of goodwill along with some rare products of Central Asia as gifts. Next year Khwaja Nasir was sent by Nur Jahan with a letter and some presents.[16] That this restoration of diplomatic relations should have taken place in 1621 was quite natural, since Persian preparations for a campaign in the East had reached an advanced stage and both the Uzbeks and Jahangir must have been afraid that they were to be the victims of a Persian attack. An English factor, writing on 18 November 1621, actually thought that both the Uzbeks and the Mughals were to be attacked by the Shah.[17]

The serious proportions which the Persian threat assumed for both the empires in 1622, led to an exchange of full-fledged embassies between the Uzbek and Mughal emperors. Imam Quli now sent an envoy with a letter and some presents. Curiously enough, this embassy is not mentioned in Jahangir's memoirs or other Mughal chronicles, and the only information that we have about it comes from the Uzbek chronicle, *Tazkira-i-Muqim Khani*.[18]

In fact, far from scorning Imam Quli, Jahangir was seeking his friendship. He now sent an embassy under Saiyed Mir Barkah which is briefly referred to in the *Ma'asir i-Jahangiri*.[19] The *Tazkira-i-Muqim Khani* gives a detailed account of this embassy, although it confounds Mir Barkah with Hakim Haziq, who was actually sent later by Shah Jahan as an ambassador to Imam Quli in 1628.[20] It tells us that the envoy came bringing from Jahangir for Imam Quli Khan presents and gifts worth a full year's revenue of India. We are told that Imam Quli was then so annoyed with Jahangir that he neither saw the envoy nor accepted the presents for six months. When he was finally persuaded to grant an audience, he did so while hunting and made use of the occasion to taunt the envoy obliquely about Jahangir's military weakness.[21] It is difficult to accept all the details of the story as the

Uzbek chronicle gives them. But it is quite possible that by this time Imam Quli might have really lost all interest in an alliance with Jahangir, so as to view with coolness the latter's attempt at being friendly. The Persian seizure of Qandahar near the end of 1622 made it clear that it was the Mughals against whom Persians military preparations had been directed. The quick success the Persians attained also showed up the weakness of the Mughals. Imam Quli must, therefore, have hesitated to annoy the Persians unnecessarily by accepting any overtures from Jahangir who was now useless as an ally.

IV

It is a curious lacuna in most modern accounts that the hostilities which broke out between the Uzbeks and the Mughals almost immediately after the fall of Qandahar and posed a menace to the Mughal possession of Kabul for two years, have been ignored. As a result, Nazr Mohammad's raid on Kabul in 1628 is considered the first Uzbek action against the Mughals,[22] while in fact it had been preceded by two invasions during the reign of Jahangir. These two invasions themselves have generally been ignored in modern studies.[23]

It is not difficult to see why the Uzbek attitude towards the Mughals should have changed with the fall of Qandahar. The Persians by their campaign against Qandahar indicated that it was the Mughals, and not the Uzbeks, against whom their warlike preparations had been directed. This must have dissipated the Uzbeks' fear of a Persian invasion. Thus in 1625 we find Nazr Mohammad sending Nazir Mirza Bashi as ambassador to the Shah to establish good relations with the Persians.[24]

The Mughal loss of Qandahar, followed immediately by Shah Jahan's rebellion, made the Mughal position in the north-west extremely vulnerable. While Shah Jahan's long-lasting rebellion made it difficult for Jahangir to reinforce his army in the Kabul province, the loss of Qandahar must have weakened the Mughal control over the Hazaras, who lived in the mountainous regions to the west and south of Kabul astride the Uzbek–Mughal frontier. All these considerations led to Nazr Mohammad's entertaining a sudden ambition to subvert the Mughal hold south of the Hindukush and, so to speak, share the spoils with Persia.

A crucial position in any Uzbek project of subversion was occupied by the two races settled south of Hindukush, namely the Hazaras and the Afghans. Of the two, the Hazaras' territories were geographically closer to the Uzbek frontier, and as a Persian speaking race, but claiming Mongol descent,[25] they had obvious affinities with the Uzbeks.

The Hazaras occupied a 'very extensive area of country, extending from the borders of Kabul and Ghazni to those of Herat in one direction and from the vicinity of Kandahar to that of Balkh in the other.'[26] All routes across it were most difficult to use, and were closed for the larger part of the year.[27]

So long as the Mughals held Qandahar, their control over the Kabul–Ghaznin–Qandahar route depended upon the loyalty of the Hazaras; and the Mughals generally appear to have maintained some kind of authority over them.[28] With the fall of Qandahar the importance of the route declined, and so also possibly the traffic out of tolls on which the friendship of the Hazaras used to be purchased. The most important Mughal-held town on the edge of the Hazara country was now Ghaznin, which stood at the point where the Hazaras mingled with the Afghans who inhabited the country to its east.[29] Ghaznin lay about a hundred miles south-west of Kabul, and was connected with that city by a fairly passable route, that is the section of the road from Qandahar to Kabul, which as a whole was remarkable for the easy passage it provides in a rugged, mountainous land.[30]

It appears that the Uzbeks found Kabul quite well defended, and their first strategic plan was to turn the flank of the Mughal position by penetrating into the Hazara country and seizing Ghaznin. They would then have commanded an easy route to Kabul from the south.

In the spring of 1624 the plans of the Uzbeks appear to have matured, and Yalingtosh, who was the leading commander of Nazr Mohammad, began to mount pressure upon the Hazara clans encamped near Ghaznin. The Hazara leaders till now had owed allegiance to the Mughals. They, therefore, approached Khanazad Khan, who was then governing Kabul on behalf of his father, Mahabat Khan, and sought his protection and submitted that failing such protection they would have no alternative but to submit to Yalingtosh. Thereupon Khanazad Khan sent a strong force to the succour of the Hazaras. They defeated the Uzbeks, Yalingtosh's nephew being killed and the fort of Chatur demolished. This reverse and the loss of his nephew greatly provoked Yalingtosh who asked for leave from Nazr Mohammad to raid the borders of Kabul. In the beginning Nazr Mohammad Khan and his leading nobles were not agreeable to this dangerous proposal, but after repeated persuasion Yalingtosh got sought-after permission. Thereupon Yalingtosh collected a large army consisting of Almans[31] and Uzbeks and marched towards the Mughal frontier. On the other side, Khanazad Khan made his preparations, and hearing of Yalingtosh's approach encamped at village Sheer at a distance of two karohs (five miles) from Ghaznin and arranged his army in battle formation. Khanazad Khan placed Mubariz Khan Afghan, Ani Rai Singh Dalan and Saiyid Haji in the vanguard. The Uzbek army encamped at a distance of three karohs from Ghaznin. The Mughal army was expecting the encounter the next day but suddenly the Uzbek army appeared and the battle started. After a sharp engagement in which Khanazad Khan used his artillery to great effect, the Mughals inflicted a crushing defeat upon the Uzbeks, and Yalingtosh fled from the battlefield.[32]

Pelsaert, the Dutch chronicler, has also given a very detailed account of this attack, generally confirming Mutamad Khan's account, which we have followed above. It is interesting that Pelsaert appears to have believed that the Uzbeks were intending a direct assault on Kabul, and Ghaznin was merely on their way. He adds certain other details as well which are significant.[33]

This resounding military success of the Mughals might have deterred any further encroachments of the Uzbeks but for the continuance of Shah Jahan's rebellion and the straining of relations between the Mughal court and Mahabat Khan. Thus, soon after this battle, Kabul was taken away from Mahabat Khan and given over to Khwaja Abul Hasan. As a result Khanazad Khan, who was deputizing for his father, left the province with his troops to take up his charge of Bengal. Meanwhile, Abul Hasan sent his son Zafar Khan to govern the province on his behalf.

In the administrative and military dislocation which followed Khanazad Khan's recall, the Uzbeks saw an opportunity to try their hand again. This time they sought the aid of the disaffected elements from amongst the Afghans. This was a policy which Abdullah Khan Uzbek had followed four decades earlier to checkmate Akbar,[34] and now his successors tried to use it to undermine Mughal rule in Kabul. Accordingly, Ahdad, a Raushanai leader, who had repeatedly organized rebellions among the Afghans against Mughal rule, was incited by Yalingtosh to rise and engage the Mughals, while he himself marched to the neighbourhood of Ghaznin (1625).

Zafar Khan heard of this fresh attempt of the Uzbeks to subvert Mughal authority as soon as he reached Kabul. He immediately advanced against Yalingtosh. Yalingtosh, seeing that the Mughals first meant to deal with him, made peace with Zafar Khan, abandoning his ally Ahdad to face the Mughals single-handed. Ahdad thereupon fled to the Lawagh mountains and sought refuge in a fort there. He was pursued by the Mughals and his fort was stormed. Ahdad was killed in the fight, and his head was sent to Jahangir.[35]

V

These two successive failures in two years (nineteenth and twentieth regnal years of Jahangir) seem to have convinced the Uzbek rulers that there was no chance of penetrating the Mughal defences despite continuing disturbances in the Mughal Empire. As a result, they reverted to their earlier attempts to make an alliance with Jahangir, in view of the increasing might of Persia. Since Jahangir, on his part, could hardly have entertained any aggressive designs against Central Asia at this time, there was no reason why he should not respond to these friendly overtures.

Naturally enough, the first step in this direction was taken by Nazr Mohammad, who had just been carrying on hostilities against the Mughals. In the beginning of the twenty-first regnal year of Jahangir, Nazr Mohammad sent Shah Khwaja as ambassador to the Mughal court. Shah Khwaja presented a letter of Nazr Mohammad to Jahangir. The letter contained professions of sincerity and friendship to Jahangir and was probably intended as an apology for Yalingtosh's conduct. Shah Khwaja also presented gifts worth Rs 50,000 on behalf of his master to Jahangir. Jahangir in return gave Rs 30,000 to Shah Khwaja as *inam*.[36]

Soon afterwards Imam Quli sent Khwaja Abdur Rahim as his ambassador with Khwaja Hasan as his deputy. Jahangir received the ambassador with great honour. He ordered the leading nobles of the empire to go out to receive the ambassadors. Khwaja Abdur Rahim was exempted from taslim and *kurnish* and from all formalities of court etiquette imposed on ambassadors. At the time of his audience Jahangir asked him to sit near the imperial throne, which was a very rare honour. A robe of honour and a jewelled dagger were bestowed on the ambassador and Rs 50,000 in cash were given to him as *inam*.[37] Imam Quli in his letter to Jahangir praised the noble descent of Khwaja Abdur Rahim and also drew the attention of Jahangir to the old agreement directed against Persia that had been concluded between Akbar and Abdullah Khan Uzbek. He asserted that since there was an understanding between Abdullah Khan and Akbar to conquer the road to the Holy Places (Mecca and Medina) and since, being blessed by courage, faith and enterprise, they brought their intention to fruition, they were able to conquer the whole of Khurasan and most of Iraq and 'Ajam'. Thus even now, the letter continued, the swords and lances of the soldiers of Turan bore marks of the blood of the braves of Iran. Imam Quli then referred to his father's drinking the cup of martyrdom at the hands of the Persians at the battle of Herat. He was, therefore, doubly resolved to take up arms against Persia: first, in order to clear the path to Mecca and, second, to avenge the death of his father. He professed to believe that Jahangir too wanted to proceed against Persia in the footsteps of Akbar and that he was only prevented from doing so by Khurram's rebellion. Imam Quli attributed Khurram's conduct to the rashness of youth and advised Jahangir to forgive him, while he counselled Khurram to desist from rebellion. In conclusion, he requested Jahangir to appoint Khurram, after conciliating him, along with other princes, to lead a campaign to conquer the route to Mecca, and assured him that he would collaborate with him in such a venture.[38]

It is not possible to judge how far this proposal was meant to be taken seriously; probably it was offered chiefly as a courteous reminder of the friendly relations subsisting formerly. Jahangir certainly made no formal commitment, but did his best to show his regard for the ambassador.

Jahangir died while Abdur Rahim was still at the court. He witnessed the events that followed, but died soon after Shah Jahan's accession. The new emperor ordered a befitting funeral for the Uzbek envoy.[39] In the meantime Mughal–Uzbek relations took yet another turn, since Nazr Mohammad saw an opportunity in the disorder and threat of civil war after Jahangir's death to make an inroad into Mughal territory. This was his well-known, but unsuccessful, attack on Kabul, made early in 1628.

A study of Jahangir's relations with the Uzbeks shows a number of twists and turns. But if we bear in mind the political developments in the three major powers involved, namely the Mughal Empire, the Uzbek Empire and Safavid Persia, most of them can be satisfactorily explained. On the whole, Jahangir appears to have followed a cautious and defensive policy, and he must be given the credit of keeping secure the Mughal position on the Hindukush even in the very difficult years that followed the loss of Qandahar and the rebellion of Shah Jahan.

NOTES

1. The construction of the fort of Attock was completed in 1586. 'Attock is a town situated on a promontory where two great rivers meet. It is one of the best fortresses of the Great Mogul, and they do not permit any stranger to enter it if he does not hold a passport from the king' (Jean-Baptiste Tavernier, *Travels in India*, tr. V. Ball, ed. W. Crooke, London, 1925, I, p. 76).

2. *A'in-i-Akbari*, II, p. 192; pp. 408–9 (tr.), 'Qandahar is known as the gate of Persia' (Sujan Rai Bhandari, *Khulasat-ut-Tawarikh*, ed. Z. Hasan, Delhi, 1918 p. 84). The Hindukush was considered to be the northern boundary of India (*Tarikh-i Alfi*, f. 5; typed copy Dept. of History, AMU, Aligarh); see also *Baburnama*, tr. A.S. Beveridge, London, 1921. I, p. 204; *Tuzuk*, ed. Sayyid Ahmad, Ghazipur and Aligarh, 1863–4, pp. 21–2; Sujan Rai Bhandari, *Khulasat-ut-Tawarikh*, p. 88. Cf. Tavernier, I , pp. 73–6.

3. Nizamudin Ahmed, *Tabaqat-i-Akbari*, Nawal Kishore (Lucknow), 1875, p. 365; Muhammad Yusuf, *Tazkira-i-Muqim Khani*, Royal Asiatic Society MS 160, ff. 27a–b.

4. *Akbarnama*, III, p. 466.

5. *Insha-i-Abul Fazal*, Kanpur, 1872, p. 4.

6. *Akbarnama*, III, pp. 736, 739. *Tazkira-i-Muqim Khani*, ff. 32a– b.

7. *Tuzuk*, p. 11; Iskandar Munshi, *Alam Arai Abbasi*,Tehran, 1313–14 AH., pp. 576, 588–9; *Tazkira-i-Muqim Khani*, ff. 35a–36b.

8. *Tazkira-i-Muqim Khani*, ff. 37b, 42a.

9. *Tuzuk*, p. 11; *Alam Arai Abbasi*, pp. 576, 588–9; *Tazkira-i-Muqim Khani*, f. 42a.

10. *Tuzuk*, p. 11; *Alam Arai Abbasi*, pp. 588–9; *Tazkira-i-Muqim Khani*, f. 44a.

11. *Iqbalnama*, Bib. Ind., Calcutta, 1865, III, pp. 40–1; *Alam Arai Abbasi* pp. 591–9; Mirza Tahir Wahid Mir Munshi, *Tarikh-Abbas Nama*, Subhanullah Coll, no. 955–3, Azad Library, AMU, Aligarh, ff. 26–7; *Tazkira-i-Muqim Khani*, ff. 44a–45a. These accounts differ as to the assistance Wali Mohammad received from Persia.

12. Lahori, *Badshah Nama*, Bib. Ind., Calcutta, 1866–72, I, pp. 220–1; Amin Qazvini, Aligarh MS, f. 269a; *Alam Arai Abbasi*, pp. 588–91; *Tazkira-i-Muqim Khani*, f. 45b.

13. *Tuzuk*, p. 11.

14. *Tazkira-i-Muqim Khani*, f. 52a.

15. *Alam Arai Abbasi*, pp. 677–8.

16. *Tuzuk*, p. 330. Neither of these embassies is referred to in the Uzbek chronicle, *Tazkira-i-Muqim Khani*.

17. W. Foster (ed.), *The English Factories in India, 1618–1621*, Oxford, 1906, p. 33.

18. *Tazkira-i-Muqim Khani*, f. 51a.

19. *Ma'asir-i-Jahangiri* (Dept. of History AMU, typed copy), p. 10.

20. Lahori, *Badshahnama*, I, pp. 233–6.

21. *Tazkira-i-Muqim Khani*, ff. 51a–52a.

22. B.P. Saxena, *History of Shah Jahan of Dihli,* Allahabad, 1958, p. 183; Abdul Rahim, 'The Mughal Relations with Persia and Central Asia', *Islamic Culture*, vol. IX, p. 188.

23. For example, neither of the raids is mentioned in Beni Prasad, *History of Jahangir*, 5th ed., Allahabad, 1962, or Abdur Rahim, 'The Mughal Relations with Persia and Central Asia'. But see R.P. Tripathi, *Rise and Fall of the Mughal Empire*, p. 391, where the first invasion is described, though with a few inaccuracies.

24. *Alam Arai Abbasi*, p. 715.

25. *A'in-i-Akbari*, pub. Nawal Kishor, Lucknow, 1892, II, p. 192.

26. H.W. Bellow, *The Races of Afghanistan*, Calcutta, 1880, pp. 113–14.

27. Holdich, *The Gates of India*, London, 1910, pp. 216, 515–16.

28. *A'in-i-Akbari*, II, pp. 190–1.

29. Cf. *Baburnama*, tr. Beveridge, I, p. 218.

30. Holdich, *The Gates of India*, p. 512.

31. A nomadic Turkic tribe, described in detail by Lahori, *Badshahnama*, II, pp. 515–16, 618–19.

32. *Iqbalnama*, III, pp. 207–9; *Ma'asir-i-Jahangiri*, Lytton no. 56, AMU, Aligarh ff. 82b–83a; *Tuzuk*, pp. 386–7; *Ma'asir-ul-Umara*, I, p. 740.

33. Pelsaert, *A Dutch Chronicle of Mughal India*, tr. and ed. by Brij Narain and S.R. Sharma, Calcutta, 1957, pp. 66–7.

34. *Akbarnama*, III, pp. 477–8.

35. *Iqbalnama–i–Jahangiri*, III, pp. 228–9. Cf. also Kami Shirazi, *Fathnamai-Nur Jahan Begam*, Bib. Nat., Paris, MS. Blochet, III, 1874, Suppl. Pers. Cat. 506; ff. 19a–20a.

36. *Iqbalnama*, III, p. 242; *Ma'asir-i-Jahangiri*, MS 31, Dept. of History. AMU Aligarh, p. 8. This embassy from Nazr Mohammad has neither been mentioned by Beni Prasad in his *History of Jahangir* nor by Abdur Rahim, 'The Mughal Relations with Persia and Central Asia'.

37. *Iqbalnama*, III, p. 259; *Tuzuk*, p. 416 (Mohammad Hadi's continuation); *Ma'asir-i-Jahangiri*, MS 31, Dept. of History, AMU, Aligarh, pp. 10–12.

38. *Ma'asir-i-Jahangiri*, pp. 10–14. MS 31, Dept. of History, AMU, Aligarh. (Typed copy of fragment from the 20th R.Y. of Jahangir till the end of Jahangir's reign. Copied from the MS of Khuda Baksh Oriental Library, Patna.)

39. Lahori, *Badshahnama*, I, p. 193.

26

The Objectives Behind the Mughal Expedition into Balkh and Badakhshan, 1646–7

Shah Jahan's expedition to Balkh and Badakhshan, marking one of those very rare events—and it may even have been unique—when an army from India crossed the Hindukush, has excited widespread interest among students of history. There are competent modern accounts of the expedition from the pens of Sir Jadunath Sarkar[1] and B.P. Saxena;[2] and aspects of the diplomatic history have been dealt with by Abdur Rahim.[3] In the present paper an attempt is made to analyse the Mughal objectives, by considering first the geographical factors, and, second, the contemporary evidence, some of which has escaped the notice of modern scholars.

The first question to be asked is whether the Mughals had any compelling reason, from the point of view of military geography, to press their frontier beyond the line they already held. In other words, we should examine whether the replacement of the Hindukush, which they had been holding for about eighty years, by the Oxus as the new frontier would have served their security interests any better.

The military significance of the Hindukush was well recognized by the writers of the Mughal period. Perhaps the description of this range from a contemporary and a modern writer might suffice to show how formidable a wall it forms. First, there is the detailed description by Abul Fazl:

The country of Kabul is surrounded on all sides by lofty mountains, so that the sudden invasion of an enemy is attended with extreme difficulty. The Hindukush separates Kabul from Badakhshan and Balkh, and seven routes are employed by the people of Turan in their marches to and fro. Three are by the Panjshir (valley), the highest of which is over the Khawak Pass; below this is Tul, and the next lower in succession, Bazarak. The best of these is Tul, but it is somewhat long as its name implies. The most direct is over the heights called Haft Bachah (the seven younglings). From Anderab two roads unite at the foot of the main pass and debouch (on

Parwan) by the Haft Bachah. This is extremely arduous. Three other roads lead by Poran up the Ghorband valley. The nearest route is by the pass of Yangi-Yuli (the new road) which leads down to Waliyan and Kinjan; another is Qipchak Pass, also somewhat easy to traverse, and the third is the Shibertu. In the summer when the rivers rise, it is by this pass that they descend by the way of Bamian and Talikan, but in the winter the Abdorah route is chosen, for at this season, all other routes but this are closed.[4]

Among the modern authorities on the subject, Holdich judges the Hindukush to be an almost inviolable line of defence, for a defender who is properly wary of his enemy's doings: 'We may rest content with the Hindukush barrier as a defensive line which cannot be violated in the future as it has been in the past by any formidable force cutting through Badakhshan, without years of preparation and forewarning.'[5]

We may now pass on to a consideration of the usefulness of the Oxus as a military barrier. The river Oxus formed the traditional boundary between Iran and Turan, that is between the Persian-speaking and Turkic-speaking people. Despite this traditional political significance attaching to it, the value of the Oxus as a military barrier was very limited, and it is not surprising that it has seldom served as an actual boundary between kingdoms.[6] However, in its upper reaches, north of Badakhshan, it was undoubtedly not easy to cross. In its 'immense sweep round Badakhshan, flowing north, then west, and finally south before reaching the neighbourhood of Khulm', its volume of water was swelled by the joining of 'many great affluents on its right bank'.[7]

In winter the river used to freeze above Darwaz. The only route open to the travellers was the bed of the frozen river. This was extremely difficult in the winter season due to the biting cold of the glacier-bred winds of the Hindukush. But as it flowed into the plains near Balkh, it became fordable at many places:

The Oxus, to the North of Balkh, is well known, and the fords and passages of that river have been reckoned up with fair accuracy. From time immemorial every horde of Skythic origin, Nagas, Sakas or Jatas must have passed these fords from the hills and valleys of the Central Asian divide on their way to India. The Oxus fords have seen men in millions making south for the valleys of Badakhshan and Golden Gates of Central Asiatic ideal which lay yet farther south beyond the grim line of Hindukush.[8]

If, then, it is unlikely that the Mughals could seriously think of

INDIA'S NORTH-WEST FRONTIERS FROM THE 13TH TO 19TH CENTURY

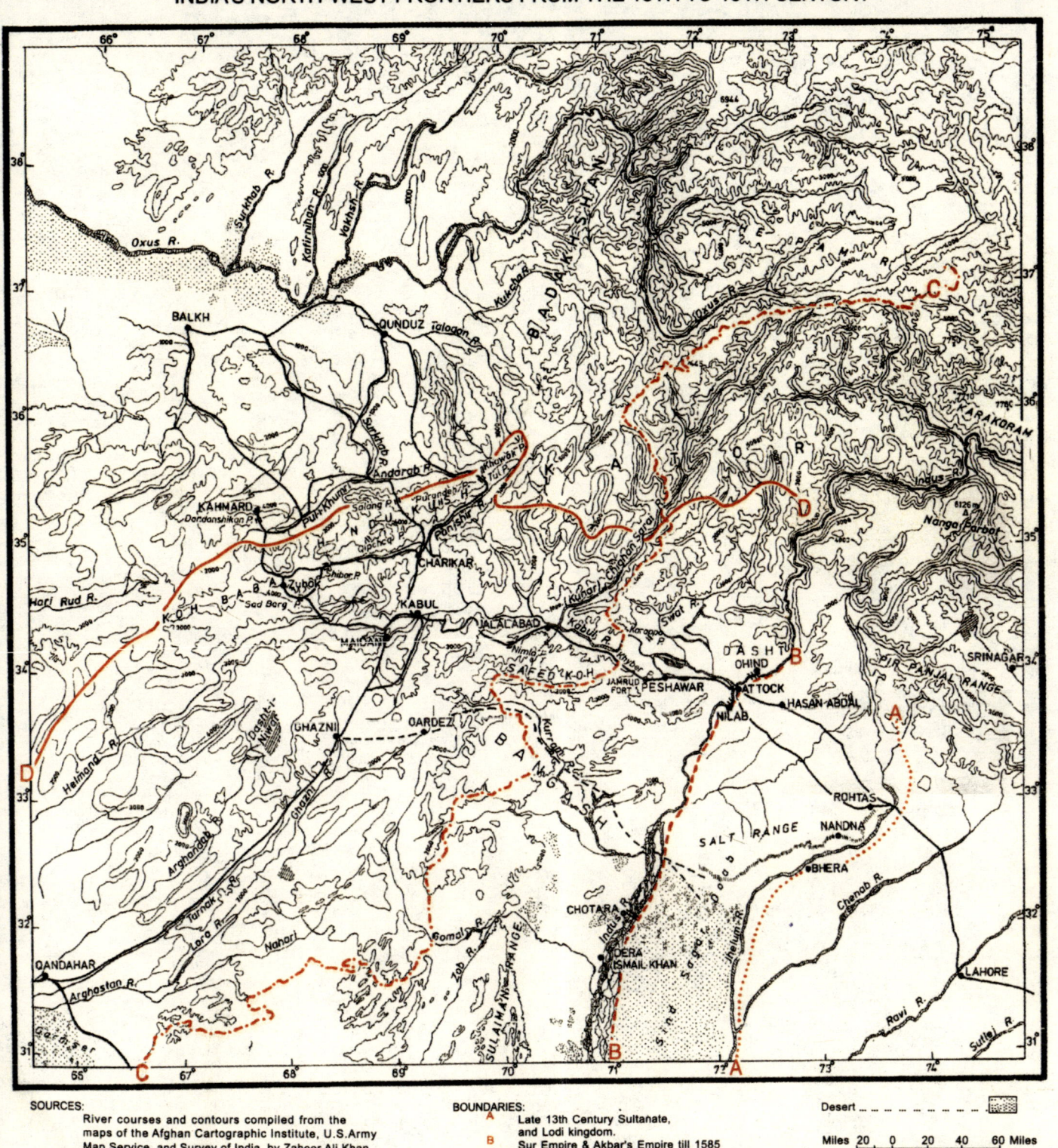

SOURCES:
River courses and contours compiled from the maps of the Afghan Cartographic Institute, U.S. Army Map Service, and Survey of India, by Zahoor Ali Khan Routes & boundary 'D' taken from Irfan Habib's Atlas of the Mughal Empire.

BOUNDARIES:

A	Late 13th Century Sultanate, and Lodi kingdom.
B	Sur Empire & Akbar's Empire till 1585
C	British-Afghan Frontier
D	The Mughal Frontier after 1586

Desert ... ...

Miles 20 0 20 40 60 Miles

Route ..—..—..—..

improving their security by taking their frontier by taking it up to the Oxus, we may consider whether the territories in between, namely Balkh and Badakhshan, could attract them.

Of these Balkh was richer and easier of access than Badakhshan. The city of Balkh is perhaps the oldest town in the basin of the Amu (Oxus) river. Muslim geographers call it the 'Mother of towns'. The plain of Bactria of which Balkh was the capital lies south of the Oxus river, extending east and west for some two hundred miles parallel to the river after its debouchment from the mountains of Badakhshan. The territory of Balkh, outside the district of the capital, was divided west and east between the two great districts of Jurjan and Turkistan, the rich irrigation of which rendered it famous.[9]

Badakhshan lay on the left or south bank of the Oxus, being almost encircled by the great bend of the river beyond Turkistan. It was and is, as noted by Istakhri, 'very populous and fertile, with refreshing streams and numberless vineyards.'[10] The capital in the earlier days was of the same name as Badakhshan, while the Badakhshan river (or Gulchah) was known as the Dirgham to the Arabs. The position of Badakhshan city is no longer known, but its capital in later medieval times was Faizabad, which still stands. Both the capitals probably stood in the same valley, 'seeing the inaccessible nature of most of the country'.[11]

The kingdom of Badakhshan was well protected by nature. If any army entered the gorges and surmounted the passes of the Badakhshan ramparts, it was confronted with a new set of military problems. The narrowness and the isolation of its cultivated valleys, the rough ranges and the passive hostility of the uplands make it extremely difficult to keep an army alive during its passage. No human tide had ever migrated into Badakhshan either from east or from the west. From the east the kingdom was guarded by the heights of the Pamirs and there is no evidence of any migration from India.[12]

Taking in everything, the territories did not have sufficient revenue-yielding capacity to justify Mughal designs. According to Lahori the revenue of the two provinces hardly provided resources enough to pay one of the grandees of the empire.[13] Besides, as we have seen, Badakhshan consisted of difficult country.

One must, therefore, reject as inadequate any explanations of the Mughal advance into Balkh and Badakhshan on grounds of military geography or economic considerations.

We may then consider the Mughal official explanations—for there was not one, but many.

First of all, there was the proclaimed desire on the part of the Mughal emperors to recover their ancestral lands—Trans-Oxiana in general, and Badakhshan, which the Timurids had lost only in 1585 in particular. Jahangir had expressed this ambition in the *Tuzuk*,[14] and Lahori too makes a point of it.[15]

Second, the Mughal court attributed its decision to invade Balkh and Badakhshan to a desire to punish Nazr Muhammad for the earlier raids. Nazr Muhammad, the ruler of Balkh and Badakshan, had attacked Kabul in 1628 and since then the emperor was thinking of punishing Nazr Muhammad. The only deterrent to the realization of the wishes of the king was the fact that the emperor was reluctant to cross swords with a neighbouring Muslim power.[16]

Sa'dullah Khan too, in a letter to Hasan Lafabeli of Khurasan wrote that the main cause of the Balkh campaign was the audacity of Nazr Muhammad. In the beginning of Shah Jahan's reign, Nazr Muhammad had the audacity to attack Kabul and plunder the suburbs of the city. The emperor postponed the punishment of Nazr Muhammad for a suitable time. When the opportunity arose an army was sent to Balkh and Badakhshan to punish Nazr Muhammad.[17]

But then, third, in obvious contradiction to the second, the Mughals professed to go into the Uzbek kingdom in order to protect Nazr Muhammad against his son Abdul Aziz Khan in 1645–6. Together with this they justified their action by a fourth motive — the desire to protect the population of Balkh and Badakhshan from the nomadic tribe of Almans who had raided the territory on behalf of Abdul Aziz Khan. This remained the standard Mughal explanation even when the Mughal prince Murad's armies had virtually driven Nazr Muhammad out of Balkh.

A few passages may be cited to illustrate how the Mughals quite seriously put forward this particular view. In a letter to Sultan Muhammad, the Ottoman emperor, Shah Jahan stated that Nazr Muhammad had expelled his brother Imam Quli Khan from Balkh and Badakshan. The people of that area and specially the Uzbeks, had resented this cruel act of Nazr Muhammad and revolted against him. Abdul Aziz, the son of Nazr Muhammad had also joined the rebels. The Almans, taking advantage of the situation, had plundered the provinces of Balkh and Badakhshan and had harassed the inhabitants of that area. The Almans in their audacity had demolished places of worship, desecrated the mosques, burnt copies of the holy Quran and massacred Saiyids. There was complete lawless-ness and the Mughal army had been sent to restore law and order there.[18]

In a letter written by Sa'dullah Khan on behalf of Shah Jahan to the Shah of Persia, it was stated that the Uzbeks, tyrants and sinners that they were, had created disturbances in Balkh and Badakhshan and had revolted against their sovereign. They were massacring people and were desecrating the places of worship. It was obligatory on the Mughal emperor to defend the life, honour and property of the people from the tyranny of the Uzbeks. Prince Murad Bakhsh had been deputed to punish the Uzbeks and to restore law and order in Balkh and Badakhshan. The prince had occupied Badakhshan in less than a month and Samarqand and Bukhara would also be conquered.[19]

It is in conformity with this official attitude that Lahori says that the Mughal army was sent to Balkh and Badakhshan to crush the Uzbeks and to suppress the Almans because they had committed all sorts of atrocities and there was no law and order. The emperor wanted that once law and order was restored in Balkh and Badakshan, the province of Balkh would be handed over to Nazr Muhammad, but he fled to Persia.[20]

We are thus confronted with a medley of motives and reasons put forward by the Mughals, none of which alone seems to carry conviction.

One motive which they did not put forward, and has, therefore, escaped the notice of historians, seems to us, however, to be the simplest, and is suggested here for the consideration of historians, as a tentative hypothesis.

From 1611, under the mild policies of Imam Quli, the Uzbek Empire had disintegrated, though its nominal territorial extent remained very large. True, the forays Nazr Muhammad had launched at moments of crisis had been repulsed by the Mughal troops with comparative ease. But, in 1641 a new development occurred. The Uzbek Empire was reunited, not only in name but in fact, when Nazr Muhammad replaced his brother Imam Quli as the Khan of Bukhara. The Mughals followed with alarm, as the detailed account of Lahori shows,[21] the vigorous attempts of Nazr Muhammad Khan to unify the vast Khanate. Visions of a second Abdullah Khan must have been resurrected. Under the new impulse, the Uzbeks even raided the Hazara country that was under Mughal control.[22] It was in such a situation that a civil war, caused by the simmering unrest among Uzbek nobility against Nazr Muhammad's despotic measures, broke out in 1645. The powerful Khan was suddenly in flight. But was his flight really the end of the rejuvenated Uzbek power? The new rival, Abdul Aziz Khan had proved successful and measures were needed to be taken to weaken him, or, better still, keep the Uzbek Empire divided by propping up Nazr Muhammad. If possible, Badakhshan, not very important in itself, but not to be scorned either, might be secured for the Mughal Empire as a byproduct of such an enterprise.

If we adopt this view, the Mughal campaign makes sense. Possibly, the comparatively easy success of Murad in 1646 inflamed Shah Jahan's ambitions beyond those suggested above. But the fact that the two territories were too difficult and too expensive to hold, soon asserted itself to cool the enthusiasm of the Mughal court.

The compromise that the Mughals sought to achieve pending their withdrawal, namely the continuation of Nazr Muhammad as the ruler of Uzbek territories south of the Oxus was, therefore, not as disgraceful or useless as it is sometimes made out to be. If success is to be judged by consequences, the point cannot be ignored that no Uzbek army crossed the Hindukush into Mughal territory after 1647.

NOTES

1. *History of Aurangzeb*, vol. I, Calcutta, 1912.

2. *History of Shah Jahan of Dihli*, Allahabad, 1958

3. 'The Mughal Relations with Persia and Central Asia', *Islamic Culture*, vol. VII and IX (1934–35).

4. *A'in-i Akbari*, II (tr. H.S. Jarrett, rev. J. Sarkar, Calcutta, 1949), p. 405.

5. *The Gates of India*, London, 1910, pp. 525.

6. See H.A.R. Gibb, *Arab Conquest of Trans-Oxiana*, London, 1923.

7. G. Le Strange, *The Lands of the Eastern Caliphate*, Cambridge, 1936, p. 435.

8. Holdich, *The Gates of India*, pp. 501–2.

9. Ibid., p. 76.

10. G. Le Strange, *The Lands of Eastern Caliphate*, p. 435.

11. Ibid.

12. Holdich, *The Gates of India*, p. 78.

13. Lahori, *Badshahnama*, Bib. Ind., Calcutta, 1866–72, II, p. 543.

14. *Tuzuk*, ed. Sayyid Ahmad Ghazipur and Aligarh, 1863–4, p. 11.

15. *Badshahnama*, II, p. 598.

16. Ibid., pp. 598–9.

17. *Jamial Insha*, compiled by Munshi Bhagchand, B. L. MS Or. 1702, ff. 4b–5a.

18. *Jamial Insha*, ff. 143b–148b; *Badshahnama*, ɪɪ, p. 436. For the rebellion of Almans against Nazr Muhammad, see ibid., p. 620. For the revolt of the Qalmaqs, see ibid., p. 438.

19. *Makatib-i 'Aiya ✔n Umara-i Mughalia*, ff. 9–11; Abdul Salam Coll., 328/98, Maulana Azad Library, AMU, Aligarh. Shah Jahan's own letter to Shah Abbas containing similar arguments is to be found in *Badshahnama*, ɪɪ, p. 438.

20. *Badshahnama*, ɪɪ, p. 529; see also Sadiq Khan, *Shah Jahan Nama*, B. L. MS Or. 174, f. 127a.

21. Ibid., pp. 252–6.

22. Ibid., pp. 295, 401–2.

THE PASSING OF THE EMPIRE

The Passing of the Empire
The Mughal Case

There have been numerous attempts to explain the fall of the Mughal Empire; and I truly feel great hesitation in adding myself to the long list of its exponents. To historians like Irvine and Sarkar, the decline could be explained in terms of a personal deterioration in the quality of the kings and their nobles. The harem influence grew—and women, for some strange unscientific reason, are always supposed to be a bad influence. The kings and nobles became more luxury-loving, though no-one has yet established that the Mughals during the sixteenth and seventeenth centuries enjoyed a less luxurious mode of living than their eighteenth-century successors.[1]

Sarkar, in his monumental *History of Aurangzeb*, also elaborated upon the traditionally recognized factor, namely, Hindu–Muslim differences; Aurangzeb's religious policy is thought to have provoked a Hindu reaction that undid the unity that had been so laboriously built up by his predecessors.[2]

Recently, there has been an attempt at a more fundamental examination. Satish Chandra sought to find the critical factor in the Mughals' failure to maintain the mansab and jagir system whose efficient working was essential for the survival of the Empire as a centralized polity.[3] Irfan Habib, on the other hand, has sought to explain the fall of the Mughal Empire as an effect of the working of this very system. The jagir transfers led to intensified exploitation; and such exploitation led to rebellion by zamindars (rural superior right-holders) and the peasantry.[4] With all these factors is sometimes compounded yet another—the rise of 'nationalities', subverting and shattering the unified empire. The thesis, developed by Soviet scholars like Reisner and maintained by a school of popular Indian Marxist writers, has received strange corroboration from 'young and youngish' American scholars who have found new regional power groups in the states that arose during the eighteenth century.[5]

It is easy to be lost in the welter of these 'factors'. It is also perhaps possible to reconcile contradictions by propounding a complex cause–sequence–cause chain and by simply disowning the search for the single ultimate cause. Such a synthesis is yet to be attempted; I do not profess any ambition to make the attempt here. I should like simply to relate the entire text to what I conceive to be the proper context.

In following the scholarly discussions over the break-up of the Mughal Empire, I have been struck by the fact that the discussions should have been conducted in such insular terms. The first part of the eighteenth century did not see the collapse of only the Mughal Empire: The Safavid Empire also collapsed; the Uzbek Khanate broke up into fragments; and the Ottoman Empire began its career of slow, but inexorable decline. Are all these phenomena mere coincidences? It seems to me straining one's sense of the plausible to assert that the same fate overcame all the large empires of the Indic and Islamic world at precisely the same time, but owing to quite different (and rather miscellaneous) factors operating in the case of each of them. Even if the search should ultimately prove futile, one must see whether it is possible to discover some common factor that caused more or less stable empires to disintegrate and created conditions in which new political structures which look large enough on the map, like Nadir Shah's empire, the Afghan (Durrani) empire or the Maratha confederacy, emerged and then almost immediately splintered into fragments.

There is one remarkable point too, which may serve as the guide-post in our search. The break-up of the empires distinctly precedes the impact from the armed attack of the western colonial powers, notably Britain and Russia. But it precedes the impact with such a short interval that the question must arise whether the rise of the West was not in some ways, not yet properly understood, subverting the polity and society of the East even before Europe actually confronted the eastern states with its superior military power.

It is a regrettable gap in our study of the economic history of the Middle East and India, that no general analysis has been attempted of the changes in the pattern of trade and markets of these countries, as a result of the new commerce between Europe and Asia. There is a tendency to belittle the significance of the great commercial developments of the sixteenth and seventeenth centuries for eastern economies, owing to the small volume of goods that entered international, or long-distance, trade at that time. But the real question is not of volume, but value. In terms of value, long-distance trade must have accounted for a sizeable portion of the gross product in all the economics with which we are concerned.

The major event between 1500 and 1700 was certainly the rise of Europe as the centre of world commerce, with its dominance over the New World and the high seas, and its total monopoly of the Cape of Good Hope. Recent estimates suggest an increase in the population of Europe from about 50 million in 1450 to 120 million in 1700,[6] an outstanding achievement particularly when we bear in mind the demographic debacle of the Thirty Years War in Germany and the slow decline of population in Spain. No similar estimates exist for Asia. But it would seem that the Indian population remained largely stable between 1600 and 1800. Moreland's estimate of 100 million for 1600 has been properly questioned, and the figure of 150 million probably is nearer the truth.[7] The Census of 1868–72 disclosed a population of less than 230 million. India thus saw an increase of barely 66 per cent in 270 years, whereas Europe enhanced its population by some 240 per cent in a period of 250 years. This contrast in population growth suggests that a real shift in the economic balance between Europe and Asia had already occurred by the end of the seventeenth century.

This shift found its true repercussions in international trade. The discovery of the Cape of Good Hope was certainly an important event, and in giving a direct, unhampered route to India, it had important military consequences in the eighteenth century. But the major economic change was not represented only by the new route (indeed, it is likely that the older, Red Sea route remained as important a channel as the Cape until well after 1700). It was, above all, represented by the emergence of Europe as the principal market for the luxuries and craft-manufactures of the world. Economic historians have so far remained immersed mainly in Europe's problem of payments, a preoccupation inherited from the mercantilist controversies of the period. The other complementary aspects, that is the increase in demand for the products of the world and the effect of this on *other* markets of these products, appear either to have escaped notice or to have not received the attention due to them.

In other words, we have to consider not only the export of large quantities of gold and silver (especially the latter) from Europe to the East, but also the fact that a large part of the luxury manufactures and high-value products of the East were diverted from their other, hitherto 'traditional' markets, and carried to Europe. Unfortunately, owing to the lack of fuller investigations, and partly to the limitations in our sources, it is difficult to set this shift in quantitative terms. But wherever we look in Asia near the end of the seventeenth century, the European demand was exercising its pull, strong or feeble, direct or indirect.

The fact that Iran no longer remained the principal market for a whole range of Indian commodities (indigo, pepper, chintz), and India and Iran, together, no longer for a number of Chinese exports (silk, porcelain), speaks volumes for the relative economic decline of these countries. This decline, was, however, not only relative; it could not but be absolute as well. One-third of the Bengal silk was already exported, through the Dutch and the English, before 1667, and one-third through Persian and Armenian merchants (much of it presumably for overland transport to Mediterranean port), and only a third remained for Indian markets.[8] The European, companies obtained a virtual monopoly of the pepper of the western coast, and they became the principal buyers of India's finest chintz, that of Masulipatam. It is not very likely that production expanded sufficiently to meet the European demand without reducing the share of the other markets. Indeed, if the production did expand to some extent, in conditions of stationary technology, costs and prices must have gone up, relatively to the general price level.

My suggestion is that these developments caused a serious disturbance in the economics of the eastern countries, and intensified the financial difficulties of the ruling classes. The Great Silk Road no longer carried the great caravans; and this must have distinctly impoverished Central Asia (the Uzbek Khanate). In India and Iran, too, the costs of luxury articles rose—and, after all, for members of the ruling class it was these luxuries that life was all about. The income previously obtained no longer sufficed. Here was a factor for an attempt at greater agrarian exploitation; and when that failed, or proved counter-productive, for reckless factional activities for individual gain, leading to interminable civil wars. Such conditions would, of course, spell the end of the great empires.

While, obviously, what I have suggested is replete with speculation, and requires much detailed investigation for its substantiation, I should like to consider another important historical factor that emerges from a consideration of the Europe–Asia relationship. The European imports of eastern goods were paid for mainly in gold and silver; and these, especially the latter, came from Latin America in hitherto unprecedented quantities. But the European demand for these commodities was generated, not so much by the possession of the specie, as by a distinct qualitative and quantitative development of craft production, leading to the enrichment of the entire economy and a notable expansion of its urban sector. At the beginning of the seventeenth century, towns like Lahore or Agra dwarfed the European cities of the period. By 1700, European towns like London and Paris had populations (at over half a million) exceeding those of all Indian cities, except perhaps Agra. According to Deane and Cole's estimate, 13 per cent of the people of England and Wales were living in towns of 5000 and above, in 1701.[9] This percentage had not been reached in India even by 1901.

This spurt in European urban growth was the first product of the new science and technology that was generating small advances in a number of sectors, the cumulative effect of which was phenomenal. A completely different picture was presented by Asia, especially India. One need not be a follower of Marx's theory of the unchangeableness of traditional Indian society to accept the fact that there was no conscious spirit of technological innovation (and scientific enquiry) here and in the Islamic East to match the spirit already motivating a large part of European society in the seventeenth century. This does not mean that no mechanical innovation was propagated or spread in the East during the sixteenth and seventeenth centuries. It has been shown that such 'generalization' did take place.[10] But what we are concerned with is its pace and scope. The pace was certainly slow, and the scope severely limited. This is manifested, above all, by the utter absence in the literature of India of any satisfactory descriptions of even the most important products of Europe's new technology, e.g. the clock, the telescope, and the flint-lock.

Whether the source lay in some structural fault of Indian and Islamic society, which perpetuated the divorce between intellect and manual labour, or whether it lay in some peculiar inhibition against science in Islamic (and Hindu) ideology is difficult to decide. The intellectual aridity is manifest; it causes are obscure.

The aridity is relevant to us because of its economic and political consequences. If technological growth resulted in urbanization, this meant that the expansion of towns could provide a safety-value at times of agrarian crises. Since a similar process did not occur in India and other countries of the East, this safety-value was missing. As has been pointed out, the Indian urban population was parasitical, based upon the expropriation of agrarian surplus.[11] A corollary of this is that if the expropriation of that surplus was affected, the scope of urban employment also declined. This means that, so long as craft production did not obtain an independent base, as it did increasingly in Europe from the sixteenth century, there was no possibility of the absorption of the shock of an agrarian upheaval. In that sense, the Mughal Empire, in spite of its splendid professional army, was peculiarly vulnerable to the ill-armed but million-headed zamindar and peasant rebels.[12]

Here, another point suggest itself. If there was anything that was affected most speedily by technological changes throughout the world it was the army. Artillery-making was the 'heavy industry' of the time. In Europe it attracted the ingenuity of scientists and mathematicians from the sixteenth century onwards. But, as one moved eastward from Europe, the pace of its development in each country would have appeared to be slower and slower. India saw no conscious attempt to design new artillery weapons; the making of muskets and guns remained a mere craft, with no touch of science; and accordingly by 1700 these were almost completely out-dated. The Mughals continued to rely upon bow and sword-wielding cavalry when its days were long over. It is, perhaps, this that led to their major debacle at Karnal in 1739, when they had to face Nadir Shah, who had better artillery, copied from the Europeans and the Ottomans.[13]

To me, then, the failure of the Mughal Empire would seem to derive essentially from a *cultural* failure, shared with the entire Islamic world. It was this failure that tilted the economic balance in favour of Europe, well before European armies reduced India and other parts of Asia to colonial possessions, protectorates and spheres of influence. It was this cultural failure again that deprived the empires of the capacity to grapple with their agrarian crises. These twin economic consequences were themselves the causes of the political and military debacles; but as we have just seen, even military weaknesses flowed from the intellectual stagnation that seems to have gripped the eastern world.

Of course, the word stagnation is relative. It is quite possible that if we were not in the compelling necessity to have to be looking over our shoulders at what was being thought and written in Europe at the same time, we might have regarded the Islamic East and India during the sixteenth and seventeenth centuries as fairly productive in the matter of literature and rational sciences. But while we my admire the poetry of Hafiz, the rationalism of Abul Fazl, the religious eclecticism of Dara Shukoh, the astronomical observations of Raja Jai Singh, the fact remains that of modern science there is hardly a trace. This is so very clear in the *Zij-i Muhammad Shahi* (1732), the celebrated work of Jai Singh. Here the entire theoretical text is virtually borrowed verbatim from the *Zij-i Ulugh-khani*, composed nearly 300 years earlier. Only the tables are changed. Jai Singh is interested in European astronomical observations, and he refers to them in his preface. But

Newton might not have lived, so far as he is concerned. Thus the entire framework of reasoning and thought, and, indeed, the limits and scope of reflection, remained the same as had been defined by the great Arabic writers before the twelfth century. The stirrings were there and were important; but, unluckily, they brought out only ripples, where a flood, a breakthrough, was needed in order to put men's minds into new moulds.

II

The polities that emerged upon the collapse of the Mughal Empire were of demonstrably two kinds. In one class were the 'succession states' like Hyderabad, Bengal and Awadh, which were really fragments of the Empire, that had to stand upon their own feet as the central government decayed and became powerless to assist or assert. They inherited more or less the entire Mughal machinery of administration in a working order. In the second category were the Maratha confederacy, the Jats, the Sikhs, and the Afghans. Their origins as polities were independent of the Mughal Empire, though they might occasionally come to terms with it, or, indeed, in the case of the first two, even acknowledge the nominal supremacy of the Mughal emperor. They were clearly the products of the crisis that we have touched upon. While they might use certain Mughal administrative institutions for their own purposes, their mode of government was by and large antithetical to that of the Empire, and could not be reconciled with it. Mughal professional cavalry could indeed survive within the Maratha confederacy, but only as Pindaris, that is as real historical Draculas, who drank up the blood of their new masters. The entire contradiction is summed up in the protest expressed by Azad Bilgrami in 1761 that the Maratha leaders, in spite of their conquests, were not behaving as rulers, but as zamindars.[14]

Mysore under Haidar Ali and Tipu Sultan stood outside these two categories, and was in some ways the most remarkable. On the one hand, it represented a conscious attempt at implanting Mughal administrative institutions in an area that had only been nominally a part of the Mughal Empire. This was most clearly to be seen in the organization of land-revenue administration, as well as the army (notably under Haidar Ali). On the other hand, it was the first state in India to make a beginning towards modernization, first and foremost in the realm of the army and arms manufacture, but also in commerce, where the English East India Company's practices were sought to be imitated.[15]

This preliminary classification of eighteenth-century polities is important, because some writers tend to speak as if, irrespective of these large differences in their essential natures, we could still find some common basis for them. The theory that these polities were reflections of the emergence of 'regional élites', or gave opportunities to certain groups previously enjoying only limited prominence, to become co-sharers in power, are either statements of the obvious in sociological terms, or are based upon rather untenable assumptions about the Mughal Empire.

Thus, if the Mughal Empire broke into certain fragments, with each fragment an autonomous or independent state, its ruling class must, of course, ipso factor have been regionalized. No longer could an officer serving in Awadh be sent to the Deccan in course of time. But this is an effect, not a cause; and it is an enforced regionalization, if anything. The case of Bengal that is often cited,[16] is rather peculiar. Here the nazims, or governors, first carried out what in an earlier period would have appeared as an act of extreme centralization. Murshid Quli Khan obtained imperial sanction for the conversion of jagirs into khalisa, and thus secured the withdrawal of all Mughal jagirdars or commanders from Bengal. Then, because he combined his office of nazim with that of diwan, or provincial revenue minister, he henceforth managed the khalisa; and he and his successors remitted enormous amounts to the Mughal Emperor.[17] By 1740 this practice ceased. Thus, the Bengal nawabs became masters of the entire revenues of Bengal without having to share them with the jagirdars, that is without there being any true remnant of Mughal nobility continuing in Bengal except for the nazims themselves. For managing the khalisa, the nawabs recruited revenue-farmers and officials from amongst the local zamindars and merchant-bankers. This phenomenon has given rise to much misunderstanding about the emergence of a new élite. No such emergence is discernible in Hyderabad or in Awadh, where the jagir system continued to be in vogue.

Information about the merchants' role in administration is rather too readily seized upon as evidence of their increased political participation. In fact, their role in the Mughal Empire was equally important.[18] Quite obviously, the Gujarat merchants in the seventeenth century exercised a degree of influence at the Mughal court that even the *nagarseth*s of Bengal in the eighteenth century might have envied.

The Maratha confederacy, as I have said, cannot be grouped with the succession states for any political analysis. That it was a failure as an attempt at Empire building is admitted by all serious historians.

While succeeding so brilliantly in the field, at least until 1761, the Marathas failed to evolve even those minimum conventions—or fictions, if you like—that are essential for building an empire. The slogan of *Hindu-pad-Pad-Shahi* died an abortive death, possibly because the Peshwas were not too keen to give undue weight to their titular sovereign, the raja of Satara. In their attempt to make themselves independent of their own nominal masters, the Peshwas seemed always prepared to accept the nominal sovereignty of the Mughal emperor, so long as the actual gains were theirs. But just as they had reduced their raja to a titular status, the Peshwas, too, were subsequently to be reduced to a titular status by Nana Phadhis (Fardnawis). Thus there was a simple failure to establish even a stable repository of sovereign power.

The second difficulty faced in the working of the Maratha polity arose out of the fact that plunder remained an essential element for its continued functioning. It too often seemed that *chauth* and *sardeshmukhi*, and in lieu thereof, a general devastation of a country, rather than its direct conquest, constituted the acme of Maratha ambitions. Thus, when a full-fledged Maratha administration was established anywhere (and, if Muhammad Ali, author of *Mirat-i Ahmadi*, is to be believed, it could on occasion be excellent), the country had already been so ravaged that the Marathas could only replenish their resources by extending the range of plunder.

I do not wish to enter into similar details for the Abdali or Durrani Empire of Afghanistan, which during the latter half of the eighteenth century came to include the whole of present Pakistan, as well as Kashmir. But in some essential features, especially the dependence upon plunder, it exhibited similar aspects.

One might then say that once the limits for plundering activities were reached, either because of geography, or of opponents, the tide was bound to turn; and civil war, that is really the plunder of the internal parts of these states, was thereupon bound to break out. This can be a plausible explanation of the break-up of both the Maratha and Afghan systems.

But here I should like to draw attention to another factor that might have introduced an element of exceptional economic strain precisely at a time when these states were otherwise vulnerable to centrifugal tendencies. In 1757 the British won the battle of Plassey and within seven years they were complete masters of eastern India. This conquest was not simply a mere political event. It changed the entire complexion of India's commerce. The revenues of Bengal and Bihar became the source of 'investments' of the English East India Company, and with these enormous resources, the English changed the entire direction of the exports of Bengal and Bihar, as well as Coromandel. The exports soon exceeded £5 million.[19] This complete diversion of commerce must have resulted in the upsetting of the whole pattern of Indian commerce. The commercial decline of Gujarat and Agra, which imported silk and cotton stuffs from Bengal, was inevitable. Similarly, the overland trade through Afghanistan was bound to suffer. As the English advanced further inland at the beginning of the nineteenth century, the decline would become still more marked.

How adversely this economic process affected the political strength of the Maratha confederacy and the Afghan Empire is obviously difficult to establish with any degree of confidence. One is struck by the fact that the sudden collapse of the Afghan Empire, in 1809, should have followed so soon after the English advance up to Delhi in 1803. Elphinstone, who led a mission to the court of the Afghan ruler Shah Shuja and who was a witness to the dissolution of his authority, himself observed the decline of the trade and the abandonment of commerce by Afghan tribesmen in favour of agriculture.[20] The decline in commerce is thus established: What is still to be proven is its link with the British conquest on the one hand, and its role as a factor in the decline of the Afghan Empire. My plea is that both the processes occur in such sequence that, at least tentatively, the link ought to be accepted. Perhaps, closer scrutiny of the evidence would some day put us on surer ground.

Finally, a question about these 'transition regimes'. Why is it that when faced directly with British power, they attempted no, or very little, modernization? The case of Mysore under Haidar Ali and Tippu remained unique. Maratha sardars, like the Sindhias, would go no further than having some regiments trained and commanded by European officers.

What is singular is that at the ideological level the English influence should have made such little dent. It is true that information about western sciences begins to appear in some Persian works; but on inspection they are all found to have been written at the direction and wishes of an English official or clergyman. In the main, the Persian literature continued in its well-established grooves. Indeed, the eighteenth century saw its maximum progress in India. Checking through the works listed in C.A. Storey's monumental *Persian Literature: A Bio-bibliographical Survey*, Vol. I, I found that whereas there were only six Hindu writers who wrote one book each in Persian during the seventeenth century, there were during the eighteenth century no less than thirty-two Hindu writers who wrote as many as forty-nine books. This is a tribute to the strength of the cultural tradition bequeathed by the Mughal Empire. But it also partly explains, I think, why the new culture, coming from Europe, held so little attraction, and was, therefore, almost wholly ignored by the educated in India.

III

The author of *Siyar-al Mutakhirin*, himself a protégé of the English, presented in his work an idealized picture of the Mughal administration which he set before his masters as a model. He was writing in 1781. The debate that subsequently occurred between Grant, Shore and Cornwallis, reproduced in the celebrated *Fifth Report*, shows how to the new rulers, too, the rights and institutions established under the Mughal Empire were of abiding interest. Their claim to land-revenue, in particular, derived from Mughal precedent and practice. It has been urged that even the Permanent Settlement was not totally exotic and was rooted in the practice of the Mughal government in Bengal during the seventeenth century.[21] Munro's Ryotwari system was even more clearly a development of the Mughal system of zabt assessment that he found in vogue in areas seized from Mysore. Asiya Siddiqi has commented on how the British administrators of the Ceded and Conquered Provinces greatly relied upon Indian land-revenue expertise, which, as reflected in a work like *Diwan-pasand*, was simply a survival of Mughal land-revenue practices.[22] In so far as the Mughals had established a uniform system of administration all over the country, and a single official language (Persian), the English were helped thereby in creating an administrative machinery that was not too varied in character to render centralized control difficult, and yet was in some harmony with existing conditions.[23]

While saying all this, I should like to refer to a parallel. When the Spaniards captured the Inca emperor of Peru and stepped into his shoes, they used the highly centralized structure of the Incas to quickly establish and extend their rule. But it can hardly be said that the Inca Empire survived in any form through the Spanish colonization. Similarly, the entire basis of British rule in India was so different from that of the Mughal Empire, that one can hardly speak of the former as being in any sense a continuation of the latter. The conception of the revenues of the country, as gross profits of the English East India

Company, was the basic principle on which English dominion was founded; and the drain of wealth to England, through public as well as private channels was the ultimate object to be realized. Thus the survival of the Mughal Empire was subverted to a new use, and not employed to resurrect anything resembling the old Empire. That empire had its own inequities, but these, to be fair to it, were of a different form and content altogether.

NOTES

1. William Irvine, *Later Mughals*, ed. Sarkar, 2 vols, and J. Sarkar, *Fall of the Mughal Empire*, 4 vols, *passim*.
2. J. Sarkar, *History of Aurangzeb*, III, Calcutta, 1916, 283–364.
3. Satish Chandra, *Parties and Politics at the Mughal Court*, 1707–1740, Aligarh, 1959, pp. xliii–xlvii.
4. Irfan Habib, *Agrarian System of Mughal India, 1556–1707*, Bombay, 1963, pp. 317–51.
5. Cf. M.N. Pearson in *IESHR*, IX, 114 and n.
6. The estimate for 1850 is that of J. Russell (*Fontana Economic History of Europe*, vol. I, p. 36) and for 1700 that of André Armengaud (ibid., vol. 3, p. 27).
7. Shireen Moosvi, *IESHR*, x, 194.
8. Tavernier, *Travels in India, 1640–67*, tr. Ball, ed. Crooke, London, 1925, II, p. 2.
9. Phyllis Deane and W.A. Cole, *British Economic Growth, 1688–1959*, Cambridge, 1962, p. 7.
10. Irfan Habib, *Technology and Economy of Mughal India*, Devaraj Chanana Memorial Lectures, 1971 (mimeo).
11. Irfan Habib, *Enquiry*, NS III (3), 55.
12. On the composition of the Maratha army, see Satish Chandra, *IESHR*, x, p. 217 and n. Cf. Irfan Habib, *Agrarian System*, pp. 346–51.
13. Cf. Irvine, *Later Mughals*, II, 352 (Sarkar's addendum).
14. Azad Bilgrami, *Khizana-i Amira*, Kanpur, 1871, p. 47.
15. Mohibbul Hasan Khan, *History of Tipu Sultan*, Calcutta, 1951, pp. 344–7.
16. Phil Calkins in *Journal of Asian Studies*, XXIX, pp. 799ff.
17. Cf. Z. Malik in *IESHR* IV, pp. 269–70.
18. Cf. M.N. Pearson in *IESHR* IX, pp. 118ff.
19. The British imports from 'East India' amounted to £5,785,000 in 1797–8 (Deane and Cole, *British Economic Growth*, p. 87). These imports included imports from China; but the China trade was itself financed by exports from Bengal.

20. Mountstuart Elphinstone, *An Account of the Kingdom of Caubul*, London, 1839, I, pp. 383, 387–8, etc.

21. Irfan Habib, *Agrarian System*, pp. 175–9.

22. A. Siddiqi, *Agrarian Change in a North Indian State*, Oxford, 1973, pp. 178–9.

23. See the perceptive remarks of Eric Stokes in *Past and Present*, no. 58, pp. 144–5, 146–7.

28

Recent Theories of Eighteenth-century India

Until recently, historians tended to view the eighteenth century in two distinct parts, separated by two dates representing two important battles. One was 1761, the year of the third battle of Panipat, which signified both the military irrelevance of the Mughal Empire and the immense setback to the Marathas, who might conceivably have replaced the Mughals. The other landmark was 1757, the year of the battle of Plassey, from which the dominance of the English in India could be conveniently held to begin. Historians concerned with the history of these three Empires are generally agreed upon this bifurcation of the eighteenth century. To the historians of the Mughal Empire, the death of Aurangzeb in 1707 marked the beginning of the decline of that Empire, which was hastened by Nadir Shah's sack of Delhi (1739). Historians concerned with the Marathas could see the eighteenth century as the Maratha century, but the really great successes seemed to occur before 1761, after which stagnation and divisions tended to set in. To the Anglo-Indian historians, 1757 is a very firm benchmark, setting the triumph of Clive as the first step in the realization of the manifest destiny of the British in India.

Along with the bifurcation of the eighteenth century, there has been another view, namely that it was the 'Dark Century' of modern Indian history. I have not seen the actual use of this term by any historian in so designating that century, but Irfan Habib comes very close to doing so when he describes it as a period of 'reckless rapine, anarchy and foreign conquest'.[1] This is clearly a combination of V.A. Smith's view of Maratha polity as a 'Robber State' and the opposite, nationalist conception of British conquest as the ultimate calamity. In a sense, Irfan Habib's brief aside on the eighteenth century would seem to represent a summary of conventional thinking as it prevailed during and before 1960s; the decline of the Mughal Empire in the first half of the eighteenth century marked a setback to the strength of the Indian political, social and economic structure; this enabled the British conquest to take place, which eliminated all such elements of internal growth as the previous regime might have contained. It was, therefore yet another, though perhaps a more profound, version of the simple textbook bifurcation of the eighteenth century.

The entire conception has been challenged by C.A. Bayly in *Rulers, Townsmen, and Bazars*.[2] It is not easy to summarize his basic arguments because of the numerous qualifications he continuously introduces. But one would not be wrong if one were to say that he believes that the Mughal Empire, by its fall, in fact, rendered a service by letting a large number of indigenous groups develop and so enabled a number of networks—established by local castes and communities and immigrant groups, together with merchants and moneylenders—to flourish. British expansion might in the beginning have hurt some of these groups, but, ultimately, represented a compromise with many of them. Thus 1757 (Plassey) or 1764 (Buxar) did not constitute a break: rather, a continuity ought to be discerned.

Bayly's views deserve detailed examination. He is not alone in challenging the older theories of the eighteenth century, though others have not dealt with the issue over such a range. Muzaffar Alam, for example, has been concerned with the first half of the century;[3] and Frank Perlin with Maharashtra.[4] Satish Chandra's essay, though insightful, is brief and concentrates again on Indian polities.[5] In many ways, however, these writings represent departures from the older views, though their authors do not necessarily agree with Bayly. André Wink is among those who totally accept Bayly's view of the Empire and the Marathas.[6]

At first sight, Muzaffar Alam's work offers much promise. Here is the opportunity to study the nature of transformation in the first half of the eighteenth century in specific terms by appealing to detailed local evidence from Awadh. The effort is, however, marred by a very obvious bias in favour of Mughal administration, to an extent that even the use of the word 'Crisis' in the title of his book seems unwarranted by the text. The empire in its heyday had contributed to prosperity, and its autonomous segments continued to do so in the eighteenth century. He speaks as if this last is an incontestable fact: 'Both the Punjab and Awadh registered unmistakable economic growth in the seventeenth century. In the early eighteenth century in both provinces, politics and administration appear to have moved along similar lines.'[7]

Muzaffar Alam's evidence of 'economic growth' is extremely slender. He offers a comparison of jamadami (estimated revenue) statistics in the *A'in-i Akbari* with an 'eighteenth-century revenue roll', to establish that it 'almost doubled' in the intervening period.[8] He admits that the increase seems cancelled by the much greater rise in prices. Yet, at a later point in his book he insists that 'the rise in jama had a bearing on the increase in agricultural production', which he now seems to regard as being established by the increase in the jama, forgetting altogether the increase in prices.

If the evidence for Muzaffar Alam's basic thesis is so poor, much of what he describes—and it is in the description of various incidents culled from sources that his work attracts the reader's interest—has no relevance to his conclusion, namely that the first half of the eighteenth century was a period of progress. Thus the supreme illogicality of the last sentence of his book:

The growing tendency among the nobles and officials to hold *jagirs* on a permanent and quasi-permanent basis, the struggle to convert *madad-i ma'ash* (revenue grant) holding into *milkiyat* (private property), the emergence of the *ta'alluqa*, *ta'ahhud* and *ijara* contracts as the most acceptable forms of government, and the consensus among the regional powers to maintain the Mughal imperial symbols to obtain legitimacy and thus stability and security of their spoils—all indicated the eighteenth century endeavour to make use of the possibilities for growth within existing social structures.[9]

If one were to adopt this line of argument, the Wars of Roses and the Thirty Years' War could also be proof of an 'endeavour to make use of possibilities for growth', for every potentate was seeking his own 'growth' in those wars just as in eighteenth-century India.

Frank Perlin's position on the Mughal Empire is different from Muzaffar Alam's, though his argument is not easy to understand. He tends to discount the influence of the Empire—as a 'system'—on Indian society and deplores 'Mughal and Maratha centric treatments of economic history'. He maintains:

It is (rather) necessary to describe those other aspects of society and state formation which lie beyond and incorporate such system-making and which arguably contradict the latter, lead to their constant mutation and compose a space of events, acts and even structured relationships and consequences which transcends the frontiers within which contemporary attempts at systematization occurred.[10]

Perlin appears to argue that the failures of the Mughals or Marathas as centralizing systems were not of central significance, in view of 'the stubbornness of the intermediary ground', that is the structures of grass-root political, legal and social institutions and rights. In that sense, there would appear to be no disaster in store for the Indian economy in the passing of the Mughal Empire.

Perlin thus dismisses all too easily the significance of an imperial system for the economy, and so seemingly overlooks the implications of the rent-extracting state. Bayly wrote before Perlin, and he too tends to avoid giving the Mughal Empire a central place in the picture of Indian society, say, in 1700. Yet, he acknowledges that the Mughal Empire 'was more than a mere umbrella raised over virtually autonomous local groups'. He observes:

It was more like a grid of imperial towns, roads and markets, which pressed heavily on society and modified it, though only at certain points. The system depended on the ability of the Mughal state to appropriate in cash as much as 40 per cent of the value of the total agricultural product. A sophisticated money and produce market must have existed to make this possible, and men who recognised the supremacy of the Emperor must have had influence in small towns and *bazaars*.[11]

Surely, the extraction of rent (40 per cent of the value of produce), 'grids of imperial towns' and 'a sophisticated money and produce market' could not be unimportant elements in an economy. And if we are looking at the scale of commerce and the size of the urban sector as indicators of economic 'development' (especially keeping the ultimate arrival of capitalism in view), then a decline of the Empire, to which these elements were tied, could well represent an economic decline as well.

Indeed, this is supported by Ashin Das Gupta's finding about the contraction of the hinterland of Surat during the first half of the eighteenth century without its displacement by any other port.[12]

Bayly's own position on the Mughal Empire is not very definite. After admitting that the Empire implied a certain amount of development of commerce and markets, he does not draw the conclusion that would seem to be inescapable: such development could be seriously affected by the decay of the Empire. On the other hand, he speaks as if the decay released forces, presumably so far suppressed, which 'benefited and consolidated the intermediate classes of society — townsmen, traders, service gentry — who commanded the skills of the market and the pen'.[13]

This is one of the weak links in Bayly's argument. The point at issue is not whether towns remained (or new ones were established while the old decayed still more) and commerce was conducted and the bureaucracy functioned at some levels, but whether there was a greater efflorescence of these activities than in the Mughal century (seventeenth). Bayly offers no such comparison. His narratives of the emergence of the Bhumihar zamindars in Banaras and further east, the Rohilas in the middle Doab and trans-Ganga tract (Rohilkhand), and the Jats and Sikhs, in terms of Hindu and Muslim, 'indigenous' and 'external', are all very interesting, but they really lend little weight to his thesis that the Mughal decline reinforced the position of the urban classes and the bureaucracy.

Once the Hindu/Muslim, indigenous/external categories that Bayly plays with are disregarded, as least for the moment, and we focus on the genesis of the new forces stepping into the vacuum created by the declining fortunes of Mughal power, the zamindari antecedents of the bulk of these become clear enough. One uses the term zamindar here in the sense established by Irfan Habib—the hereditary, largely caste-bound, rural class with control over part of the produce of land and served by armed retainers.[14]

Bayly's description of the Bhumihar chieftains as zamindars and Muzaffar Alam's survey of Awadh and the Punjab in the first half of the eighteenth century show how the zamindar clans rose in uprising after uprising. S.P. Gupta, in his recent study, has shown how the Amber ruler strengthened his position in the first half of the eighteenth-century in eastern Rajasthan, and thus essentially converted a zamindari into a local sovereignty.[15] Where, as in the case of the Rohilas, there was an immigrant group, it too tried to sink its roots into the soil by replacing old zamindars (for instance, Rajputs in Rohilkhand, with whom the Rohillas came into persistent conflict).[16] The zamindar origins of the Maratha rulers have been investigated by Satish Chandra.[17]

One may note that the emergence of zamindar power on the ruins of the Mughal Empire is implicit in Irfan Habib's analysis of the crisis of the Mughal Empire.[18] Harbans Mukhia, who seldom finds himself in agreement with him, has come to the same conclusion:

It is thus that even when the Mughal Empire was collapsing, one gets the impression that the class of *zamindars* at various levels was turning out to be the main beneficiary. It was, in other words, an older form of property that was re-emerging in strength.[19]

Wink concedes the same process, despite his assertive observation of continuity between the Mughals and the Marathas, when he sees the Marathas as representing the 'intermediary gentry or zamindari stratum' and the eighteenth century, therefore, as 'the century of the "gentrification of the Muslim Empire"".[20]

Clearly, a reassertion of the zamindars' power over a large part of the country could not lead to a restoration of conditions that prevailed before the Mughal Empire or the Sultanate. It would not be in the zamindars' own interest to give up the right to collect the bulk of agricultural surplus as land revenue once they stepped into the shoes of the preceding Mughal administration, whether as nominal jagirdars, revenue contractors, ta'alluqdars or simply usurpers. What happened now was a great admixture of state rights with hereditary landed rights, seen pre-eminently in a steady decentralization of political authority, which was marked as much in Mughal polity in the first half of the century as in the Maratha polity in the second.

It would be hard to argue that the mutually conflicting small political units into which India was divided in the eighteenth century were individually stronger than the Empire they had supplanted. Bayly does not take up this point at all: what he suggests is that these units were more strongly based on the soil either because they were composed of local elite or based on compromises with them, as could be illustrated by the liberal policy pursued by the surviving Mughal satrapies towards a wide range of Hindu warriors and administrative groups.[21] But, apart from the fact that the Mughal Empire too had promoted an 'eclectic culture' (witness Akbar and Dara Shukoh),[22] many of the compromises that the Mughal satrapies made with the zamindars were signs of weakness, and not of strength; that a zamindar, in his locality, was strong is, of course, the reason why he could step into the shoes of the contracting Mughal authority. It did not mean that the sum of zamindar-based powers that now arose could be stronger than the unified Empire they had supplanted.

Yet, because of the very fact that the new political units were admixtures, continuing all the essential features of the Mughal land-revenue system, while often combining possession of revenue rights with private zamindari rights, the fundamental nature of the state as a rent-extracting institution was preserved. This necessitated that association of rulers with merchants, which revenue collection on any large scale must demand. As the potentates' courts on local scale continued, and large armies were maintained, a large portion of the agrarian surplus flowed into towns, and much, though not all, of the urban glory of the past could survive. Faizabad, Farrukhabad and Lucknow were representative of this urban survival, when Delhi and Agra were fast declining. While the fact that there was still resilience in the Indian economy should not be forgotten, it is not easy to understand how any important new elements can be discerned in the economy of the first half of the eighteenth century, as Bayly's description would lead one to infer.[23]

There is one further element which tends to be forgotten about the eighteenth century—the cultural. In an essay on the decline of the Mughal Empire, I had commented on the cultural failure of the ruling class in not responding to the European challenge on the plane of technology and science. The cultural distance between India and Europe continued to lengthen in the eighteenth century; none of the regimes seemed capable of even attempts to bridge it.[24] Potentates like Haidar Ali and Mahadji Sindhia saw the challenge in military terms and tried to organize modern armies with French assistance; only Tipu went a little further by trying to develop commerce and production. But none thought in terms of establishing schools or institutions to absorb western learning or arranging for translations. In other words, not only did the eighteenth-century regimes continue with the revenue system of the Mughals, they also continued with the same ideological apparatus. It is characteristic that Shah Waliullah (d. 1762), the famous Muslim jurist and thinker, does not even show that recognition of European learning and science which was present a hundred and fifty years earlier in Abul Fazl.[25] Unaided by any conscious endeavour, Indian crafts remained supremely uninfluenced by the proto-industrialization of Europe.[26]

Little of substance has thus been presented to justify the view that there was an internal momentum towards progress or 'growth' in the first half of the eighteenth century. The picture still remains of a society in decline, despite the possible accusation that one is 'Mughal-centric' in saying so.

The second major point about the eighteenth century is whether the second half, encompassing British expansion from 1757 to 1807, can be regarded as a continuum of the first, rather than as part of a separate period. Essentially, it raises the question whether the British regime can be regarded, in its initial phase, at any rate, as one which maintained the traditional institutions and policies of the contemporary Indian states. There has been a strong belief that the '1757 Revolution' was a compromise between the English East India Company and the Hindu bankers and merchants to control the *nizamat* for mutual profit.[27] This has been built into a theory of the British conquest as an act of collaboration between the Company and powerful indigenous groups.[28]

Bayly finds the thesis 'cliché-ridden' but then goes on to express considerable sympathy with it.[29] All this finds an echo in Harbans

Mukhia's observation: 'The view that colonial society was the creation of the colonial state is also being slowly questioned.'[30] Mukhia, probably unconsciously, does us good service by putting the whole matter in such terms as to make the weakness of the position most apparent: colonial society was not the product of colonialism, but rather colonialism was the product of colonial society. How, else, would the society be 'colonial' at all?

From such an extreme statement of the case we may return to the less radical suggestion that English power was dependent on compromise and collaboration with certain indigenous groups and classes. Even this suggestion is hard to accept. There are two possible kinds of collaboration: (a) where two powers meet on an equal plane; and (b) where one power is dominant and the other collaborates because this is the only opportunity for survival or profit. In history, examples of the first are so rare as to be virtually absent, while those of the second abound. Clearly, the collaboration secured by the English from Amin Chand and Nand Kumar was of the second type; and we know what end they came to: one was defrauded, the other was hanged. If the Permanent Settlement is viewed in the light of a political compromise, such a view also needs reconsideration. Cornwallis argued for it because he thought that without a deal with the zamindars, agriculture would continue to decay and the commerce of Bengal would correspondingly contract, leaving little possibility of further growth of the Company's revenues. There was to be no collaboration between the Company and the zamindars as equals in any sense of the term. This applies to all other 'allies' of the Company as well. The merchants and bankers, whom the Company graciously allowed to continue because revenue collection was helped thereby as well as remittances of funds arranged, found their spheres of activity far more narrow than under the previous regimes. Overseas trade was closed to them, and so also much of the trade in muslin, silk, indigo and saltpetre in eighteenth-century Bengal. Finally, in the case of Subsidiary Alliances, the collaboration was decidedly one-sided. Awadh was compelled to pay a 'massive annual tribute (more than Rs 50 lakh)',[31] and in 1801, was to lose more than half of its territory to its protector.[32]

Such weighted 'collaboration' could hardly justify one's designating the British conquest as a joint Anglo-Indian enterprise. If any other view is to be dubbed 'Eurocentric', as Bayly warns us,[33] let it be so dubbed. Colonialism had blue-blooded European ancestry; and it will be wrong to make the ancestry dubious in the interest of international understanding.

One must remember that the expansion of British power in India was not simply the expansion of a politically centralizing system, a mere successor to the Mughal and the Marathas, as a rent extracting state. It was the expansion of a colonial power, essentially different in its nature and objectives from all previous regimes. The Upper Gangetic basin, that is the focus of Bayly's study, had not, unlike Bengal and Bihar, come under British control before 1801–7. Yet, already the effects of the Tribute were manifest in this area. The 'want of specie' felt in Upper India after 1770, with disastrous results for long-distance trade, which Bayly recognizes,[34] was the direct consequence of the Tribute, since it stopped all imports of specie and compelled its export to China. Bayly absolutely fails to see this connection, and thus fails to discern the impact of Colonial Tribute even in areas outside formal British control.

The inherent contradiction in Bayly's approach is, perhaps, brought out best by two passages in André Wink's *Land and Sovereignty in India*. In his introduction he acclaims Bayly's thesis of 'the indigenous component in European expansion', which brought about 'a balanced redistribution of resources rather than any overall significant corrosion'.[35] His epilogue, however, has a totally different conclusion: 'the Maratha documentation shows that it was not the "rapacity" of revenue farmers but rather the impact of the colonial government, which interfered with the circulation and diffusion of money, credit and resources.' If Wink remained unconscious of the implications of his conclusion, while framing his introduction, his reader is under no obligation to do the same.

We must therefore harbour much doubt about any theory which seeks to view eighteenth-century India as a single whole. The conventional bifurcation, as presented in old text-books, might seem to have been very formalistic, based on mere dates of battles. But it was objectively, perhaps, far closer to the realities of the social and economic history of India than the many recent theories endeavouring to present us with vistas of continuity and progress in that troubled century.

NOTES

1. Irfan Habib, *Agrarian System of Mughal India*, Bombay, 1963, p. 351.

2. C.A. Bayly, *Rulers, Townsmen, and Bazars: North Indian Society in the Age of British Expansion, 1770–1870*, Cambridge, 1983. Bayly presents his views on the eighteenth century most conveniently in the introduction, pp. 1–35.

3. Muzaffar Alam, *The Crisis of Empire in Mughal North India: Awadh and the Punjab, 1707–1748*, Delhi, 1986.

4. Frank Perlin, 'State Formation Re-considered', *Modern Asian Studies*, XIX, pt. 3, Cambridge, 1985, pp. 415–80.

5. Satish Chandra. *The 18th Century in India: Its Economy and the Role of the Marathas, the Jats, the Sikhs and the Afghans,* Calcutta, 1986, pp. 1–40.

6. André Wink *Land and Sovereignty in India—Agrarian Society and Polities under the Eighteenth-Century Maratha Soarajya*, Cambridge, 1986.

7. Muzaffar Alam, *The Crisis of Empire in Mughal North India*, p. 12.

8. Ibid., pp. 103–4. How Muzaffar Alam obtained figures for 'Moradabad-Bareilly' from the *A'in-i Akbari* is not at all clear. No such *sarkar* or administrative region existed at that time.

9. Ibid., p. 318 (italics mine).

10. Frank Perlin, *Modern Asian Studies*. p. 429.

11. Bayly, *Rulers, Townsmen, and Bazar*, p. 10.

12. Ashin Das Gupta, *Indian Merchants and the Decline of Surat, 1700–50*, Wiesbaden, 1979, p. 134f.

13. Bayly, *Rulers, Townsmen, and Bazar*, p. 14–15.

14. Irfan Habib, *Agrarian System of Mughal India*, ch. v.

15. S.P. Gupta, *The Agrarian System of Eastern Rajasthan, 1650–1750*, Delhi, 1986, pp. 1–37.

16. Iqbal Husain, *The Rise and Decline of the Ruhela Chieftances*, Delhi, 1994.

17. Satish Chandra, *Medieval India: Society, the Jagirdari Crisis and the Village*, Delhi, 1982, pp. 126–38.

18. Irfan Habib, *Agrarian System of Mughal India*, pp. 334–8.

19. *Feudalism and Non-European Societies*, ed. T. Byres and H. Mukhia, London, 1985, p. 275.

20. André Wink, *Land and Sovereignty in India*, p. 8.

21. Bayly, *Rulers, Townsmen, and Bazar*, pp. 26–7.

22. M. Athar Ali, 'The Passing of Empire: The Mughal Case', this volume, pp. 324–35. See also M. Athar Ali 'Towards an Interpretation of the Mughal Empire', this volume, pp. 54–69.

23. I cannot trace any particular remark in Bayly, where this is stated, but the entire trend in his introduction is to describe many developments in this period as if they were innovations.

24. M. Athar Ali, 'The Passing of Empire', this volume, pp. 24–35.

25. Abul Fazl was aware of the European discovery of the New World (*A'in-i Akbari*, pub. Nawal Kishore, Lucknow, 1892, vol.III) and the achievements of European learning (*Insha-i Abul Fazl, daftar*, i); see also M. Athar Ali 'Towards an Interpretation of the Mughal Empire', this volume.

26. See Tapan Raychaudhuri's remarks in *Cambridge Economic History*, vol.II, part I, ed. Dharma Kumar, Cambridge, 1982, pp. 1–25.

27. K.M. Panikkar, *Asia and Western Dominance*, New York, 1953, p. 99.

28. Cf. R.E. Robinson in *Studies in the Theory of Imperialism*, ed. R. Owen and B. Sutcliffe, London, 1972, p. 120, quoted by Bayly, *Rulers, Townsmen, and Bazar*, p. 2.

29. Bayly, ibid., pp. 3–4.

30. *Feudalism and Non-European Societies*, p. 248, n. 13.

31. Bayly, *Rulers, Townsmen, and Bazars*, p. 27.

32. The relations between the Company and Awadh have been studied by Richard B. Barnett, *North India Between Empires*, Berkeley, 1980, pp. 223–39.

33. Bayly, *Rulers, Townsmen, and Bazars*, pp. 3–4.

34. Ibid., pp. 65–6.

35. André Wink, *Land and Sovereignty in India*, p. 4.

SOURCES

29

History in Indo-Muslim Tradition

It is often said, though inaccurately, that history came with the Muslims to India. The existence of dynastic annals is attested in the epigraphic prasastis from the fourth century, and Bana's *Harshacharita* of the first half of the seventh century and Kalhana's *Rajatarangini* (twelfth century) represent important landmarks of the pre-Islamic historical tradition. But so far as we can judge, this tradition existing mainly in Sanskrit did not exercise any traceable influence on the Muslims' pursuit of *tarikh* in India, such as, let us say, the *Shahnamah* tradition exercised on Perso-Muslim historiography.

The Islamic phase of history-writing in India began with a remarkable Arabic work of unknown title and authorship, its Persian translation made, *c.* 613/1216–17, by Ali bin Hamid Kufi, now known as the *Chachnama*. The work consists essentially of two parts, an account of the Brahman dynasty of Sind preceding the Arab conquest, and a narrative of the Arab conquest 710–14. The former part is seemingly a translation of a local dynastic chronicle, and the latter and larger portion, a collection of narratives of the nature of those contained in Tabari's great history with the Arab and tribal biases of individual narrators being fairly well manifest. Except for one interpolation, at the end, the original Arabic text seems to have been completed during the ninth century, though some material may indeed be much earlier.

Indo-Persian historiography proper begins with Hasan Nizami's very ornate work, *Tajal Ma'athir*, completed 1217, dealing with the first two Sultans of Delhi. But the first major work is Minhaj bin Siraj Jjuzdjani's *Tabaqat-i Nasiri*, completed 1259, a history of Islamic dynasties, but very rich on the Ghorid dynasty, the early Sultans of India and their nobles and on the contemporary Mongol empire, for which too it constitutes a valuable contemporary record.

A series of historical works by the poet Amir Khusrau, (d. 1325), namely the *Qiran al Sa'dain* (1289), *Miftah al Futuh* (1291), *Khazain al Futuh* (1311–12), *Duwal Rani Khadir Khan* (1316), *Nuh-sipihr* (1318) and *Tughluqnama* (1320) give rather uneven glimpses into the history of the period, especially the Khalji dynasty (1290–1320).

Despite their contemporariness to the events they describe, the poet's proneness to verse, stylistic digressions, words with double meanings and complicated rhetoric deprive his works of much substance, and flattery overshadows insights and truth.

A totally different kind of work, and, perhaps, one entitled to be treated as a true history under any definition of it is Ziya Barani's *Tarikh-i Firuz Shahi*, completed 1357, treating of the history of the Delhi Sultanate from Balban's accession in 1265 to Firuz Tughluq's early years. Barani has a definite theory of history, in which the Sultan's natural urge to aggrandize is seen as a threat to the stability of the nobility, which in his view, must be based on respect for station according to birth. Barani is masterly in his sketches of character, brilliant in his insights on complicated economic situations and administrative measures. His fluent and trenchant style, unaffected by any attempt at ornateness, makes him one of the great Indian masters of Persian prose.

Compared to Barani, the other two histories of the Delhi Sultans, Isami's versified *Futuh-al Salatin* (1349–50) and Yahya Sirhindi's *Tarikh-i Mubarak Shahi* (1434) are prosaic works, though furnishing us with much information derived independently of Barani. Shams Siraj Afif has left us a history of Firuz Shah (r. 1351–1388), written after Timur's invasion (1398)), which manages to be factual (though somewhat weak in dates) despite much rhetoric.

The fifteenth and early sixteenth centuries saw the production of a few histories of provincial dynasties, such as the anonymous *Tarikh-i Muzaffar Shahi* (1484) and *Zamima-i Ma'athir-i Mahmud Shahi* (1511)) relating to Gujarat and Shihab Hakim's *Ma'athir-i Mahmud Shahi* (completed before 1500), relating to Malwa. Rather surprisingly, no history of the two Afghan dynasties, the Lodis (1450–1526) and the Surs (1540–1556) was written during the period of their rule. Of the Lodis, there is the later *Waqi'at-i Mushtaqi*, by Rizq Allah 'Mushtaqi', (d. 1581), a work of an anecdotal character but the main source for later accounts of the Lodis; and for the Surs, Abbas Sarwani's *Tuhfa-i Akbarshahi* (written after 1579) remains the main source.

The establishment of the Mughal dynasty, with Babur's victory at Panipat (1526), inaugurated a new era in history writing. Babur (d. 1530) continued the writing of his Turki memoirs in India, so that he has given us a fascinating account of India and a frank description of the events of a large part of his reign of four years in India. These memoirs were translated into Persian with commendable accuracy by Abdur Rahim Khan-i Khanan (1589–90).

With Yazdi's *Zafarnama* setting the model for Timurid history writing, the greatest historical work which took it for its model but undoubtedly went much beyond it is Abul Fazl's *Akbarnama*, first text completed in 1004/1596. This official history of Babur, Humayun and Akbar not only used a large amount of archival material, but also a number of especially commissioned memoirs among which only few survive, such as those of Gulbadan Begam and Bayazid Bayat as well as historical narratives especially sponsored to provide material, of which Abbas Sarwani's work mentioned above is one. Abul Fazl has a much larger vision of history than mere annals, and he therefore appended to his narrative history, what came to be considered a separate work, the *A'in-i Akbari* containing massive fiscal, financial and social data, a detailed provincial gazetteer and a cultural history of India. The work provides a fairly firm baseline for a quantitative history of India. It is also remarkable in being without any religious bias and in treating Indian culture as a composite one to which both Hindu and Muslim traditions have contributed.

Akbar's reign saw the production of the first general history of India, Nizam al-Din Ahmad's *Tabaqat-i Akbari* (1593–94). Especially notable was his endeavour to reconstruct the history of provincial dynasties as part of the political history of India. He was followed by Qasim Hindu-Shah 'Firishta', who in his *Gulshan-i Ibrahimi* (1015/1606–7) gave a still more detailed history of the country, and showed considerable critical sense in using his sources. Abd al-Qadir Badauni completed his *Muntakhab al-Tawarikh* in 1595–96, another history of India which draws much of its information from Nizam al-Din's work. But he concentrates on Akbar's reign, of whose events he gives a trenchantly critical interpretation from an orthodox Muslim point of view. His biographical sketches of scholars and other celebrities in his concluding portion forms a special feature of his work.

Jahangir (r. 1605–1627) followed Babur in writing his memoirs. These are in Persian and appear to have begun to be written like a diary soon after his accession to continue up to 1624. Jahangir writes in simple but literary prose with a surprising degree of frankness; and his deep interest in art and in natural history as well as the life of ordinary people particularly enlivens his memoirs for the modern reader.

With Shah Jahan (r. 1628–1658) begins another series of official histories. First, Muhammad Amin Qazwini was commissioned to write the *Padshahnama*, based on official records. His account covered the first ten years of Shah Jahan's reign. A shift from the solar to lunar calendar for dating events, and perhaps other reasons, led Shah

Jahan to commission Abdul Hamid Lahauri to write the history of these ten years afresh. Lahauri ultimately produced a very detailed account of the twenty years (lunar) of Shah Jahan's reign under the title *Padshahnama*. The account of the third decade was prepared, as a continuation by his pupil Muhammad Waris. Aurangzeb (r. 1659–1707) had the history of the first ten years of his reign, entitled the *Alamgir Nama*, written by Muhammad Kazim. All these official histories have some features in common. They are accurate as to dates and details, for which official records are their main source; they pay much attention to geography; and their authors are anxious to convey to the reader the imperial view, whether in commendation or criticism of individuals or on assessment of causes and consequences of various events. Their model is Abul Fazl, for the narration of events, though they obviously do not share his views on religion (now no longer official), nor his very large vision of history that had embraced, as we have seen, the full range of economic and cultural life.

Since Aurangzeb did not allow any further official history to be written after 1668, the era of private histories began. The most notable was Abul Fazl Mamuri's untitled history, which was almost entirely incorporated in Khafi Khan's well-known *Muntakhab al-Lubab* (1731), a general history of India. Mamuri's critical approach was shared by Bhim Sen, a Hindu officer, whose *Nuskha-i Dilkusha* (1709) is a combination of history and memoirs, written with much candour and insight (e.g. his discussion of the agrarian roots of the Maratha uprising). Saqi Mustaid Khan's *Ma'athir-i Alamgiri* (1710–11) is designed to provide an ostensibly official history of Aurangzeb's reign, and therefore follows the style of such histories, but is much briefer. Aurangzeb's reign is also marked by the appearance of Hindu historians writing in Persian: besides Bhim Sen, we have Isardas Nagar and Sujan Rai Bhandari.

Historical works in Persian became still more numerous in the eighteenth century. Khafi Khan's history has already been mentioned. An anonymous work, *Tarikh-i Shivaji*, written before 1777, consciously presents the Maratha point of view on Shivaji, which is based on a Marathi narration or *bakhar*.

Perhaps the most interesting historical work of this late phase is Ghulam Husain Khan Tabatabai's *Siyar al-Mutakhirin* (completed 1781), covering the period from 1707 in great detail. Its close account of the English East India Company's conquests and government, and strong criticism of the practices of that government have assured it of a large readership, especially through Hajji Mustafa's celebrated translation (1789). It belongs partly to the genre of works produced under Englishmen's patronage, such as Ghulam Ali Khan's *Imad al Sa'adat* (completed 1808), relating to Awadh, and Lachhmi Narayan 'Shafiq's' *Bisat al Ghanaim* (1799), a history of the Marathas down to 1761.

Modern historiography began to exercise its influence in the nineteenth century. Sayyid Ahmad Khan wrote the *Athar al Sanadid* in Urdu in 1847 on the buildings of Delhi; and his young friend Zakaullah produced the first history of India in Urdu containing results of modern research and first published in 1898.

A discipline which followed a tradition distinct from history was that of biography. The biographical notices of twenty-five slave-officers of Sultan Iltutmish (*maluk-i Shamsi*) that Minhaj Siraj gave in the *Tabaqat-i Nasiri* find no sequel in historical works of the succeeding generations. But with the Mughals a new tradition of bureaucratic biography began: on Abdur Rahim Khan-i Khanan was written a long biographical work, the *Ma'athir-i Rahimi* by Abd al-Baqi Nahavandi in 1616; and Ni'matallah included in his *Tarikh-i Khan Jahani* (1613), a full biography of his patron, Khan-i Jahan Lodi, another officer of Jahangir. The pioneering step towards compiling a comprehensive biographical dictionary of the Mughal nobility was taken by Shaikh Farid Bhakkari in his *Zakhirat al Khawanin* (1060/1650), the result of extensive reading and collection of oral information. Much of his work was incorporated, along with other massive data independently collected from other histories, epistolary collections and records, in the *Ma'athir al Umara* of Shah Nawaz Khan, Azad Bilgrami and Abd al-Haiy (finally completed, 1780), which contains over 730 biographies. A much smaller work of a similar kind, but earlier, was Kewal Ram's *Tazkirat al-Umara*, 1727–28.

The biographical literature on religious divines begins with Mir Khurd's *Siyar al-Auliya* (completed before 1387), a fairly detailed and reliable narrative of the lives of the Indian Chishti saints from Muin al-Din Chishti (d. 1236) onwards. A subsequent work on fourteen Chishti saints, the *Siyar al-Arifin* of Shaikh Jamali (d. 1536), is less reliable but obtained considerable popularity. With Abd al-Haqq's *Akhbar al-Akhyar* (1591) began the tradition of compilation of biographical dictionaries of Indian saints without distinction of mystic affiliation. Ghausi Shattari's *Gulzar-i Abrar* (1613) is a similar but much more comprehensive work, beginning with saints of the thirteenth century, and is undoubtedly the result of great care and industry.

Sadid al-Din Aufi's *Lubab al-Albab*, with biographical notices of some three hundred poets, technically belongs to India since it was written (1221–22) under Qubacha, the ruler of Sind. But the first major work of this genre was Ala al-Daula Kami's *Nafais al-Ma'athir* (begun 1565–66), written under Akbar, giving notices of some 350 poets, all of his own century (sixteenth). Subsequent biographical dictionaries of poets include Sher Khan Lodi's *Mirat al Khayal* (1690–91), Brindabandas's *Safina-i Khwushgu* (1734–35), Azad Bilgrami's *Sarw-i Azad* (1752–53) and Lutf Ali Beg's *Atishkada* (begun 1760–61). They are poetry selections as well, since each biographical notice is invariably followed by the author's selection of verses from that poet. It was partly by reliance on such biographical dictionaries of poets, besides the information personally collected, that the *Ab-i Hayat* by Muhammad Husain Azad came to be written (1880), combining the biographical dictionary form with a truly historical treatment of the Urdu language and literature.

Among the more general biographical dictionaries covering scholars, mystics, theologians and poets, possibly the most noteworthy is that by Muhammad Sadiq, the *Tabaqat-i Shahjahani* (1637), containing the lives of some 871 celebrities. A different kind of work is Mirza Muhammad's *Tarikh-i Muhammadi* (completed 1776) giving obituary notices of prominent men in chronological sequence, according to the years of their death.

With the introduction of the results of modern Indological/Orientalist research in Indian historiography, it becomes very difficult to demarcate the Indo-Muslim stream from the general stream of South Asian historiography. Two trends may, however, be identified: the Indian nationalist, which emphasized the Muslim contribution to a composite Indian culture, and the separatist, which insisted on the study of Muslim community as an independent political, social and cultural entity. The nationalist point of view found early expression in Mohammad Habib's *Mahmud of Ghaznin* (1924), a critical tract on that conqueror, and in Tara Chand's *Influence of Islam on Indian Culture* (1922). The most comprehensive statement of the nationalist viewpoint perhaps occurs in M. Mujeeb's *Indian Muslims* (1967). The opposite school came to be represented particularly in the writings of Ishtiaq Husain Qureshi, especially in his *The Muslim Community of the Indo-Pakistan Subcontinent 610–1947*. The debate continues at various levels of historical writing in India, Pakistan and Bangladesh, with the Aligarh School of historians making its own contribution.

SELECT BIBLIOGRAPHY

The major work on Indo-Islamic historical works remains H.H. Elliot and J. Dowson, *History of India as Told by its Own Historians*, 8 vols, London, 1867–77. The sources in Persian are surveyed in C.A. Storey, *Persian Literature-A Bio-bibliographical Survey*, I, Parts I (London, 1927–39) and II (London, 1953). Other relevant works include Peter Hardy, *Historians of Medieval India*, London, 1960; Mohibbul Hasan (ed.), *Historians of Medieval India*, Meerut, 1983; Harbans Mukhia, *Historians and Historiography During the Reign of Akbar*, New Delhi, 1976. See also M.Athar Ali, 'The Use of Sources in Mughal Historiography', this volume, pp. 355–72.

30

The Use of Sources in Mughal Historiography

India during the period of the Mughal dynasty (sixteenth-eighteenth centuries) is exceptionally well illuminated by a large body of historical literature, mainly in Persian. This literature followed the traditions of classical Persian historiography, the models of which like Yazdi's *Zafarnama* (a history of Timur) and Mir Khwand's *Rauzatu's Safa* (a history of the world), both written in the fifteenth century, were widely read in India. By its very volume, if nothing else, Mughal historiography has, however, to be studied and assessed separately. It may be recalled that when C.A. Storey made his great survey of Persian historical literature, works written on Indian history accounted for a major part of it providing 475 items, by authors (nos 612–1087), as against 299 (nos 312–611) concerned with Persia, Central Asia and countries other than India.[1] And among the works written in India those written in Mughal times again account for the overwhelmingly larger part.

Indo-Mughal historical literature is not only large, but also varied: histories of India, dynastic and regional histories, memoirs, biographies, biographical dictionaries, historical gazetteers, collections of historical letters and administrative documents are all well represented.[2] What we are concerned with here is how their authors acquired their information, from what kinds of sources and with what exercises of the critical faculty. In turn this may help us to assess the accuracy of the information that comes to us from such a large body of professedly historical writing. We can, of course, treat only of a few of these works, by way of illustration, so that some tentative conclusions may be hazarded.

I

It may be useful to proceed from the most secondary (or general) to the more primary or detailed works. In dealing with the secondary works, one must recognize the tendency in many of them of incorporating earlier texts, often without acknowledgement, which today would be regarded as gross plagiarism, but which enabled the author then to transmit to his reader a more authoritative narrative of an earlier period than he could himself presumably construct.

A very notable example of this is offered by Khafi Khan, author of the well-known history of the Mughal dynasty, the *Muntakhabu'l Lubab*, completed in 1731. He seems to have come across a little-known work, the *Shahjahan-Nama* of Sadiq Khan, containing a history of Shah Jahan's reign (1627–58) and its continuation by Abul Fazl Mamuri containing an account of Aurangzeb's reign (1659–1707). The work has survived independently (British Library MS Or. 174) as well as with its continuation (British Library Or. 1671, and Raza Library, Rampur). Both authors gave numerous personal details, some so patently fictitious that one is led to think that the authors have adopted pseudonyms. Now Khafi Khan, perhaps knowing of this fact, bodily incorporated these two works into his book, personal details and all, to form his chapters on Shah Jahan and Aurangzeb. British Library MSS Add. 6573 and 6574, appear to represent the first phase of this incorporation. Subsequently, while revising the text for his final version, contained in most MSS of his work as well as in the printed edition,[3] Khafi Khan weeded out many (but not all) of the plagiarized writers' personal details, changed the wordings, made condensations, altered opinions and substantially added to the narrative of the later years of Aurangzeb's reign. If Sadiq Khan's work and Abul Fazl Mamuri's continuation had not survived, one would have always wondered about the sources of Khafi Khan's information for the reigns of Shah Jahan and Aurangzeb, since with an obvious lack of ethics, Khafi Khan conceals from his reader the text from which he has borrowed wholesale.

Yet this lapse was not universal. The first history of India (as claimed by the author himself) now known is the *Tabaqat-i Akbari*, written in 1594, by one of Akbar's best educated officers, Nizamuddin Ahmad Bakhshi. In his preface, Nizamuddin lists twenty-nine works (virtually all surviving) from which he has drawn his information.[4]

How Nizamuddin Ahmad uses his sources may be seen from his account of Ghiyasuddin Tughluq's death in 1324.[5] First he gives the account as he had found in his main source, Zia Barani's *Tarikh-i Firuz Shahi*[6] (completed in 1357). The Sultan was returning from Bengal and was to be received at Afghanpur about three kurohs (about six miles) from Tughluqabad (Delhi), where a pavilion had been rapidly constructed for the purpose of his reception by his son, Ulugh Khan (Muhammad Tughluq), coming from the south. After they met and a

meal had been taken, most nobles came out to wash their hands. At
that time suddenly the roof fell, and the Sultan, who was sitting beneath
it, was killed. Nizamuddin omits Barani's reference to this having
been caused by lightning, perhaps because he thought the words 'sky-
sent thunderbolt of fate' to be mere rhetoric. For the cause of the fall
of the roof he shifts to another source ('some histories'), which
happens to be Isami's *Futuh us Salatin* (completed, 1351), which he
lists in his Preface as a source along with Barani's *Tarikh*. Isami, who
was hostile to Muhammad Tughluq, says the roof fell because the
Sultan ordered elephants to be driven at speed in front of the pavilion,
whereupon the newly constructed structure collapsed and a pillar fell
upon the Sultan killing him.[7] Nizamuddin takes this to be the true
cause of the accident, but then he adds a comment, showing that he
is not satisfied that the death was purely accidental:

From the discerning ones it would not be hidden that it was not at all
necessary to construct the pavilion. One is led to suspect that Ulugh
Khan conspired to kill his father. It seems that the author of the *Tarikh-i
Firuz Shahi* (Zia Barani), writing in the reign of Sultan Firuz, who had great
attachment to Sultan Muhammad Tughluq, did not write (the truth) out of
regard for him.[8]

Here then, is a criticism of his source as well as an explanation why
the source has departed from the truth. It is all the more remarkable
since Isami does not explicitly make Muhammad Tughluq the murderer.

The same incident is also examined by the next important author
of a history of India, Qasim Hindu-Shah Firishta, who completed his
history, the *Gulshan-i Ibrahimi (Tarikh-i Firishta)* in 1606–7, then
revised it in 1609–10. His history is remarkable because he uses the
Mahabharata (in Persian translation) to attempt a reconstruction of
pre-Islamic Indian history. All in all, he lists in Preface some thirty-
two texts (a list which is, indeed, not exhaustive), which he had used
for writing his history.[9] These included Nizamuddin Ahmad's history.
Firishta, describing Ghiyasuddin Tughluq's death, says he perished
under the falling roof with five other persons and then adds:

In some histories it is written that the pavilion was newly built and collapsed
because of the fast tread of the elephants. Some historians have stated
that there was no need to construct such a building, so that one is led to
suspect that Ulugh Khan conspired to kill his father, and that Zia Barani,
who lived in the time of Firuz Shah, who had great attachment to Sultan
Muhammad (Tughluq), did not write the truth out of regard for him. But it
would not be concealed from the discerning ones that this story does not
stand to reason. For Ulugh Khan was present at the meal along with his

father. How would he have the miraculous power to make the roof fall the moment he himself came out? More colourful still is the story given by Sadr Jahan Gujarati in his *Tarikh* that Ulugh Khan had erected the building by magic. When the magic was broken, the roof fell! Haji Muhammad Qandahari in his *Tarikh* writes that when the Sultan was washing his hands, lightning fell from the sky and piercing the roof struck his head. This story seems to be nearest the truth. But God knows best![10]

It is obvious that Firishta had, first, the text of Nizamuddin Ahmad before him, relying on his reading of both Barani and Isami (whether Firishta had access to the latter is not clear: his work is not listed in his Preface). He then weighs Nizamuddin Ahmad's theory and finds it implausible. And when he turns to Sadr Jahan's version,[11] he absolutely rejects magic as an explanation. He accepts Muhammad Qandahari's attribution of the accident to lightning, which, of course, is not his, but the contemporary historian Barani's version (overlooked by Nizamuddin Ahmad).

These two standard authors' treatment of sources for one incident brings out both the strength and weakness of Mughal historiography. Its strength was that it was eminently rational. In his scepticism over the death being accidental, Nizamuddin Ahmad points to the irrationality of the pavilion being constructed. In his rejection of the conspiracy theory, Firishta raises the question of the technical impossibility of so setting up a structure that it should collapse at the precise time desired. The weaknesses in both historians' treatment are also obvious. Nizamuddin Ahmad speaks vaguely of 'histories' when he means Isami's *Futuh-us Salatin*, a work written twenty-six years after the incident. He fails to highlight the fact that its account is virtually contemporaneous. Firishta shows much sloppiness in ignoring the contemporary Zia Barani's reference to 'lightning', though he was closely familiar with Barani's History and censures him a few pages later for omitting the account of Tarmashirin's raid.[12] In rejecting one source for another he does not at all consider which source is early: for Qazi Muhammad Qandahari, of whose copying of Barani Firishta is not aware, was writing much later, though, since his work is not extant, his exact date of writing is not known.

II

Hitherto we have considered the treatment only of historical works as sources. For the more general works, the source-material of the historian would naturally be confined to such texts. But for pioneer writers of detailed works, concerned with the history of a region or of a single recent reign, it would not be possible to depend only on other secondary works. The historian would then certainly need to use primary documents or archival sources.

In the Mughal period it was quite customary to collect the documents, including letters, of a historical nature. This was done partly with a view to studying the style of such documents, so as to train the reader in *insha*, or the science of drafting, and partly with a view to satisfying the interest of those who were historically inclined.

A major collection of this genre was made by Abul Qasim Khan Namkin under the title of *Munshat-i namkin* in 1594, containing an exceptionally large number of diplomatic and political letters, farmans (imperial orders) and administrative documents.[13] A smaller collection of documents and letters drafted by Akbar's minister and court-historian Abul Fazl was made in 1606–7.[14] The reign of Aurangzeb is marked by a number of important collections, such as those of his own letters, notably, the *Adab-i Alamgiri* compiled by Muhammad Sadiq[15] and *Kalimat-i Tayyabat*, collected by Inayatullah Khan.[16] In the 1680s Malikzada collected a large number of documents, diplomatic and historical, in the *Nigarnama-i Munshi*.[17] It is not possible to list many other such collections that exist in MS. Suffice it to mention the anonymous collection of documents relating to all sorts of matters, administrative, commercial, agrarian, private, judicial, mainly of Surat and its environs of the period *c.* 1590–1647/48, made by a person who was presumably a local Mughal official,[18] and the collection of letters of a local revenue official of Haryana made into part of a book by the author, Balkrishan Brahman, in the early 1660s.[19]

The actual use of such documents for historical purposes by Mughal writers is fairly common. One can cite as an illustration, the history of the Mughal suba of Gujarat, the *Mirat-i Ahmadi*, written by Ali Muhammad Khan in 1759–60. He says that he reconstructed the history of the province by using the detailed official histories of successive reigns, by drawing upon the memory of older people, and since 1708–9, upon his own observations. He states that upon his own appointment as diwan (finance officer) of Gujarat (by now a largely nominal post), he came into possession of the depleted archives of the office, and in 1748, with his assistant Mitha Lal Kayasth, he began to compile a comprehensive record of the resources and revenues of Gujarat which presumably forms the Supplement of his History.[20]

What is of great interest from our point of view is that Ali Muhammad Khan intersperses his narrative by copying into it in strict chronological order numerous documents, notably farmans containing fiscal and other regulations, most of which, not being found in any other known collection, must have been collected by him from other persons. After copying a farman issued by Aurangzeb to Muhammad Hashim, 'diwan' of Gujarat, he mourns the fact that 'despite imperial instructions accompanying such Imperial farmans that whenever the office of diwan was transferred to another person, the farmans, which contain the basic administrative regulations should be transferred to the new appointee, with receipt taken, yet owing to certain circumstances and the ensuing disarray, these farmans are no longer in the (diwan's) office.'[21] It is, therefore, considerably to Ali Muhammad Khan's credit that he should have obtained and reproduced so many official documents, with their rich information on the agrarian and commercial conditions of Gujarat. Where he has not, presumably for reasons of space, been able to reproduce documents, he summarizes their import and describes their context fairly competently.[22] Generally speaking, Ali Muhammad Khan is successful in reproducing documents accurately, despite the damaged state or bad transcription of some of the papers or copies he had at hand, which he laments.[23] But he seldom offers any helpful commentaries on many of the terms used or clarifies obscurities. And, generally, while conscientious in setting each document within his narrative by its date, he seldom allows himself the leisure to speculate on its cause or consequence or the effectiveness of implementation.

It is much to the credit of Mughal-period compilers of documents and of historians, like Ali Muhammad Khan, who reproduce them, that, except for copyists' errors, the reproductions are faithful. Such faithful reproductions might have been encouraged by the system in the Mughal Empire, where the copy of a document to be usable in litigation or representation had to have the attestation with the seal of the qazi, or local judge. The only case where the reproduced text diverges substantially from the original is the reproduction of the imperial farman of Shah Jahan of February 1632 sent to be inscribed on the Srinagar congregational mosque. The text, as reproduced by the official historian, Amin Qazwini in the *Padshahnama*, when compared with the actual inscription turns out to be a heavily 'sanitized' version, toning down the censure of the preceding governor.[24] But in fairness it may be said that Amin Qazwini does not explicitly claim to reproduce the farman and does not, for example, have the first person plural which the text of the farman, if exactly reproduced, would have required.[25]

For most official histories, the basic documentation was provided by waqai or reports of the proceedings at the court and events in the provinces, the letters sent by the *Waqai Navis* posted in the provinces, to the central minister, designated *bakhshi ul mamalik*, who presented these to the emperor. When Saqi Musta'id Khan was offered the task of writing a surrogate official history for the reign of Aurangzeb (after the tenth regnal year, till which the reign had already been covered by the officially compiled *Alamgirnama*), he argued that 'if the sheets of the news-letters (waqai) of the court and the provinces be collected, then the work of the composition may be accomplished with ease'.[26] The waqai prepared in the Deccan provinces have been preserved in the archives at Hyderabad, and a selection of them for the period 1660–71 has been published.[27] The waqai of the *suba* of Ajmer for over two years, 1678–80 have also come down to us.[28] Unfortunately, the archives of the Mughal central government have not survived, and the waqai of the imperial court are not extant, although their nature can be established from both the provincial waqai and the *akhbarat* from the imperial court (for which see below).

It is manifest that the official histories, beginning with Abul Fazl's *Akbarnama* (to whose use of sources, a separate section will be here devoted), the *Padshahnamas* of Amin Qazwini, Abdul Hamid Lahori, and Waris, and the *Alamgir Nama* of Muhammad Kazim, all drew their chronology and information on court movements, appointments, conferments of ranks and titles, major events of the campaigns, etc. from the waqai of the court and the provinces.[29] It is also likely that Jahangir's celebrated memoirs were also written with the waqai kept in front of the imperial diarist.[30] All these texts often begin individual passages with the words *az waqai*, which can be rendered either as 'from the *waqai*' or as 'among the reported events'.

Non-official historians could have had access to a species of reports called akhbarat, which are often confused with the waqai. The akhbarat were not really records of the Mughal government proper, but news-reports sent by nobles and high officers' agents (*wakils*)) at the imperial court and at governors' headquarters in the provinces. The wakils were allowed to be present at the court or headquarters and to witness the proceedings, hear the waqai and petitions being read out and the orders issued by the emperor or governor thereon. When sent by wakils posted at the court these were known as *Akhbarat-i Darbar-i Mu'alla*. A large collection of the akhbarat sent by the wakils of the rulers of Amber from the beginning of Aurangzeb's reign have survived, reposing partly in the library of the Royal Asiatic

Society, London (James Tod having removed these from the archives of Jaipur), and partly in the Rajasthan State Archives. A selection from these has been published.[31] The *akhbars* sent from the Mughal court in the eighteenth century by Maratha wakils have been preserved at Pune and partly published. Stray akhbarat are also widely found. Apparently, these were also passed on to non-officials such as bankers, merchants, etc. Thus, in 1717 the English East India Company appointed 'Mittersein' (Mitra Sen) as its 'vakile at the kings Durbar', but without divulging his position, 'his business being to transmit the Durbar news' twice every month along with the *'wackas'* (waqai) to Bengal.[32] Akhbarat from the court are copied wholesale into Itimad Ali Khan's diary, the *Mirat ul Haqaiq*, carried on till 1139/1727, and kept mainly at Surat.[33] Since he was a retired official, these were presumably obtained from local bankers (*sarrafa*) whose messengers regularly arrived from Delhi, and who needed to have such akhbarat for their business purposes.

It is important to remember that unlike the waqai, the akhbarat were not properly official documents. They recorded the proceedings (including reports given and orders issued) at the court, as the wakil heard and recorded at the time.[34] These sometimes contain errors, e.g. of spellings of names or titles or discrepancies in numbers of ranks which would be inconceivable in the official waqai. Still, in most cases of unofficial historians who offer us day-to-day details of the happenings at the court, e.g. Hadi Kamwar Khan in his account of events after Aurangzeb's death (1707) to 1724 in the early part of Muhammad Shah's reign,[35] it is not always clear whether the author has direct access to the waqai (or *sawanih*), or whether he is mentioning their contents as they were presented at the court and recorded in the akhbarat.

III

Much stress is currently being laid on 'oral history'. It is, of course, worth recalling that much of the history that has come down to us through the pages of Mughal-period writers was not simply built up from written records, but was based on the writers' own memory of events of which they were witness or on mere hearsay. By their very nature narratives so constructed would span a wide range of degrees of reliability.

First of all, we have the memoirs of a man who was barely literate, and so unable himself to use any records at all. This was Mehtar

Jauhar Aftabchi, an attendant of the Mughal emperors Humayun (reigned, 1530–56) and Akbar. He seems to have written or dictated his memoirs soon after Humayun's death (1556), since to him the capital was still Delhi, and the later rebel, Abul-Maali is still spoken of in sympathetic terms.[36] He says in his preface that he began to write in 1587 for presentation to Akbar; but this must refer to his handing over the manuscript to Ilahdad Faizi Sirhindi, who was himself to write a history of Akbar's reign. Faizi Sirhindi was asked to 'rewrite the manuscript in the manner of histories and in proper style'.[37] Faizi Sirhindi presented his polished version of Jauhar's memoirs (*Tarikh-i Humayun*) to Akbar on the night of 18 June 1590. The emperor asked immediately: 'Jauhar does not know how to write; how have you prepared his memoirs?'[38]

Faizi Sirhindi's version, when compared to Jauhar's artless original, shows how 'oral history' can lose much of its charm and truth when handled by a 'professional'. Sirhindi edited out many of the lively and informal pieces of information found in the original, especially in the report of Akbar's birth. Inaccuracies too were introduced: Jauhar in his original had spoken of the people of Panjhir who were like the Siyah-posh Kafirs; now they became the Siyah-posh Kafirs themselves.[39] Yet, it was not the original semi-colloquial version of Jauhar, but Faizi Sirhindi's polished and sanitized text, which was more widely read and, presumably, used. The King's College MS shows by its fly-leaf endorsements that it went into the libraries successively of Akbar's aunt, Gulbadan Begum, Jahangir, Shah Jahan and Dara Shukoh between 1603 and 1651.

Unlettered, Jauhar had relied mainly on his memory, which must have been fresh enough at the time he first dictated his memoirs. But with the more educated memoir-writers, memory and reading of record went together. Babur (reigned 1526–30) seems to have kept a diary in later years on which his celebrated autobiography was constructed; the earlier portion with all its details (but few dates) was purely based on memory.[40]

Jahangir (reigned 1605–27) did not aim at full autobiography, but a continuous narrative of his reign. He thus obviously used the waqai and other documents and secretarial resources of the court to write successive parts of his memoirs, which always possess the quality of close contemporaneity.[41] Fasciculi of these memoirs seem to have been distributed among officers, from time to time. Ni'matullah, writing the biography of his patron, Khan-i Jahan Lodi, as early as February 1613, was able to use as a source 'the history called

Jahangirnama, which His Majesty had been writing as diary (*roznamcha*)'.[42] Upon completion of twelve years of his reign, Jahangir had volumes of copies prepared for distribution, as he himself says.[43]

Jahangir's memoirs, because of the access they give us to many facts which could never have been put in the waqai or akhbarat, such as Jahangir's relations with individual nobles, and to his own private ambitions, opinions, beliefs and judgement, are a unique document. As Ni'matullah shows, they became, while they were in the process of writing, a source for contemporary historians. They, therefore, called for rival accounts of Jahangir's reign, more suited to the point of view of his son and successor Shah Jahan (reigned 1629–58), whose conduct Jahangir had heavily criticized. Thus Mu'tamad Khan, to whom Jahangir had dictated his memoirs in his later years, wrote a separate history of Jahangir, which also became the third volume of his historical work *Iqbalnama-i Jahangiri*.[44] Even more than Mutamad Khan's work, Kamgar Husaini's *Maasir-i Jahangiri*, completed in 1630, is little more than a shorter version of Jahangir's memoirs with the addition of some facts and omissions of others, designed to produce an effect hostile to Jahangir's influential queen, Nur Jahan, and favourable to Shah Jahan.[45] Thus, through these summaries Jahangir's memoirs became the quarry for facts of other 'secondary' historians, e.g. Muhammad Yusuf Ataki, who wrote his *Muntakhab-ut Tawarikh* in 1646–47.[46]

A contrary process, where an existing 'secondary' history is heavily added to from memory and current observation is offered by Abdul Qadir Badauni. What Badauni did for his history of Akbar's reign (forming the second volume of his *Muntakhab-ut Tawarikh*) was to take volume two of his friend Shaikh Nizamuddin Ahmad's *Tabaqat-i Akbari*, containing a year-by-year account of Akbar, summarize or rewrite it and add heavily what he had himself, as a scholar with influential friends and patrons and subsequently as a courtier, observed or heard, providing a parallel, heavily critical and even (at times) scandalous version to the detriment of the reputation and integrity of Akbar and other notables.[47] He admits that for the last two years covered by his history, he did not have the benefit of Nizamuddin Ahmad's history, which had closed in 1594, its author having died then. He confesses that he had been compelled to offer 'more summary annals' thereafter.[48] He makes up for it, however, by a more richly gossipy account of what was happening at Akbar's court at Lahore, and of what heresies he himself as an orthodox theologian was being compelled to witness. Similarly, for his third volume, Badauni seems to have relied heavily on the biographical dictionary of contemporary scholars and poets, the *Nafaisul Ma'asir* of Alaud Daula,[49] and then to have added massively from his own knowledge of many of the persons included in the collection of biographies, while adding notices of others not included there, especially mentioning incidents of which he was witness or of which he had heard.

Badauni's work, by so enriching and embellishing the dull annals from which he drew his skeleton of facts, became the favourite source for all historians looking for lively or critical versions of the liberal religious environment at Akbar's court. The first author who actually cites him is 'Mobad', who wrote in 1653 his great work on the various religions of the world, the *Dabistan-i Mazahib*.[50] Badauni's influence in constructing a hostile portrayal of Akbar does not, however, seem to have been strongly felt in the seventeenth century; it seems to have grown later with time, attaining its height not in Mughal historiography, but in its Anglo-Indian successor.[51]

IV

In visualizing the way historians sought to reconstruct the past in Mughal India, there is no better illustration than the fashion in which Akbar's counsellor Abul Fazl prepared his history of the Mughal dynasty, but principally of Akbar's reign. Its third daftar or volume, comprising the *A'in-i Akbari*, treated as a separate work, was to deal with Akbar's administration and empire and the culture and cultural history of India.[52] Abul Fazl was directed by Akbar to prepare such a history in 1589, and he says he took seven years over it, closing the work in 1596, but then continuing to work on the *A'in-i Akbari* till 1599, and carrying on the *Akbarnama* narrative to 1600.[53]

In the conclusion appended to the *A'in-i Akbari*, but which actually is the conclusion to the entire work, Abul Fazl describes how he collected material for his work:

In many of these occurrences I bore a personal share, and I had a perfect knowledge of the undercurrents and secrets of state, to say nothing of the ordinary drift of public affairs. And since the insinuation of rumour had prejudiced me, and I was not sure of my own memory, I made various enquiries of the principal officers of state, and of the grandees and well informed dignitaries, and not content with numerous oral statements, I asked permission to put them into writing, and for each event I took the written testimony of more than twenty intelligent and cautious persons.[54]

One may smile at the author's boast that for each event he had so many recorded testimonies. But we know for a fact that memories of persons who were expected to know of events of the earlier period (Akbar's early years of life and reign) were especially tapped. Thus, Bayazid Biyat, an old officer now employed as Superintendent of the imperial kitchen, tells us in the preface of his memoirs:

His Glorious Majesty Jalaluddin Muhammad Akbar Padshah ordered that whoever from amongst the Imperial servants has the capacity of recording history should do so. Especially they should record any thing that they remember from the times of His late Majesty Humayun Padshah, and complete it, dedicating it in Our name. This order was delivered to this humble Bayazid Biyat by His Highness the exalted Shaikh Abul Fazl, son of Shaikh Mubarak. At the time I was *Kolbegi* I spoke and the scribe of the Shaikh (Abul Fazl) wrote it down, while I was also deciding upon the affairs of the kitchen, though I had not the capacity to write, nor did I have any written record.[55] Matters of AH 949 (AD 1542–3) that had taken place at Zankan in His Majesty Humayun's camp are now written down in the city of Lahore in AH 999 (AD 1590–1). Since my youth had gone and old age had come, my memory is not very strong. If I have made slips, let the reader overlook them.[56]

A far better-known text of personal memoirs (but unfortunately extant only in fragment) similarly written on Akbar's orders for Abul Fazl's work, is that by Akbar's aunt, Gulbadan Begum.[57] Both these sources were used by Abul Fazl, since many events mentioned there also occur in his work. It is less certain whether Abbas Khan Sarwani's *Tuhfa-i Akbarshahi*, written at Akbar's orders to provide a history of the Sur usurpers (1540–56), was written for Abul Fazl, or earlier.[58] It does seem, however, that he did put it to some use. As for Mihtar Jauhar's memoirs, prepared independently, it is not clear if Abul Fazl was able to use the original or the polished version that had been presented to Akbar in 1590; but it seems that he did use one of them as a source for at least one event identified by Mukhia.[59]

Abul Fazl in his Preface to the *Akbarnama* speaks of the large amount of archival and documentary material used by him. Akbar had established his system of waqai or news reporting and recording in 1574,[60] and thus from that time at least, Abul Fazl would have had the benefit of access to a rigorously chronological record of events at the court itself, as he himself notes.[61] He also collected texts of all the orders which Akbar had issued since his accession.[62] Abul Fazl seems, indeed, to have prepared first a text which closely followed the waqai, and, therefore, had much more numerous dates than in the final version. Fragments of this first or earlier draft have survived in a MS in the British Library, which also contains fragments of the final version and of the *A'in-i Akbari*.[63] This version contains full texts of such documents as Todar Mal's memorandum on revenue administration and Akbar's orders thereon (1582), Sharif Sarmadi's report on Man Singh's campaign in Orissa (1590), and Prince Murad's queries and Akbar's replies on administrative and other matters (1591).[64] The final version omits the latter two documents, and offers a polished summary of Todar Mal's memorandum.[65] The archival base is still stronger in the *A'in-i Akbari*, whose provincial and local statistics, revenue and financial data, information or regulations of various departments, rates of prices and wages must have been drawn from a very large number of official sources and collected and screened by a veritable secretariat.

In his conclusion Abul Fazl emphasizes a problem every historian faced with a multiplicity of sources has to confront and resolve:

The flagrantly contradictory statements of eye-witnesses had reached my ears and amazed me, and my difficulties increased. Here was an event distant, the functionaries of (the office of) *Waqa'i* and *Sawanih* present, the Sovereign testing me, and I with my eyes open observing these manifold discrepancies! ... By deep reflection and a careful scrutiny, taking up the principal points in which there was a general agreement, my satisfaction increased, and where the narrators differed from each other I based my presentation of facts on a footing of discriminate investigation of exact and cautious statements, and this somewhat set my mind at ease. Where an event had contrary accounts from equally credible persons, or anything reached me opposed to my own view of the question, I submitted it to His Majesty and freed myself from responsibility.[66]

Abul Fazl says he prepared five successive drafts, to improve each stylistically. A comparison with the earlier version, as contained in British Library Add. 27, 247, shows that in this process there was much loss of detail and of the touch of original source material. Apparently, as the re-drafting progressed, the differences in original testimonies were also set aside in favour of either the consensus approach, or of a decision adopted by Abul Fazl himself or obtained from his sovereign. One can only regret this gradual 'alienation' from the original sources (which Abul Fazl does not usually even deign to quote or acknowledge by name), which prevents us now from checking whether Abul Fazl's choice among divergent reports was reasonable or biased.

Despite these weaknesses, Abul Fazl's work still constituted a model for Mughal historiography, both in its insistence upon accurate record based on archival and other sources, and in its broad vision of history which encompassed annals, biography, polity, administration, economic life and culture. At these levels, it was a model which official and quasi-official historians of the next century constantly sought to imitate though it was never even remotely approached by them.

Our exploration of source-use in the works of Mughal historians shows that they attached considerable importance to primary documents and eyewitness accounts in order to reconstruct history. This was apparent in their wide use of official news reports and memoirs. Where they were concerned with distant events, they had certain canons of source-criticism to apply, namely rationality and plausibility, as we can see in the treatment of the issue of the death of a Sultan of Delhi in 1325. Confronted with multiple versions of the same event, they like Abul Fazl invoked the doctrine of inherent probability. All these were important achievements; and one regrets only that these canons were not systematized in even a single theoretical text written during the Mughal period.

Yet, with all its achievements, Mughal historiography is not a direct ancestor of modern Indian historiography, for the simple reason that it did not sufficiently develop criticism of documents nor truly antiquarian interests. There is nothing like the Renaissance exposure of the Donation of Constantine; nor like the West European pursuit of Roman coins and inscriptions from the sixteenth century onwards. In fact, it is strange that with such profusion of inscriptions, even in the Persian language in which the Mughal historians wrote, and of coins of all periods, the Mughal historians hardly ever turned to them to establish or corroborate any fact. Thus, though nineteenth-century India inherited a fairly high order of narrative history dating from the thirteenth century, the earlier historical tradition had no capacity for reconstructing ancient Indian history, where epigraphy and numismatics had to play a crucial role. It was, therefore, European historical science, applied and adapted in India in the nineteenth century, with which modern Indian historiography really came into being.

NOTES

1. C.A. Storey, *Literature—A Bio-bibliograpical Survey*, section II, fasciculi 1-3 (London, 1935, 1936, 1939). Nos 101–311 cover General History

and the history of the Prophet and the Pious Caliphs and *Imams*. Of these too, many works were written in India. From these items biographical literature is excluded, which Storey catalogued in a separate volume, coming after section ii, fasciculus 3, as part ii of volume i (London, 1953).

2.   For a fairly comprehensive survey of Persian and other literature of Mughal India, in which such works are listed, see D.N. Marshall, *Mughals in India: A Bibliographical Survey, I: Manuscripts (but including works now printed)*, Bombay, 1967.

3.   Kafi Khan, *Muntakhabu'l Luba ✓b,* ii, ed. K.D. Ahmad (Calcutta, 1860–74).

4.   Nizamuddin Ahmad, *Tabaqa ✓t-i-Akbari,* Lucknow, 1875, p. 3.

5.   Ibid., pp. 98–9.

6.   Barani, *Tarikh-i Firuzshahi*, ed. Saiyid Ahmad Khan, W.N. Lees and Kabir al Din (Calcutta, 1862), pp. 452–3.

7.   Isami, *Futuhn's Salatin*, ed. A.S. Usha, Madras, 1948, pp. 418–20.

8.   *Tabaqat-i Akbari*, i. p. 99.

9.   *Tarikhi-i-Firishta,* Lucknow, 1281/1864–65,i, pp. 4–5.

10.   Ibid., p. 132.

11.   Sadr Jahan began writing his History in 1497. The statement quoted by Firishta occurs in the *Tarikh-i Sadr-i Jahan* (account of the Sultans of Delhi), ed. Iqtidar Husain Siddiqi, Aligarh, 1988, p. 54.

12.   *Tarikh-i Firishta*, i, p. 134.

13.   As yet unpublished, see Aligarh Muslim University Library MS Lytton Farsiya 3–26, 27 (2 vols).

14.   *Maktubat-i Allami* or *Insha-i Abdul Fazl* (Lucknow, 1262/1864) and several other edns.

15.   *Adab-i-Alamgiri*, ed. Abdul Ghafur Chaudhuri, 2 vols (Lahore, 1971).

16.   Pub. as *Ruqat-i Alamgiri* (Lucknow, 1260/1844): numerous MSS.

17.   *Nigarnam-i-Munshi*, Lucknow, 1882.

18.   MS Bib. Nat., Paris: Blochet Suppl. Pers. 482.

19.   MS British Library, Add. 16,859, ff. 270–109b, 122b–127a.

20.   *Mirat-i-Ahmadi*, ed. Nawab Ali, I Baroda, 1928, pp. 8–13. The same editor published vol. ii , Baroda, 1927, and Supplement, Baroda, 1930.

21.   *Mirat-i Ahmadi*, i, p. 272.

22.   See, for example, orders issued in respect of coining lighter copper coins (*dams*), *Mirat-i Ahmadi*, i. pp. 265, 267, 288.

23.   Ibid., pp. 272, 283.

24.   For Amin Qazwini's text, see Aligarh CAS in History Library transcript, pp. 509–10. For the text of the actual inscription as found on the

mosque, see Pir Ghulam Hasan Khoyhami, *Tarikh-i Hasan*, Srinagar, n.d., II pp. 500–1.

25. These versions are studied by Shireen Moosvi, 'Administering Kashmir, an Imperial Edict of Shahjahan', *Aligarh Journal of Oriental Studies*, III (2), 1986, pp. 141–52.

26. Saqi Mustaid Khan, *Ma'asir-i Alamgiri*, ed. Agha Ahmad Ali, Calcutta, 1871, p. 69.

27. *Selected Waqai of the Deccan (1660–1671, A.D.*, ed. Yusuf Husain, Central Record Office, Hyderabad Govt. (now AP State Archives), Hyderabad, 1953.

28. A.P. State Archives MS (Asafiya, *Fan-i Tarikh* 2242), transcript, Aligarh CAS in History Library, nos 15–16.

29. Of these histories the following have been published: Abul Fazl, *Akbarnama*, Calcutta, 1873–87; Lahori, *Padshahnama*, Calcutta, 1866–72; Kazim, *Alamgirnama*, Calcutta, 1865–73.

30. *Jahangirnama (Tuzuk-i Jahangiri)*, ed. Syed Ahmad, Ghazipur and Aligarh, 1863–4.

31. G.H. Khare and G.T. Kulkarni, (eds.), *Aurangzebachya Darbarache Akhbar* (Persian texts with Marathi calendars), Pune, 1973.

32. C.R. Wilson, (ed.), *The Early Annals of the English in Bengal*, II (2): *The Surman Embassy* (1911, 1963), pp. 282–3.

33. MS Oxford, Bodleian 257 (Fraser 124), ff. 129a–489b, which largely comprises material from *akhbarat* from Delhi, given under separate entries for each day.

34. Cf. S.R. Sharma, *A Bibliography of Mughal India (1526–1707 A.D.)*, Bombay, n.d., pp. 9–10.

35. *Tazkirat-us Salatin-i Chaghta*, ed. Muzaffar Alam, Bombay, 1980. Cf. the editor's remarks in the English introduction, pp. 5–7 for this author's sources.

36. British Library, Add. 16, 711, ff. 141a, 145b–146a.

37. *Khatima* (Epilogue) of Faizi Sirhindis's recension of Jauhar Aftabchi's memoirs, King's College, Cambridge MS 84, ff. 134a–b. India Office MS Ethe 222 (I.O. 788) is also a copy of this recension.

38. Faizi Sirhindi, *Akbarnama*, Br. Lib. Or., 169, ff. 194b–195a.

39. King's College, Cambridge, MS 84 ff. 55b, 88b.

40. 'The book might be described as consisting of annals and a diary which once met within what is now the gap 1508–19 (914–925 A.H.)', A.S. Beveridge in the preface to her translation, *Baburnama* (London, 1921), p. xxxiii.

41. *Jahangirnama*, ed. Syed Ahmad, Ghazipur and Aligarh, 1863–64.

42. *Tarikh-i Khan Jahan Lodi*, ed. S.M. Imamal Din, Dacca, 1960, II, pp. 704–5.

43. See account of the thirteenth regnal year in *Jahangirnama*, p. 239. Cf. Elliot and Dowson, *The History of India as told by its Own Historians*, London, 1866–77, VI, pp. 278–9.

44. The separate history was published as *Jahangirnama*, Lucknow, 1898. The *Iqbalnama*, a history of the Mughal dynasty till Jahangir's accession (1605), was written earlier in Jahangir's reign in the fifteenth regnal year (1620) (Nawal Kishore edn, Lucknow, 1870, p. 479), in two vols. The history of Jahangir came to be treated as its third volume, and was published as such in the Nawal Kishore edition of the whole work (Lucknow, 1870), and in the Bib. Ind. edn of this volume only (Calcutta, 1865).

45. *Maasir-i-Jahangiri*, ed. Azra Alavi, Bombay, 1978.

46. Br. Lib. Add. 16,695, ff. 211b–245b, contains Ataki's account of Jahangir's reign.

47. The standard editions of the two works are: Badauni, *Muntakhab-ut Tawarikh*, ed. Ali Ahmad and Lees, 3 vols, Calcutta, 1864–9; Nizamuddin Ahmad, *Tabaqat-i Akbari*, 3 vols, ed. B. De (vol. iii partly ed. M. Hidayat Husain), Calcutta, 1913–35. In his work *Nijatur Rashid*, ed. S. Moinul Haq, Lahore, 1972, p. 82, Badauni himself modestly styles his *Muntakhab-ut Tawarikh*, 'a summary' of 'the late' Nizamuddin Ahmad's history.

48. *Muntakhab-ut Tawarikh*, II, p. 389.

49. MS Aligarh Muslim University Library, Subhanullah Coll. Suppl. Farsiya 920/45. For a few of Badauni's references to this work, see *Muntakhab-ut Tawarikh*, III, pp. 76–7, 97, 323.

50. *Dabistan-i Mazahib*, Bombay, 1292/1875, p. 266.

51. Thus H. Blochmann allowed it to influence heavily his translation of the chapters on Akbar's religious views in Abul Fazl's *A'in-i Akbari*. Not satisfied by rendering, for example, *A'in-i iradat qazinam* (Rules for Spiritual Disciples) as Ordinances of Divine Faith, Blochmann proceeds to insert the translation of a whole series of passages from Badauni. See *A'in-i Akbari*, tr. H. Blochmann (orig. pub., Calcutta, 1864–73), rev. D.C. Phillott, Calcutta, 1927, p. 175 (Ordinances of Divine Faith), 177–218 (extracts from Badauni). By and large, Mughal historians even in the eighteenth century, e.g. Khafi Khan in *Muntakhab-ul Lubab*, vol. I, remained great admirers of Akbar and his achievements, ignoring his religious heresies.

52. The standard editions of the two works are: *Akbarnama*, ed. Ahmad Ali, 3 vols, Calcutta, 1873–87; *A'in-i Akbari*, ed. H. Blochmann, Calcutta, 1867–77.

53. These dates are best discussed in Shireen Moosvi, *Economy of the Mughal Empire*, Delhi, 1987, pp. 5–8.

54. *A'in-i Akbari*, III, tr. H.S. Jarrett, rev. Jadunath Sarkar, Calcutta, 1948, p. 472 (translation modified after checking with text ed. H. Blochmann, op. cit. II, p. 255); see also *Akbarnama*, I, p. 9 (Abul Fazl's preface).

55. I assume *nadanist* (did not understand) is a misreading here for *nadasht*.

56. *Tazkira-i Humayun wa Akbar*, ed. M. Hidayat Husain, Calcutta, 1941, pp. I–2.

57. *Humayun Nama*, ed. and tr. A.S. Beveridge, London, 1902, from the only known MS, in Br. Lib.

58. India Office Library, Ethe 219 (I.O. 218) seems to be the best MS copy of this work.

59. Harbans Mukhia, *Historians and Historiography during the Reign of Akbar,* New Delhi, 1976, pp. 68–9.

60. *Akbarnama*, III, p. 118.

61. *Akbarnama*, I, pp. 9–10.

62. Ibid., I, p. 10.

63. Br. Lib. Add. 27, 247.

64. Add. 27, 247, ff. 331b–332b; 400a–401b; 401b–404b.

65. *Akbarnama*, III, pp. 381–3.

66. *A'in-i Akbari*, III, tr. Jarrett, rev. Sarkar, pp. 472–3: translation substantially corrected after checking with text, II, p. 255.

31

The Correspondence of Aurangzeb and its Historical Significance

This chapter attempts to discuss the nature of information contained in various collections of the letters of Aurangzeb and their historical significance.

Chronologically, the first place among the collections of Aurangzeb's correspondence belongs to the *Insha-i Zubdatul Araiz*. It was discovered by Professor S. Nurul Hasan, who possesses a unique manuscript of it. The collection contains letters written by Aurangzeb to Shah Jahan and some important nobles, relating to the Qandahar campaign of 1652.

The most important of all collections, and in chronological order the second, is that collected by Shaikh Abul Fath Qabil Khan Thattawi and Muhammad Sadiq, under the title *Adab-i Alamgiri*. These include the letters of Prince Akbar as well and the collection was given its final form by Muhammad Sadiq, 1115 /1703–4. Out of this collection the letters written by Aurangzeb to Shah Jahan, Jahan Ara and the princes have been published in the *Ruqa'at-i 'Alamgiri* edited by Sayyid Najib Ashraf Nadvi.

The *Adab-i Alamgiri* was collected and edited by Muhammad Sadiq of Ambala (then a town under Sirhind) of Hanafi persuasion. He says in his preface that he came across the papers of Munshi al-Mumalik Shaikh Abul Fath (later raised to the title of Qabil Khan), comprising letters written by Aurangzeb before his accession, to Shah Jahan (and princes), ministers, nobles and religious men, *hasbul amrs* written by Abul Fath which are in the form of *arzadashts* or letters from himself, but containing Aurangzeb's instructions, to princes, and, finally, Abul Fath's own letters. These Sadiq collected and added, confessedly from his own pen, but derived in fact entirely from the *Amal-i Salih* and *Alamgir Nama*, an account of the war of succession, ending with the death of Dara Shukoh. He then gives letters written by Aurangzeb to Shah Jahan during his captivity, but makes no reference to these in the preface. Lastly he gives letters written by prince Akbar to Aurangzeb and other princes and his nishans to various nobles written or drafted by Muhammad Sadiq himself while in the service of that prince. They belong mostly to the short period of the Rajput War. The date of the collection is given in a chronogram at the end of the preface yielding 1115/1703–4.

The *Adab-i Alamgiri* is an extremely valuable source, in particular for the period of Aurangzeb's second viceroyalty of the Deccan. It contains very important material on the system of jagir assignment, mansabdari regulations, general and incidental references to the agrarian situation, etc. It also contains very useful information regarding the Deccan problem and the arguments advanced by Prince Aurangzeb to adopt a forward policy towards the states of the Deccan. There are also some interesting data on the financial crisis with which the Mughal nobles posted in the Deccan were faced; and a discussion on the problem of supporting the Deccan war through the resources of the occupied Deccan only.

Apart from the above two collections, all the others contain letters belonging to the last twenty years of Aurangzeb's life. The first of these is the *Raqaim-i Karaim*, containing Aurangzeb's letters to Mir Abul Karim, Amir Khan, governor of Kabul. The *Raqaim-i Karaim* is a collection of Aurangzeb's letters mostly addressed to Amir Khan arranged by his son Saiyid Ashraf Khan, Mir Muhammad Husaini, who adds a short preface at the beginning. There seems to have been a basic text of the original compilation to which later transcribers added further as other copies of letters or supposed letters of Aurangzeb came into their hands.

The *Raqaim-i Karaim* contains some useful information, having some bearing on the administration of the Mughal Empire and forms of court etiquette.

Kalimat-i Taiyabat, or Notes for letters, to be drafted on behalf of Aurangzeb were collected by Inayatullah Khan, and arranged by him in 1131/1722. Inayatullah states in his preface that owing to the kindness of Aurangzeb he had reached a position where he enjoyed personal contact with the emperor.

As explained by Inayatullah himself, the present work is a collection of notes written by Aurangzeb to form the basis for orders and formal letters to be drafted by Inayatullah. They are, therefore, by their very nature obscure and the compiler has not helped us by omitting all headings and dates, thus retaining the original *kalimat* in an almost undisturbed form. From references to the events and doings of the officers found in the kalimat, they can all be said, with some confidence, to belong to the last decade of Aurangzeb's reign. On the whole, they are a valuable source for the study of administrative forms and methods of the period, but almost entirely fail to provide any important material and sidelights on the political and administrative system of the day.

Inayatullah Khan also compiled another collection, the *Ahkam-i Alamgiri*. Of all the collections of Aurangzeb's letters in the later years of his reign, this is by far the most important historically and is as authentic as, if not more than, the *Kalimat-i Taiyabat* and the *Raqaim-i Karaim*. The author of the *Mirat-i Ahmadi* explicitly acknowledges his indebtedness to this collection in writing his account of the events in Gujarat during Aurangzeb's last few years. This is amply confirmed by the most perfunctory reading of his account, in which he makes references to or quotes words and sentences from a number of hasbul hukms embodied in the present collection.

The letters in the *Ahkam-i Alamgiri* were almost all written in the last two or three years of Aurangzeb's life. All the dates in the letters and references to current events, without exception, belong to this period. Thus Aurangzeb writes to Bidar Bakht that since his departure from Ajmer he had spent twenty-five years waging the holy war in the Dakhin. The events in Gujarat covered by the letters are chiefly the defeat of Hamduddin Khan, diwan of the province, at the hands of the Marrathas, which took place late in AH 1706, besides the events that followed it and a conflict with the Dutch at Surat and the release of Fakhrul Islam and Shaikhul Islam from their ship in 1707. C.A. Storey is mistaken in implying that there is any portion in common between this collection and the *Ahkam-i Alamgiri* translated by Sarkar as *Anecdotes of Aurangzeb*. There is no connection between the two works at all.

The letters are classified according to the persons they were addressed to, and though a few headings are missing, the arrangement is generally consistent and free from that anarchical confusion found in some other collections of the emperor's letters. It is, therefore, much easier to handle the information contained in this collection.

The *Dastural Amal-i Agahi* is a collection of Aurangzeb's letters, collected, as stated in the preface, at the desire of Raja Aya Mal in 1156/1746, the twenty-ninth regnal year of Muhammad Shah. Many of the letters of this collection are to be found in the *Ramz o-Isharahai Alamgiri*,[1] also compiled at Ayahmal's desire four years earlier and in the popular collection of the *Raqa'at-i Alamgir* (Kanpur edn. AH 1267), while at least some of its letters are taken directly or indirectly from the *Raqaim-i Karaim*. The letters of Aurangzeb to Shah Jahan at the beginning are identical with those preserved in the *Adab-i Alamgiri*, and were probably taken from that work. Not at all to be despised, finally, is the so-called bazar collection of Aurangzeb's letters, printed under the title *Ruqa'at-i Alamgiri*.

This is, or perhaps, was till recently, the most common collection of Aurangzeb's letters. In its final arrangement it may not, however, be a very old one and this probably explains the paucity of its manuscript copies in the major libraries. Indeed, the larger part of it is taken bodily from the *Ramz-o-Isharaha-i Alamgiri*, compiled in AH 1152 at Ayamal's desire. In its later portion it adds a number of letters taken from the *Raqaim-i Karaim*. It omits the alleged last letter of Dara Shukoh and the will of Aurangzeb.

The subject matter of the contents is generally similar to that of the *Kalimat-i Taiyabat* and *Raqaim-i Karaim*. They all seem to have been written in the last two decades, mostly in the last one, of his reign.

There exists in English translation a collection, whose Persian original has not been traced. This translation bears the title, *Letters of the Emperor Aurangzeb to his sons, grandsons, his ministers and principal nobles, to which is prefixed his will*, translated by Joseph Earles, Calcutta, 1788. The will is obviously fabricated, though it is probably the one included in the *Ramz-o-Isharaha-i Alamgiri*. The translation itself does not reveal any document of singular value. Many, if not most of what are presumably the originals are found in the better known and more authentic collections.

There can be no doubt that the correspondence of Aurangzeb is extremely useful from the point of the view of reconstructing the narrative and administrative history of the period. At some points it is more reliable than the contemporary chronicles. Aurangzeb has narrated the events of these letters as he saw them and comments freely problems with which he was faced. If all these letters are properly classified, annotated, edited and calendared, a great service would surely be rendered to the cause of Medieval Indian History.

NOTE

1. I owe this information to Dr Irfan Habib.

Index